ARAGON
ISSUES IN
PHILOSOPHY

PARAGON ISSUES IN PHILOSOPHY

THE PARAGON ISSUES
IN PHILOSOPHY SERIES

At colleges and universities, interest in the traditional areas of philosophy remains strong. Many new currents flow within them, too, but until recently many of these—the rise of cognitive science, for example, or feminist philosophy—often went largely unnoticed in undergraduate philosophy courses. The Paragon Issues in Philosophy Series responds to both perennial and newly influential concerns by bringing together a team of able philosophers to address the fundamental issues in philosophy today and to outline the state of contemporary discussion about them.

More than twenty volumes are scheduled; they are organized into three major categories. The first covers the standard topics—metaphysics, theory of knowledge, ethics, and political philosophy—stressing innovative developments in those disciplines. The second focuses on more specialized but still vital concerns in the philosophies of science, religion, history, sport, and other areas. The third category explores new work that relates philosophy and fields such as feminist criticism, medicine, economics, technology, and literature.

The level of writing is aimed at undergraduate students who have little previous experience studying philosophy. The books provide brief but accurate introductions that appraise the state of the art in their fields and show how the history of thought about their topics has developed. Each volume is complete in itself but also aims to complement others in the series.

Traumatic change characterized the twentieth century, and the twenty-first will be no different in that regard. All of its pivotal issues will involve philosophical questions. As the editors at Paragon House continue to work with us, we hope that this series will help encourage the understanding needed in a new millennium whose times will be as complicated and problematic as they are promising.

John K. Roth
Claremont McKenna College

Frederick Sontag
Pomona College

WORLD RELIGIONS IN A
POSTMODERN AGE

WORLD RELIGIONS IN A POSTMODERN AGE

HENRY L. RUF

PARAGON HOUSE
ST. PAUL, MINNESOTA

First Edition 2007

Published in the United States by
Paragon House
1925 Oakcrest Avenue, Suite 7
St. Paul, MN 55113

Library of Congress Cataloging-in-Publication Data

Ruf, Henry L.
World religions in a post-modern age / Henry L. Ruf. -- 1st ed.
    p. cm.
Summary: "Presents an introduction to religion and shows how religion differs from
    metaphysics, provides interpretations of Asian religions, Middle Eastern and Western
    religions, and provides a declaration of religious freedom for the post-modern age"--
    Provided by publisher.
Includes bibliographical references and index.
ISBN 1-55778-866-9 (pbk. : alk. paper) 1. Religions. I. Title.
BL80.3.R84 2007
200--dc22
                          2006037685

Manufactured in the United States of America

The paper used in this publication meets the minimum requirements of American
    National Standard for Information Sciences—Permanence of Paper for Printed
    Library Materials, ANSIZ39.48-1984.

10 9 8 7 6 5 4 3 2 1

For current information about all releases from Paragon House,
visit the web site at http://www.paragonhouse.com

To Marion E. Olbrantz

Beautiful and Loyal Sister

ACKNOWLEDGMENTS

July 2006 saw the death of two religious and philosophical giants whose influence on my writing of this book is immense, although they never were aware of this: Thomas English Hill and Dewa Zephania Phillips. The first taught me in person through his spoken words and presence and the second through his written words. Both embodied a fusion of religious faithfulness and critical, intellectual integrity.

There are a host of debts that need to be acknowledged to people who determined that all my philosophical concerns would be centered on religious issues that could be addressed only if I kept my eyes fixed on the sameness and differences in the world religions. My mother, Emma Ruf, without ever once talking about religion, faithfully practiced her faith and channeled me so as to not wander too far from religious involvement. Rev. Ray Kiely and Rev. Mason Ellison of the Presbyterian Church in Wausau, Wisconsin, again and again made in possible for me to become re-involved. During four years of service in the Air Force as a chaplain's assistant, the Lutheran, Presbyterian, Methodist, Disciples of Christ, and Jewish chaplains with whom I worked convinced me that dialogue across religious divides was both possible and profitable. Spending three years serving in Japan strengthened this conviction as I was introduced to Shinto shrines, Buddhist temples and gardens, and nondenominational congregations of Japanese Christians. At Macalester College this conviction was further strengthened as I was introduced to Kierkegaard by Hugo Thompson and to Asian religions by David White. Presbyterians, Methodists and Congregationalists in Rockford, Minnesota; Chamblee, Georgia; Burdett, New York; Burlington, Massachusetts; and Fulton, New York, who were my students over three decades in groups studying world religions and the Bible, showed to me that quite ordinary people could engage in such dialogue. My American undergraduate students in philosophy of religion and philosophies of Asia classes proved the same point.

What cemented my convictions about the sameness and differences among the world religions were the things I learned from my students in Japan, Thailand, Pakistan, and China. I thank the Fulbright Program for allowing me to meet, teach, and learn from these people with their different forms of religious faithfulness. I thank Father (Dr.) Reimer at Nanzan University, a Roman Catholic University in Nagoya, Japan, for introducing me to the creative thought of the Buddhist philosopher, Keiji Nishitani, whose works were being translated at Nanzan's Center for Buddhist-Christian studies, and for sharing with me his admiration of the Christians martyred over centuries in Kyushu, Japan. I thank Dr. Wariya Chinwanno, chair of the Humanities Department at Mahidol University in Thailand, as she made it possible for me to spend a year learning from the Buddhist monks who were students in my graduate seminars and from the professors who were teaching Hinduism and Buddhism. I thank Hakim Mohammed Said, president of the Hamdard Foundation in Pakistan, for making it possible to lecture at the University of Karachi, Pakistan, where I was able to deepen my understanding of the work of Dr. Mansoor Ahmad, who drew upon the history of Islamic law to demonstrate that Muslims in good faith can respect other religions. I thank Dr. Basharat Tayyab, chair of the Philosophy Department at Karachi University, for coming to spend a year at West Virginia University and taking time as she taught me about how Islam provides room for a women's liberation movement. I thank Dawa Jial in the Language Department at Tibet University for enabling me to spend time at his university and to learn from him and his students how Tibetan Buddhism is re-creating itself in the new Tibet. I thank Xiao Xingzheng, a teacher of English and a student in my graduate seminar on comparative philosophy at Xiamen University, China, for revealing to me how a number of Chinese intellectuals are now rethinking Taoism and Buddhism in the light of their study of recent European philosophy.

I have to thank Dr. Huston Smith for forty years of dialogue with me. We will never agree on the issue of whether or not religion needs metaphysical, ontotheological postulations, but I will never cease thinking of him as one of the most saintly persons I ever have met and as a religious philosopher who has so much to teach us about the religions of the world.

Finally, I have to thank Dr. Gene James, Rev. Ray Kiely, and Dr. John Vielkind for reading and commenting on the manuscript. I thank the staff at Paragon House for preparing the manuscript for publication.

An abbreviated version of parts of section one of this book appeared as an article, "Encounters and Responses: Sameness and Differences in World Religions," in the *International Journal on World Peace,* September 2005.

Contents

Section One

THE WORLD'S RELIGIONS AS FINITE RESPONSES TO THE CALL OF THE INFINITE

Hindus, Buddhists, Taoists, Jews, Christians, and Muslims are all religious people. Why are they all called "religious"? Do they all share a common core, or do they bear only family resemblances to each other? Why are they seen by themselves and others as being different from one another? Are they really radically different, or are they just singing variations of the same tune, climbing different paths to the same mountaintop? In this book I will assert and attempt to show that people living faithfully in these six ways are responding in six distinctive, irreducibly different, religiously not unjustified, socially and culturally constituted ways to encounters with the nonfinite, infinite, other to all finite objects, events, and subjects constituted by social and cultural practices that are not faithful responses to the call of the infinite. There are human worlds properly called secular because they neither recognize not seek to respond faithfully to anything other to their world of objects and subjects.[1] There also are religious worlds that are radically different from secular worlds. These religious worlds also are different from one another because, although people in each of these religions hear a call from the infinite that is transcendent of all secular worlds, they faithfully respond in different ways to this call, in ways that preserve the sacredness of the infinite other of all merely secular objects and subjects but that also reflect the specifics of the social and cultural worlds into which people have been thrown.

Characterizing these six major religions of the world as different, socially constituted, faithful responses to encounters with the infinite is not the way many, perhaps most, people in our world would characterize them. As the word "religion" is used by many people today,

1

especially by those in the mass media, many social phenomena, personal beliefs, and actions are designated as religious even though these six religions would brand them as mere pretenders. One of the reasons why many people say that it is improper to introduce the topic of religion into polite conversation is that people radically and sometimes violently disagree about what religion is and about what distinguishes authentic from inauthentic religious talk and practice. Additionally, and perhaps more significantly, many people steer clear of religious talk because religions often condemn what many of us are doing, and because one places oneself in danger when one judges that someone else's religious talk is inauthentic. Some people find themselves at a loss for words when they try to give verbal expression to their religious faith, and most people find it extremely difficult to carry on a respectful dialogue with people who do not share their faith. Therefore, before even attempting to show the manner in which these six world religions are different faithful responses to the call of the infinite, it is necessary to say something about why religious talk is dangerous talk, why it is so difficult to locate authentic religious linguistic practices within religious worlds constituted as faithful responses to encounters with the infinite. It is also necessary to show how talk using the word "infinite" does and does not work in religious talk. This I will do in the five parts of this opening section, before I present interpretations of six of the major religions of the world in sections two and three. In the final section, I will attempt to show what kind of religious freedom this understanding of the religions of the worlds calls for us to tolerate, respect, and cherish.

1. The Dangerousness of Religious Talk

Religious talk is dangerous talk for two major reasons. In its authentic voice it stands as a dangerous threat, first, to the perpetrators of injustice and, second, to all religious pretenders. Authentic religious talk has been voiced around the globe by prophets, priests, seers, and gurus in their condemnation of the mistreatment of people and the unjust practices present in the societies in which they lived. Hindus have condemned making the pursuit of economic, political, or social power the ultimate goal in one's life. Buddhists have condemned all the cravings that cause human suffering. The Hebrew prophets again and again condemned social and personal forms of injustice. Christians have called for a love that finds injustice intolerable. Muhammad and the Qur'an enunciate Allah's demand for righteousness and mercy. Entrenched holders of dominating and oppressive power have always found the authentic voices of the world's religions to be dangerous threats to themselves and the practices supplying them their power.

These same voices also have condemned religious fakes who are judged to be dangers to justice and religious faithfulness. Inauthentic religious talk by religious pretenders and by people trapped in fly bottles of confusion and misunderstanding is dangerous for three different kinds of reasons. First, it is often used to make domination, oppression, and unwarranted denials of freedom seem justified and appropriate. Second, it is used to motivate violent and vicious attacks on people with different forms of religious faithfulness. Third, it drains authentic religious talk of its ability to oppose the misuse of power and the mistreatment of people, and it prevents people from reaping the religious rewards of gaining liberation from self-inflicted misery and from the inability to acquire joyous, blissful lives.

Religious spokespersons condemning injustice always have had to face, in turn, the danger of retaliation from the abusers of power and from those who have acquired power, profit, fame, and glory because of oppressive social practices. In addition, priests and prophets condemning religious fakery and pretentiousness always have risked the danger of having their religious faithfulness denied by religious pretenders and their critical appraisals of religious pretensions demonized as "anti-religious." Since many of the participants in unjust social practices are skillful manipulators of what sounds like religious talk, religious pursuers of justice and authenticity must continually take on the dangerous task of driving the corrupt pretenders out of the temples of the world's religions. Being religious is dangerous. Prophetically criticizing injustice is dangerous. Attacking religious fakery is dangerous. Because being religious is a danger to injustice and religious fakery, inevitably religious people are challenged to have the courage to live dangerously.

Our twenty-first-century world desperately needs the religions of the world to become ever more dangerous threats to injustice and the misuse of religious talk. Avoidable wars, starvation, disease, and denials of freedom and respect devastate hundreds of millions of people each day. Talk that runs counter to what is fundamental in all religions but which claims to be religious has contributed to these disasters. It has constantly underwritten unjust political, economic, and social practices, and has fostered hatred and fear that has produced violence and disrespect. Kings and emperors have been said to have a divine right to rule, a divine duty to imperialistically colonize the world. The economically powerful have been honored as God's favored people, and talk of karma has been used to legitimate keeping the powerless in their oppressed class. Bloody crusades have been fought, cruel inquisitions have been carried out, witches have been burned, and millions have been enslaved and marginalized, all in the name of religion. The cry "It is God's will" has been sacrilegiously used again and again by fearful and resentful people to legitimate dangerous totalitarian, intellectual, political, and social efforts to gain oppressive power over others and by elevating all-too-human creations into some absolute to be served without question or reservation.

In order to empower the religions of the world to better perform their prophetic tasks of resisting injustice and religious pretense, it is crucial that people come to understand how to distinguish authentic religious life and talk from the inauthentic fakes making so much dangerous noise today. It is the purpose of this book to help people gain this understanding. The book will talk about what is fundamental in religion, what is common to all the world's religions, and it will talk about what is specific, uniquely different, fundamental, and precious in each of these religions. It will do so not just to satisfy idle curiosity or to engage in enjoyable, intellectual puzzle solving. The rhetoric in this book is not directed by an objective, interest-free depiction of the world's religions. Such depictions, as we shall see, are impossible. Rather, the book is written out of a passion to resist injustice and the debilitating effects of religious quackery. It aims at interpreting religious faithfulness so that it can be respected and cherished for what it is: a dangerous threat to injustice and service to false gods and an indispensable dimension of ways of life filled with so much joy and happiness that not even injustice and suffering can challenge life's meaningfulness.

Resisting injustice and rejecting all attempts to make some finite, secular object or subject into an absolute to be served without reservation are the two inseparable sides of the core that is common in all of the world's religions. When authentic religious voices speak from the first side of this core they threaten all people misusing power and profiting from dominating and oppressive social practices. All the religions of the world call for compassion and justice; and they condemn all failures to cherish that in people which is other than what oppressive secular social practices have constituted them to be—to cherish them as what the Hindus call Atman or as what the Hebrews, Christians and Muslims call the created images of God. They condemn all the social practices and institutions that result in coercing people into social roles which deny respect for their unique otherness to all such roles or identities . Authentic religious talk always has been inalienably tied to a universal ethical call to respect all people and to recognize that one must justify to each and every person any and all restrictions on their freedom to live. The world's religions call for the merciful and loving treatment of all people (family members, widows, orphans, neighbors, strangers, enemies).

This common ethical aspect in all the world's religions is inseparably tied to the second side of the common core in all religions. All of the world's religions reject worshiping anything merely finite, either in the form of false idols or in the form of a materialism or humanism that sees the secular finite as the ultimate. They reject treating as exhaustive and self-sufficient the nonreligious social worlds in which people generally find themselves located historically. This is a constant, even though religions differ about how to live out this refusal to absolutize any facet of such human worlds. The world's religions reject living as though there is no other to all the socially constituted objects, subjects, practices, words, and concepts that exist. The faithful in all the world's religions live in response to encounters with the other to everything socially constituted, encounters with the other to every finite object or event. The different religions are themselves social phenomena historically constituted, thus accounting for their specificity and the differences among them, but common to them all are their encounters with the nonfinite, the infinite. Religious people strive to live in faithfulness to encounters with what is radically other to any finite objects or subjects, radically other to anything describable by any socially constituted words and concepts.

In responding to the call of the infinite, religiously faithful people in different social, economic, political, and cultural worlds have spoken out against making any such finite world, and the finite objects within them into graven images or "gods" to be worshiped. Authentic religious talk always is a dangerous threat to kings, presidents, CEOs, priests, preachers, and philosophers who forget their socially, historically, personally limited and finite status. Hearing the call of the infinite is hearing the command that nothing created by people should be worshiped with the absolute surrender called for by the infinite. One of the things that talking about God creating everything signifies is that one is not to make into a god anything created by people. No political institution, economic practice, conceptual schema, or intellectual theory is to be mistakenly confused with the infinite. The infinite calling people to religious faithfulness is other than anything that people can think of as a being of a certain describable kind. The infinite is not a being, not even a supreme being. Talking religiously about a supreme being is really talking about what is other to all beings and the being of all beings. The call of the infinite comes not in human words, but through encountering the incompleteness and absence of self-sufficiency of that which is conceivable and describable, and of encountering joyfully, thankfully, ethically, contritely, hopefully, lovingly that which conceiving and describing cannot touch. Genuine religious talk is quite properly a dangerous threat to all the images, all the theoretical or postulated objects, all the theoretical books that people have tried to elevate beyond the human, all-to-human, world of the finite.

Authentic religious talk is even a dangerous threat to all those aspects of the lives of religiously faithful people that have not yet been transformed by their hearing the call of the infinite. People are not blank tablets on which the voice of the infinite can write a pure narrative of total faithfulness. All people have been socialized and culturally nurtured into specific, nonreligious social worlds filled with confusion, corruption, and injustice before they can ever come to respond to the voice of the infinite, a response that begins in hearing the voice of the infinite. In some religions this is called bad karma, in others original sin. Our social inheritance, which is so heavily secular, molds us before we can seek to remold it in faithful response to the call of the infinite. Without thinking, we take part in many unjust social practices and much inauthentic religious talk, and we perpetuate so many of the nationalistic, political, economic, racial, sexual, and metaphysical ideologies that authentic religious faithfulness indicts. It took years for us to be constituted as the acting, thinking, believing, valuing, fearing, craving people that we are. Hearing authentic religious talk is painfully difficult because it involves hearing what is a dangerous threat to much of what we unfortunately still are. Religiously faithful people are always on a spiritual pilgrimage as they aim at fuller and deeper faithfulness, even as they sense the danger and feel the intense anguish of having to surrender so much that they unfortunately have held so dear for so long.

The dangerousness of religious talk is tied to the difficulty of religious talk. In all of the world's religions, one hears again and again that no words are adequate to describe the infinite other to the finite, that other that has been encountered. They affirm the limitation of human language and thought, even as they use the language of a specific world religion to report these encounters, to point out how to permit these encounters to occur, and to talk about the impossibility of describing what is encountered. Meditating, worshiping, and praying take place as responses to what is understood to be infinitely other than anything describable. As we shall see in the sections that follow, the attitudinal, behavioral, and linguistic responses to encounters with the infinite take on different forms in the different religions of the world, but they all warn against thinking that one can linguistically box in the infinite.

The religious imperative is to respond faithfully to the call of the infinite that we encounter, and this inescapably always involves an ethical imperative. Throughout this book that ethical imperative will be characterized as a responsibility to justly and compassionately respect and cherish the singular uniqueness of all persons, no matter how much any person differs from other people physically, socially, or psychologically. It especially involves respecting and cherishing those who are different from the powerful of the world, respecting and cherishing those who are weak and vulnerable, those who are poor and sick, those who are ostracized and marginalized, those who are homeless and stateless, those who are orphans, widows, and strangers. This ethical imperative is part of the core shared by all the religions of the world. In part five of this first section, it will be pointed out that a host of postmodern thinkers endorse this ethical imperative and use it to open space for religious faithfulness even though the metaphysical god is dead. Emmanuel Levinas, for example, points out that people are different from one another because they are unique; they are not unique because they are describably different from one another.[2] People are other than all the social masks they wear. The uniqueness of people makes them indescribably different. Saying that people are indescribably unique is saying that they are other than anything finite. It is saying that they are infinite. Encountering the indescribable uniqueness of people is a paradigmatic example of hearing the call of the infinite. We are called to be unreservedly responsible to others. This is a fundamental that is common to all of the world's religions. Authentic religious talk is partly a faithful response to this ethical call of the infinite. This is why religious talk stands as a dangerous threat to the many faces of injustice existing in the world, to all the social practices and institutions that result in the domination and oppression of people. It is also one of the reasons why religious talk is so difficult.

2. The Difficulty of Religious Talk

Religious talk is so easy and so unbelievably difficult. Some speakers seem unable to stop talking religion. Others find it extremely difficult to put into any words what they are doing within a religious tradition and extremely difficult to know how to talk about religion in general. Some people have become so sick and tired of hearing any kind of talk about religion that they automatically tune out whenever talk goes religious. As Jean-Luc Marion puts it, we have to avoid the noisy talk that silences the call of the infinite so that we can learn to hear this call in the silent voice of the infinite, which is unnameable, inconceivable, and ineffable to those with worldly ears and noisy mouths.[3] It is crucial, therefore, to see through the inauthenticity of the easy talk and to understand that the difficult talk is not impossible. This will not guarantee that people will not willfully tune out the demanding call of the infinite, but it at least removes one serious roadblock preventing many contemporary people from hearing religion's cry for justice and the promise of joy.

Without hesitation or any apparent difficulty, religious words by the millions are written and spoken twenty-four hours a day, 365 days a year. These religious words are spread around the world in publications, radio, and TV by persons who locate themselves in one of the world's religions. Religious words pour out of the mouths of priests, rabbis, imams, preachers, faithful worshipers, politicians, warriors, crusaders, and evangelists. Although obviously skillful in participating in these religious linguistic practices, it often is the case that very little reflection about the presuppositions or implications of this easy religious talk has been done by people talking that way. It is when people start reflecting seriously about how religious words actually function in religious talk that so much religious talk is found to be inauthentic, and that many people sincerely interested in religion find it so difficult to talk about the religions of the world or even to keep talking within a particular religion's traditional way.

Reflecting on how words function in religious talk requires asking the following questions. In what human forms of life and in what linguistic practices can and do words like the following have functions to perform: God, Yahweh, Brahman, Christ, Boddhisattva, Allah, Veda, Upanishad, Sutra, Bible, Qur'an, creation, revelation, salvation, prayer? It is very difficult to answer these questions and not only because they function very differently in different religious traditions. The problem is more fundamental than that. The problem is that of trying to use finite words to talk about encountering the infinite other of everything finite. The problem is made even more difficult by the fact that for centuries metaphysicians have been trying to reduce religious talk to their talk about infinite and eternal beings. It is crucial, therefore, to understand how words in general work, why words cannot be adequate to describing the infinite other that religious people encounter, and how words can be used to acknowledge such encounters and religiously respond to these encounters.

Words are social tools people have produced and used to do many different things. People use them to describe what things are like or to relate what is happening; they also use them to wonder about what things might be like or what did or will happen. They use them to direct people to do things or to supply answers to their questions, and they use them in making promises and expressing feelings of joy or sorrow. They use them to start ball games, call pitches, strikes, and runners out. They use them to pronounce people married and to sentence people to death.[4] Most of the things people do with words in our contemporary world are linguistic actions that are not in any way manifestations of any religious faithfulness. The contemporary social and cultural worlds in which we live generally and for the most part are nonreligious worlds, and the way we use words shows this. Most people, most of the time, talk about lakes and plains, flies and ants, french fries and hamburgers, tables and chairs, computers and cars, town governments and business corporations, rising inflation rates and populations, mall openings and military actions, and they do so in totally nonreligious ways, in totally secular ways. These beings and events are just there in their secular worlds. The significance to us of all beings and events comes from the significance they have in the social and cultural worlds in which they and we are constituted. Generally and for the most part, in our daily living and talking we do not experience them or describe them religiously.

This book, however, is an expression of the conviction that in addition to the beings and events that we experience and describe in non-religious ways, there is that which is other to anything that might be experienced or described this way, other to anything that could ever be conceived as being experienced or described in a purely nonreligious manner. Also, in the world's variety of religious ways of life, there are objects, events, and personal identities religiously constituted in faithful responses to encounters with the infinite. Religiously constituted objects, events, and subjects are different from what is secularly constituted, and beings in both sorts of worlds are different from that which is other to anything describable. It is failure to acknowledge this otherness that makes secular descriptions what they are, and it is as faithful verbal responses to this otherness that makes authentic religious descriptions what they are. The difficult challenge is to show what encounters with the indescribable other to anything describable could be like and how words can be used in responding to such encounters.

Describing anything, whether one is doing it in secular or religious ways, always is describing something finite and limited. Descriptions not only say what something is like and how it is the same as other things of the same sort, but they also show what it is not like and how it differs from other things. Apples are not oranges, colors are not shapes, and Pearl Harbor is not Victory in Europe Day. A boddhisattva is not a messiah, and the exodus is not the resurrection of Jesus Christ. Describable beings and events are finite, but people in all the world's religions report encountering that which is not finite, that which is infinite, that which is in principle beyond description. It is in faithful responses to these encounters that religious words like Yahweh, boddhisattva, and Allah have come to mind and been given a religious use.

Running through the religious linguistic practices in the major religions of the world, as we shall see in detail in sections two and three, are some significant linguistic constants. One can distinguish talk within a secularly constituted world of finite objects and subjects, a world that treats itself as exhaustive and self-sufficient and which acknowledges nothing other to itself, from talk about the secular, finite world's other, the nonfinite, the indescribably infinite, that which transcends the world of secular objects and subjects. Levinas goes even further and charges that the indescribably infinite is an immanent necessary presupposition of secular subjectivity.[5] As we shall see in part five of this section, talking about this division is possible only because human life and human consciousness does not consist only of thinking and talking about or experiencing describable beings, socially constituted objects, events, and subjects. People can encounter the otherness to such a world of conceivable beings and classifiable people. Encounters with this otherness, with the infinite, consists of many kinds of behavioral, attitudinal, affective, desiring, and linguistic responses.

In faithfully responding to the call of the infinite, different kinds of religious objects, events, subjects, and linguistic practices get socially and culturally constituted. People in nontheistic religions constitute the infinite as Brahman without characteristics, as Atman, as no-thingness, or as the transcendent Tao that cannot be named. People in theistic religions constitute the infinite as a personal god to be praised, thanked, confessed to, and asked for guidance, and as a strengthening of the desire to be ever more fully faithful. Constituting the infinite as Yahweh, Elohim, God the Father, Allah, or Brahman without characteristics is always done while also attaching the irremovable warning not to let this constitution slip over into worshiping some finite idol or graven image. In addition to these constitutions of the infinite, in some traditions religious beings get constituted as incarnations of these different transcendent objects of religious faithfulness. In the Bhagavad Gita there is Krishna. In Buddhism there are bodhisattvas. In the Hebrew/Jewish tradition there are the ark, the tabernacle and the Torah. In Christianity there are Jesus the Christ and the church as Christ's body filled with the Holy Spirit. In Islam there is the Qur'an. In addition, in all of these religions of the world, people report in words specific to their religious traditions mystical experiences with the infinite other of all constituted worlds.[6]

At the common core of all the religious talk in all of the world's religions are encounters with the infinite. It is in their faithful responses to the infinite that different religious objects, events, subjects, and linguistic practices get constituted. The differences between the world's religions and their linguistic practices are due to the different ways people have responded to their encounters with the infinite otherness of all descriptive beings and events. In different religious ways of life, some people talk of divine creations and acts of God, others talk of finite incarnations of an infinite that cannot be described, others talk of finite drops in an ocean of infinity, and still others talk of mountains resting on no-thingness. In all times and places, but particularly in our contemporary world, major portions of human talk has been and is thoroughly nonreligious. Even so, authentic religious talk has not been extinguished, although it often is either marginalized or transformed into metaphysical or superstitious talk. Religious descriptions of religiously constituted objects and subjects are different from nonreligious descriptions, because the former are linguistic responses to encounters with the infinite while nonreligious linguistic talk is not.

Religious vocabularies are different from one another because the people encountering the infinite are located in different social, cultural, and historical worlds and because they drew upon their cultural heritage in constituting their responses to their encounters with the infinite. Differences in the linguistic practices present in different authentic world religions are merely different historical responses to the infinite that is one without any possibility of there being a second. Secular talk, on the other hand, is radically different from all forms of religious talk. One of the reasons religious talk is so difficult is that it is very hard to distinguish the difference between secular talk and religious talk from the differences existing between the talk present in the different religions of the world. On the one hand, there is our all-too-common secular way of talking, and on the other hand, in the religions of the world there are the many different religious ways of talking, acting, and being a person. There is something universally the same in all the world's religions and something specifically different and unique within each one. It is the thesis of this book that it is possible and religiously and morally imperative to respect what is universally the same in all religions and what is uniquely different in each faith, and that one can do this even as one remains faithfully loyal to the specifics of one's own religion. Faithfulness to one's encounter with the infinite requires both faithfulness to one's own faith and respect for all other religious faiths.

Let's look again at the question of why it is that religious talk, upon reflection, seems so difficult. First, it is important to reemphasize that it is very difficult to separate authentic religious talk from talk that is only pretending to be religious. A great deal of talk that people call religious may not be religious at all because it does not remain faithful to encounters with the infinite. It is so difficult to keep religious talk faithful to its fundamental core. Many religious people do not realize that finite, sacrilegious weeds, in massive numbers and varieties, have invaded the fields of authentic religious faithfulness to the infinite, and thus have corrupted authentic, verbal responses to encounters with the infinite. Many people have been trained and nurtured to talk in ways they think are appropriate responses to the call of the infinite, but which in fact are expressions of human cravings for metaphysical or superstitious explanations and justifications of things and for magical control over events. With respect to all the world's religions, outside as well as internal critics have denounced both superstition and the desire to magically control what happens to oneself or those one loves. It is difficult and dangerous, however, to talk religiously to superstitious people craving for reassuring answers and magical solutions to their problems, especially when they see this as the heart of their religious faith. It is understandable that people will experience fear, resentment, and anxiety when they hear talk about distinguishing the pretentious weeds from the religiously nourishing grain, and when they are called to rip out the weeds by their roots, no matter how unsettling and painful that might be. Calling for people to remain faithful to universal religious fundamentals, and also to the fundamentals definitive of specific authentic religious traditions, does involve calling people to reject superstition, magic, and intolerant and disrespectful dogmatic fundamentalisms. Often it calls on people to give up long established taken-for-granted beliefs, feelings and hopes that prove to be nothing but religious pretensions hiding out in the temples of the world's religions. Authentic religious calls are difficult for people to hear and thus dangerous to those religious speakers calling people to reject the religious pretenders and to come back to religious fundamentals. The call of the infinite, however, requires the religiously faithful to live through these difficulties and dangers.

Another reason why it is so difficult to talk about religion is because it is difficult for the faithful participants in one of the world's religions to talk about their religious way of living as being just one among several religious ways of living. Religious talk is always located within a specific religious way of life that has at its defining center a specific way of responding to encountering the infinite other to the secular features of the specific social and cultural world into which one was thrown. Living within specific religious ways of life, with their individually unique ways of religiously constituting objects, subjects, and events, religious people come to see and interpret everything in a religiously specific way. Within a religious tradition, constituted by attempts to faithfully respond to the call of the infinite, the ideal of seeking to describe everything in terms of this faithful response seems to require describing other so-called religions using only one's own distinctive way of talking. Faithfulness to one's faith requires interpreting everything in one's own specific way. The faithful within any specific religious tradition and community rightfully worry about being unfaithful to their faith were they to step outside their circle of faith to talk about religious ways of life, whether their own or that of people in other religions. They worry that doing so would give some external point of view precedence over their own way of religiously understanding things. It is difficult to distinguish the way secular talk about religions reduces the distinctively religious to something secular (psychology or sociology) from ways of talking that simply distinguish religious ways of life or the ways people in one way of life might talk respectfully about another religious way of life. This is the case when one understands that for historical reasons different people have constituted different responses to the call of the infinite, and thus also that a religious person still quite properly can live faithfully in one specific religious tradition.

This difficulty, however, only constitutes a challenge and not an impossibility. It challenges people deeply committed to the fundamentals of a particular religious faith to proceed carefully, cautiously, courageously, and respectfully. It does not call for fearful denial or a panicky effort to build an impregnable fortress protecting one's own faith and faithfulness. It does not call for seeing self-examination as religious betrayal. Religious talk responding to the call of the infinite not only does not need to fear self-examination or critical interrogation, but it demands it so that pretentious religious emperors can be shown to be wearing no clothes. Because it is so easy for religious faithfulness to fall into idolatry, self-interrogation, reformation, and reconstruction are continually needed. It is never enough for religious reformations to be one-time occurrences. They are continually needed because it is so difficult for religious verbal responses to the infinite to not fall back into talk about secular finite beings, and because it is so tempting for the holders of political, economic, and social power to try to manipulate religious talk and authentic religious faithfulness in order to legitimate dominating and oppressive practices that reap material rewards for the holders of power. Religious faithfulness requires constant resistance against those who would corrupt loyal religious responses to the call of the infinite so as to support their self-serving interests.

Religious talk that responds in one specific way to the call of the infinite need not fear recognizing that others have found other ways of responding in words and deeds to this call. The call is universal but the responses are many and varied. Total faithfulness to one's way of responding not only permits but requires respecting other ways of responding. Otherwise, one is confusedly replacing the infinite with one's particular way of responding to the infinite. One is transforming a religiously appropriate way of responding into a religiously inappropriate worship of a humanly constituted tradition. One is turning it into a false idol to worship. A definitive part of any religious response to the call of the infinite is an affirmation that one's response is only a historically, socially, and personally finite response, and that there are other possible ways of responding. Total faithfulness to one's own faith requires total faithfulness to that affirmation. Different authentic religious traditions do not war with one another, either militarily or culturally. Authentic religious traditions do not use the coercive power of the state or oppressive social practices to force people to be faithful to their particular religious tradition. Religiously faithful people move far beyond merely tolerating other traditions; they respect and cherish the way different sorts of socially and culturally constituted people respond to the call of the infinite.[7]

In addition, encounters with the infinite are not one-time events. A religious tradition is a living tradition only if its participants are continually encountering the infinite and seeking to respond to this call. This means that religious traditions are never frozen in ice. They are historical and subject to modification. Reflecting on the universal fundamental in all religions and the different fundamentals in different religions may very well deepen, broaden, and strengthen one's own faithfulness to the call of the infinite. Dialogically listening to the faith affirmations of other religions may well produce reconstruction of one's own tradition, but it can do so without destroying differences between the world's religions, differences that must be respected and cherished if those constituted by and living within those traditions are to be respected and loved.

In spite of the fact that the world's religions place encounters with the indescribable infinite as the yardstick measuring the faithfulness of all religious responses, many intellectuals and scholars who want to talk about the world's religions ignore that yardstick and talk instead only about the concepts, language, beliefs, experiences, and practices being measured. They proceed as if these phenomena were not responses at all but were by themselves exhaustively definitive of these world's religions. Sociologists accent differences in social practices. Psychologists accent differences in religious experiences. Philosophers and many historians of religion accent differences in concepts and beliefs. When these religious practices, beliefs, and experiences are divorced from what makes them distinctively religious, scholarly studies of religion end up reductively describing religious responses in a merely secular manner.[8] When the heart and soul of religion is cut out in this manner, the world's various religious forms of life get destroyed and the way religious language functions in these ways of life becomes totally lost to sight. Taking such an approach not only makes it difficult to understand authentic religious talk, it makes it impossible.

The problem of understanding religious talk becomes especially acute for scholars and non-scholars alike when differences in religious practices are seen as stemming from differences in religious beliefs torn out of the religious way of life that gives them their identities, when the religious faithfulness of people to encounters with the infinite is reductively taken to be a matter of merely holding certain beliefs about supernatural or metaphysical beings and events. Many people today claim that in some religions people believe that there is one supernatural god while those in other religions believe that there are many such gods. Some people believe that they will be reincarnated, while others believe that they will be punished or rewarded in an everlastingly long life after death. Religion, they claim, is fundamentally a matter of subscribing to such beliefs.

This metaphysical intellectualization of religion is apparent also in the kinds of questions many ordinary people ask when talking to one another about religion. What do you believe? Do you believe that there is a God, a supreme being? Do you believe that Jesus Christ is the son of God? Do you believe that there is a higher power? Do you believe that there is a hell or a heaven? Do you believe that everything written in the Bible is true? How about what is written in the Qur'an or the Vedas?

Once such talk is torn out of its religious home in faithful responses to encounters with the indescribably infinite, only two nonreligious ways of interpreting such talk seems possible. Either the religious phenomena being talked about are nothing but secularly describable psychological or sociological phenomena or they are secularly describable supernatural or metaphysical phenomena with respect to which one can be a believer, an atheist, a skeptic, or an agnostic. Tragically, the continual debates among these four positions drown out investigations of the place of religious concepts, beliefs, experiences, and practices in the religious forms of life constituted in faithful responses to the call of the infinite.

Disagreements about the answers to the above questions are what often lead to vicious arguments and violent conflicts. Without doubt, religiously faithful people do hold religious beliefs, but these are beliefs about religious beings and events socially constituted by worshiping communities responding to encounters with the infinite. Religious faithfulness is what gives religious beliefs their content, and it is not beliefs about metaphysical beings that constitute, generate, or justify such faithfulness. Prioritizing beliefs over faithfulness is a mark of religious confusion or of a religious pretense that favors loyalty to nonreligious beings, supposedly designated in metaphysical or supernatural terms, over faithfulness to encounters with the infinite. It is the prioritizing of beliefs about beings or events not constituted as part of a faithful response to the infinite that leads to intellectual and violent conflicts between the holders of conflicting beliefs of this sort, beliefs often offered as religious but which are not tied back to the universal core of all authentic religions.

There are a number of interconnected reasons why so many people think that religion is a matter of beliefs about metaphysical or supernatural beings, and why there are so many weeds and pretenders in the fields and temples of religion. First, it is difficult to talk about an infinite other to everything finite without ending up once again describing some supposed being or event. Every being or event remains inescapably finite and cannot be the infinite other to the finite. So much of our talk is about nonreligious finite beings and events—apples and oranges, shapes and sizes, countries and corporations, human actions and unforeseen events—and therefore is difficult to drop when talking about encountering the infinite and about one's proper linguistic and nonlinguistic responses to such an encounter. Rather than using a language of creation to express our joyous acceptance of the elements of wind and water with which we live, it is difficult not to end up talking about a powerful, supernatural being creating nature the way a potter creates a vase or a dancer creates a dance. Rather than simply living faithfully in response to encounters with the infinite by interpreting everything using an exodus or resurrection faith, it is difficult not to construct a narrative of miraculous acts performed by a supernatural actor. This is especially the case when creation talk is transformed into metaphysical talk about unmoved movers, and eternal life and happiness talk is contaminated by metaphysical talk about immaterial souls or bodiless spirits. If one were to talk about a super being and its acts, or about metaphysical souls, spirits, or minds, however, one still would be talking about humanly constituted, finite beings or events. This is fine if the being is religiously constituted in response to encounters with the infinite, but it is human self-deification if beliefs about such beings or events are prioritized over encounters with the nonfinite. Saying that a being is infinite is not sufficient to make it so. This is because all talk about beings or events is human talk, and all such talk is done using humanly constructed concepts governed by human, social criteria of applicability. Thus, all such talk is about humanly constituted, finite beings and events, even when it is presented as talk about supposedly immortal souls or supernatural beings, powers, or activities. All concepts of beings or events apply only to identifiable objects of thought different from other identifiable objects of thought. Each such being or event is finitely limited by the others from which it is different.

It does not help to say that one is talking only metaphorically or allegorically when one is talking about supposedly supernatural beings. When one uses language metaphorically, one is drawing upon similarities existing between things. Saying "John is a pig" is saying that John lives the way one believes that pigs behave. That which is other than all finite things cannot be a thing that is similar to finite things. Besides, one must already assume that it makes sense to say that there exists a supernatural, infinite being in order to be able to say that one can use language metaphorically to describe this being. This same critique applies to efforts to use language allegorically in order to give descriptive content to the expression supernatural, infinite being. There can be point-by-point similarities between elements in an allegorical narrative and the nature and activities of an infinite being only if makes sense to talk of an infinite being and if there can be similarities between the finite and its other. Neither makes sense.

What rescues religious talk about the infinite other to all finite beings and events from the same criticism of reducing the infinite to the finite is that such religious talk is not about some describable and identifiable being, some object falling under some concept. The infinite is not any such being or event. Talking about encountering the infinite is talking about human life and subjectivity in a way that shows that there is more to them than what can be conceptually classified and individuated. In part five of this section, an attempt will be made to show how we can encounter that which transcends the conceptual and describable without turning it into some infinite being. The finite, conceptualized, symbolic, descriptive world shows that it is neither exhaustive of human life nor self-sufficient. It points to what is ungraspable by human language, thought, and conceptualized experience, but still is a necessary precondition for such grasping. That which is other to all beings and events is not one more being or event. The call of the infinite is a cry and not the assertion of a proposition, and hearing and faithfully responding to this cry is not in the first instance coming to believe some propositions, but rather it is a matter of moods and desires. It is a matter of being thankful for life and repentant for what one has been socially constituted to be. It is a matter of desiring to be responsible to people in their unclassifiable uniqueness, desiring what is most worthy of desire, desiring to ever strengthen one's desire to be responsible. It is a desire that is not aimed at meeting a lack in a constituted subject, but rather a desire transcending the interests of oneself as such a subject in order to be passionately interested in rebuffing threats to the infinitely precious, unique singularity of other people.

The whole debate with fundamentalists about whether one is to take religious texts literally or not is grounded in confusion about what religious texts literally are saying. Of course one is to take religious texts literally. The question is, "What is the literal meaning of religious texts?" What is the form of life and linguistic activities in which these words are being used? These texts are not secular scientific or historical texts. The *Bible* and the *Bhagavad-Gita* are not CNN nonreligious reports of nonreligiously constituted people and events. Neither are religious texts metaphysical texts trying to talk about a supposed infinite, supernatural being and its actions. Secularists are correct in saying that religious texts should not be taken as literal, secular scientific or historical texts. Religious liberals are incorrect when they say that these texts are metaphorically pointing from secularly described beings and events to a supernatural being and the actions of such a being. "Fundamentalists" are correct when they say that religious texts are not to be dismissed because they are not secular texts dealing with secularly described beings and events. They are incorrect when they say that these texts are to be read as non-metaphorical descriptions of metaphysical souls or a supernatural being and its actions. Such "fundamentalists" are not literalists; they do not let religious texts mean what they literally mean. In their talk about religious texts they do not remain faithful to the fundamentals of religion in general or the fundamentals of the religions of the world in their specifics. They keep interpreting religious texts metaphysically.

There is no doubt that many persons worshiping in religious communities labeled as "fundamentalist" are striving to live lives of religious faithfulness. They often are among the most committed of religious people. This is why it is so tragic that their religious desires and commitment get tied to confused theoretical assertions about the meaning of religious texts and to claims about supernatural beings and events that are religiously unnecessary and counterproductive. What is wrong with "fundamentalists" theorizing is that it make incoherent and unjustifiable metaphysical claims, and then too often uses these claims in an attempt to justify restricting freedom and acting cruelly. "Fundamentalist" opposition to sex education, stem cell research, abortion, reducing AIDS by promoting use of condoms, family planning, sex education, homosexuality, ending clitoridectomies, ending coercive dress codes, and ending coercive caste systems generally and for the most part is grounded not in religious faith but in metaphysical beliefs parading as religious beliefs.

Understanding what is involved in remaining faithful to encounters with the infinite and to the world's religious responses to the infinite requires moving beyond reductions, by so-called "literalists," of religious speech to journalist type reports of supernatural events, and moving away from metaphysical claims about some supreme being transcending secular beings. It requires understanding how the words and sentences in religious texts, prayers, and acts of worship function in the religious linguistic acts and forms of life in which they function. This book is an attempt to aid readers to gain such understanding by looking at the religious responses constitutive of six of the world's religions.

3. The Metaphysical God

To understand what faithfulness to encounters with the infinite involves it is necessary first to understand what the infinite in religion is not. It is not the metaphysical god which so many philosophers and theologians have tried to prove exists, and which Nietzsche has proclaimed to be dead. It is important to note that almost all philosophers who defend what they call "atheism" are thinkers who are defending their belief that metaphysical gods do not exist. If religious faithfulness also excludes beliefs in metaphysical beings, then the religiously faithful also quite appropriately are such metaphysical"atheists." Because of the Buddha's noble silence on issues of metaphysical speculation, Buddhists often have been called "atheists". This not only does not prevent them from being authentically religious, but it is a necessary condition for such authenticity. As we shall see in part five of this opening section, a number of modern defenders of religious faithfulness, such as Levinas, Derrida, Caputo, Marion, Zizek and D.Z. Phillips, have explicitly written that the God whom one is to faithfully serve is not some supreme being who makes it possible to give super-scientific metaphysical explanations for why all other beings exist and are as they are. This book attempts to show that all the religions of the world are metaphysically atheistic. Their responses to encounters with the infinite are not tied to beliefs in the existence of a metaphysical ultimate being. Unfortunately many intellectuals in these traditions have planted so many metaphysical weeds in these fields of religious faithfulness that it now is difficult for many of the faithful to separate their religious faith from these metaphysical beliefs. This book aims to help people achieve this separation.

For many contemporary Western philosophers of religion, the very idea that religion might not involve belief in a metaphysical god seems incredulous. A huge scholastic industry is now flourishing as philosophers publish books and papers sometimes defending some version of a supposed proof of the existence of a metaphysical god and sometimes arguing that all such versions are unsound. Sometimes the arguments pro and con are centered on the issue of whether traditional metaphysical characterizations of such a god are consistent or coherent. These metaphysical philosophers of religion even interpret all of the thinkers about religion who reject the whole metaphysical project as people still talking about a metaphysical god but doing so in confused, incoherent, self-contradictory, unjustified and irrational ways. For example, Nicholas Everitt, in a book presenting powerful, carefully constructed arguments criticizing traditional concepts of a metaphysical god and classical and contemporary attempts to prove the existence of such a god, limits his attention only to metaphysical philosophers of religion.[9] He examines carefully none of the texts of interpreters of religion who reject the whole metaphysical project.

In a very cavalier manner, Everitt criticizes Kierkegaard and Wittgenstein because the former says it is futile to engage in metaphysical reasoning about the existence of god and the latter says that if there were evidence supporting belief in God this would destroy the whole religious business. Everitt thinks that the fact that theologians and philosophers for centuries have been presenting arguments pro and con for the existence of the metaphysical god shows that Kierkegaard and Wittgenstein are wrong.[10] He does not even entertain the possibility that they are not talking about a metaphysical god, a supreme, supernatural being. When Kierkegaard says it is religiously futile to play the metaphysical game, this is because that game is played in the subjective mode of objectivity (an objectivistic way of life focusing on secularly conceivable objects) while religion is a matter of living in a subjective more of subjectivity (a subjectivistic mode of life focused on finding a true mode of living which works for people who are both finite and

infinite). When Wittgenstein says that talking about evidence supporting beliefs in a metaphysical god would destroy religious life, this
is because religion deals not with beliefs about secularly conceivable
beings but with taking up attitudes towards the whole world of secular
beings and happenings. Everitt is convinced that the word "god" gets
its meaning from the metaphysicians and metaphysical theologians
who have been using the word in their debates about the existence
of the metaphysical god.[11] Those who reject the metaphysical project
claim that it gets it meaning from its use in the practices of worship
and prayer in which it is used, a use which this book will try to show
is not tied to efforts to refer to a metaphysical being because it is used
in faithfully responding to encounters with the other of everything
merely finite, an other that cannot be a being or it would be finite.

It is because it is so difficult to distinguish talk about encountering
the infinite from talk about some supernatural being that metaphysicians have been so successful in sowing their corrupting, speculative and
theoretical weeds in the fields of religious faithfulness. The metaphysical
project begun by Aristotle over 2000 tears ago in ancient Greece does
not give priority in human life to responding faithfully to encounters
with the nonfinite. It gives priority to responding intellectually to contingencies in life by constructing theories about how things necessarily
and timelessly are. It is a project in which finite people attempt to use
finite reason to give final explanatory answers to the questions: Why
is every contingent thing as it is rather than otherwise and why do all
contingent events occur as they do rather than otherwise? It attempts
to answer these questions with a theory about ultimate reality, a theory
about some necessary, infinite, unchanging being causing all contingent,
finite, changing beings and events to be as they are. It is a rationalistic
project which gives ultimate allegiance to a principle of sufficient reason which claims that there must be a reason why every possibility that
is not actual remains a mere possibility. The metaphysical claim that
there must be a reason for everything unfortunately was seized upon by
many religious thinkers, and thus religious responses of thanksgiving
and hope were mutated into beliefs that there is a supernatural purpose
for everything that exists and happens. Religious talk grounded in faithful responses to encounters with the infinite was transformed into talk

about an infinite and eternal being having a reason and purpose for causing all contingent beings to exist and all contingent events to occur. It is this intellectual project that has corrupted in many different ways the religious talk of Hindus, Jews, Christians and Muslims. It is one of the aims of this book to tear out these weeds and to show how religious faithfulness thrives without them.

Since the ancient Greeks, philosophy has defined itself as love of wisdom. This wisdom is an intellectual kind of wisdom. Aristotle claims that wisdom is knowledge of the ultimate reasons why everything is as it is and not otherwise.[12] The religions of the world offer a different kind of wisdom. Their passion is not knowing what finite objects and events are like, when described in nonreligious terms, or why they are as they are. The wise religious person knows how to relate and respond to the finite objects and events in the world, how to construct a way of living, evaluating, feeling, and thinking about the finite, a way that consists in a faithful response to encounters with what is other than such finite beings and events. Aristotle says that wonder is what brings people to philosophy. This again, however, is wondering why things are as they are. It is not the wonder religious people experience when religious people respond thankfully to the wonderfulness of their own existence and their dependence upon elements which are the source of their most basic enjoyment. It is not the wonder religious people experience when they encounter other people face-to-face, encounter them in their infinite, singular uniqueness and immeasurable ethical value and significance. Aristotle's world is an intellectual world of descriptions, beliefs and explanations of finite beings and events. Religion's world is a world of responses to encounters with what is other to all descriptive beings and events.

Since all beings and events of which we can have sensory knowledge exist only contingently, metaphysicians have felt compelled to produce rational arguments which supposedly prove that there exists some necessarily existent, ultimate reality in terms of which all contingent beings and events can be explained. Since sensory descriptions only apply to the finite and contingent, the only descriptions of this ultimate reality that are possible are the ones that must be postulated in the effort to give such metaphysical explanations. To answer the question why something is as it is one must say that it is because of something else. In the metaphysical project these "becauses" are called "causes." It is not possible to satisfy the metaphysician's principle of sufficient reason by simply saying that one contingency caused another contingency, by saying that Sally's parents are the cause of her birth or that John's drunkenness was the cause of the automobile accident. These types of answers simply invite more "whys?" The principle of sufficient reason can be satisfied adequately only if a final cause can be stipulated which could not be otherwise. The final cause, the final answer to the string of "Why?" questions, which leaves no room for any more "Why?" questions, has to be something necessary, something for which there is no alternative possibility that has to be explained.

Right at the beginning, therefore, the metaphysician faces the problem of specifying a meaning for the word "necessary" and the supposed relationship holding between such a necessary being and the contingent beings and events in the world, specifications which will meet the requirements of the principle of sufficient reason. The notion of physical necessity used by scientists in characterizing what is required by laws of nature such as the law of gravity won't meet the need for a final necessity because such laws might be different from the way these laws are. The notion of necessity used by logicians, who claim that certain propositions are necessarily true, won't meet the need because from logically necessary truths only logically necessary propositions, and not contingent truths, can be deduced. The notion of necessity involved in saying that something is causally necessary for everything else and nothing is causally necessary for it requires specifying some notion of cause which will meet the requirements of the principle of sufficient reason. However, is such a notion of cause any more possible than the notion of necessity just examined?

Since all events occurring in time occur only contingently and might not have happened, no event in time can be the ultimate cause. Science for centuries now has understood causality in terms of causal laws governing the occurrence of events in time, laws which specify how things do behave or how they would behave if scientists were to make experimental changes in the occurrence of such events. For example, all bodies gravitate towards each other directly proportional to their mass and inversely proportional to the distance between them. Such causal laws, however, are contingent. The law might have said that all bodies gravitate towards each directly proportional to the square of their masses. The laws of science can't give the metaphysician what is desired, a reason or cause why the law is as it is and not as it might have been. One must try to go outside all sequences of events in time in order to postulate a metaphysical, ultimate cause. The problem is finding some notion of a causal relation holding between a supposedly unchanging, nonfinite being and all the finite beings and events in the world.

Metaphysicians have turned from the notion of scientific causality to the notion of causality involved in saying that people make things happen.[13] They have postulated that there is some necessarily existent, eternal agent that is this kind of cause of all contingencies. We do talk about agents causing things to happen. The scientific talk about causal laws is not our only causal talk. The metaphysician claims that one must postulate some agent existing outside of time but causing things to happen in time, if all contingencies are to be explained. One must turn to a necessary, timeless, eternal agent timelessly causing all contingent beings to exist and all contingent events to occur. The demands of the principle of sufficient reason can be satisfied with nothing less. Metaphysicians often have called such an agent "god," and metaphysical theologians unfortunately have interpreted religious talk about creation in terms of such an agent.

The problem, of course, is making any sense out of the notion of a timeless act causing any and all events occurring at some time, of an eternal "god" "creating" a world of contingent beings and events in time.[14] This agent often was called by metaphysicians "A First Cause," but, of course, they did not mean a first cause in time but a cause that was first or ultimate in the sequence of explanations satisfying the principle of sufficient reason. In this metaphysical scenario, talk about God acting in history (saving the children of Israel from slavery in Egypt) has to be interpreted as meaning that this act eternally is a part of the agent's timeless act. History gets swallowed up in this one timeless act. To make this eternal agent the cause of everything is to say that only one agent is responsible for everything that happens. This generates all the problems tied up with notions of eternal predestination and the task of reconciling talk about human freedom and responsibility with this talk about the metaphysical god causing everything. If one takes seriously the claim that some metaphysicians/theologians make, that the unmoved mover causes space for freedom to exist, then either this "freedom" is a mere appearance (really the unmoved mover is causing things to happen) or free actions are not metaphysically explainable. Postulating the metaphysical god as the ultimate cause of everything also generates the metaphysical/theological problem of suffering. If the metaphysical god causes everything, then this ultimate cause is responsible for suffering caused by tornados and cancer and by the people who are what they are and are behaving as they behave because of this one timeless act. The metaphysical god, however, as we shall see, cannot do anything wrong or let anything wrong happen; it must be a good, all knowing, all-powerful god. Why then is there suffering?

The principle of sufficient reason is not satisfied by merely postulating a timeless agent. We still need to ask why such an agent created the finite world in time to be as it is. In our ordinary talk about agents, they create things and cause things to happen in order to achieve a certain result. If the eternal agent were limited in knowledge about what things would be like after his causal act, then there would be a need to explain why there is such a limitation. The eternal agent must be infinitely unlimited in knowledge; it must be omniscient, knowing all possibilities and all actualities. Of course, this must be a kind of knowledge radically different from all forms of human knowledge. This agent cannot be changed by sensory input from finite objects. In one eternal "moment" this agent must know all past, present, and future events. Since this agent is unchanging, we can't say that what we do in any way affects or changes this metaphysical god. There is no response in it to human joy or suffering because responses are events occurring in time. Also, even though this God is said to be all knowing, we cannot say that it knows what we will do before we do it or what the consequences of out actions will be before they happen. We have to say that this agent timelessly knows all events, just as it timelessly causes all events. One shouldn't say that the metaphysical god predestines everything, because the prefix "pre" suggests that god knew before we acted what would happen. Locating such knowledge at a time before we act is to locate this god in time and thus to deny its eternal character. The metaphysician needs to say that its god, in its timeless act and knowledge, eternally destines everything to happen as it does. The problem then arises whether our ordinary use of the word "knowledge" can be modified in this way and still be used in the way we ordinarily use it, to mark justified and not unjustified beliefs.[15] We also face the problem of whether such metaphysical talk can do any kind of justice to what people in theistic religions mean when they say that God acts in history or that God knows their suffering.

The principle of sufficient reason also requires that there be no limitations on the ability and power of this agent to select which possibilities to make actual. The infinite, eternal, omniscient agent must be omnipotent. Again, problems arise when the metaphysician tries to specify how the word "power" works in the case of this infinite, eternal agent. In the science of motion, "power" is defined in terms of the time it takes to accelerate a mass through a specified distance, with such acceleration always being caused by another object acting upon it. The metaphysician's first cause, however, cannot be an object in space acting at a time. We can talk about people having the power to move things, the power to overcome obstacles, the power to get people angry, the power to think things through. All these exercises of agency power, however, are carried out by finite, embodied persons existing in space and time and acting on beings likewise located in space and time. None of these notions of power carry over when talking about an unlimited, infinite, unembodied agent causing at one timeless moment all finite beings to exist and events to occur. There seems to be no difference between saying that everything simply happens as it happens and everything is caused to happen by an all knowing, all powerful eternal agent. Only by using anthropomorphic language to talk about this ultimate cause does it seem to make sense to talk about action, knowledge and power here. This is only an appearance of meaning, however, because we have no clue how to use such language to talk about this cause. The problem becomes even worse when the metaphysician says that this ultimate cause is good and perfect.

The principle of sufficient reason requires that we answer the question why one set of possibilities is timelessly actualized rather than a different set. This question can be given a final answer only if the best set of possibilities is actualized and the all knowing, all powerful, eternal, unlimited, infinite, first cause is perfectly good. If the best possible world is not created, then it is necessary to explain why the metaphysical god was prevented from producing the best results. Such a god, however, could not be the final explanation for everything contingent. If the set of possibilities actualized is the best possible set, then one has the best possible reason for this actualization. This gives us a sufficient reason for actualization only if the agent actualizing these possibilities is perfectly good and has no reason or motive for doing anything else. This goodness, therefore, must be a necessary feature of this infinite agent, just as must its omnipotence, omniscience, eternity, and limitless. It these were only contingent features, the question why this agent has these features would have no sufficient answer.

The metaphysician's god, were one possible, would have to be the way the principle of sufficient reason requires it to be. Using this principle to answer the question why everything is as it is requires that this god be described this way. It is this intellectual project of seeking to give ultimate explanations that supplies the description of this supposedly ultimate answer to the philosopher's intellectual wondering. Talk about such a supposedly final and first cause of all contingencies, about such a metaphysical god, however, is not religious talk. It is an intellectual substitute for the words of prayer and worship. One can talk as a metaphysician without ever having encountered the infinite other to all things finite and without responding faithfully to such an encounter. One can say that one believes in such a metaphysical god without passionate commitment to justice, respect for the indescribable singular uniqueness of people, and without responding in worship and prayer with thankfulness, contrition, and hope. Actually, worship and prayer would be meaningless if such a metaphysical god existed. Everything simply is as it must be, and even acts of worship and prayer would be eternally destined by the unmoved mover. The same holds for the metaphysical project itself. As Hegel pointed out, the unmoved mover would be the cause of people believing in the unmoved mover; coming to believe in the metaphysical god would be just a predestined moment in the movement of the eternal Absolute from potentiality to actuality. It is the metaphysician's commitment to the principle of sufficient reason and thus to his own intellectual practices of wondering and seeking ultimate explanations that is the ruling force in his life. The finite, human intellect is raised to the level of an ultimate, and it is just such a deification of the finite that encounters with the infinite denounce as worship of idols.

In spite of all the problems inherent in explaining the meaning of the descriptive terms applied to the metaphysician's postulated ultimate reality, attempts have been made by metaphysicians to prove that their explanatory god exists. Many religious people, responding to encounters with the other to all finite beings and events, find all talk about proofs not only unnecessary but as symptoms of the metaphysician's effort to deify human rationality. Metaphysicians need rational proofs to demonstrate that they can masterfully represent ultimate reality and provide explanations of all contingencies. Also, this is their only descriptive access to their god. Just as their efforts to describe their god face insurmountable problems, so do their attempted proofs of its existence. There are specific reasons why each particular "proof" fails,[16] but the general, overall reason for their failure is their dependence upon the principle of sufficient reason, which produces the incoherence mentioned above and which is totally unjustified. Before examining the reasons why specific proofs fail, it will be useful to see what is wrong with the metaphysician's whole project of finding sufficient reasons for why all contingencies exist.

The metaphysician's effort to explain all finite beings and events in terms of an ultimate reality is an intellectual attempt to transcend the finite conditions which govern the use of the words "explain" and "real". In our ordinary use of the word "explain," explanations are needed only when anomalies appear, when we believe that situations are present that cannot be explained by our current general beliefs about how things happen. It is against a background of general beliefs that expectations are formed. When an anomaly appears that is not expected, then the question "Why?" has work to do. The question is answered when background beliefs are modified so that the anomaly disappears and the unexpected now becomes the expected. The pragmatics of the human situation determine when explanations are needed and when they have been successfully given. There is no need to try to do what we have seen as impossible, specify an eternal, infinite being causing any and all contingencies to be as they are. All that is needed to explain events that need explaining is finding a general but contingent account of how finite things behave which for the time being leaves no unexplained anomalies.[17]

Attending to the pragmatics governing the use of the word "real" also shows that there is no need to postulate some ultimate reality. The word "real" has work to do on those occasions when one wants to rule out the possibility that some describable thing is not real, is a fake, or imitation, or pretense, or phoney. Saying that something is a real diamond is just saying that it is a diamond, saying this in some context in which doubts have arisen about whether it is a diamond at all. Only if one has some reason for thinking that the whole finite, descriptive world is only an appearance or an imitation does it make sense to talk about an ultimate reality.[18] Only if one already assumes the truth of some general metaphysical claim, such as the principle of sufficient reason, can one find our whole descriptive world to be an anomaly needing explanation. Since the question "why?" also always needs pragmatic conditions in order to have a use and meaning, and thus the search for first or final causes is not necessary for explaining things needing explanation, then there is no need to treat finite contingencies as mere appearances of an "ultimate reality." Examining the specific problems present in the proofs offered to demonstrate the necessity of postulating a metaphysical god will provide additional reasons for rejecting the whole metaphysical project of seeking final explanations of contingencies in some ultimate reality.

The cosmological argument is offered by Aristotle[19] and Aquinas[20] and purports to prove that observable changes in the finite world can be explained only if they are explained in terms of an eternal, infinite being of the sort metaphysicians postulate. They claim that all motion needs a cause and that there cannot be an infinite series of such causes. If the word "motion" is taken to designate the motion of a physical object through space, then the argument is claiming that there cannot be an infinite series of such motions, with one motion causing the next. There has to be a first motion, a "big bang." This argument does not work, however, for three reasons. First, it is not rationally necessary that a series of past or future motions come to an end. If the present is numbered zero, then there could be an unending series of negative numbers for the past and an unending series of positive numbers for the future. Second, treating a metaphysical god as the agent causing the "big bang" first motion, steals from this god its eternal character. It now acts at the first moment of time and not timelessly. Thirdly, motions of objects do not always need a causal explanation, as Newton's first law of motion points out. Bodies in motion simply stay in motion unless acted upon by an external force. Only the acceleration or de-acceleration of bodes needs explanations and these are explained by the force of other bodies acting upon them. The ancient Greeks were unaware of this law of inertia.

Newton scientifically pulled the rug out from under this cosmological argument. Kierkegaard religiously did the same thing when he showed that such objectivisitic attempts to prove the existence of an object fail to understand that these attempts are part of a subjectivisitic form of life that is anti-religious because it gives primary loyalty to human intellectual efforts rather than to a worshipful faithfulness that indicts all worship of such finite, man-made idols. In spite of its argumentative, scientific and religious inadequacies, a huge intellectual industry has developed attacking and defending this argument. This is an industry that does not produce any products that authentic religions need. Its products simply spread harmful contaminants in religious environments.

Aristotle and Aquinas generally did not use the word "motion" to refer to such movements of objects through space. They used a biological notion of motion. "Motion" for them meant "growth," moving from potentiality to actuality the way an acorn grows to be an oak tree or a baby moves or changes as it matures. They argued that explanations for the existence of finite beings and the occurrence of contingent events ultimately depend upon giving explanations of potentialities becoming actualities. For Aristotle, the whole world of contingencies is to be explained as striving to reach a certain final actual form, striving as if it were in love with the unmoved mover, the pure form which governs the whole process of growth in the finite world. For Aquinas, the metaphysical god is a very special kind of agent, one which is pure actuality, without any potential for change, but still one governing the actualization of potentialities in finite beings. Using this biological notion of motion in a proof for the existence of the metaphysical god, however, begs the question. It assumes what it is trying to prove. It assumes that the finite world really is a world of potentialities seeking actuality and that such growth can only be explained in terms of an infinite, eternal un-growing grower. We have no reason to think that the finite world as a whole is a living, growing thing. To have such a reason the metaphysical thinker must assume that the only way to explain biological growth is by postulating such an unmoved mover governing such a growing world. In contemporary biochemistry, however, we have excellent explanations in terms of DNA and proteins why living things mature as they do, and these explanations do not themselves require explanations in terms of an unmoved mover. In addition, only if we assume that we could escape our finitude, and stand outside like a disembodied mind, could we know that the whole world is such an evolving organism moving from potentiality towards an eternally destined actuality. Hegel thought that metaphysicians could rationally reach such a transcendent position, that they could through reason actualize divine knowledge in themselves. It is just such self-deification that religiously faithful prophets like Kierkegaard have denounced.

There have been many recent attempts to reconstruct the cosmological argument for the existence of a metaphysical god, but they also fail to escape the objections just given to Aristotle's and Aquinas's original formulations. In order not to get lost in the polemics involved in the philosophical industry engaged in debating the pros and cons of supposed cosmological proofs of the existence of the metaphysical god, examining only a few recent efforts to defend the cosmological argument should be sufficient to show how old difficulties with these proofs reappear in modern dress. William Craig[21] has argued that it is incoherent to talk about there being actually an unending series of events prior to the present, causing the present to be as it is, because mathematics shows that in an actual infinite set of numbers any subset of numbers is equivalent to the whole infinite set. Thus, he concludes, if there were an actual infinite set of past events, yesterday would be the same thing as an infinite number of yesterdays, and if yesterday were wiped out, then all time would be wiped out[22]. Rather than showing that today's changes couldn't be the causal result of an endless series of earlier changes, however, Craig only shows that mathematical talk about actual infinite sets must be kept distinguished from non-mathematical talk about things always have been happening. It was confusing mathematical talk with empirical talk that led to the Zeno's paradoxes. (Achilles can't pass the tortoise because he must pass through the infinite set of points separating him and the tortoise, and this can't be done in the finite number of moments of time available to Achilles.) We can run past turtles, however, and every yesterday could be preceded by a previous yesterday without ever forming the mathematical actual infinite set that creates the paradoxes Craig mentions. Talk about a mathematically closed infinite set is a radically different kind of talk from talking about a historically unclosed, unending series of yesterdays. As Paul Draper points out, none of the things that Cantor has to say in his theory of transfinite numbers entails that there has to be a first moment of time.[23] There is no conceptual incoherence in saying that things endlessly have been and will be happening.

Although it is not incoherent to talk about happenings having no beginning or end, perhaps it is empirically false to say that they do. Astronomers seem to be saying just that in presenting their "big bang" theory. Craig uses this astronomical theory to give what he calls a scientific argument in defense of the claim that an infinite personal being had to be the cause of our worlds of stars and atoms. He thinks that astronomy's big bang theory of the origin of the universe shows that it was caused by a personal infinite god. He charges that the only way to explain the big bang is by postulating an unchanging metaphysical being who chooses to begin the big bang. The problems with this "proof", as with all such "proofs" of metaphysical beings, are threefold: [1] the metaphysical postulation is scientifically untestable and thus is not a scientific proof at all, [2] No criteria for the application of the words "cause," "began," "being," and "choice" can be supplied[24], and [3] a variety of alternative scientific explanations are possible. As far as scientific evidence is concerned, saying that an unchanging, nonfinite being caused the big bang to occur cannot be conceptually distinguished from saying that the big bang just occurred without any cause. We have no way of identifying such a being, of specifying the difference between saying there is one such being or many such beings, or of giving content to the notion of a causal relation between a nonfinite, non-material, non-temporal being and the universe of finite, material, temporal events. Besides, an uncaused big bang is a scientific possibility. Theordore Schick Jr.[25] has pointed out that quantum mechanics has shown that some things occur which are uncaused. Just as electrons, photons, and positrons appear spontaneously in vacuum fluctuations, so our big bang might have been just a fluctuation in some larger space.[26] There is no need to claim that such a possibility is what actually happened. That it might have happened is enough to show that postulating an infinite being as the universe's cause is not necessary. Also, our big bang might have been just one among an indefinitely large number of big bangs. Our expanding universe might be only one among many such universes. Although there isn't enough mass in existence for everything to be oscillating back and forth in an expanding, then condensing, and then expanding universe, it is quite possible that our universe is but one among many universes each of which is repeatedly expanding from a very small dense core [a black hole] and then contracting back into a black hole again, with gravitational potential energy equalizing mass-energy. The point is not whether Schick's theorizing is correct (that is the business of astrophysics) but that the use of the "only possible explanation" tactic is inherently flawed. It only indicates a very limited scientific imagination.

None of this cosmological debating is really relevant to authentic religious faithfulness. One could subscribe to any one of a number of astrophysical or metaphysical explanations of subatomic and astronomical phenomena without in any way being a person living in a religious way of life, without living with religious humility, joy, trust, hope, responsibility and love. Beliefs about big bangs not only do not guarantee a religious mode of life, but making theorizing about big bangs the central focus of one's life guarantees adulation of one's intellectual powers rather than faithfully responding to that infinite which is other than all objects of conceptual and theoretical treatment. Beliefs about metaphysical gods never guarantee religious life. They indicate instead glorification of ourselves rather than the religious faithfulness to that which is other than ourselves and other than anything that people have constituted as objects falling under their nonreligious, descriptive concepts.

Sensing the inadequacy of the cosmological argument, especially after Newton established the law of inertia, metaphysicians from Descartes to Hegel turned to the ontological argument to prove the existence of the metaphysical god. The best known versions of the argument are found in the writings of Anselm[27] and Spinoza [28]. This argument purports to demonstrate that the possibility of the existence of the metaphysical god is sufficient to guarantee that this is not a mere possibility, but that this god actually exists. Anselm enunciates this "proof" in his prayers in order that it might help him understands the god he is worshiping. Anselm defines the metaphysical god as the greatest possible being. He then argues that no contingently existing being could be such a greatest being. Only a being that necessarily exists could be a greatest possible being. He claims that if it is possible that there be a being describable as "greatest possible being," then necessarily it exists and it exists as a necessary and not a contingent being. It is not possible that this possibility be a mere possibility.

This form of the ontological argument, however, faces serious difficulties. Usually when talking about something existing [protons exist], we are not describing what we claim exists. Rather we are saying that the word "proton" can be correctly used to describe something. Similarly, when we say that dragons do not exist, we are saying the word "dragon" cannot be correctly used to describe anything. Saying that the greatest possible being exists is not like saying that protons have mass, and saying that it does not exist is not like saying that dragons are not ice cream bars. "Exists" is not a descriptive term and it cannot be part of the description "greatest possible being." It makes no sense to say that A is greater than B because A exists and B does not exist.

If "exists" is not a descriptive term, can "necessarily exists" be such a descriptive term and can it be used to prove that the greatest possible being does necessarily exists? Alvin Plantinga[29] has argued that there is a version of the ontological argument that is valid and would be seen as sound by anyone who believes that it is possible that there is a greatest possible being, when this predicate "greatest possible being" is defined in a certain way. Since it probably makes no sense to say that there exist merely possible beings, does it make sense to say that it is not possible without contradiction to describe anything with the two supposed predicates "is greatest possible being" and "does not necessarily exist?"[30] Assume "greatest possible being" means having maximal greatness (omnipotence, omniscience, moral perfection) and "having necessary existence" means that these two predicates can be correctly and jointly applied to some x in every possible world. This means that in no possible world do these two predicates fail to be applicable to some x. Since the actual world is one of these possible worlds, we cannot say without contradicting ourselves that there isn't in our world a greatest possible being, a god. However, Plantinga points out that this argument can only be used by someone who independently believes that it is possible that there is a greatest possible being, and thus can only be used by them to show to themselves that their religious faith is not irrational. The person who does not believe that there exists in our actual world a greatest possible being would not believe that it is possible that there exists a greatest possible being in all possible worlds. This version of the ontological argument fails to prove the existence of the metaphysical god. Only by assuming its conclusion as a premise in the argument does it turn our to be formally valid and sound.

There is one other version of the ontological argument worth examining. By "necessary existence" one might mean "a being that is necessary for everything else and nothing is necessary for its existence and thus nothing is sufficient for its non-existence." This is basically Spinoza's definition of substance, his metaphysical god. Spinoza uses this definition, plus his version of the principle of sufficient reason, in constructing his "proof" for the existence of this god. Spinoza claims that not only actualities need an explanation but also possibilities, which, when they remain mere possibilities, need a reason why they are not actual. Since by definition, however, Spinoza argues, nothing could be a sufficient cause for the possibility of this substance not existing, it must exist.

Why, however, accept Spinoza's version of the principle of sufficient reason? As we have seen, only some actualities need explanation, those that are unexpected anomalies given our background general beliefs. Why do un-actualized possibilities need an explanation for being mere possibilities. If something is possible in this formal sense, then it is necessary that it is possible. There is nothing strange about there being such mere possibilities. We are aware of so many things which might have happened but didn't happen. Every choice among possibilities leaves un-actualized possibilities. There are uncountable possibilities that remain mere possibilities. Spinoza's "proof" begs the question. Only by assuming that everything, including all possibilities, is necessitated, and nothing is contingent, is his version of the principle of sufficient reason and the ontological argument acceptable. Of course, then this principle has no work to do because there are no mere possibilities to be explained; there is only one necessary actuality, substance, the metaphysical god. Spinoza's ontological argument becomes the *reductio ad absurdum* of proofs for the existence of an ultimate cause of all contingencies.

Other attempts have been made by metaphysicians and theologians to prove the existence of a metaphysical god, but they also show themselves to be unsound. Design or Teleological Arguments were offered by Aristotle[31] and William Paley[32], supposedly proving that the nature of finite objects can be explained only by postulating the existence of an eternal agent making them be the way they are. Aristotle's favorite example is our teeth, some designed for cutting and some for chewing. Paley sees the whole world, and its parts, such as eyes, as an intricate machine like a clock with carefully coordinated parts. Aristotle claims that only by postulating an unmoved mover moving the growth of teeth towards a destined end can this growth be explained. Otherwise one would have to say it just happened by chance or coincidence, which is highly unlikely. Paley also sees chance as the only alternative to postulating a maker producing things according to an intelligent design. Both claims are false.

The following maxim needs repeating. Whenever someone argues for a position by saying that it is the only alternative to sheer chance, one should suspect that this person has a very limited ability to think of alternative possibilities. Biochemistry and evolutionary biology have provided well verified explanations of biological phenomena such as teeth and eyes.[33] Besides, trying to construct a coherent idea of such a metaphysical designer would face all the problems pointed out already. The designer is timelessly eternal, but the designed product is in time. Designing and producing the designed object occur at a time, but the designer never acts in time because it is eternal. An eternal design either preprograms all the details or it cannot be used to explain why everything is as it is and not otherwise. Either human freedom and history, the heart and soul of religious concerns, get swallowed up by metaphysics, or metaphysical explanations fail to give the explanations promised. In spite of the incoherence of the theory, the scientific demonstration that it is not needed, and its threat to authentic religion, a huge service industry of Sunday morning preachers prosper economically by constantly presenting this discredited argument. The religiously faithful need to understand that their faithfulness in no way depends on believing in the soundness of this argument.

Two recent efforts to argue from the nature of the perceptual world to the existence of the metaphysical god are worth analyzing, because they do not claim that they can deductively prove that such a god exists. Instead, one uses an argument from analogy, and the other argues that postulating such a god gives the best possible explanation of the phenomena being considered. First, Richard Swinburne claims that the only rationally acceptable explanation for the laws of nature is hypothesizing that they are the result of the actions of a rational agent whose body is the whole of the universe, even as some of the order in our world—the placement of books in a library, for example—is the result of the actions of human persons.[34] The hypothesis that interprets all occurrences in the world as actions (some human and some divine) is simpler than a nontheistic hypothesis that interprets some occurrences as the results of human actions and some occurrences as instances of unexplained natural regularities. Swinburne claims that simpler hypotheses are rationally preferable to more complex hypotheses, and thus that is reason to believe in theism. Second, Robert M. Adams has argued that the hypothesis that the metaphysical god exists provides the best explanation for the existence of both brain states and sensory states, because leaving the two kinds of states as brute facts explains nothing, and materialistic identity claims only deny the phenomena being considered, the sensory states. Postulating a metaphysical god can account for the existence of both kinds of states and the orderly relationships holding between them.[35]

The problem with both of these projects is that they seek explanations in situations in which there is no reason to do so. In Swinburne's case, only if one endorses the metaphysical principle of sufficient reason is there any reason to seek explanations of natural regularities. They do not constitute some anomaly needing explanation. One can simply point out, that is simply how things are. That human brains allow human beings to organize libraries is also not surprising, although scientists do want to know much more than we now know about how the brain is functioning when we do such things. There is no need to get trapped in trying to metaphysically solve the metaphysically constructed free-action/natural-determinism problem. Seeing people do things is as primary as seeing things happening to billiard balls and brains. Without the first we would never have the scientific activity of theorizing about the second. No story about the causal relationships between neurological events can invalidate talk about people doing things. As Martin Heidegger has pointed out, beings merely present on hand are constituted by people who care about such beings.[36] Talking about being free to do something is parasitic upon talk about doing things; it is talking about not being compelled to do something (which still is talk about actions). That humans care about talking about what people do and about natural correlations among events does not present a need for a theory that talks instead only about what people do and what a rational being with the universe as its body does.

There also is no need to postulate, as Adams does, a metaphysical god to solve the metaphysically constituted body/mind problem. This is a problem that needs dissolving and not solving. There is no anomaly needing explanation. When animals develop a certain sort of neurological system, then they have sensory states. That these states are not identical with the observable neurological states is not a surprising anomaly needing explanation. It happens with hundreds of species of animals. That these sensory states only appear when certain sorts of neurological states exist is interesting and even exciting, but it only indicates that these neurological conditions are necessary for the presence of these sensory states. That a certain kind of complex neurological condition is necessary for the occurrence of these sensory states is simply a general fact about how things are. Why shouldn't a different kind of state, a sensory state, appear when a certain kind of neurological state appears? As John Searle points out, having brains that enable us to have sensory states is as natural as having a digestive system.[37] The story about conceptualization and intentionality may need to have a social story added to the sensory/neurological story, but this, too, can be done without postulating a metaphysical god who causes mental and physical states to occur in ordered series.

One other proof for the existence of the metaphysical god is worth examining because it shows once again how metaphysicians get trapped in fly bottles of confusion when thy do not attend to the pragmatic, contextual conditions determining the use of words. In his fourth way of proving the existence of the metaphysical god, Aquinas argues that we can say that things are more or less good only if there is some perfect being of which these things are diminished resemblances. Only if there is a perfect yardstick of goodness can we measure how good some imperfect thing is. Examining how our words "good," "better," and "best" (and "bad," "worse," and "worst") work, however, shows that this argument is unsound. These words are professional grading words. We grade all sorts of things using them: cars, apples, days, tastes, prices. This practice of grading things has arisen for many different reasons. The reasons for grading these sorts of things at all provide us with the criteria we use in doing the grading. Some things are better than zero and some are worse. Some good things are better than others, and some bad things are worse than other bad things. Sometimes we want to say that given these criteria, nothing could be better or nothing could be worse; it's the best day I've ever had, or it's the worst day in my life. No yardstick of perfection is needed to make these comparative evaluations. The practice of grading and the words used in this practice are thoroughly human and can be understood as thoroughly human. There is no need to postulate an eternal perfect being to understand the grading practice and our use of grading words.

A number of recent philosophers have offered moral arguments for the existence of God derived from reflection on what they think Kant said about practical reasoning requiring the postulation of the existence of a metaphysical god and the immortality of people. Kant argued that we have an idea of the perfectly good life, which would be the life chosen by all rational persons if these people were in no way limited in their power to get what they were to choose.[38] This perfectly good life would consist of a morally virtuous life (refraining from doing what no one could conceive and be willing for all people to be free to do and for all people to be actually doing as if in accordance with a law of nature) and a thoroughly happy life. During their lifetime on earth, however, people neither attain the holiness that consists of always restraining themselves in the mandated ways, nor achieve a completely happy life while being thoroughly, virtuously obedient to moral prohibitions and requirements.[39] Therefore, Kant argued, it is reasonable for rational people to act on a belief that they can complete the project of attaining a perfect life only if they make two postulations: (1) that people will live forever so that they can make endless progress toward moral holiness, and (2) that there is a good god able and willing to unite in a life of perfect goodness both moral holiness and thorough happiness.[40]

The necessary conditions for the reasonableness of believing that one can complete the project of attaining a perfect life, however, do not entail that these conditions do obtain or that the project is attainable. Kant points out that his reflections about what is necessary to complete this project do not prove theoretically that a metaphysical god exists or that people are immortal. His reflections do show what ideal (the perfect life) we should aim at in this life, even if one cannot complete the project of attaining it. In his criticisms of Epicurus, who claims that pursuing happiness successfully guarantees the attainment of moral virtue, and the Stoics, who claim that pursuing moral virtue successfully guarantees attaining happiness, Kant points out that neither moral virtue nor happiness guarantees the other.[41] They are only contingently related. He also points out that we have reasons for being morally virtuous even if we do not attain happiness. (We cannot conceive of anyone being morally free to steal or force their will on others, and we cannot be willing for all to be exercising a supposed moral freedom to deceive or ignore people in need of help.) Pure practical reasoning about what can be conceived as morally free and willed as morally free demonstrates that we are morally obligated regardless of our state of happiness. Kant does add that people can not theoretically know that humans will not live forever, that the metaphysical god does not exist, or that the perfect life is not attainable. The postulates of practical reason do not prove, however, that we do live forever or that such a god does exist.

George Mavrodes has attempted to use Kant's claims about the necessary postulates of practical reason to conclude that life in a world in which there were no correlation at all between moral obligations and human happiness would be an absurd world.[42] As we shall see, all the religions of the world proclaim that some sort of happiness can be obtained, even when meeting our moral obligations requires sacrificing all sorts of personal interests, but asserting this does not require asserting the existence of the metaphysical god. Hindu bliss, Buddhist nirvana, Christian heavenly life in the body of Christ, the Christian church, or Levinas's enjoyment of the elements are not removed by the sacrifices required when meeting moral obligations. Mavrodes claims that our world is meaningful and not absurd only if morality is built right into the core of that world. As we shall see, Levinas affirms just this when he claims that the infinite, nonclassifiable other of face-to-face ethical encounters holds priority over all ontologies, including ones that affirm that god is some supreme being guaranteeing harmony between moral requirements and any forms of nonreligious happiness. In doing so, he rejects the idea that a supernatural or metaphysical god exists. Mavrodes himself backs off from the attempt to argue from morality and happiness to religion; he elevates religion above morality. He sees morality as a necessity only because people do not live in an economy of gifts and sacrifices, in which every good thing is either self-created or a gift that is something one is to be ready to sacrifice as a good gift given to someone else.[43] As we shall see, the world's religions also recommend going beyond the moral law to live in a spirit of compassion and sacrificial love, but this life also does not require belief in the existence of a metaphysical god. As Nietzsche has pointed out, only the nihilists who do not find living itself meaningfully exciting need to postulate a metaphysical god in order to avoid seeing life as absurd.[44] Kant didn't say what Mavrodes initially claims and Nietzsche shows, that life is not meaningless simply because it is filled with such necessities and chanciness that morally good people suffer and morally evil people gain wealth, power, and pleasurable lives of tennis, boating, and living in beautiful mansions in South Florida.

In addition to the mind/body argument already considered, Robert Merrihew Adams also presents moral arguments for the existence of a metaphysical god.[45] There are things about morality, he claims, that are best explained by postulating the existence of a loving metaphysical god. First, he claims that treating all moral statements as commands issued by a loving god best explains how such claims can be interpreted as true claims about something other than the phenomena studied in the sciences, descriptions of which never entail any claims about what ought to be the case since they only talk about what is the case. Treating moral claims as intuitions of moral facts, he charges, explains nothing, because such talk about intuitions is just a way to stop requests for reasons why things ought to be done. Treating moral utterances as emotive expressions or imperatives, he continues, simply robs such utterances of their status as claims that can be true or false. The best alternative, Adams claims, is treating them as commands issued by a loving god.

There are, however, alternatives to Adam's proposal that do not require postulating the existence of a metaphysical god and which do not keep religious talk enslaved to metaphysical talk. Analyzing talk about the truth of claims pragmatically as double negatives, the rejection of rejections of moral claims, avoids all the problems tied to Adams's assumption of a correspondence theory of truth in which there must be some external fact to which moral claims must correspond.[46] Moral claims need not be reduced to mere emotional utterances, imperatives, or divine commands in order for us to say that some of them are true. Also, morally perceiving people as cruel or sacrificially compassionate is as basic and natural as the nonmoral perceptions by physicists and chemists of metal balls rolling down inclining places. Neither mysterious moral intuitions nor metaphysical claims are needed for there to be claims reporting such moral perceptions, or for people, when their claims are rejected, to reaffirm these claims by saying that they are true. Finally, as we shall see, we can draw upon Levinas's insight that interpersonal ethical encounters of people face-to-face, encounters not boxed into any symbolic or socially constituted conceptual world, are the basic core of all moral claims. Not making claims about commands from a metaphysical god but making verbal expressions of faithful responses to interpersonal ethical encounters is what gives to moral talk its unique status. When such core moral claims are challenged, we can insist on our position by claiming that they are true. Being able to say that a certain moral claim is true does not require postulating that what is being claimed is a claim being made by a metaphysical god.

Adams's second moral argument for the existence of a metaphysical god stems from his reading of Kant's discussion of the postulates of practical reason. Adams claims that people will be demoralized unless they believe there is or will be a correlation between doing one's duty and meeting one's self-interests, and metaphysical theism provides the best theory about there being such a correlation. Seeing one's moral efforts contributing to a larger good, he claims, provides additional motivation for meeting one's obligations, and it serves as a bulwark against demoralization. This practical advantage gained by believing in a metaphysical god gives us a good reason, Adams claims, for agreeing with William James, for thinking that our belief is true when intellectual grounds cannot settle the matter, when the matter is of urgent importance, and when it gives one reason for doing something one wouldn't otherwise do. Believing in such a god and its guarantee of a correlation between moral virtue and happiness, Adams asserts, will contribute to the cheerfulness and single-heartedness of a person's devotion to morality.

Adams does not show, however, that people will be motivated to aim at the ideal of moral holiness and perfect happiness only if they believe in the existence of a metaphysical loving god. Kant never claimed that such a theoretical belief was a practical necessity. Kant points out that people can be rationally motivated to do their duty simply because they know that they are morally free to do something only if they can conceive and will all other people to be likewise free. Sartre makes the same point when he claims that we are free to live any life we choose as long as we can conceive and be willing for all other people to be free to choose the same kind of life.[47] There is no reason for thinking that people will not be motivated to strive to gain a life closer and closer to perfection (more adequately meeting one's obligations, more completely finding happiness) if they do not believe that this ideal will be realized in the lives of all people or even in their own lives. We know that in these two cases, more is better than none, and that is sufficient to motivate people to better themselves both in morality and in happiness. Besides, we do not need to believe that a perfectly heavenly life must be guaranteed in order to be motivated to reduce the hellishness of our own life or the lives of those about whom we care. Besides, human living is filled with so much joy and potential for joy that seeking to remove personal and social barriers to such enjoyment will be more than adequately motivated, especially when we understand our involvement in the constitution and maintenance of such barriers and our possible involvement in their removal. In fact, thinking that some metaphysical god will do what is necessary to progress towards the ideal may sap the motivation in many people to make the sacrifices necessary to remove themselves as the causes of so much suffering in the world. Finally, as we shall see, encountering the infinite in the many ways that we do, none of which involve encountering a metaphysical god, can produce faithful religious responses of thankfulness, trust, commitment, hope, and loving care, which can provide motivation for going beyond merely meeting socially constituted moral obligations. It provides motivation for living in a spirit of sacrificial compassion and loving acceptance of unlimited responsibilities.

No ultimate metaphysical explanations are needed and no metaphysical embodiments of perfection are needed. Thinking they are needed is simply a refusal to recognize what we and our situation are like. We are finite. Our words are finite. We and everything in our world are contingent. We cannot escape our world. Trying to escape is trying to be infinite rather than living in faithful response to what is other than the finite and all our finite descriptions. Getting locked into the metaphysical explaining business is locking oneself out of the religious worshiping and praying form of life. Religious faithfulness in one of the world's religious faiths is not a matter of having correct beliefs about metaphysical beings or acts. It is not a matter of being trapped in that sort of fly bottle of confusion and incoherence. Religious faithfulness is a matter of living a certain form of religious life and becoming a certain sort of religious person.

Although the classical arguments for the existence of the metaphysical god are unsound, they can be interpreted as expressions of religious faith once they are no longer taken to be talking about some supreme metaphysical being. The ontological argument can be taken as the prayer Anselm offers it as, a prayer in which he acknowledges that only foolishness would lead one to say that the finite does not have an infinite other. The cosmological argument can be interpreted as saying that conceivable finite beings always point to the nonfinite that never can be conceptually exhausted. The teleological or design argument can be taken as saying that enjoying the elements, experiencing the awesome sublimity of nature, habitating interpersonally with others, ethically meeting people face-to-face, conceptualizing beings, or living on in one's cultural and ethical legacy can exist only because of the infinite that is the atmosphere surrounding and penetrating everything finite. The moral argument can be religiously interpreted as saying that all justifiable moral principles, codes, and virtues depend upon our face-to-face encounters with that ethically infinite dimension of every person which gives to people the unique, unlimited responsibilities that make them into infinitely unique ethical individuals.

Many proponents of these arguments probably were motivated as much by their religious faith as by the temptation to participate in the metaphysical theorizing practices so popular at various times. It is important therefore to show that people's lives of religious faithfulness do not require beliefs about a metaphysical being or faith in the soundness of the various metaphysical proofs for the existence of god as a metaphysical being. There is no doubt that many people today have come to believe that living a religiously faithful life requires believing that a metaphysical god exists and that one or more of these proofs is sound. Showing that their faithful religious lives will flourish without this metaphysical baggage must be done in such a way that it will not damage their faithfulness. This will be attempted in this book by providing detailed interpretations of the major religions of the world that are free from making any claims about a supernatural or metaphysical being. This will be done by showing that the various religions of the world are different faithful responses to the encounter with the infinite other of all finite beings and events, an infinite that is not an infinite being. Reconstructing the arguments for the existence of a metaphysical god, by locating them in a framework of encountering the infinite other to all worlds of beings and in a framework of responding faithfully to these encounters, requires getting as clear an understanding as possible of what all such talk about encounters with the infinite is saying.

The Reformed tradition in Protestant Christianity comes very close to the position being advocated here, except that many of its proponents still adhere to the belief that Christianity's God is a supernatural, metaphysical god. Nicholas Wolterstorff points out that the Reformed thinkers feel a revulsion for all proofs for the existence of a metaphysical god, finding such proofs useless and pernicious and idolatrous acts of serving a false god of reason.[48] Alvin Plantinga has argued that the religious person's beliefs that god has created the world, that god disapproves of his sinful actions, that god exists are as properly basic and epistemologically groundless, though not unjustified, as our beliefs that we see trees and other people and that we remember things we just did.[49] Religious beliefs, Plantinga charges, are not beliefs epistemologically justified by any reports of nonreligious experiences or any cosmological, ontological, or design arguments for the existence of god.

There are significant similarities between the two kinds of beliefs to which Plantinga makes reference—first person perceptual and memory beliefs and religious beliefs that God created the world—but there are also significant differences. If Kant is correct, we can establish the general reliability of perception and memory as a necessary presupposition of thinking about the distinction between true and false judgements, justified and unjustified judgements. Given their general reliability, specific perceptual and memory beliefs are not unjustified whenever we have no reason to doubt them. Beliefs about a metaphysical god, however, would be beliefs comparable to scientific beliefs about theoretical entities (e.g., quarks, black holes). In the absence of any justification, beliefs about such entities could be doubted for good reason, and therefore they need justification.[50] Speculations about the existence of unobservable entities many times have been shown to be confused or proven to be false. Metaphysical beliefs about a supernatural being cannot be a properly basic belief.

Plantinga would be right about religious beliefs, however, if these were not interpreted metaphysically. Linguistically responding in faithfulness to an encounter with the infinite can yield properly basic beliefs, beliefs about Brahman, the Tao, Yahweh, Jesus Christ, Allah, or the Qur'an. These beliefs would be properly basic, not justified by any speech not part of such a faithful response, and not unjustified because no nonreligious beliefs can put them in doubt. They are not metaphysical beliefs about some being. They are religious beliefs that people not responding faithfully to encounters with the infinite cannot epistemologically evaluate. Religious talk is sui generis as Wittgensteinians like D.Z. Phillips have proclaimed.[51] Phillips's position has been criticized by philosophers who assume that talk about god as creator or savior must be interpreted as talk about a metaphysical god for which no criteria can be supplied for identifying it.[52] The rest of this book consists of an effort to show how the talk in the major religions of the world can be interpreted without it being taken as talk about such a metaphysical god. The effort will attempt to show that when this talk involves expressing religious beliefs, these beliefs will be not-unjustified, properly basic religious beliefs.

4. The Death of the Metaphysical God

Today in the twenty-first century, thank god, the intellectually created gods of the metaphysicians are dead in the lives of many people. Today, thank god, we can respond with religious passion and intellectual honesty to the call of that which is wholly other to our secular, social worlds, to ourselves as socially constituted persons, to all the objects of our secular, socially constituted descriptions and theories. We can recognize the nonreligious finite as what it is: finite, limited, contingent, lawful, chancy, and power driven. We also can let people and their lives be what they are: more than secular beings, but more without being some other kind of metaphysical substance. We can let people be infinite in their ethical uniqueness and significance, even while they remain descriptively finite in their physical, social, and psychological constitution. We can let human living be what it is: something more than conceptually constructed thoughts, perceptions, memories, desires, feelings, and actions, with such conceptualization itself being socially constituted, usually in nonreligious ways. We can let people respond religiously to their encounters with that which is other than what is secularly constituted, responses that can liberate people from their all-too-human, secular forms of self deception and adulation, from harmful cravings, secular and metaphysical confusion, and incoherence. We can let people realize their ability to encounter the infinite and to be passionately faithful to such encounters and the worlds of religious practice constituted in response to such encounters.

We can let people be free to proclaim in many different religious idioms: "Here I am, a grateful hostage of the infinite. Thanks and praises be to what is other than what is secularly constituted. Thanks for life and that joyous abundance in life that no forms of suffering can tear away from us. I confess my failings to recognize what is other to what I can conceptualize. I confess my failings to recognize that what I have been socially constituted to be has brought great harm to the oppressed, dominated, suffering multitudes in the world. I confess my failings to respond to the infinite in all people by accepting my responsibilities to them and by acting justly toward them. Continually strengthen my desire to meet these responsibilities, even though I can never fully do so. Show me what and how to love in my loving devotion to the infinite."

We now can proclaim: The metaphysical god is dead. Long live Yahweh, the "I am who I am," who never can be pigeonholed into any descriptive box. Long live the Yahweh community of the Hebrews, faithful to its memory of exodus from spiritual slavery; of journeying into a promised land; of a joyous affirmation of life in the face of unwarranted suffering; of settling down in an age crying out for prophetic rejection of false idols and justice for the orphans, widows, and strangers we all are, steadfastly trusting in a messianic future always still to come. Long live Brahman, proclaimed by Hindus to be radically other than all humanly conceivable, secular, natural, or supernatural beings; and long live Atman, the singularly unique, and thus linguistically and conceptually indescribable, person that each of us is, different from all the social masks we wear and thus identical in our infinity with Brahman. Long live moksa, the liberation of ourselves as Atman from our socially constituted and continually counterproductive Jiva tendencies to absolutize our nonreligious, physical and social desires. Long live what Buddhists call Sunyatta or Mu, that empty sky, that

no-thingness which is that other to all the things we experience or talk
about, that no-thingness which we must encounter and remain faithful to if all secularly describable things are to be allowed to be what
they are, and thus self-inflicted suffering is to be ended and compassionate and joyful living is to be gained. Long live Nirvana, the condition remaining when Tanha is extinguished (Tanha, those life-defining cravings of ours for social status), the condition in which we are
enabled to respond compassionately to others who are wholly other,
to let them be as they are without their social masks. Long live the
bodhisattvas, historically constituted by faithful Buddhist communities in their worshiping efforts to extinguish Tanha. Long live the Tao,
the unnameable other permeating everything finite and making possible the relative sameness of all things finite and nameable, same in their
social constitution. Long live the Tao, the way of living harmoniously
with the infinite other about which those who know don't speak, the
way of living religiously with our finite selves and environment, which
we honor with the deepest respect. Long live the Chan or Zen tradition, constituted through dialogue with faithful voices speaking out of
the Buddhist and Taoist traditions. Long live their ability to move past
seeing and living with mountains as merely socially constituted objects
of human utility, past seeing them as mere appearances of some more
ultimate metaphysical reality, thus seeing them as they and all of nature
is, the elements we enjoy prior to ever talking about them.

Now that the metaphysical god is dead, we can proclaim: Long live
the Christian God who remains indescribable except as what can be
said by means of the Christian church's constitution of Jesus as God's
resurrected son and Messiah. Long live Christ, the Messianic embodiment and promise of religious salvation from our all-too-worldly lives.
Long live the Christian church, the community that is the body of
Christ filled with messianic spirit, the Christian community of faithful worshipers. Long live the church's resurrection faith, integral to
their constitution of Christ as Messiah, the faith that all people can
rise from spiritual death to passionate commitment to the pursuit of
an eternal, timeless happiness through agape love, a happiness found
in the unreserved pursuit of such happiness, a timeless happiness that
remains untarnished in worlds of unjustifiable suffering. Long live the

Christian mystics who, in order to prevent confusion over the meaning of what is being said by Christians interpreting everything through the lens of their resurrection faith, never allowed Christians to forget the indescribable, infinite godhead that transcends even what Christians faithfully have to say about God.

We can proclaim: Long live Allah, the infinite who wears no finite mask. There is no god but Allah. Long live Islam, the spiritual peace and compassionate charity coming from surrendering totally to the infinite. Long live the people in Muslim communities who constitute themselves as communities by listening to the Qur'an as Allah, speaking through the transmitter, Muhammad, calls for religious and ethical righteousness. Long live the Muslim Sufi mystics who, like their Jewish and Christian counterparts, keep reminding the faithful that faithfulness to encounters with indescribable Allah remains the supreme obligation of all Muslims.

The metaphysical god is dead, and if the religiously faithful people of the world can understand this, then all the religions of the world will be liberated from a terrible burden they have had to bear. Liberating religion from metaphysics will mean liberating people from the plague of metaphysical wars, from the oppression and domination caused by trapping religious discourse in metaphysical prisons. Liberating religion from metaphysics will mean liberating the religions of the world to carry out their prophetic critiques of injustice; liberating people from self-imposed suffering; liberating them for lives of bliss and joy. The death of the metaphysical god allows the world's religions to be faithful to their common core. Faithfulness to encounters with the nonfinite other to all describable beings and events remains the common mountain peak that makes authentic religious talk be what it is. The different religions of the world, with their different forms of worship, prayer, service, and discourse, are different responses to these peak encounters. There are so many not unjustified religious proclamations that the death of the metaphysical god will enable people around the world to hear. No longer trapped in the ultimate explanation game, people can religiously offer praise, express thanks, confess guilt, forgive and accept forgiveness, seek the wisdom to understand their responsibilities to all others, receive the strength to pursue justice, and live with a sense of peace, joy, and hope found no other way.

Many different kinds of thinkers are responsible for the death of the metaphysical god, and some of these same thinkers have provided us with the understanding needed for religion to prosper once it is freed from metaphysical corruption. Perhaps better than ever before we can understand now what encountering the infinite and living faithfully to such encounters is all about. Martin Luther helped kill the metaphysical god when he condemned the manner in which intellectual clerics, craving for Greek metaphysical theories, contaminated faithful worship of the Christian God. Most people know about the ninety-five theses that Luther posted on the castle church in Wittenberg, Germany, on October 20, 1517, which condemned what he saw as corruption in Christian church practice, especially the selling of indulgences. Not so well known are the ninety-seven theses that he set forth six weeks earlier on September 4, 1517, in an effort to protect the biblical proclamation from the confusion caused by the medieval introduction into Christian thinking of Aristotelian metaphysics.

The eighteenth-century philosophers, David Hume[53] and Immanuel Kant[54] helped kill the metaphysical god when they wrote in an effort to show that all philosophical proofs for the existence of the metaphysical god are unsound. In the nineteenth-century, Ludwig Feuerbach[55] helped kill it by pointing out that serving a metaphysical god is just serving a fetish projection by people of their own flawed, idealized self-images. Unfortunately, his materialism prevented him from acknowledging the possibility of encountering the infinite that is not a metaphysical being. Otherwise, instead of talking about people creating metaphysical gods as fetish projects, he might have talked about people constituting religious foci of worship while faithfully responding to encounters with the infinite. Kierkegaard showed that all attempts to worship an ontotheological, metaphysical god are pagan, objectivistic approaches to an object humanly constituted by our anxiety-ridden conceptual efforts to be god, our efforts to stand outside and beyond our social and historical skins, observing all times and places and explaining everything.[56] Kierkegaard showed that such an objectivistic way of life produces only sickness unto spiritual death, because the only life that works is one in which people passionately welcome the infinite other of all constituted objects.[57] Karl Marx[58] helped kill the metaphysical god when, in his ruthless critique of everything oppressive, he showed that commitment to a metaphysical god is an opiate used to perpetuate domination by nurturing people to worship economic fetishes, and by turning people into merely docile workers, consumers, and citizens of finite economic systems and national states claiming an absolute sovereignty that never belongs to anything finite. Nietzsche[59] killed the metaphysical gods, whether they be explanatory, moral, or scientistic gods, by showing that people serving such false gods are nihilists afraid to celebrate life with all its finite chanciness and infinite otherness to all socially constituted norms. Nietzsche, of course, said that he was not the one who actually killed off the metaphysical gods; he was only describing and analyzing what science, business, politics, and art had done to the culture of his day. In spite of the metaphysical/religious rhetoric that some philosophers and preachers were still using, generally and for the most part people were living totally secular lives that needed no metaphysical postulations or attempted proofs.

The twentieth century pounded additional nails into the metaphysical god's coffin. Heidegger showed that the meaning of beings is the meaning that it has to people who care about the significance of beings, and that the being of beings is not another being, a supreme being responsible for the existence of all other beings. Rather, beings are beings because they are one of the following three sorts of beings: (1) either beings constituted as tools people use and actively live with (hammers and farmlands) or useless items that get in the way of living with tools (dust under the bed), (2) works of art and literature that radically modify existing cultural worlds, that come to be as socially and culturally constituted people cease trying to control things, but instead let themselves be changed so that new worlds come to be through them, (3) people themselves who are Dasein, being there as persons who are both historically constituted by their social and cultural inheritance and yet free to realize some and leave unrealized other potentialities present in their inheritance. Talking about a metaphysical god who is the ultimate cause of the existence and significance of all other beings is in fact concealing from oneself the radically human character of human existence, the worlds in which we live, and the beings present to us in such worlds.[60]

Derrida, in undercutting the whole idea that anything (meanings, beings, properties) simply can be present to the mind showed that the identities of all meanings, objects, and subjects are inescapably related to holistically interdependent, historically developing social and cultural practices, which enabled their constitution and are inescapably related to presently unpredictable future practices that will affect their future identities.[61] To specify the identity of any meaning, object, event, subject, fact, one has to interpret the historical development of a whole cultural and social world. But even then one would not succeed in specifying that identity because identities are thoroughly historical, and one can't predict how any of these identities might change in the future while still being taken by people to be remaining the same. This pulls the rug out from under the feet of metaphysical realists who think that objects and properties are just there present, for us to talk about, and of defenders of correspondence theories of truth who think that "facts" are just there for us to picture and represent in our assertions. When we perceive something with our senses, we always conceive what we perceive in a certain way, and thus all perceived objects depend upon the historical, social, and cultural constitution of ourselves and all our concepts. If cars and games are not just there completely present before us at this present time, then neither are supposed metaphysical first causes. If the truth of descriptions of cars and trees is not a matter of the correspondence of statements to "facts," but rather has to be interpreted in terms of claims, rejects, and counterclaims, then the same holds for religious statements. If thinking and talking about everything depends on interpreting human cultural and social practices, then so does all religious talk. Once one has ruled out the idea that it is talk representing metaphysical beings and facts, then we are left with the question: "How are we to interpret the place of religious talk in the various social and cultural worlds in which it is practiced?"

Finally, the psychotherapist, Jacques Lacan, and his interpreter and appropriator, Slavoj Zizek, add their swords to the slaying of the metaphysical god who supposedly provides reasons why everything is as it is and not otherwise. They show that all linguistic, symbolic, and conceptual efforts to refer to the metaphysical gods and their surrogates deconstruct themselves, given that there is an inescapable void in socially constituted objects and subjects. It is a void that calls for people to respond to the wholly other, the nonfinite that is inescapably calling us to be responsible to all people in their singularity and not to unjustly ignore that they are wholly other to all pigeonholing.[62]

Many of these thinkers, in killing off metaphysical gods and tearing out these weeds sapping religious faithfulness of its energy and dignity, are affirming that respecting the radical otherness of people means respecting the different religious communities constituted by people seeking to be faithful to their historically particular encounters with the infinite. It means that the religious pursuit of justice and religious authenticity must continually battle with all totalitarian, political, or metaphysical projects striving to turn this otherness into sameness, trying to coercively force on all people some one human image of a heavenly or earthly paradise. Hume, Kant, Marx, and Nietzsche primarily were killers of metaphysical weeds, whereas Kiekegaard and the postmodernists have added valuable nutrients for the growth of authentic religious life.

5. Existential and Postmodern Interpretations of Religion After the Death of God

Rather than killing off religion, the death of the metaphysical god has produced in many philosophers a renaissance of interest in and radically creative reflections on the possibility of religion without such a god. Kierkegaard's nonmetaphysical interpretation of Protestant Christianity is the founding voice in this renaissance, a voice that has spoken to Jewish thinkers such as Martin Buber, Emmanel Levinas, and Jacques Derrida; Roman Catholic thinkers such as Jean-Luc Marion and John Caputo; and difficult to classify Christian thinkers such as Jacque Lacan and Slavoj Zizek. Here is not the place to offer detailed analyses of the interpretations of the finite and the infinite found in the texts of Kierkegaard and these postmodernist writers. I have attempted to do that elsewhere.[63] Highlighting some of their interpretations, however, will be helpful in presenting the interpretations of the world's religions that will be offered in this book.

Kierkegaard. Four aspects of Kierkegaard's thinking are especially important to highlight, given how they form the horizon locating the interpretations of the world's religions contained in this book and how they have heavily influenced the postmodern thinkers being interpreted here. First, there is Kierkegaard's interpretation of the religious as a way of life rather than a set of metaphysical beliefs about a supernatural being. Second, there is Kierkegaard's dialectical, critical interpretation of the internal conflicts in nonreligious ways of life. Third, there is Kierkegaard's interpretation of religious ways of life as being constituted by people whose desires, passions, practices, happiness, and identities have been transformed as they faithfully responded to the call of the infinite. Fourth, there is Kierkegaard's interpretation of Christianity as a subjectivistic way of life of people in the Christian church who have constituted the infinite as God the father and Jesus as God's Messiah, their Christ and Savior, thereby becoming the body of the resurrected Christ filled with the loving and saving spirit of their God. These four aspects need a closer look.

First, in *Concluding Unscientific Postscript*[64] Kierkegaard charges that it is on ways of life, religious or nonreligious, that one must focus if one is coming to gain any understanding of how words, concepts, beliefs, standards, norms, rationales, and ideals are functioning. He calls such ways of living modes of subjectivity (ways of conceiving, perceiving, judging, reasoning, valuing, feeling). Different ways of life function with different horizons locating different expectations and different possibilities. Kierkegaard focuses on two such ways of life, two such modes of subjectivity. First, there is the objectvitistic mode of subjectivity in which people live lives focused on beliefs about, desires for, and attitudes towards conceptualizable, perceptible objects and events. For Kierkegaard, Hegel, in his pursuit of total knowledge of nature and human history, best exemplified the metaphysical deification of such an objectivisitic way of life. Scientism, with its absolutizing of the empirical sciences whose descriptions are intersubjectively shared and whose explanations are acceptable to the scientific community, likewise is an effort to restrict human life to an objectivististic way of life. Living as a mere social conformist, binding oneself slavishly to carrying out the requirements of the social roles assigned to oneself by existing social practices, is another example of an objectivistic way of life.[65] Kierkegaard charges, however, that there is a second subjectvisitic mode of subjectivity in which people live lives focused on how they are relating themselves to all the objects focused upon in objectivistic ways of life. The religious way of life, he claims, is a subjectvisitic mode of subjectvity. According to Kierkegaard, all interpretations are formed within one of these two forms of life. Kierkegaard's interpretation is formed within a subjectvitistic way of living focused on such ways of living. This means that what is scientifically or metaphysically possible and impossible is determined by a horizon of expectations that cannot be justified scientifically or metaphysically. The objectivistic and subjectivisitic ways of life are simply two different ways of living. The crucial issue is whether a way of life truly works. For Kierkegaard the truth of a way of life is found in the living of it. He charges that such living truth can be found only in a subjectvitistic mode of subjectivity.

Second, Kierkegaard points to a number of places in an objectvitistic way of life where it is in conflict with its own horizon of possibilities. Kierkegaard applies to objectvistic ways of life a Hegelian dialectical analysis which shows that there lies within the thesis of such a way of life its own conflicting antithesis. First, its exclusive focus on objects located within its way of life prevents it from understanding that it itself is a mode of subjectvity. It is structurally prevented from understanding that what it takes to be possible, impossible, and necessary are only contingent modalities. By failing to recognize that what it takes as impossibilities can be possibilities in a different way of life, it fails to realize its goal of providing a total picture of all possible actualities. Second, the whole objectvisitic way of life has to presuppose what it cannot prove, the reliability of its procedures for gaining knowledge. As Kierkegaard reminds his readers, Plato had pointed out that people, if they think they are self-sufficient in gaining knowledge, must assume that they innately possess the ability to recognize the truth, that they can properly work with criteria of meaning, truth, and justification which they simply possess.[66] Third, the need in objectivistic forms of life to treat everything as an object falling under a concept prevents people in such a form of life from understanding that they themselves are not such objects, but rather are the very ones giving constitutional identity to the objects being perceived. They are the very ones who have the capacity to endorse a particular way of life, whether it be objectivistic or one of the subjectivistic ways of living. One despairingly falls into a sickness unto existential death if one either sees oneself trapped by one's objective physical, biological, and social inheritance or if one confuses one's wishes for future possibilities not tied to such an inheritance with the range of actual options still possible to a person with such an inheritance.[67] Kierkegaard insists that one cannot avoid such conflictual despair as long as one tries to maintain autonomous control over one's life. Instead, one must surrender oneself to an infinitely passionate pursuit of the absolute goal of an eternal happiness found in the pursuit of such a happiness. Pursuing eternal happiness is losing the self that has been constituted by one's social and cultural inheritance and by one's cravingly seeking such finite goals as power, fame, interesting experiences, or pleasure. It consists in becoming a new person, whose way of living is defined by absolutizing nothing finite, by seeking a timeless form of happiness that is not subject to destruction by the suffering caused by the necessities and chances present in our inheritance or our environment or by the frustrations of our pursuit of finite goals.[68] The motivation for pursing eternal happiness with infinite passion cannot come from one's constituted self, but comes only by encountering the infinite as a loving, suffering, saving God.

Third, Kierkegaard claims that a subjectivistic mode of subjectivity permits one to live in a way of life that consists of responding with unrestricted and unconditional (infinite) passion to a call that cannot come from anything that can be classified as a constituted object, subject, practice, or event describable with the concepts used in an objectivitistic way of life. In a subjectivisitic way of life, and only in a subjectivisitic way of life, can one passionately commit oneself to the pursuit of a goal that is other than any goal that can be aimed at in an objectivisitic way of life. The person who is passionately pursuing the absolute goal of eternal happiness is a person who is responding to a call to worship nothing finite, responding to a call to be willing to give up everything not determined by the pursuit of eternal happiness, responding to a call to be someone who is required to find's one's singular identity in such responding, responding to a call let all people live as the infinitely significant and singularly unique individuals they are.[69] In hearing and responding to this call, we are encountering the infinite, which for Kierkegaard is God, and praying to God is praying to do everything required in order to pursue with infinite passion the absolute goal of eternal happiness. Again and again, Kierkegaard proclaims that God is not an object, not an externality, and that God exists only for subjectivity[70] and comes into being only for people who rub the lamp of freedom and choose eternal happiness as their absolute goal.[71] Worshiping God is faithfully responding to this call, praising and being thankful for this call, meaningfully interpreting everything in terms of this call, loving all people in their singular uniqueness, and recognizing that one has the power to faithfully respond only because the call proclaims that all people are lovingly cherished in their individual uniqueness.

Fourth, Kierkegaard rejects all efforts to interpret Christianity in terms of beliefs about something in an objectivisitic way of life. One should not think that one must or can establish in such a way of life that Jesus is the Christ, the Messiah. Neither the Bible nor church confessions nor the impact of Christians on world history can provide reasons in an objectivistic way of life for believing that Jesus is the Christ. These are meaningful only to Christians living in a Christian subjectivistic way of life. Even if one could objectivistically prove something about the Hebrew exodus from Egypt or about the life and death of Jesus, this would prove nothing about whether the Christian way of life was the truth of successful living. Likewise, if one objectively proved that the Red or Reed Sea did not open before Moses, or if one found evidence of Jesus's body lying in a cave different from the one his followers went to after his death, this would say nothing about the truthfulness of the Christian way of life.[72] Christianity is grounded in Christology and not Jesusology. For Kierkegaard, Christianity is a way of life constituted by Jesus and Christians responding to the call of the infinite God and recognizing that people are not innocently unaware of the infinite and its call, but are in fact rebelliously closing their ears to this call because they do not desire to make the sacrifices involved in loving all people in their singular uniqueness, especially the sacrifice of their cravings for power and control over things. People need to be motivated to put to death one way of living in order to be reborn in a new loving way of life, relating to Jesus as God's suffering servant and to his resurrection as the Christ as the defining center of the Christian community's faithful worship of and service to God and God's call.[73]

The Christian church in its resurrection faith has constituted Jesus as Christ, Messiah, savior, son of God, incarnation of the infinite. Just as Paul could encounter this resurrected Christ, although he had never met Jesus, so every person can encounter the resurrected Christ through the constituting and sustaining work of the Christian church, Christ's body. Christianity is a historical religion, not because it is based on historical beliefs about Jesus or metaphysical beliefs about a supernatural being magically making things happen in history, but because it is grounded in a community's historical project of constituting Jesus as the Christ through its self-constitution in a resurrection faith and a life of worship of and prayer to the infinite in the name of Jesus Christ. Such a faithful religious response to encountering the infinite by constitutively raising a finite man who died into an incarnate, loving, saving son of God is, Kierkegaard confesses, doubly absurd in an objectivistic form of life. How can the infinite call out to finite people? How can something be finite and infinite at the same time? Kierkegaard points out that in a subjectivistic religious way of life, however, we can understand that what is socially constituted and thus finite does not exhaust what can be encountered. From Kierkegaard we can learn that in some religious ways of life, the infinite is constituted as God and in Christianity Jesus is constituted as the incarnation of god, as the Christ, the son of God.

Two other voices need to be heard from in order to begin to understand how recent postmodern thinkers use Kierkegaard's thoughts as the springboard for the religious revival now taking place in their thinking. These are the voices of Nietzsche and Heidegger.

Nietzsche. Kierkegaard in his critique of the objectivistic character of his time focused on the restricting effect of leveling and social conformity on the freedom of people to determine their individual identities and to be free to respond to the call of the infinite. Nietzsche, however, critiqued his time for its nihilistic, resentful, ruthless, dominating, exploiting service to a will to power in its construction of social and cultural practices, especially moral and so-called religious practices.[74] To appreciate the dangers that postmodern thinkers find in our present objectivisitic worlds, we need to add to Nietzsche's critique the critique

by Marx of economic exploitation, the critique by Frankfurt social critics of cultural hegemonies servicing exploitive power[75], the critique by
Heidegger of the technological enframing of most things, including
people, in a pursuit of power for the sake of enhancing power,[76] and
Foucault's micro-physics analysis and critique of the mini-practices
that make possible political, economic, and social domination.[77] For
postmodern thinkers, objectivisitic worlds are cruel and unjust worlds
from which people need the deliverance or at least the hope of deliverance that subjectivisitic religious modes of life can provide. Although
most postmodern religious thinkers appropriate Nietzsche's diagnosis
of the present world's ailments, they are less willing to appropriate his
prescribed medicine. Nietzsche's own attempt to find salvation in a
Dionysian celebration of spontaneous play seems to lack the accent on
heading that call for the ethical care for people in their singular uniqueness which Kierkegaard and most postmodern thinkers accent.

Heidegger. Appreciating three aspects of Heidegger's thought will
be helpful here. First, there is Heidegger's development of Kierkegard's
prioritizing of subjectivistic modes of subjectivity in his analysis of the
manner in which the meanings that objects have to people is their
significance to people as constituted tools ready on hand to be used,
or as objects merely present on hand and either getting in the way of
people's use of tools or as objects stripped of their toolish characteristics
in order to be scientifically studied so as to be returned to efficient use.
Furthermore, our toolish world forms a holistic interdependent network
of tools. Just as Hegel had shown that social, cultural, economic, and
political practices are functionally related to one another, so Heidegger
shows that hammers can exist as hammers only because nails, boards,
furniture, houses, and people exist as users of them.[78] Heidegger's
accent on the primacy of our practical understanding of things will be
echoed by postmodernists who claim that it is religious practice that
gives meaning to religious language and thought. Heidegger will be
praised for critiquing and rejecting the theoretical, metaphysical god of
ontotheology, even if his own accent on people's (Dasein's) constitution
and use of objects still exhibits the will to power of the all too worldly
world into which people are thrown, and in which people try to maintain control over everything, even over how they will die, this dying

that is the possibility and necessity of no more possibilities.

Second, as already has been mentioned, there is Heidegger's analysis and critique of the "technological" way of living in the present world in which everything in nature and people themselves are treated as nothing but standing reserve (natural and human resources) available for use in the pursuit of power for power's sake. Heidegger will be praised by postmodern thinkers for identifying the danger he see in our present world, but he will be critiqued for failing to appreciate what must be done to prevent this destiny of the West from becoming its unavoidable fate.

Third, Heidegger in his later writings chooses not to accent merely how individual persons are to seize the openings in their social and cultural inheritance and to heroically face the future as they live and die in their own freely chosen way. Instead, he focuses on how people can let themselves be used in a project that opens up radically new possibilities that remain impossible as long as existing social and cultural practices determine the horizon of living possibilities. Given how people are already socially and culturally constituted, they cannot by an act of their will create new social and cultural worlds. If they just live within their inherited horizons, it will be decided that their destiny given current trends will become their inevitable fate. People, however, Heidegger charges, can cease trying to control things, and they can become poets who let new social and cultural practices and thus new worldly horizons come to be through them.[79] Postmodern religious thinkers will appropriate Heidegger's call for people to release themselves into the activity of freeing the being of beings from currently existing, oppressive horizons of possibilities. They will critique, however, his focus on merely freeing the being of beings so that different worlds of beings may arrive. Heidegger, they claim, ignores the call to ethically care for people, a call that when heard will lead people to place ethical horizons of possibilities above all ontological horizons, a call that comes from beyond Heidegger's constituted beings and the cultural worlds in which they are located. It is the call of the ethical that is being heard by the postmodern thinkers who are involved in the revival of religion after the death of the metaphysical god.

Because the word "postmodern" is used in many different ways by different recent thinkers, some of the writers being classified below as postmodern do not want to be so labeled. The expression "postmodern" is being used here to identify certain critiques, rejections, and movements beyond a number of modern intellectual and cultural tendencies prevalent since the seventeenth century. Since traces of these modernist movements existed as far back as the Greeks and continue to exist today, and since they were being critiqued before the seventeenth century, it is important not to treat these expressions as picking out specific historical periods.

By postmodern thought and practice what is meant here is the rejection of the metaphysical project of giving ultimate explanations of contingent events; the rejection of the epistemological project of giving ultimate justifications for beliefs about conceptualized objects; the rejection of the theoretical ethics project of giving ultimate justification of rules and principles prohibiting or requiring actions, character traits, or ways of living; and the rejection of all the dominating and oppressive social and cultural practices that tried to use these metaphysical, epistemological, and theoretical ethics projects to legitimate themselves. John Caputo asserts that it is with Kierkegaard's accent on the singular individual that postmodernism begins.[80] The postmodernist religious thinkers we will examine are all post-Hegelian thinkers who celebrate the death of the metaphysical god, even though they, like Kirkegaard, appropriate other aspects of Hegel's thinking.

They all take as a given the death of the metaphysical god and instead appropriate Kierkegaard's claim that religion is primarily a matter of a religious way of living that is other than living merely with socially constituted objects or tools not definitively linked to the infinite. Derrida claims that religion begins with a faithful response embodied in a belief beyond proof and an experience of sacredness and holiness.[81] It begins with a radical welcoming of all people regardless of their social identities.[82] Caputo, Derrida's most faithful interpreter and appropriator, claims that living with the event that is God is a matter of living in time, and the name of God is forged in the joys and sorrows of ordinary life.[83] God, he claims, is the name of what we love, desire, pray for, our hope for a justice to come.[84] Jean-Luc Marion asserts that God is no being and that religious faith in God as agape love is a mode of human existence, is a way of life to be contrasted, for example, to a way of life dominated by bore-dom.[85] Slavoj Zizek builds his position on an appropriation of Paul's distinction between two existential positions, death and life,[86] and he asserts that Christianity is a matter of living a life of love that is radically other than ordinary life.[87] Emmanuel Levinas locates the birth of religion in the desire religious people have for the most desirable, the desire to meet one's unlimited responsibilities to other people who always are different from and other to other people because of their singular uniqueness.[88] Levinas supplies an analysis of human life that attempts to show that living consists in much more than beliefs about and desires for socially conceivable and perceptible objects and events by socially constituted subjects. And in that more we find the enjoying, interpersonal habiting and ethical encounters with people in their singularity that supply the raw materials for religious encounters and responses.[89] Levinas's accent on the primacy of ethical encounters and responses, over beliefs about or desires for objects socially constituted without dependence on such encounters and responses, is present in all these postmodern religious thinkers in their accents on agape love and the hope for a justice that transcends worldly social prohibitions and requirements. What distinguishes them from one another is the manner in which they appropriate Hegel's dialectic, Edmund Husserl's phenomenology, and Western negative theologies.

Derrida. Jacques Derrida's move beyond modernism begins with his interpretation of the nature of human language and the way words get those uses that make them meaningful to us in our writing, speaking, and thinking. Derrida draws upon Hegel's, Heidegger's, and Ferdinand de Saussere's demonstration that words are functional units in a holistic world. He rejects, however, the Hegelian and structuralist claim that our linguistic practices have an overall unchanging formal character. We use the word "word" to refer to two different sorts of things. Words have a socially organized physical identity. The word "dog" is a signifier, a set of sets of written marks (printed, in script, big or small, dark or light, in blue, red, or black) and of sets of sounds (with different pitches, loudness, accents). In addition, words have uses, meanings, what they signify. Both with signifiers and signifieds, they are what they are only because of the social customs differentiating them from one another. These customs are historical, with current practices both carrying with them traces of past customs and being open to future changes as current practices carry unspecifiable potentials for being grafted into unpredictable future practices. Derrida coins the word "differance" to point out the way that signifiers and signifieds differ from each other and defer to past and future signifiers and signifieds. Customs governing signifieds often can be traced back to changes in signifiers and the same influence most likely will occur in the future.[90] The net effect of Derrida's interpretation of language is the strengthening of Heidegger's critique of Husserl: Meanings or signifieds cannot be simply present to the mind for intellectual inspection. Meanings, in fact, have no timeless meaning; they have only historical identities that can never be fully specified since they are tied to a past which is never totally recoverable and to an unpredictable future. Since the language of concepts has been constructed to deal with the condition that different words can have the same meaning, concepts, like meanings, cannot be present for inspection. Since objects and events can be thought about, perceived or, desired only as objects and events conceived of in a certain way, they, too, never can be present to some thinking, perceiving, desiring subject. The flaw in all forms of a metaphysics of presence is a failure to appreciate the holistic and historical character of language, thought, perception, and desire.

To his interpretation of the world of human language and conceptualization, Derrida adds the Hegelian insight that this world contains within it conflicting theses and antitheses and the Kierkegardian and Levinasian insight that these conflicts arise because people constitute these worlds, people who neither singularly nor in their interpersonal and ethical relationships with one another are objects that can fall under such socially constructed concepts. Kant had talked about ideas we can have (god, immortality, freedom) that are neither empirical concepts nor concepts of objects of which we can have theoretical knowledge, but which can function as ideals we can strive toward in our behavior. Similarly, Derrida identifies areas of language dealing with other people (forgiveness, giving, hospitality, friendship, justice) that seem impossible to use in our current world of signifiers and signifieds, given the way our linguistic practices are tied to the kind of extralinguistic

practice that Nietzsche condemned of treating all interpersonal trans-
actions in terms of debts incurred and paid off. In a world of practices
in which people are forgiven only when they repent and show they
are sorry, forgiveness becomes impossible, because such people have
earned by their repentance and sorrow their reinstatement. The only
thing that could be forgiven is that for which repentance and being
sorry is not good enough, but that makes it unforgivable.[91] In a world
in which recipients of gifts are obligated to be thankful for the gift and
in which givers of gifts are paid off with the pleasure of giving and/or
the receipt back of a gift of comparable worth, gifts are impossible.[92]
Because one is not being friendly or polite if one is simply doing what
one does as prescribed by socially established rules for personal interactions, friendliness and politeness require rising above such socially
constituted worlds.[93] An ethic that calls for respecting all people in
their singularity is an ethic calling for all people to show welcoming
hospitality to all people. But such hospitality can be concretized as
more than an empty utopian ideal only if all these people could be
welcomed into specific social, political, and legal worlds of established
communities. But no community can do this, however, to all possible
immigrants and refuges without destroying themselves as a specific
community. Pure hospitality is impossible.[94]

Derrida recognizes, as Hegel did, that Kant's formal moral requirements need the concrete social norms of a historical community, but he
also recognizes that these norms need to be ethically critiqued because
they are often unjust. Having rejected with Kierkegaard Hegel's
ontotheological absolute, something else completely outside socially
constituted worlds and their mandates and possibilities is needed. An
event of moving to a new horizon of possibilities, one ethically focused
on the unique singularity of people that is always other than social
roles, meets this need. Letting die off one world and the social identities of people in it is needed in order to receive the gift of a new world
in which people are loved without restriction. In this event we find the
origin of true religion, distinct from the kinds of socially constituted
religions that are not founded on this event.[95]

The whole point of the project of deconstructing intellectual positions and social practices inescapably linked to ontotheologies or meta-

physics of presence is to show the contingency of the horizons of current possibilities. This is done in order to show that it is possible to move on to think and desire new possibilities that are impossible given the old horizons. As Kierkegaard pointed out, moving to a religious horizon of possibilities can only be viewed as madness by those who have not made the move. The event of moving from a nonreligious horizon to a religious horizon is not one that people acting in terms of nonreligious social proprieties, rationales, and identities would make. A decision to faithfully meet the higher ethical responsibilities that the unique singularity of other people place upon each person is one that people will make only as they recognize that they too are being similarly loved in their personal uniqueness. In the Abraham/Issac story, which Derrida sees as the central core of the three Abrahamic religions (Judaism, Christianity, Islam), he reads this proclamation: Because Abraham is loved by God, he is able to obey God's call to sacrifice the life of one world in order to receive the gift of that other world and the promise of living with a new ethical horizon of possibilities.[96] Now victims offer forgiveness whether or not repentance takes place, thereby making peace with people who are encountered in their infinitely valued singular uniqueness and not as thieves, murders, sex offenders, or war criminals.[97] Gifts are given even when it is not enjoyable, even when it is painful to give them; they are given without any expectation of return, even a return of gratefulness; and they are gifts especially when they are given to those who will never know who the giver is and who are so in need that they never will be able to give anything in return. Giving gifts in this new horizon of possibilities will not even be seen by the giver as giving something away, but simply be the manner in which the agape way of life is lived.[98] The desire to hospitably welcome all people, embodying a recognition of one's responsibility to do so, will be the ideal of justice one operates with when judging how best to implement it in concrete political, economic, and social practices.[99]

Derrida locates the origin of religion in two factors. First, there are the irremovable, dialectical tensions and holes in any and all historical worlds of words, concepts, and social practices, which he names "khora," appropriating and reconstructing the word Plato uses in the *Timaeus*. The khora keeps all social worlds from becoming closed totalities and thus always keeps open the possibility for impossibilities, for new horizons of possibilities.[100] Second, there is the messianic desire for the coming of justice. Although the Messiah will always be yet to come,[101] since we never can know what new horizons of possibilities will arise, it is this desire that keeps hope alive.[102] The khora makes god talk of prayer and worship possible and the promise of the Messiah gives it prophetic content.

Caputo. John Caputo develops Derrida's reflections into a complete biblical theology.[103] Many of his religiously powerful interpretations of biblical texts will be drawn upon in section three where the Abrahamic religons will be examined. For Caputo, who rejects all ontotheologies and all forms of a metaphysics of presence, "God" is not the name of a supreme being who is the ultimate cause of nature or of miraculous suspensions of the laws of nature; neither is he/she a powerful monarch who forces things to happen in human history. God is a loving call crying out of weakness, and not an all-powerful cause dominating nature and history. God is the name of the event that replaces the horizon of the world of beings, subjects, and objects constituted in the exercise of a will to power and producing incalculable suffering through domination and oppression. The desire of God is both the desire for the event that will make possible a kingdom of God in which justice is desired, and it is the desire of God for loving treatment of all people in their precious uniqueness, especially the weak, presently dominated, oppressed, and those excluded from the circles of power. This desire is the defining center of this new way of life. Praying to God is praying for this event to come.

Zizek. Slavoj Zizek also appropriates Hegelian themes, which he integrates with insights borrowed from the psychotherapist Jacques Lacan, as he presents his interpretation of Christianity freed from metaphysical gods.[104] The prohibitions in Abrahamic religions against making any graven images of God were needed, Zizek claims, so that the God constituted through personalization would not be interpreted as a metaphysical being, thus violating the need to keep the infinite indescribable.[105] Drawing upon Hegel's analysis of the contradictions in our social world and our own subjectivity, Zizek claims that within the world of the socially constituted objects and subjects that we treat as reality, there is radical dislocation, a primordial abyss, a void, a black hole that dissolves all supposed identities. This dislocation or gap is what Lacan calls the "Real" known only by its effects, an otherness within sameness that produces social and personal traumas that most people use ideologies and fantasies in an effort to fill in the black holes and thus end the trauma.[106] Zizek's interpretation of Christianity builds upon Lacan's account of human subjects who begin at a mirror stage by imagining that they are like other people, then proceed to view themselves in terms of the social roles and identities supplied through social nurturing, and who then find themselves traumatically encountering conflicts and gaps in their social and psychological identities and interpersonal encounters,[107] gaps that people try to fill with ideologies and fantasies, efforts that always turn out to be inadequate.

Christians, Zizek claims, make a Kierkegaardian decision to leap beyond the antagonisms inherent in social orders, illusions, and fantasies.[108] They recognize that there always will be a void in social reality and personal subjectivity that denies any dignity to people living only in such modes of life.[109] Instead of trying to find a way to deny the inescapable vulnerability of all people, Christians make a radical decision to focus their lives on a finite person, the crucified Jesus, who becomes for them the Truth that transcends anything meaningful in social reality or our ideologies and fantasies and that determines their commitments and actions.[110] Jesus becomes for them the absurd and comical Truth who is the Christ, the Messiah, the concrete, unique individual who is both infinite God and finite man.[111] The crucified Jesus is performatively transformed from a living teacher with a universal message into the absolutely singular crucified Christ, savior,[112] the finite one whom Christians love more than anything else,[113] and who through that love is constituted as infinite God, other and more significant than anything finite in social, ideological, or fantasy worlds.

Christians such as Paul transformed the trauma of Jesus's crucifixion, the suffering and death of their beloved teacher, into life-transforming and community-formation decisions, commitments and actions that constitute Christ as the God-man who is at one and same time finite and infinite. Inseparably interwoven in this ending of one way of life and the beginning of a radically different life are a whole series of radically new threads.[114] The reality of the suffering of the crucified Jesus witnesses to the death of the metaphysical god who is revealed to be impotent to prevent the crucifixion.[115] This impotence makes clear the meaninglessness of suffering in all social and psychological worlds of meaning.[116] Constituting the crucified Jesus as the Christ solves the problem of the relation of God to suffering and evil; God is a suffering God.[117] Constituting God as a suffering god involves many different lines of thought and action. The crucified Jesus becomes for Christians the Suffering God as they form a community of people who love all of the outcasts from their earlier social world, outcasts such as beggars, lepers, prostitutes, and Jesus himself, and who embody in that love the Holy Spirit of the Suffering God whom they now love with all their hearts, minds, and spirits.[118] Christians understand that one can see God only in the fleeting appearance of an earthly face, that it is in the Christian love of one another that God abides in them.[119]

By forming and living within this new community, this new body of Christ, Christians themselves become outcasts who are seen as comical and absurd by those living by old social rationalities, ideologies, and fantasies. Becoming outcasts, however, is powerfully liberating. Rather than living by desires to gain what people in the old way of life think we lack in order to satisfy the socially constituted desires of others, Christians can admit and accept the unfillable gaps in themselves, the vulnerability they cannot escape, the miserable excrement from social reality that they are.[120] Christians can do what is impossible in worlds defined by desires grounded in lacks, and that is to love themselves and others, in spite of and because of inadequacies that always will remain, but which do not undermine the singularly unique identities they now gain as members of the community of Christians, whose past social identities are wiped clean as each begins fresh from a zero point.[121] In the new community, the old logic of revenge and punishment is fractured, and the old scale of values is revolutionized as the lowest in the old world are given highest honor in the Christian community. Becoming worldly outcasts in the new Christian community also involves actively loving the world's outcasts in ways which are very demanding, in ways that show that one understands that there are causes for which it is worth dying.[122] What binds Christians together in their new community is a love grounded in the sharing of a common cause, inactive, militant political resistance to the social order's treatment of people as useless or nonconforming excrement to be turned into outcasts.[123] Zizek sees this mistreatment resulting from the law of our current social order, the relentless pursuit in capitalism and state socialism of ever increased productivity. Relentless attack upon this economic foundation of the existing, oppressive social order is the radical political act called for by those living by agape love in the Christian community, which is the body filled with the Holy Spirit of Christ, the suffering God. This puts Marx in the same lineage as Christ.[124]

Through its liberation, commitment, and action, the Christian community of outcasts, the living body of Christ filled with the Holy Spirit, is the authentic psychological community and the ethical, revolutionary political community.[125] The community of Christian faithfulness becomes the resurrected body filled with the spirit of agape love.[126] Authentic Christian fundamentalists, Zizek claims, are so militantly committed to their agape way of life and so engaged in living it that they can let the black holes in social worlds and personal psyches just be what they are. They do not need to fill these holes with metaphysical beings, and they do not feel any of that horror and envy towards people living differently by which inauthentic fundamentalists are existentially driven.[127]

In Zizek's interpretation of Christianity, a new community is constituted, filled with people with new identities, and bound together in agape love by a commitment to serve the suffering God and a Crucified Christ, which was constituted in their constitution of their community and themselves as living members in it. It is not difficult to discern the Hegelian ring to this interpretation. Hegel had claimed that the Absolute, God, is actualized only in the lives of people who actualize God's potential. Zizek claims that God actualizes himself only through human recognition and that divine otherness needs man as its place of revelation.[128] In utilizing Hegel's analysis of human subjectivity, however, Zizek rejects the common interpretation of Hegelianism, which sees it as claiming that there is an eternal law of historical development. For Zizek, the Christian Absolute is a very fragile absolute. The Christian community was chosen and not necessitated. Its continued existence depends upon agape love, whose presence is rare and too easily extinguished, needing constantly to be regained again and again.[129] There is no guarantee that the body of Christ will continue to live filled with the Holy Spirit. This god, too, can be killed off by people if commitment, action, and agape love die off.

Marion. Jean-Luc Marion presents an interpretation of Christianity in which God as agape can be encountered even though God is without being.[130] Seeing all concepts as humanly constituted, Marion turns to the Western tradition of mystical theology (according to Marion, misnamed as negative theology) in order to make his point that God cannot be any conceptualizable being, and thus cannot be a being at all since all beings must be conceptualizable. He agrees with Nicholas of Cusa that infinity is all we can discover of God, that infinite which is other than any finite being, remembering that all beings must be finite.[131] Marion points out that many of the early Christian and Jewish thinkers (Justin Martyr, Athengoras, Clement, Origin, Philo, Athanasius, Basic, Gregory of Nyssa, John Crysostam, and John of Damascus) claimed that there is no name for the ineffable God, that the form of God cannot be uttered, and that God is incomprehensible, invisible.[132] Utilizing Husserl's analysis of experience in terms of conceptual intentions of objects of which one can have intuitional (non-inferential) knowledge, Marion points out that conceptualized beings are always beings at which we gaze, beings we dominate and control with the concepts and intentions through which we do our gazing. Treating any conceptualized object as an ultimate, a metaphysical god, is worshiping a graven idol.[133] Marion turns Anselm's argument against those who talk of God as such a conceivable being. God as agape love is greater than any conceivable god, even as the agape way of life is greater than a way of life whose definitive center is a will to power blind to its finiteness and oppressiveness.[134] To know God is to know that one cannot have propositional knowledge of God. To know God is to hear the call of agape love, to hear it in such a way that oneself and one's lived world are transformed as one lives with a new horizon of possibilities, living now by desiring to love and not to maintain power and control. Hearing the call of God is to cease making assertions about ultimate realities and to begin to praise and pray, to say "hallelujah" and "Here I am, take me."[135]

The Christian way of life, according to Marion, is definitively centered on constituting icons that point to new horizons of life beyond the will-to-power world of beings, icons that we can religiously experience as gazing upon us and our lives of idiolatry, icons that call us to live agape ways of life, icons to which we and others faithfully respond thereby forming a radically new religious community.[136] For Marion, "God" is the name without conceptual content that people hearing the call of agape love utter in their faithful praising and praying linguistic response; Jesus Christ is the icon of the agape love named God that transformed people constitute in their faithful response; and the Eucharist is the icon of Jesus Christ constituted as the Christian faithful constitute themselves as a community that is the body of the resurrected Christ filled with his spirit, God's spirit, the spirit of agape love.[137] Although in Husserl's phenomenology meanings, concepts, and intentions always contain an excess over any object falling under them (thus enabling conceivers to maintain constituted control and power over that at which the gazer gazes), Marion charges that in the Christian way of life, Christians can indicate that they are encountering and responding to God, Jesus Christ, and the Eucharist, which exceed what any concept or intention can capture. In the Christian way of life, living is much more than intending intuitable beings, and Christians can point this out in a kind of phenomenology that deals with this new Christian horizon of possibilities, which deals with Christian saturated phenomena.[138] Wittgensteinians are saying something very similar when they call for religious utterances to be interpreted not metaphysically, psychologically, or sociologically, but as moves in religious linguistic practices located in religious ways of life.[139]

There are many themes that most of these postmodern thinkers have appropriated from the writings of Levinas. The infinite is the indescribable other to all finite socially constituted objects and events. The unique ethical singularity of people as the key example of what is infinite and never an object falling under a concept. Ethically encountering people who call out to be allowed to live in their uniqueness, one responds to this call in a way that radically transforms the respondent as one recognizes and accepts both that one has unlimited responsibilities to those one encounters and that being called to these responsibilities signifies that one is being respected and loved in one's own uniqueness. People use such ethical encounters and responses as the yardstick by which the justice of all social orders may be judged as one engages in the endless task of realizing such a messianic future.

Levinas. Aspects of life can have meaning to people, Levinas claims, when such meaning is not conceptual meaning.[140] Many philosophers, according to Levinas, suffer from the professional illness of over-intellectualizing human life. There is much more to living than conceptual subjectivity, much more than thinking about, perceiving, desiring, or fearing conceptualizable objects. Even consciousness of oneself as a concept using subject is not all there is to consciousness.[141] There is an implicit consciousness preceding all of Husserl's conceptual intending of intuitable beings.[142] There is a unique kind of intentionality other than conceiving of objects.[143] Claiming that he still is a phenomenologist, Levinas offers a phenomenological indication of those dimensions of life that are other than conceptual; he proposes to point out things in Husserl's lived world that are excluded through his reduction of attention to conceptual meanings and acts using such concepts.[144] Levinas thinks that there is an intelligibility older than that present in conceptual experiences of being.[145] When he is indicating that which is older than conceptual beings, Levinas is not talking about what is temporally prior, but rather what is presupposed by our conceptual living. He identifies five aspects of human life that possess such alterity and transcendence of the conceptual aspects of our lives. It is out of these five aspects of alterity that religion originates and the idea of God comes to mind, and since alterity is the presupposition of conceptual worlds, religion provides the ultimate structure for human living.[146]

First, analytically prior to our experience of objects, there is our encounter with the brute otherness of an environment from which we cannot escape, an otherness that fills us with the horror felt by children alone in their silent, dark bedrooms, an otherness that the constituting of tools and other beings tries to control and make safe.[147] Rudolph Otto writes of a sense of the holy that is derived from the dread and fascination we feel when encountering a numinous other to all concept-constituted phenomena.[148] By this indescribable alterity we are both horrified and fascinated. Levinas is not claiming that there is some metaphysically amorphous stuff being classified by us as objects and subjects. He is only reminding us that all vocabularies are historically contingent and changeable, including any confused metaphysical talk about stuff, and that we can sense this contingency in our silent, dark bedrooms. Levinas's "there is" is not far from Derrida's "khora," which for Derrida is one of the originating sources of religion.

Second, other than and analytically prior to living with constituted objects, there is our joyous living from the elements: drinking cool water, eating food, walking and running, feeling the wind in one's face, or losing oneself in sunrises, sunsets and starry nights. Enjoyment is absorbing the energy of one's environment in order to nourish oneself. The horror of the darkness of the other is more than matched by being enjoyably nourished by the other.[149] This is the dimension of enjoyment, jouissance, of which Lacan speaks, which never can be fully controlled by our conceptual practices. This is the joy of living that gives people a love for life, which accidental tragedies and human injustice cannot destroy. This is the dimension of life that generates myths of paradise.[150] This is the dimension of life that motivates people to be thankful for being alive so as to enjoy the goodness of life. To the infinite other of all conceptually constituted beings, when constituted as God, one offers up hymns of praise and thanksgiving. As we shall see, this is the heavenly way of life that Judaism, Christianity, and Islam promise, and Taoism and Zen seek to liberate us back into.

Third, because enjoyable living from the elements faces many threats and thus is very chancy, there is another dimension of human living that, although still other to tool using and conceptual and intellectual life, prepares the way for such living. People, Levinas points out, habitat together interpersonally in the gentle intimacy of the home, suspending immediate enjoyment as they, in practical, nontheoretical ways, take possession of things and labor to postpone death, suffering, and the blocking of enjoyment.[151] Tool using presupposes possession practices developed while inhabiting together.[152] Out of this dimension of living gently in the home arise myths of utopia[153] and messianic desires and hopes. For Levinas, these myths of paradise and utopia always need to be protected from being projected as metaphysical, supernatural heavens or as temporal, end-of-the-world scenarios.

On the one hand, these are the joys and pleasures people can have here and now, if they will not cravenly constitute false gods to worship. This is the living in the land of milk and honey promised to the Hebrews if they will allow themselves to participate in the exodus from spiritual slavery, and this is the joyous life in the Kingdom of God that Christians find in their communal worship. On the other hand, this is the messianic future that still is always yet to come, as Derrida points out, given our inability to be masters of the necessities and chanciness of our environment, and given the never ending pursuit of justice that is required if we are to live ethically in our power-hungry world.

Fourth, people encounter the nonfinite, the infinite alterity to the world of tools and conceivable beings, when they individually and existentially encounter the possibility of their own death, the possibility for oneself of the impossibility of any further possibilities. One's own death is something one cannot represent to oneself, but this is a possibility one encounters continually, even if one uses one's intellectual apparatus to deny that it really is so. One can stand at the grave site of one's loved ones and grieve at their death. One can imagine that one is doing the same as one's own body is about to be cremated, but then, of course, one is imagining that one is not dead but is a living observer of one's body. Death, as the final limit of all possibilities, is not a possible event that one can experience or even represent.[154] This perhaps is one of the reasons why people believe that they do not die and that they live on as some sort of metaphysical soul or resurrected spirit. The impossibility of representing one's own death, however, provides no reason for believing such metaphysical claims. People do die. You and I will die. That we cannot represent our own death only shows that all representing requires an existing person doing the representing, and since in death there is no living person to represent, there is no living person to do the representing. What the impossibility of representing one's own death shows is the finite limitations of representations. It shows the need to remain humble about human conceptual capacities. It shows that we encounter the nonfinite, nonconceptual other of conceptualizable, representable objects and events. Levinas does defend a nonmetaphysical claim that people are immortal, but to understand that claim one must understand his claims about our ethical encounters with the ethical nonfiniteness of people, because one's identity lives on after death only in the lives of the people one has parented to continue to meet one's ethical responsibilities...

Fifth and most decisive of all of Levinas's examples of encountering the infinite are our ethical encounters with other people face-to-face.[155] These are our encounters with the singular ethical uniqueness of people that give to us our singular uniqueness, an ethical uniqueness of having acquired responsibilities that cannot be transferred to anyone else. Encountering people face-to-face is something other than just seeing them only as mortal and vulnerable, seeing them as dominated, oppressed, hungry, cold, in pain, humiliated, homeless, stateless. Face-to-face encounters are not mere sightings by cognitive subjects of suffering human beings. Face-to-face encounters are all that, but also something radically more and different, something occurring against an ethical and not merely an ontological horizon. Our encounters with people face-to-face are ethical encounters in which our very identity is defined, not by fingerprints or DNA, but by a unique set of moral responsibilities to the person we encounter, a person who has a singularly unique status in an ethical world no matter how the person can be physically, socially or psychologically described as a human being. These are responsibilities that define us whether we acknowledge them or not, and this is an ethical status that all encounterable people have regardless of what others think of them or what they think of themselves. Primordially, prior to our existence as human beings in a world of conceivable beings and conceiving subjects, we exist as ethical individuals defined by our ethical encounters with other ethical individuals whom we are ethically bound to permit to live in their ethically unique otherness, whom we are bound to care for so that they can so live.[156] When our ontological existence threatens their ontological well-being and their ethical existence, then we are obligated to justify to them taking up this space that threatens them. Encountering people face-to-face makes us an ethical hostage to them. No matter how we historically constitute worlds of conceivable beings and conceiving subjects and thus structure the world of finite beings, this timeless, nonfinite, infinite, ethical world remains as the horizon of all ontological horizons.[157]

It is in these face-to-face ethical encounters, of persons in their infinity with other persons in their infinity, Levinas claims, that religious responses get constituted and that God comes to mind. It is because people in face-to-face ethical encounters are also related to third and fourth persons that ethical encounters demand the pursuit of justice, demand resistance to the injustices of oppression and domination, demand respect and help for orphans, widows, strangers, and enemies.[158] The prophetic indictment of injustice is an essential part of religion. Levinas would certainly endorse the rhetorical question, "How can you love God whom you cannot see if your cannot love people whom you do see?" Levinas says that the desire for God is the desire for the most desirable, the most worthy of desire, the fulfillment of one's ethical responsibilities.[159] The fear of God is the fear for the helpless, the orphan, widow, and stranger. The word "God" has no meaning apart from our search for God, our search for ways to act upon our desire for the most desirable.[160] The word "God" is not used to make statements about some being, some all-powerful supreme being and ultimate cause. It is used performatively to give thanks and praise for the joy of living; to seek assurance in the face of horror and inexplicable suffering; to call out to be permitted to exist in one's uniqueness; to prayerfully ask that one's desire for the most desirable be ever more strengthened and that one gain the wisdom and strength to act on this desire; to ask for forgiveness for the unforgivable crime of ignoring one's responsibilities; and to give thanks for receiving the impossible forgiveness that wipes away the past without forgetting it, so that one can ever anew live joyously and act lovingly in a way faithful to one's desire for the most desirable so that one can seek justice.

The metaphysical god is dead, and space has been opened up by postmodern, post-metaphysical thinkers for religion to enjoy a powerful renaissance. Those who have been responsible for killing off or deconstructing the metaphysical god are to be thanked for liberating religion. Yes, the metaphysical gods are dead, thank god, but alas, their rotting corpses still lie around, contaminating massive amounts of the world's politics, cultures, and religions. Never was the sanitizing and cauterizing power of religion needed more, and never have metaphysical assumptions and claims, posing as religious beliefs, made religion's work more difficult and caused so much hatred of not unjustified differences. So many dreadful and destructive metaphysical claims are proclaimed daily to be religious truths by self-appointed spokespersons for religious fundamentals that they too often drown out the voices of the great religions of the world that call for lives of self-interrogation, humility, transformation, trust, joy, justice, and compassion. Today, as much as ever, the faithful in all the world's religions must proclaim the words of religion that are dangerous to all graven images. Faithfully responding to encounters with the infinite obligates us to expose, oppose, and drive out the dangerous pretenders in the temples of the world's religions. It requires showing how the great religions of the world can survive and prosper once all the metaphysical trash has been cleared away. In the chapters that follow, that is what this book will try to do.

One final introductory word. The servants of a decaying and diseased corpse, whether they be self-serving opportunists or confused victims of a metaphysically contaminated culture, must not be allowed to exempt themselves from criticism and rejection by claiming that their claims are religious and thus protected by the mantle of religious freedom. It simply is not true that one has a right to believe anything one wants to believe once one has labeled it one of one's religious beliefs. One has no epistemological right to believe what cannot be justified when it is indicted for being incoherent or unjustifiable. One has no moral right to ignore or violate the obligation every person has to respect the unique singularity of people, violations that are the heart of all unjust and oppressive actions and practices. No metaphysical beliefs called religious can justify such a failure to respect people, and yet so often efforts are made to justify restricting people's freedom by offering nothing but such metaphysical claims. One has no religious right to privilege one historically constituted religious community by coercively rejecting or marginalizing, on metaphysical grounds, all other such communities. One has no moral or religious right to use the power of the state or any social group to coerce people to belong to any specific religious community. Because it is impossible to coerce anyone to faithfully respond to encounters with the infinite, certainly not in the case of people who willfully or confusedly deny having such encounters, coercion must never be attempted to get people to be religious.

Long live religious faithfulness. Cremate, however, as long as it is necessary, the metaphysical corpses, and let their ashes become nothing but library dust reminding us of the danger involved when people fail to respond faithfully to the infinite, but pretend instead that their finite, self-serving efforts are themselves divine. No single book can burn away these corrupting metaphysical weeds. Seeing the crops and flowers in the fields of the great religions of the world, once the metaphysical weeds are torn out, may help, however, in building the needed funeral pyres. Praise be to religions that are a danger to human efforts at self-deification. Long live Yahweh, Brahman, Sunyata, Tao, Christ, and Allah. Long live the religious communities constituted in response to the call of the infinite. Some respond by constituting a personal God and incarnations of God, and some do not. Encountering the infinite remains the same in all the religions of the world, but responses to these encounters are historically and culturally varied. Praise be to the call of the infinite, however, which remains a danger to any community that fails to remain religiously humble. In order to avoid getting lost in some metaphysical graveyard, let the faithful in every one of the world's religions remember the words of the Zen master who said, "When you see the Buddha, kill the Buddha." Authorities, certainly not objectivistic, metaphysical authorities, cannot provide a person with a religious way of life. Nothing can be a substitute for a passionate, prayerful, worshiping response to the call of the infinite.

Section Two

THE RELIGIONS OF ASIA

In presenting these interpretations of Hindu, Buddhist, Taoist, and Zen religions, no attempt is going to be made to duplicate the wonderful studies of the religions of Asia or the philosophies of Asia that already exist.[161] Rather, an attempt will be made to show how each of these religious traditions develops distinct religious responses to encounters with the infinite. An attempt will be made to show that these religious faiths do not depend upon any of the metaphysical speculations and theorizing that sometimes infiltrated their religious practices. An attempt will be made to show that in these religions, as with proofs for the existence of the metaphysical god, such metaphysical considerations can be reconstructed as religious insights. Each of these religious traditions provides valuable insights into the pitfalls people fall into when they try to live without listening to the call of the infinite. All four of these religious traditions make major contributions to people's understanding of what is involved in encountering the infinite and living in faithful response to these encounters. In presenting these interpretations, the hope is that people in other religious traditions will strengthen their appreciation of and respect for these four traditions. Although no attempt will be made to motivate people to change their specific religious faiths, the hope is that dialogues can be started between the different worlds of religious faith that will enrich all the faith communities.

1. Hinduism

Within the Hindu religious tradition, there is a well-developed analysis of the various ways humans live their lives. Similar to Kierkegaard,

Hindus focus not on conceptualizable objects that one might perceive or of which one might have theoretical beliefs. Rather they focus on human modes of subjectivity, different ways people relate themselves to the finite factors they must deal with daily. Hindus claim that whole ways of life are determined by what people think they want most of all in life, by the ultimate goal they desire to achieve. As Lacan points out, desire is the key to the human constitution of the finite self and to the whole symbolic world and all the conceivable objects in it. Hindus have been saying this for more than two-thousand years.

The Hindu tradition lives out of faithfulness to its interpretation of the Vedas, a collection of poems, hymns, and prayers circulating orally for centuries before being collected in a written form around 800 BC In the "Hymn of Creation"[162] it is written that desire is the seed of which thought is the product. Without such desire one cannot think any distinction between being and nonbeing, air and stones, the sky and the earth, between death and life immortal. Without desire, driven thought, there are no distinguishing marks, and ordinary light and darkness are covered by a primordial darkness. Desire motivates the conceptual constitution (creation) of all distinctions and distinguishable beings and events, the finite world and all the gods constituted by people. The religiously wise understand that what has being (finite objects and events) cannot break its bond to what is nonbeing (the nonfinite, the infinite). Hindus focus their attention on people's desire-driven modes of subjectivity because only one of them, the religious mode of subjectivity, gives people what they really desire. For the most part, people live unsatisfying lives grounded in a practical, preconceptual, misunderstanding of what they really desire.

What one thinks one desires determines one's whole way of life, whether it is objectivistic or subjectivistic, whether one prizes above everything else pleasure, power, fame, fortune, social virtue, or spiritual liberation from enslavement by the merely finite. Since making rational and reasonable judgements is framed within desire-structured ways of living, the Hindu tradition takes it for granted that one cannot be argued into or argued out of what is functioning as one's ultimate goal in life. What will be accepted as a reasonable thing to do will be determined by what one prizes above everything else. The person wanting pleasure above all else cannot hear the advice given about how to sacrifice pleasure to gain power or fame. The person pursuing power above everything else will not listen when told to take time out and relax or to not use people as mere means in one's pursuit of one's goals. The person wanting to be a responsible father above everything else will find it repugnant to even think of seeking personal pleasure, fame, wealth ,or power by failing to meet one's duties to one's children. The person wanting spiritual liberation will be like Abraham, unable to even entertain the possibility that his faithfulness should be sacrificed in order to avoid the pain of losing Isaac or his ability to be the leader of a people, or in order to obey social prohibitions against murder. One's ultimate desire determines one's criteria of reasonableness. When it comes to ultimate desires and goals, reasoning is powerless. One must discover by oneself that one does not really desire what one has been taking as one's ultimate goal. One must discover that personal satisfaction cannot be gained in any of the ways of life other than the religious. Not rational argumentation, but dissatisfaction, disappointment, frustration, despair, absence of contentment, and peace motivate people to move from absolutizing the finite to living faithfully in response to encounters with the infinite.

In the Hindu analysis of the human situation, there basically are four goals that different people live with as their object of ultimate concern. There is *kama* (pleasure and enjoyment), *artha* (success, fame, power), *dharma* (moral duty), and *moksa* (liberation from pursuing finite goals and liberation for living faithful to encounters with the infinite). Given that striving for one of these goals is an expression of one's ultimate desire, one cannot mix and match elements from the various ways of life. There will be times when seeking pleasure will conflict with seeking power, and seeking power will conflict with doing one's moral duty, or any and all three of these will conflict with religious faithfulness. When facing such moments of conflict, what one desires most will settle the question of what to do. The Hindu will claim, however, that once kama, artha, and dharma cease being one's ultimate goal in life, then the pursuit of moksa will enable people to be ethical, to function fruitfully in the corridors of economic, political, and social power and fame, and to experience joyfully life's many pleasures., living with bliss, understanding, and eternal happiness and significance.

It is perfectly understandable that people seek pleasure and desire to enjoy themselves. As Levinas has pointed out, enjoying, and not concept-structured perceiving, is our primary way of relating to the elements with which we live. As Lacan and Zizek point out, the pleasure of jouissance, which never is fully controllable by symbolic life, is the other to the whole symbolic world. As hedonists have understood for centuries, living without pleasure and enjoyment is hardly living at all. Living is loving life. For the person who loves life, waking up to the rays of the morning sun is pure joy, and watching awe-inspiring sunsets is the frosting on a day filled with the simple pleasures of sight and sound, smell, taste, and touch supplied by our sensory organs. Pleasure is good, and in no sense is it evil. People and their freedom are to be respected in order that they in their own ways can find pleasure and joy. Spiritual liberation aims not at eliminating pleasure and joy from life, but at freeing us from the ways we make ourselves miserable. Much of the suffering we cause ourselves and others to bear is due to the resentment and envy we feel because others have found ways to enjoy themselves that are different from ours. We wish we could celebrate life as they do, but because we believe that we cannot, we condemn their pleasure as disgusting and corrupt. What difference should it make to anyone else what foods someone else finds delicious, what clothes or bodily markings someone finds beautiful, what music or dancing someone finds exhilarating, or how a person gains genital pleasure?

Although there is nothing wrong with pleasure itself, there is something terribly wrong if one makes the pursuit of one's own personal pleasures the ultimate goal constituting one's way of life. The lives we love and find enjoyable are located in an environment that often causes pain; threatens our pleasures, joys, and life itself; and that inescapably is dependent on receiving assistance from others when we are very young, very old, and very ill or disabled. Even the best of lives are a balance of pleasure and joy over pain and misery. To maximize pleasure and minimize pain, it is not enough to be prudent in our ways, not focusing on minor pleasures today that will give us big headaches tomorrow. We need to move beyond mere prudence and live interpersonal lives. We need to live in families, depend on one another, share the good and the bad with others, and function with others economically and politically. Living with others eventually involves confronting them ethically face-to-face and being obligated to let them be in their unique singularity. Living interpersonally and ethically is impossible if seeking personal pleasure is one's ultimate goal in life. If I am only concerned with my pleasures and my pains, then I cannot live in a family meeting my obligations as a brother or father or as a just person concerned about the widows and orphans in the world. Merely being prudent might allow one to be willing to sell one's son for the right price, but being a father makes it impossible to even consider such an option.

If my personal pleasures become gods on whose altar everything else is to be sacrificed if and when the need arises, then such a life becomes counterproductive. I, then, would continually have to be on the alert never to make any commitments to anyone else. Such constant vigilance never to be a son, father, friend, buddy, fellow worker, comrade, or citizen will produce so much misery that it would make life not worth living. In addition, on the one hand, in order to gain certain pleasures, one continually would have to pretend that one was such a relative or friend and live knowing that one is a living lie, while, on the other hand, one would have to maintain constant vigilance not to get trapped by feelings of love and friendship that carry with them obligations. Also, given the chanciness of life and the inability to control the future, unbearable suffering can hit even the most prudent of persons at any time. Living only for continuing moments of personal sensory pleasure can fill one with such fear of the future that little psychic room is left for enjoying life. Making moments of pleasure one's ultimate goal in life can never provide the peace and defense against tragedy that only can be found by passionately seeking what Kierkegaard calls "eternal happiness," a happiness found in the pursuit of it, a happiness that enables one to love life even when undeserved suffering occurs. Besides, great as pleasure and joy are, they last only as long as we last, but even the person who tries to serve only the pursuit of pleasure probably also wants some form of significance that remains after the person dies.

Seeking kama is good, but making it one's god does not leave one with a workable way of life. If people do however, think that what they want in life is personal pleasure above everything else, then there is nothing one can say to them to persuade them to change their ultimate goal in life. They can always rationalize away any of the considerations given in the last paragraph. They can always keep telling themselves, if only I had more pleasure, then everything would be fine. If only I were more skillful in gaining pleasure, then I would have what I really want. The Hindu claims that these people have to find out for themselves that they are only rationalizing things and that their chosen way of life never will work. To help them in this journey to self-discovery, the *Kamasutra* is offered. It is a manual for attaining sensual pleasure. Follow the manual! Get more pleasure than you ever imagined possible, so that you no longer can say that the problem is that you are not skillful enough. Then perhaps you will see that making kama a god to be served at whatever cost is not going to give you what you really want.

The second, life-defining ultimate goal that people desire, according to the Hindu tradition, is artha, success in getting other people to do what one wants and in receiving from other people recognition, honor, and praise. People desire power, popularity, and fame. Here is where we find most people. People want to be successful in life, with success being defined in terms of wealth, economic power, political power, or respected social status. To gain power and social approval, people will make all kinds of sacrifices of enjoyment and pleasure. They will sacrifice having fun in order to attain athletic, economic, political, and social skills and results. They will do almost anything not to be unpopular, not to live at the bottom of the social ladder with no one worse off than themselves, or to experience the shame of being seen as an economic or social failure.

It should not surprise any one of us that so many people worship the gods of power and social approval. One needs economic resources to care for oneself and those one loves. One needs political power not to be dominated and oppressed by others. Our whole social identity as persons needs the approval of others. As Lacan has pointed out, from early childhood on the one desire that colors all our desires is the desire to meet the desires of others: parents, teachers, peer groups, bosses, general social expectations, and normative requirements. "What do you want me to do?" is the anguished cry of all of us as we try to figure out what kind of a person we will be. So thoroughly do many of us commit ourselves to the attainment of economic well-being, political power, and social status that "religious" seems to be the only term appropriate for describing such commitment. Power and prestige do function as gods in the lives of many people. So many people get so caught up in the pursuit of these goals that they leave no time to enjoy themselves, and they become willing to use people as mere means to attain these ends. They become so wound up in playing the noisy social games of acquiring and retaining power and approval that they prevent themselves from hearing the still small voice of the infinite.

The problem, the Hindu tradition says, with building a life solely around the desire to attain artha is that it does not work in giving us the satisfaction we had hoped for. In a competitive world of people seeking power and prestige, the battle is continual. Unless you keep climbing, others will climb all over you. The competition is fierce. One dare not take time out. No matter how high one climbs, there is always someone right behind you to pull you down. No matter how much power and fame one gains, one always wants more. In this game, there is no time for peace and contentment. One knows that no matter how hard one tries, only a few can be successful even for a little while. Most of the players never win at all, and great is the despair of those who put all their marbles into this game and then lose. The fear of losing everything becomes ever greater the higher one climbs the ladder of success. Even when one is successful in gaining great power or fame, one is haunted by two inescapable concerns. First, what is one to do with this achievement? What does one do with power and fame, other than using them to run the treadmill ever faster in an effort to gain still more power and fame? Second, what lasting significance is achieved in this scramble to gain power and fame for their own sake. This game always ends in death. Successful living is never attained in a life consumed by a passion to succeed in this battle for supremacy.

Once again, the Hindu tradition teaches that people have to find out by themselves that absolute commitment to the gods of power and fame will not give them what they really desire. The *Artha-sastra*, written between 321 and 296 BC by Kautilya, chancellor to the emperor of the Indian Magadha empire, contains his advice to the emperor on how to gain and hold onto earthly power.[163] Kautilya's recommendations are direct and brutal. Keep you eye clearly fixed on your goal: wealth and power. Do not let temptations for sensual pleasure, feelings of sympathy, or moral considerations or ideals interfere with your pursuit of this goal. Politics and business are about power. This is the real world; don't let idealistic fantasies cloud your focus or sap your energy and determination. Since power always involves attaining power over others, do everything you can to minimize their resistance. Flatter them. Make them promises, that you have no intention of keeping. Lie to them. Get them to feel obligated to you. Get them to make sacrifices that enhance your power. Get them to fear you or feel that their entire well-being depends upon their loyalty to you. Use any kind of ideology and nurturing practices that work in strengthening your power and weakening their resistance. Never, never, however, tie your hands with your promises, claims, or ideological pronouncements. Never think that you owe anyone anything. You have one obligation only, to maximize your power and fame. Do this and you will be as successful as is possible in this competitive scramble for power and fame. Perhaps, then, when you have done everything humanly possible, you will be able to convince yourself that such a way of living is not what you really want.

Rather than seeking to be lord and master of the social world in which one lives, there is an alternative way of living as a socially constituted person in a world of people similarly participating in the social practices that give an identity to that world. One might strive to live as a perfect social functionary in such a world, with perfection being defined as making the best contribution one can to the well-being of the whole social world in which one finds oneself. This is one way of living a moral form of life.

If one's supreme desire is to serve the well-being of one's community, then social responsibilities take precedence over personal pleasure or ambition. In the Hindu tradition, such a moral way of life is specified in the Code of Manu[164] in which a person's responsibilities are spelled out in terms of each person's ability to contribute to the good of the social whole at each stage of the person's life, from youth to old age. The Code of Manu, compiled between 500 BC and 200 AD, is an example of an ethic of social role fulfillment. It is grounded in the understanding that one's social identity is a matter of the social roles that one is playing: son, daughter, father, mother, priest, ruler, administrator, warrior, skilled artisan, unskilled laborer, student, household provider, full time seeker of enlightenment, enlightened sage. The Code calls for people to be the social person they are, and thus to be true to their own social identity by desiring to fulfill the duties definitive of their social identity. Specifying a social role is specifying a set of duties and authorized actions. Being the President of the United States is not a matter of having certain physical features, certain personal ways of enjoying oneself, or certain personal ambitions. It is a matter of having the duty to enforce the laws and the authority to command the armed forces, nominate judges, and veto legislation. In a similar manner, being a mother, father, son, or daughter is not a matter of mere biology, but it is a matter of having a certain set of duties. Being morally faithful to one's social identity is a matter of carrying out the duties definitive of one's social roles.

The role assignments specified in the Code of Manu are based on two beliefs about the nature of people. First, it is understood that people have different abilities and should not be required to do what they are not capable of doing. The general moral consideration behind India's caste system is that people have different abilities that should determine what they should contribute to the common good and thus should determine their social identity. Some people are gifted in philosophical reflection. This *Brahmin* caste of people should, through reflection, keep everyone's eyes focused on what is really good for the community as a whole. Other people are good at leading and managing people to do what is necessary to achieve this good. This *Ksatriya* caste of people should listen to the wise counsel of the Brahmins and should be given the authority needed to carry out their assigned task, authority to constitute and preserve the social practices that will achieve the well-being of all the people. Other people are good producers, skilled workers, and artisans who grow things, make things, create works of art. The people in this *Vaisya* caste should be free to do what they do best within the overall planning and administration performed by those in the *Ksatriya* caste. Carrying out their responsibilities means that they must be given the authority to direct unskilled laborers and aid them in exercising their skills. Finally, there are people who are good at doing physically demanding labor, often in demanding repetitive tasks. People in the *Sudra* caste make valuable and essential contributions to the well-being of the whole community. The Code of Manu says that people's roles and duties need to be matched to their abilities for the good of the whole. This part of the Code bears striking resemblances to the class structure advocated in Plato's *Republic* and in Confucius' ethic of role fulfillment.

The second assumption behind the Code of Manu is that for the good of the whole, people should take on different roles at different times in their lives. There is a time for young people to be students, obligated to learn and study how to serve the community, but for a time exempt from other duties so they can concentrate on their studies. Then comes that productive period in one's life when one ought to use one's abilities to raise and care for a family and to work, providing the materials and services the community as a whole needs. Recognizing that the good of the social whole is furthered by people who are seeking spiritual enlightenment and by people who have attained it, two further stages in life and their accompanying roles and duties are acknowledged. Usually when one's children have become productive householders with their own children, one may drop off the householder role and one's earlier productive responsibilities. One now can take on the role of forest dweller with the duty to devote oneself full time to the pursuit of spiritual enlightenment. Finally, there is the role of the wandering sages who have the responsibility of living faithfully in response to their liberating encounters with the infinite. As with students, so with these last two categories of social life, producing householders have a duty to meet the material needs of these groups.

Unfortunately, despite the moral considerations that provide support for the caste system, its operation in practice has departed drastically from the considerations that give it ethical standing. Even many directives in the Code of Manu seem to conflict with the considerations that give it ethical standing. Differences in abilities often are not biologically inherited from one's parents or by restricting marriage to members of one's caste. Yet as practiced, caste membership often was determined that way. Differences in abilities to contribute to the common good do not mean "…a sudra…was created …to be a slave of a

Brahmin."[165] The well-being of the community may require the assignment of authority to some people to advise, administer, or provide technical directions, but that does not imply that members in higher castes are to be empowered to oppress and dominate people in other lower castes. Neither does differentiation of tasks within the home legitimate claiming that "day and night women must be kept in dependence by the males [of] their [families]," and "a woman must never be independent."[166] The ethical underpinnings of the Code of Manu certainly do not justify the classifying of some people as untouchables and thus as not having any social status in the community at all.

The actual operation of the Indian caste system is a symptom of the inadequacy of a way of life founded on a supreme desire to live merely as a socially constituted person striving to meet duties supposedly aimed at maximizing the good of the whole social world. An ethic of social role fulfillment can remain a viable ethical form of life only if it operates against a background understanding that people are not just social functionaries and that roles are constituted and duties are assigned by finite people with limited knowledge and too often with flawed motivations. If one makes serving a social morality one's ultimate goal in life, one will not incorporate in that morality an appreciation of the Hindu religious insight that people must be respected and compassionately identified with in their nonfinite, singular uniqueness. If one absolutizes existing social roles and norms, then one will not recognize the all-to-human nature of the social world. No actual social world was constituted by some all-knowing, all-powerful, perfect metaphysical god. It was constituted by people who too often are aiming primarily at personal pleasure, wealth, power, or fame. Nothing is more effective in enhancing dominating and oppressive power than to have the dominated and oppressed internalize a belief that those in power are morally authorized to possess and use such power. Even with the best of intentions, every social way of life and every form of personal, class, racial, ethnic, or gender identity must remain subject to critical appraisal, because humans do not know enough about their social environment and their complicity with unjust social practices to construct a blueprint for attaining paradise on earth. What is true of the Indian social moral Code of Manu is true of all sets of social roles and moral rules. To absolutize any of them is to treat something finite as though it were the infinite. This is worshiping a false god. Everything socially constituted must remain open to judgement and the possible need for reconstitution. This is why we will want to look closely at the Confucian ethic, which does have built into it a process of critical self evaluation and creative reconstruction. Finally, an ethic of social role fulfillment is limited in another way. The master blueprint assigning social responsibilities may be pretty good, but one still faces the problem of deciding whether one should keep doing one's duties when they seem to have lost their point because so many others are not doing theirs, and thus the common good is not going to be achieved. Perhaps the whole idea of constructing and following a master blueprint in order to maximize the good of the community needs to be replaced by a much more modest moral project of resisting unjust social practices as best one can in very specific and local social environments.

The classic Indian text that sets forth the deficiencies in a way of life ultimately centered on the desire to meet one's socially constituted moral responsibilities is the Bhagavad Gita, part of the great epic *Mahabharata.*[167] In this epic two brothers are warring for control of the land of the Kurus, because its blind and aging king decided to pass over his oldest son, whom tradition says should inherit the throne, for his younger son, who was a much more virtuous person. Moral considerations in this setting were in conflict with each other. Long-standing, assigned role responsibilities, necessary to avoid lawlessness, favor the older son, but virtuous fulfillment of these responsibilities favor the younger son. In order to dramatically accent in the epic the personal differences between the two sons, the older one seizes the throne by trickery and sets out to kill his four brothers to remove all challenges to his power. Krishna, the head of another clan and cousin to the brothers, having failed to reconcile the two brothers and their competing moral demands, releases his vassals from their duty to follow his lead and allows them to decide which warring party to support with existing morality not being able to settle the moral superiority of either side. Some support one side and some the other, and Krishna elects to join the action merely as the charioteer for the epic's hero, Arjuna, who sides with the virtuous younger brother. Arjuna is caught in a horrible moral dilemma. He has friends and relatives on both sides in this civil war. Moral considerations support both contenders. Advice is given to Arjuna by Krishna, whom the epic presents as an incarnation of the god Vishnu, constituted in the Hindu community as one of the gods to be worshiped as a way of responding faithfully to encountering the infinite, Brahman. Krisna points out that Arjuna's dilemma cannot be resolved as long as living only by a morality of role fulfillment is one's ultimate goal in life. Krishna recommends not trying to resolve the dilemma at the merely moral level. Rather, he suggests that there is a way of living that allows one to act in a morally imperfect world without personal despair. One must act not aiming at moral perfection, but rather aiming at liberation from desires grounded in merely finite considerations, aiming at liberation from making kama, artha, or moral dharma one's ultimate goal in life. Instead, recognize that faithfulness to one's encounter with the infinite allows one to keep pleasure, wealth, power, and social obligations in their proper place, and thus allows one still to find peace and bliss even in the midst of the madness of human conflict.

The problem with making social well-being, personal pleasure, or personal success one's ultimate, desired goal in life, according to the Hindu tradition, is that this fails to appreciate that people are not just finite enjoyers, competitors, and social functionaries (although, of course, they are always that). People are singularly unique individuals who desire to be liberated from living merely as finite creatures interacting only with socially constituted objects and with people who are always seen wearing social masks. People who have encountered the infinite understand that they are more than finite and that what they want more than anything else is what can only come by responding faithfully to their encounter with the infinite. Using the Hindu vocabulary, what people really desire, whether they know it not, is *moksa,* liberation from mere finite existence, knowledge, success, and enjoyment. The Hindu proclaims that this is a desire that can be satisfied. By letting oneself be what no classification system can capture, one will gain *sat, cit,* and *ananda.* One will gain sat, an identity not confined between the boundaries of birth and death. One will gain cit, unlimited understanding of the relationship between the limited and the unlimited, a nontheoretical, living understanding of how the specifiable finite lives within the unspecifiable environment of the infinite. One will gain ananda, a sense of timeless happiness and bliss that is not endangered by the contingencies of finite life. Unlimited understanding and bliss are just waiting there for people to enjoy, if only they would let themselves be what they are, *Atman,* other than merely some describable, finite being, someone who then can encounter what is other than all describable, finite beings, *Brahman.* In talking about Atman and Brahman one cannot be talking about two unlimited infinites, because there cannot be two infinites; anything countable as one or two is not infinite, given that one would be limited by the other. Atman is Brahman. The infinite other to all finite beings is the infinite person that each of us is.

Moksa is the goal that people really desire, but most people live lives chasing after impossible goals of personal pleasure, success, or social propriety. Most people just do not understand themselves or how to successfully live. Their tragic desires give them what the Hindu calls a *jiva* identity, living as though they were nothing but merely a finite biological, social, and psychological person, living with pleasure, success, or social properness as their ultimate desires and goals. Living that way means living a life of *maya,* living under the all-encompassing illusion that the finite is self-sufficient and exhaustive. Living as jiva, however, never satisfies, something one can acknowledge only when the power of maya is broken, when one is liberated from jiva, when one is liberated to live as what one always already is—Atman. We are Atman. Our singular uniqueness cannot be confined within socially constituted descriptions or roles. We are other than jiva, other than a being that can be described and therefore is finite. Our identity is tied to our encounters with the infinite, to our ethical encounters with other people face-to-face (and not merely as socially constituted beings dealing with other socially constituted beings in socially appropriate or inappropriate ways). Our identity is tied to the unique, nontransferable, and unlimited responsibilities we have to those we encounter ethically face-to-face and for the responsibilities they have to others they encounter. Our identity is tied to our enjoyment of the elements and our interpersonal cohabiting within families and homes, neither of which are parts of the jiva lives we live with socially constituted objects of perception and desire. Our identity as Atman is not limited to our biological life between birth and death. My passionate desire to fulfill my ethical responsibilities lives on in the children I parent to have the same passionate desire. My social identity stretches back into the primordial recesses of the social and cultural history that has produced the constitution of my social and psychological identity, and as Atman I accept the burden of responsibilities that my historical identity gives to me. As Atman, I cannot say that I am not ethically implicated in the American enslavement of Africans or the genocidal murder of Native Americans. Every person's life has ethical significance that is unlimited in historical time or space. Furthermore, people are not just the products of social constitution, but they are the constitutors and sustainers of all the socially constituted objects, practices and subjects that there are. To desire moksa, and thus to desire sat, is to accept responsibility for the whole constituted world and all the ethically unique people that live within it and with us.

Closely tied to the Hindu religious understanding of jiva is its understanding of *karma*, a law of causality that governs the interconnections between jiva lives. Karma often has been given a metaphysical interpretation in which it is claimed there are one-to-one causal connections between one person's spiritual success or failure at one moment of historical life and the spiritual blessings and curses that this same person has at another moment of historical time. Interpreted religiously, a very different interpretation of karma becomes possible. As the Japanese Buddhist philosopher, Keiji Nishitani, has pointed out, karma is best understood as operating primarily at the level of a social/cultural environment, and only secondarily at the level of the individual jiva, who is constituted by a social/cultural inheritance and who leaves as its legacy a modified social/cultural environment that will be the constituting inheritance of future jiva.[168]

Hinduism and Buddhism make it clear that the law of karma applies only to jiva-type lives, because religious faithfulness to encounters with the infinite guarantees liberation from the law of karma. Talking about karma reminds us that our social and psychological identity ties us to the lives of people in the past who have constituted the social and cultural practices into which we have been initiated and which thereby give us our finite identity. We do not begin living as persons who are blank tablets; the social and cultural get to us before we can modify them or recognize that there is radical otherness to. Being born into a world structured by certain sorts of unjust and antireligious practices creates specific sorts of obstacles that must be overcome to gain spiritual liberation. Born into a world with significant just and religious practices becomes a gift of grace that we have not yet done anything to deserve. Speaking of karma reminds us that the manner in which we live influences the burdens and gifts we leave for people in the future. Since our very social and psychological identity at any given time is inseparably tied to the lives of our ancestors and descendants, and our ethical identities are tied to our ethical offspring, there is a sense in which we are born and reborn again and again, with the spiritual, qualitative character of these lives being causally related. The causal linkage and the relationships of identity go from my present jiva life to an indefinitely large number of past jiva lives and lives still to be lived in the future. Liberation from jiva and the law of karma means liberation from the obstacles preventing people from gaining what they really want, and it means liberation for parenting and living on in one's ethical children who passionately are committed to meeting their infinite responsibilities and to seeking eternal happiness.

Making ultimate the desire for moksa (identity not limited by biological and social constraints; understanding not limited by finite conceptualizing, perceiving, and theorizing; bliss not limited by the threatening contingencies of biological and social life) guarantees that this desire will be satisfied. Our identity as Atman extends as far as historical time and social life extends. Encountering the other to all socially constituted objects and subjects enables us to understand the finite as being merely finite (not the self-sufficient beings of secular materialists and not the material or immaterial substances of metaphysicians). It allows us to understand the infinite as being other than the finite (but not being a super being). It allows us to understand the dependency of the human practice of social constitution of objects and subjects upon people being other than merely such subjects. It allows us to understand that people are ethically nonfinite and unique, enjoyers of the elements, cohabitors in interpersonal life. They are people who can encounter the other of the finite and live in faithfulness to such encounters. Living in faithfulness to the desire for moksa is living a life of bliss and joy undreamed of in all other ways of life. Pleasures now just can be allowed to be the wonderful things they are, without having them be compromised by trying so hard not to let responsibilities to others arise. Once one stops trying to be an all-powerful king of the hill, one can begin enjoying being in committed relationships to others, engaging in productive labor producing things of use value, and seeking and exercising power to resist unjust social practices. Once one desires something more than being a perfect social functionary serving the supposed well-being of the community, one can find joy and significance in meeting one's traditionally assigned duties as family member, employee and employer, citizen, and public official, while always resisting unjust assignments that do not recognize the unique singularity of people and the different, not-unjustified social worlds in which people function. One can find the joy and contentment of recognizing one's ethical significance, of understanding oneself, the inevitable limitations of one's conceptual and theoretical knowledge, and the other to the finite. Finding happiness in living out of the desire for moksa is finding eternal happiness, as Kierkegaard would call it. It is finding a happiness not conditional on being free from physical pain, not conditional on others not acquiring greater wealth, power, or fame, not conditional on morally evil people prospering according to jiva standards while people faithful to their encounters with the infinite are hungry and sick, oppressed and dominated. Eternal happiness is attained when one acts faithful to one's ultimate desire to have unlimited unique status and significance, unlimited understanding of the relation of the finite to its other, and a bliss not even limited by the threatening contingencies of biological and social life. Satisfying this desire for moksa is ours for the taking, if we will let ourselves be what we are, Atman.

The word "Atman" is used in the Hindu religious tradition to refer to what we are in addition to having a biological, social, and psychological identity. It is crucial to allow all of this talk about Atman to remain religious talk, talk enunciated in a subjectivistic mode of subjectivity, and not to allow it to slip into talk in an objectvisitic mode of subjectivity, in which Atman becomes some metaphysical object or being, some supernatural soul or mind, residing somehow inside of us. A similar understanding of the use of the word "Brahman" must be maintained. Brahman is used to indicate what we encounter when we encounter the finite's other, the nonfinite, the infinite, encounters we are to remain faithful to in living liberated from all limitations on our identities, our understanding, and our bliss. Talk about Brahman must remain religious talk and not be captured by metaphysical talk in an objectivistic mode of life in which it supposedly refers to some supreme being or to the being of beings. Religiously, the words "Atman" and "Brahman" come to mind as we religiously respond faithfully to encounters with the finite's other. If it is used metaphysically, we get hopelessly entangled in conceptual confusion as we are forced to ask how Atman can be infinite and yet each of us is Atman and singularly unique; or how Atman, what we are, can be Brahman, what we encounter. When the Hindu texts using the words Atman and Brahman are interpreted religiously, no such confusions need arise.

The Upanishads are a series of meditations on the meaning of the Vedas. Joined together, the Vedas and the Upanishads function in the Hindu tradition as the canonical confession that constitutes the Hindus as a religious community desiring to remain faithful to its encounters with the infinite. Although at times it seems as though metaphysical speculations crept even into the Upanisads, it is possible to interpret them as being merely religious texts, responding faithfully to the call of the infinite. The *Katha Upanishad* says a person as Atman, desiring moksa above everything else, is not anyone with any describable nature.[169] As Atman, we enjoy our ride in our bodily chariot, with our conceiving and thinking mind functioning as the driver and reins determining the sensory objects we perceive.[170] The *Brhadaranyake Upanishad* says that with respect to every describable object at which we can point, we need to say that Atman is not this and not that *(neti, neti)*.[171] The *Svetasvatara Upanishad* declares that Brahman is limitless, incomprehensible, and unthinkable,[172] and the *Chandogya Upanishad* says that Brahman is the void.[173] Finally, the *Brahman Isa Upanishad* says that trying to use language objectivistically to talk about Brahman only results in saying contradictory things (it moves and does not move; it is far and near, it is within us and outside us).[174] Interpreted religiously, this Upanishad can be taken to say that the nonfinite is beyond change but presupposed by all constituted changing things, that the closest and the most distant finite objects have their otherness, and that we finite persons are infinite and living in an environment in which we can encounter the infinite. Atman is not a thing and Brahman is not a thing, and saying that Atman is Brahman is not saying that two things are really one thing. It is saying that, when we live the moksa way of life, we live as enjoying, interpersonally related, ethical persons who are more than any descriptions can capture; and we live encountering the indescribable in ourselves, other people, and all socially constituted objects and events.

We may be Atman but we also always remain biological, social, and psychological persons. We may have encountered the nonfinite and we may desire to live in faithfulness to this encounter, but for many of us this primarily may be a matter of desiring to desire moksa as the ultimate goal in our lives. For years before sensing any encounter with the infinite, people live socially constituted jiva lives governed by the law of karma. For years people live as the social and psychological persons they have become by having their desires for pleasure, competitive success, or social propriety structure what they are like as persons. Desiring spiritual liberation may be born out of encountering the infinite and thereby beginning to desire moksa, but maturing into a spiritually liberated person and then continually living a liberated religious form of life may take time and a great deal of effort in order for old ways of living to be replaced by new ways of living that are faithful responses to these encounters. People have lived different forms of jiva life and therefore have different kinds of obstacles to overcome in order to respond with such faithfulness. Therefore, the Hindu tradition offers four different kinds of *yoga*, four different ways of strengthening people's desire for moksa, four different ways of deepening enlightenment, four different ways of responding faithfully to their encounters with the infinite. Within the Hindu tradition it is acknowledged that there can be different kinds of religious faiths, different ways of responding to encounters with the infinite, even though it is encountering the infinite and desiring moksa that is the common faithfulness shared by all the faiths.

In the Hindu interpretation of the human situation, four different kinds of yoga are offered because there are basically four different
kinds of people who can be desiring moksa. The goal sought after in
each of the yogas is living totally in faithful response to one's encounter
with the nonfiniteness of one's life. This means that all of one's ways of
thinking, acting, feeling, and sensing things must become a matter of
remaining faithful to one's encounter with the infinite.

(1) *Jnana* yoga is for the few reflective types of people whose intellectual understanding can determine the whole manner of their living,
once they have understood that they have encountered the nonfinite
aspects of themselves and everything other than themselves. What has
been written in this book is an exercise of jnana yoga.

(2) *Bhakti* yoga is the more common Hindu yoga. It is responding with loving worship of a god, constituted by one's community as
it responds in faithfulness to people's encounters with the infinite. It
does not treat such gods as metaphysical beings but as constituted focal
points in a religious mode of subjectivity. For people whose manner of
living can be determined by what they love and worship, their desire for
moksa can be strengthened and more fully realized as, in such worship,
they move beyond making kama, artha, or dharma ultimate in their
lives. Because people are different in the kind of god they can worship,
different kinds of gods get constituted in different communities. Some
people can love and worship a father god, some a mother god, some
a friend god, and some a child god. This does not make Hinduism
into a metaphysical polytheism. That would be interpreting such god
talk objectvisitically rather than recognizing it as talk that is part of a
yoga aiming at strengthening a religious response to encountering the
nonfiniteness of human life. It does recognize, however, that there can
be many different kinds of worshiping communities living faithfully
to the call of the infinite. Hindus can point out that a very similar
phenomenon occurs in Christianity as worshipers sometimes focus on
God the Father, sometimes on God the Son, sometimes on Mary the
mother of God, sometimes on Jesus as friend, and sometimes on the
baby Jesus. Bhakti yoga says, if loving worship is what strengthens and
expresses your desire for moksa, then love and worship the constituted
god that works for you and your community of similar persons.

(3) *Karma* yoga is for people who let their actions speak for them, whose way of doing things determines what their entire life is like, expressing their thoughts, feelings, and moods through what they do. There is a way of acting, the Hindu says, that for some people can construct a way of faithfully responding to encounters with the nonfinite aspects of ourselves and our environment. Karma yoga calls for one to show in one's actions one's faithful response to one's encounter with the infinite. Act without making kama, artha, or dharma one's ultimate goal in life. Act out of a desire to strengthen one's desire for moksa. Act understanding that the finite is enveloped by the infinite. Act humbly and thankfully. Act so as to meet one's unique, unlimited obligations to those one meets face-to-face. Act justly and compassionately toward all others. Karma yoga often is practiced along with Bhakti yoga and so the instruction becomes: Act not so that the will of one's jiva life be done, but act so that the will of the God one loves and worships be done. In the Bhagavad Gita, this is what Krishna advises Arjuna to do.

(4) *Raja* yoga, like Jnana yoga, will only be useful for a small number of people. This is a yoga that requires a great deal of very difficult self-discipline. It aims at allowing people to personally encounter, in a nonsensory, nonconceptual, nonsocial way the nonfinite otherness of our jiva selves and our jiva-constituted world. It aims at doing so by even going beyond our nonconceptual enjoying of the elements, beyond interpersonally cohabiting with other people, and beyond meeting people ethically face-to-face. Through focused concentration it directs people to allow layer after layer of our ordinary experiences to drop away. End all agitation in oneself caused by friction with other people. End all feelings of hate, fear, envy, and resentment. End all kinesthetic sensations, by sitting properly, breathing properly, and by not feeling any gnawing need for drugs or cigarettes. Focus one's attention so that all input from the five senses ceases. Focus one's attention so that all talking to oneself, all memories, all daydreaming, all thinking about the past, present, or future comes to an end. Now all sense of spatial distances and temporal episodes will come to an end. Now all sense of self as perceiver, thinker, rememberer, anticipator as opposed to objects of perception, thought, memory, and expectation, will end. Do not fall asleep. Now one will reside in this kind of mystical experience, a blissful, jiva-free mode of

subjectivity without any sense of spatial or temporal location. Enough Hindus say they have attained this state of subjectivity that there is very little reason to doubt that raja yoga can lead one to it. It has proven itself to be a powerful way of strengthening the desire for moksa and of producing people living faithfully in response to their encounters with the infinite. Some people have tried to use such mystical experiences as evidence proving the existence of some metaphysical being or realm. There is no need or reason to do so, however. This state, as powerful as it can be in molding a religious mode of subjectivity, is exactly what one would expect to happen if one were to peel off the ethical, interpersonal, social, sensory, conceptual, memory, expectation aspects of our subjectivity. It is the desire for moksa, motivating one to practice raja yoga, that gives to its achievement its religious significance. This is why current fads of training people in various pieces of the raja discipline, as useful as they may be for other reasons, often fall far short of acquiring religious and ethical significance.

Many epistemological and metaphysical schools of philosophy developed in India. Many of them were developed because the philosophers saw the Carvaka materialist school of metaphysics as a threat to Hindu religious traditions. Carvaka rejected the law of Karma, denied that there is any other to the describable, material beings that people and all other objects are, and instructed people to rest content in desiring kama, because attaining pleasure and avoiding pain are the only sensible goals in life.[175] Unfortunately, many Hindu thinkers decided that Hindu religious traditions needed to be defended against Carvaka's metaphysical claims. They went over onto Carvaka's turf and tried to produce better metaphysical theories. *Vaisesika* postulated a dualism of immaterial souls and material atoms with a metaphysical god coordinating what look like interactions between them.[176] *Samkhya* postulated a dualism of one soul and one material plenum evolving in accordance with a law governing their mirroring developments.[177] *Vedanta*, drawing heavily upon the final achievement of raja yoga, postulated a monism of one subject of experience, Atman, and one object being experienced, Brahman, and affirmed that Atman is Brahman.

The anti-Carvakian metaphysical schools did not appreciate adequately the Hindu analysis of human subjectivity, which provides the understanding that people cannot be theoretically argued into or out of a way of life, whether it be a kama, artha, dharma, or moksa way of life. The Hindu ways of living faithfully responding to encounters with the finite's other are subjectivitistic ways of life that are contrary to Carvaka's recommended metaphysically objectivistic mode of subjectivity. Hinduism need not lose itself in intellectual confusion by presenting competing objectivistic, metaphysical theories. Faithful Hindus only need to confess their encounters with the finite's other, and then wait for other people to acknowledge their own encounters. Jnana yoga might help the reflectively minded Hindus seeking to strengthen their desire for moksa by having them reflect on the many ways the infinite can be encountered in enjoyment, interpersonal cohabiting, and ethical face-to-face encounters. It need not present, however, a metaphysical, theoretical alternative to Carvaka. Samkara, traditionally read as a defender of the Vedanta school of metaphysics, can be read as merely practicing Jnana yoga and reflectively interpreting the Vedas and Upanishads. He proclaims that Hindu faithfulness to the infinite does not need any metaphysical proofs to support it and would not be aided if any were offered.[178] Hinduism is a religious way of living with different kinds of faithful responses to encounters with the nonfiniteness of human life.

2. Buddhism

Founded by Siddhartha Gautama (563-483 BC), Buddhism was a religious reformation movement in India. Gautama became the Buddha, the enlightened one, the one who had awakened from the sleepless dream of everyday life within which most people tragically were still trapped. His enlightenment produced in him a way of life whose resultant compassion for all people led him to condemn the corruption that had settled into Indian social practices, especially its caste system. His enlightenment included a living religious life of faithfulness to the nonfinite that called for rejecting all metaphysical theories and for letting life in all its glorious joyousness simply be what it is. The Buddha recommended a middle path between the maya and artha ways of life, on the one hand, and the total denial of pleasure and acting in the world advocated in India's third religious tradition, Jainism.[179] The Buddha rejected the social practice of empowering the caste of Brahmans as the only qualified interpreters of the Vedas and the Upanishads and as the priests required to perform rituals that supposedly could replace the hard work of the yogas and could magically give people what they wanted. The Buddha rejected the idea that only the Vedas and Upanishads could provide the enlightenment needed to encounter the nonfinite and live in faithfulness to such encounters. The Buddha recommended bypassing all the metaphysical theories of the Carvaka materialists and the metaphysical theories that viewed Atman as a metaphysical soul and Brahman as a metaphysical, supernatural being. He recommended keeping a "noble silence" on all metaphysical theorizing, because it ends up with incoherent postulations and because it feeds a craving for theoretical opinions that, like all cravings, must be removed, if the hard, practical work of gaining enlightenment and religious faithfulness is to be carried out. The Buddha proclaimed that the problem of life is a practical problem, and it needs a practical and not a theoretical, solution.

The enlightenment that people need, the living understanding that they must embody in their ways of life, according to the Buddha, is simple and understandable by anyone. Expert priests and professional philosophers are not needed. They are part of the problem and not part of the solution. Brahmin priests often are only feeding their cravings for dominating power. They claim that they are indispensable, because only they can teach how to gain spiritual liberation, and because participation in their priestly ceremonies supposedly does for people what the Buddha says people must do by themselves. Brahmin philosophers also crave another kind of power, the intellectual power to rise above finite restrictions and to rationally have an answer for everything. They live by a craving embodied in the principle of sufficient reason, a craving for opinions and theories that supposedly give epistemological reasons which end uncertainty and metaphysical reasons that do what the Buddha says is impossible to do, escape the chanciness of life and the necessity of just letting things be. They crave to be intellectual masters who know how to justify all beliefs, explain why everything is as it is and not otherwise, and justify in some big picture the daily suffering of people . The Buddha warns against "becoming enmeshed in views; a jungle of views, a wilderness of views; scuffling in views, the agitation (struggle) of views, the fetter of views."[180] He charges that speculatively positing some eternal realm is just a "puppet-show" and that it is "coupled with misery, ruin, despair, and agony, and does not tend to aversion, absence of passion, cessation, quiescence, knowledge, supreme wisdom, and Nirvana"[181] (extinguishing the cause of suffering). The religious life, the Buddha points out, does not depend upon having metaphysical beliefs about the world being either eternal or not eternal.[182]

People, the Buddha instructs, simply have to live with an understanding of the four noble truths, something anyone can come to understand, something everyone has to come to understand in a living way all by themselves. People by their practices have created the problem of life, and people in their practices have to solve the problem. Buddhism is a very practical, pragmatic religion. The four noble truths are: (1) Life, as people generally live it, is filled with suffering. (2) A sense of self and self-worth, grounded in cravings for control and social status, is the cause of this suffering. (3) These cravings and senses of self and self-worth can be extinguished. (4) There is a practical eightfold path that will lead to such an extinction, a resultant end of suffering, and a life of joyous living in which one simply is what one is rather than what one craves to do and be.[183]

In order to understand these four truths, there is a need to separate craving from desiring. Buddhism often has been incorrectly interpreted as saying that suffering can end only when all desiring is ending, hardly a joyous way of living. It is craving that must be ended, not the desiring to end craving or the desiring that remains when craving is ended. Although the Buddha understands that most people are living in misery and suffering, his is not a negative or nihilistic evaluation of life or a pessimistic attitude toward life. The Buddha understands that human life presents the potential for overwhelming joy, if only people would stop making themselves and others miserable, and he is an optimist who understands that people are able to stop producing such suffering and to live instead in joy and bliss.

Without denying the reality of physical pain caused by bodily injury and illness, it is not on this sort of suffering that the Buddha concentrates. Physical pain can be allowed to be the sensation that it is when it is allowed simply to be in a life liberated from self-caused anguish and liberated into a life filled with a cornucopia of joyous encounters with the elements with which we live, with other people with whom we cohabit, with the nonfiniteness of all subjects and objects. Physical pain does not drive people to despair and self-destruction when it is allowed to be the warning system of bodily injury that it is, or when it occurs in the context of carrying out acts of compassion or heroic effort. Mothers verify this daily in birthing and caring for their children, and military personnel prove it as they lose themselves in saving their buddies. Artistic creators and fighters against injustice prove it as they refuse to let physical pain stop them. Besides, it is the fear and dread of pain that intensifies the suffering people experience, and it is later resentment over what is seen as unjustified pain that makes people even more miserable. The suffering on which the Buddha focuses is the avoidable suffering we bring upon ourselves and others because of cravings we have due to our sense of self and self-worth.

Understanding the first noble truth requires understanding the second noble truth. Understanding the kind of suffering the Buddha is talking about is tied to understanding what we are doing to cause such suffering. Tanha is the cause of this kind of suffering. Tanha is a sense of self and self-worth that we have built up because of the cravings that feed them and flow from them. There are many things that we as Tanha people crave, but they all are tied back to a craving to be superior to other people in some way or other (or at least not to be inferior to them) and a craving to be in control. We keep comparing ourselves to other people. We want to be smarter; better looking; stronger; more skillful; more successful academically, economically, athletically, or artistically; or more popular or famous. We crave to be superior in some way at least to some people. We treat people with physical, psychological, or social handicaps as inferior. We humiliate and make fun of them. We think that people who are different are inferior, and we become racists, sexists, homophobic, and economic and social elitists. We live in fear that we might become, accidentally or through some misfortune, what we consider to be inferior. People crave not to be what they consider to be inferior to other people. Many people, buying into the very system of comparative evaluations that others use to brand people as inferior, curse the hand they have been dealt. They make themselves miserable, ashamed for being different, ugly, handicapped, old, dumb, a lousy baseball player, homosexual, poor, shy, a social misfit. Building a sense of self-worth on the basis of comparative evaluations alienates people from other people, from themselves, from the natural, social, and psychological conditions in which they find themselves, and this causes immense amounts of suffering.

Craving for social status and control leads to cravings for the things we think we must have to maintain this sense of self-worth. We crave certain kinds of clothes, cosmetics, hair styling, houses, TVs, appliances, stereo sets, boom boxes, lawns, cars, boats, sports equipment, vacations, foods, beverages, potency-enhancing pills, drugs, antiaging and death-delaying technologies. The list goes on and on. We crave material things so badly that we become willing to cause ourselves and others extreme suffering in order to get them. We feel frustrated and miserable when we can't get them. We feel shame and humiliation when we think that others know that we are what we think of as failures in life. We will tear others down if we think this is necessary for us to view ourselves as something worthwhile. When this kind of self-worth seems unattainable, people feel that life is not worth living, and they start engaging themselves in quick or slow suicide. Tanha causes suffering.

Craving for social status leads us to crave approval from others and thus to crave to do whatever we think will please them. As Lacan has recognized, so much of our desiring is a craving to satisfy the desires of others. Often the other whom we try to satisfy is the anonymous other of social norms that we are supposed to obey. Oftentimes we cry out in frustration and despair: "What do you want me to do? You parents, you teachers and coaches, you supposed friends and loved ones, you society in general—What do you want me to do? Tell me what you want me to do." However, Lacan points out, these are cravings that always lead to frustration and never can be satisfied, because other people and society in general have no unified, coherent set of desires. Other people, too, have fractured lives with conflicting desires. Different people have different fractures and conflicting desires. Social norms for the most part generate dilemmas and not coherent, satisfiable instructions. We cannot do something that will win approval from all of them. We cannot even do something that will win continual approval from any of them. If we crave to do so, we will always end up frustrated and miserable.

Being continually frustrated in efforts to do what others want us to do, it is understandable that many people will cry out, "I don't care any more what you want me to do. I am going to do what I want to do." Unfortunately, this effort also fails. In our Tanha lives, we do care what others think of us. We do evaluate ourselves comparatively. It only makes matters worse to act out the pretense that we don't care. Besides, for the most part what we want to do is what we have been socially nurtured and trained to desire, and what we are is what we have been socially coded to be. Craving to rebel against social demands is usually done in socially constituted ways, as one more way of show-ing to ourselves that we are superior to those other social conformists. Craving to be our own person usually is just one more instance of karma-structured Tanha.

Craving for comparative social status leads to craving for indepen-dence and control. We can hardly see ourselves as superior to others if we are dependent upon them, and we often lose all sense of self-worth when we become dependent. Craving to avoid dependency leads teenagers to want to rush into adulthood. It leads people to fear and loathing of illness, of becoming handicapped, of old age and dying. Many people can't see themselves as worth anything if their lives are Dependent on uncertainty and chance. They crave for certainty in their beliefs about what is going on, about how one ought to live, and about what will happen to them. In order to avoid doubt and uncertainty, they embrace dogmas and promised certainties (sacred texts, tradition-al moral codes). They use political, economic, and social instruments of power to protect these dogmas and "certainties."

Similarly, in order to escape the chanciness of life, people crave assurances that there is good reason and purpose behind everything that happens to them. Not finding certainty and purpose in their current lives, they crave for metaphysical assurances that some supreme being or power will guarantee such purpose. They crave for a life after death in which everything will finally be understood fully, in which life will face no more threats of suffering, in which goodness and evil at last will receive their just rewards and punishments. Craving such an assurance of eventual justice, but far from assured that they will receive rewards and not punishments, they suffer through a constant fear of death and a craving that someone or some thing can magically guarantee that heaven and not hell awaits them. Craving for assurances, dominating and oppressive power is given to those who convince people that they can supply such assurance, and people become willing to do almost anything to protect the very source of their own domination. People caught up in this craving for certainty and assurance, often become willing to turn to coercion and violence against any others who they think threaten their source of certainty and assurance. Craving for certainty and assurance even overpowers craving not to be dependent, as we become willing servants to the masters we have created. Sometimes we become willing to sacrifice our own lives as we take the lives of perceived enemies of our masters, in order to protect the books, dogmas, priests, and philosophers that are our masters, and to gain the "heaven" that they promise. The result is more and more and more suffering.

Unfortunately, people generally have a craving for power over other people and over what happens to them, and they have a sense of self-worth that is based upon comparing themselves to other people. Much of what we crave and are as Tanha is due to the social and cultural worlds into which we have been thrown and which have nurtured and socialized us to be Tanha-type people with these cravings that cause so much pain and suffering. This is the curse of bad karma. This curse usually, rears us to participate in a competitive battle for comparative worth. It trains us to crave what we think is necessary to succeed in this battle. It inaugurates us into social and cultural worlds that have trained us to have impossible expectations, needless fears, and thus cravings for the impossible. As Nietzsche has pointed out, much of our social and cultural life is based on resentment and fear, and most people have been reared to live as though life has no meaning unless we can see ourselves as parts of some big cosmic drama that gives to our finite lives meaning and purpose and which guarantees that death is not the end of life.[184] We crave for theoretical knowledge of how we fit into this big picture. We fear death and crave for certainty that there is in us something which will guarantee us life after death. We crave for metaphysical opinions that will satisfy these cravings. We crave to maintain theoretical control of things. Tragically, such cravings cause immense suffering. This is why the Buddha urges his followers to maintain a "noble silence" on all such theoretical issues. Do not try to solve epistemological and metaphysical puzzles, but dissolve them by extinguishing one's craving for them and their solutions. This will allow one to let theoretical uncertainties and the chanciness and finiteness of biological life simply be what they are. This, plus extinguishing the cravings for comparative self-worth, will enable one to live the life of joy and peace that results.

The third noble truth is that Tanha and its destructive cravings can be extinguished, and thus harm and suffering can be replaced with compassion and joyous living. Our problem does not lie in our physical or biological makeup. Tanha is our socially constituted and personally reinforced way of craving and living and the sense and self and self-worth that they generate in us. The moral Law of Karma only applies to Tanha. When Tanha is extinguished, the Law of Karma, which binds cravings to ignorance and injustice inherited from the past, no longer prevents compassionate and joyous living. It is possible, the Buddha instructs us, to end the causal chain of bad karma in the past (social practices instantiating ignorance and suffering-causing cravings) that cause (through social/cultural nurturing and training) present Tanha cravings, self images, and comparative senses of self worth. These in turn cause more people to live Tanha lives as our present socialization and training practices turn out more tragic cases of people craving and suffering. Our socially constituted and personally endorsed Tanha lives, together with all the dimensions of such living and all the socially constituted objects we perceive when living such lives, are holistically interconnected in one tragic drama of *dependent origination*.[185] That which we as Tanha people conceive and perceive depends upon our how we classify things and establish identify criteria for nameable individuals with these forms; and such classifying and instantiating depends upon our cravings and our existence as Tanha individuals with a certain sense of self and self-worth. Buddhist talk about dependent origination is not a metaphysical theory saying that everything has only a functional identity in some monistic whole. It is talk used to present a practical analysis of the causes of suffering and the warranted hope of ending such suffering. The Buddhist is saying that the Tanha world, with all its subjects and objects, is social all the way down. There is no need to postulate metaphysical souls to explain how the law of karma, the drama of the birth and rebirth of Tanha lives, operates. As a flame moves from one candle to another, without any unchanging soul passing from one life to the next, so socialization and nurturing practices pass on Tanha styles of craving and living from one generation to the next. This, the Buddha claims, is a causal chain that can be broken. Tanha, craving, and self-caused suffering can be extinguished.

The eightfold path is the way (the yoga) to extinguish Tanha and its cravings, and thus the way for us to be absorbed in a craving-less life of joy and compassion. This is an eightfold and not an eight-step path. We do not do eight different things, one after another. The eight practices we must initiate in our lives come as a package, and we must engage continually in all eight of them at the same time until at last our cravings are ended, our socially constituted and personally endorsed Tanha form of life and sense of self and self-worth are extinguished, and we let ourselves be what we would be if we were not trapped in such a constituted self.

The eightfold path is a practical set of activities that we carry out to put to death that about us which is causing ourselves and others to suffer. It is the set of activities that will free us to live the joyous and compassionate lives that will remain when cravings for comparative worth and power are extinguished. The eightfold path demonstrates the optimistic and anti-nihilistic character of Buddhism. The problem of life is one we have cursed ourselves with, and we have the power to undo what we have been doing to create the problem. Once we have removed the cause of our self-inflicted suffering, the life that remains is so filled with wondrous joys and interpersonal compassion and harmony that we will sense no need to look beyond life to find something that makes life worthwhile.

The first aspect of the eightfold path is *right understanding*. In a living and not just in an abstract theoretical way, we must come to understand the Four Noble Truths. We have to understand how and why we are causing so much suffering and how and why we are keeping ourselves from living joyously and in peaceful harmony with other people and with what happens to us. We have to understand what can and must be done to remove these causes and barriers. This is a very difficult kind of understanding to accept because it means renouncing so much of what we are. But accepting these truths about ourselves is what we must do if we are to correct the mess we have created. Because these truths are so painful for us at first to accept, it is crucial, if anyone is to find the courage and motivation to accept them, to understand that they are noble truths that will end suffering and release joyful and harmonious interpersonal living. Extinguishing Tanha, its cravings, and the suffering it causes, and living with the resultant joyfulness, compassion, and peace, is what Buddhists call *Nirvana*.

That joy and peace will remain once Tanha is extinguished is a vital part of right understanding for a second set of reasons. It will remove the motivation to see life nihilistically and in need of some metaphysical superpower to guarantee that life is significant. With our eyes wide open to the chanciness and finite character of life, it will allow us to celebrate life as it is. The Buddhist postulates no metaphysical cause for the way things happen in the world. Once science gives its explanations of events occurring in nature, by referring to the laws of nature which could have been different, talk about explanations comes to an end in noble silence. In the Buddhist language, everything in nature rests on *Sunyata* (no-thingness).

There is no super metaphysical being that causes the laws of nature to be as they are. Every contingent thing simply is as it is and not otherwise. They rest on nothing. One's last word on nature is, "that's just how things are." There are not even any metaphysical things, metaphysical substances that never change. There are only historically changing, socially constituted, conceivable, and perceptible objects and subjects. Everything rests on no-thingness. There is no super being that turns the accidents in life (one's child chases a balloon out between cars and is killed by an oncoming truck) into justifiable consequences of a cosmic agent's purposeful act. There is no eternal soul that lives after one's finite life is over, so that virtue can be rewarded and evil punished (another craving we have for comparative superiority). Virtuous people, of course, often fall victim to natural ailments, accidents, and human crimes, while other people who have done great harm sometimes luck-ily escape such misfortune. That is just how things are. Craving to control things only causes suffering. One cannot control completely the accidents in life. One cannot control things so as to guarantee that virtue is rewarded and vice punished, and thus guarantee that we, who think we are more virtuous than others, can also believe that we will be better off than others. One cannot control living so as to prevent one's living coming to an end. Attaining peace in the face of accidents and unpreventable crime requires understanding that this is just how things are. Peacefully facing death, the possibility of no more possibilities, is living without craving anything more than the finite life of unspeak-able joy that one can have when Tanha is extinguished and one lives in Nirvana. Living sensuously with the elements, living interperson-ally and compassionately with others, will drive out all doubts about whether life is worth living. Then in spite of what happens in our lives, in spite of the uncertainties in living and the certainty of death, we can joyfully say with Nietzsche: Well, was that Life. Let's do it again. In spite of the hand that nature happened to deal us and others, in spite of how others treat us, in spite of our shifting, historical nature with its conceptual and cognitive uncertainties and limitations, in spite of life coming to an end, we can proclaim with the Buddha, "let's celebrate the joyous life that remains for everyone when Tanha is extinguished."

The second fold in the eightfold path is *right aspiration*. One whole-heartedly has to want cravings for comparative worth and power over others and nature to end. Aspiring to achieve such an end is not an all-or-nothing matter. Almost all of our life up until now has been a matter of living in terms of such cravings and sense of self and self-worth. Our cravings will certainly resist the aspiration to have them extinguished. What we are as Tanha will not disappear just because we intellectually come to the conclusion that it should end so that suffering can end and the barriers to joyous living can be removed. Weakening our cravings and transforming our sense of self-worth will happen as our aspirations for Nirvana are strengthened, and such strengthening will occur as our cravings weaken and we are changed. Similarly, as our understand-ing of ourselves, as our critical appraisal of our Tanha way of living, deepens, so our aspiration to extinguish craving will be strengthened.

In aspiring to reach Nirvana two dangers need to be avoided. First, we need to recognize that a great deal of hard work is going to be needed. Merely wishing to be liberated will not do what is needed. A strong and determined will is required if one's life is to be completely transformed in the way that is required. Second, a special kind of aspiring, willing, and acting is needed. Wishing to be liberated from craving and a comparative sense of self-worth must not become a new kind of craving. Nirvana is not something one can grasp and take control over so that afterwards one can be proud that one has done what others have not been able to do. Our craving for Nirvana can prevent it from coming. Extinguishing Tanha will occur only when we simply let it be. Let the elements be enjoyable. Let interpersonal life be enjoyable. Let compassionate service simply occur. Let nature simply be. Craving to live in Nirvana disappears when one surrenders into such a way of living.

The third fold in the eightfold path is *right speech*. Thirty-five-hundred years ago, the Buddha recognized the crucial role that language and speech play in determining how people relate to one another. Wrong speech appears in three forms, and right speech has to replace such speech in three different ways. First, at the heart of the way we build up Tanha is the way we lie to protect our sense of self-worth and the way we use words to humiliate and tear down others. Second, at the heart of the socializing and training practices that give us our Tanha nature are our linguistic practices. Third, at the heart of extinguishing Tanha is coming to encounter and respect speakers and hearers independently of all the ways we describe them in order to serve our cravings for status and power. The three forms of wrong speech are inseparably connected. Wrong speech is responsible for a tremendous amount of suffering, and learning right speech allows Tanha to be extinguished as we compassionately respond ethically to the people whom we encounter, people who no longer are pigeonholed in linguistic categories. Right speech allows us to encounter in other people the infinite other to finite categorization. It allows us to compassionately let them be the singularly unique people they are, and it allows us to compassionately fulfill the obligations that encountering them place us under.

First, consider specific speech acts. Why do we continually lie to other people? So often we do so because we are ashamed of what we have done or because we are embarrassed to have others know something about ourselves. We fear losing face, losing other people's good opinions of us, losing popularity, losing self-esteem based on comparative evaluations. We continually lie by commission and omission to protect the self-images we crave for ourselves, self-images grounded in comparative evaluations. We not only lie about ourselves, but we also lie about other people. Why do we say things to tear other people down? Why do we laugh so heartily at jokes that demean people? We do so in the hope that this will guarantee that we are better than they are in some way we consider vital to us. We do so in the hope of gaining greater dominating power over them. Right speech means ending the game of telling lies, doing this one crucial thing to extinguish the sense of self and self-worth causing so much suffering. Lying and speaking cruelly to and about others even harms oneself, for it strengthens Tanha and it makes it that much more difficult to just let oneself live without the self-images and comparative self-evaluations one imposes on oneself.

Right speech means not lying to protect oneself. Right speech means stopping use of language to harm other people. Right speech means not speaking harmfully to and about others, and it means speaking to them kindly. Sometimes speaking compassionately in order to not harm others means keeping to oneself one's own beliefs about things. Americans so often think that speaking their minds is so virtuous that not doing so is a deception and vice. Asians often think that not harming others with their speech is more important than linguistically expressing their beliefs, if their silence is motivated by compassion and not motivated by a craving to protect their own self-image. Wrong speech builds Tanha and causes suffering. Right speech contributes to extinguishing Tanha and allowing people to live without alienation, ethically respecting and compassionately aiding one another. Switching from harmful speech to right speech will not be easy. Buddhists recommend meditating daily, asking oneself what lies one has told and what harming things one has said since one's last meditation session, seeking to understand why one felt one had to say these things. What cravings was one giving into? Why are these cravings unnecessary and counterproductive of a joyous life? At first one will note that what one is saying is only after the fact.

Then, little by little, one will catch oneself before one starts lying or saying nasty things. Finally, the motivation to lie, to belittle, to spread false rumors, and to insult will be extinguished.

Second, what is it about the language we use in wrong speech that causes so much suffering? During the past 150 years, social critics have accented again and again that language often supports unjust domination and oppression, and that training people to use a certain kind of language is nurturing them to have a socially constituted self participating in unjust practices. In the language of Buddhism, linguistic training is one of the main instruments for transmitting bad karma from one generation to the next, for constituting Tanha and its cravings that cause so much suffering. Nurturing people to use racist, sexist, homophobic, class, and handicap degradation language is constituting them as people who must exert heroic effort not to become cruel racists, sexists, elitists, and bigots. Training people to work with binary terms, as though they marked absolute, metaphysical categories rather than pragmatically used classifications, makes it that much more difficult to liberate religious faithfulness from metaphysical cravings. Binary oppositions, such as finite beings and infinite Being, presence and absence, identity and difference, mind and body, internal and external, prevent people from gaining the understanding needed to extinguish Tanha.[186] Treating as natural and normal the use of euphemisms that paper over horrible acts of cruelty numbs people to accept without question the suffering being caused. During World War II, under the justifying rubric of "strategic bombing," thousands and thousands of children, mothers, and grandparents were incinerated by firebombs at Dresden and atomic bombs at Hiroshima and Nagasaki. Under the rubric of "free-fire zones" thousands of noncombatants were napalmed in Vietnam, and under the rubrics of "collateral damage" and "smart bombs" they are being killed and maimed in Iraq. Spin doctors in political offices and public relations experts in business corporations make domination and oppression almost disappear from sight under a barrage of words. More and more Buddhists now recognize that right speech requires social and cultural criticism of the language we inherit and the language we leave as a legacy to our children. This criticism must be tied to creative replacement of the linguistic causes of suffering with linguistic instruments of respect and compassion. "Language" as used here includes all the nonverbal symbols and all the body language that is used to cause suffering, and thus the Buddhist call for right speech is a call to critique our entire symbolic world and to work patiently, persistently, and imaginatively to replace the destructive aspects of our current symbolic world with more people-friendly language and speech.

This bring us to the third way in which wrong speech must become right speech if Tanha is to be extinguished. In our current world, people generally live with an objectivisitic form of subjectivity in which they focus more on what is being said than on the people who are speaking and listening. So often, people are treated as just more objects about which things can be said. The Buddha denied that people are such objects. We are neither mere describable biological objects nor metaphysical souls. Biologically we are always changing and being changed. Our psychological makeup is fractured with a void at its center. There is no unity in either case to guarantee our individuality. Our individuality comes only through our ethical encounters with one another. The words we use to describe, individuate, or name people are simply socially convenient ways of designating people, and when it is Tanha that is doing the designating, then the ethically singular uniqueness of people is not being respected or dealt with compassionately.[187] Right speech is directed to the hearer one is encountering face-to-face, the person who places one under an obligation, transferable to no one else, to let this person live in their unclassifiable ethical uniqueness. Right speech is compassionately saying "here I am, willing to accept my responsibilities to respect you as the person you are, no matter what social names get attached to you." Your uniqueness and significance lies not in what you are (male or female; black, yellow, tan, or white; blind or deaf, well or sick, young or old, orphan or widow, etc.) or what Tanha people say you are (nigger, Chink, Jap, savage, ugly, stupid, coward, weakling, lazy, crazy, loose, delinquent, terrorist, etc.). It lies in your nondescriptive ethical individuality as a person to be encountered and loved and as a person called to be ethically bound, compassionate, and just. Right speech is vital in extinguishing Tanha and ending suffering.

As the fourth fold in the eightfold path, *right behavior* expands what is called for in right speech. Striving to meet one's ethical obligations, which underlie all appropriate social obligations, and striving to live compassionately, require acting so as not to cause death, pain, domination, oppression, or disrespect. The Buddha describes right behavior very succinctly. "Right Acts are to abstain from taking life, from stealing, from lechery."[188] Reflecting on this call for right action shows how sweeping and contemporary its implications are. Consider the prohibition against taking a life. As Levinas points out, merely by their presence, people whom we meet ethically face-to-face cry out to us, "Do not murder me; let me be; do not turn me into a controllable object; let me live free from domination and oppression; do not use me as a mere means to satisfy your cravings; respect my ethical status as a unique individual different from everyone else because I am ethically unique."[189]

Consider the injunction not to steal. It needs to be seen as a marker for a whole set of similar injunctions. As Kant pointed out, considered morally it must be wrong to steal. One cannot conceive without contradiction the idea that it is morally all right to steal. In order for stealing to be possible, it must be wrong. Saying that it is morally all right to steal would be saying that it is all right to take on the moral rights of property ownership that have been assigned exclusively to someone else, to another person as private property or to a community's government as public property. If there were good and sufficient reasons for making the original assignment of property rights, then it is now morally wrong to steal them away from someone else and take them for oneself. The institution of property can exist, and thus stealing property can become possible, only if the rule prohibiting stealing is instituted at the same time. Although there may be times when one may be justified in doing what is the morally wrong thing to do (for example, when otherwise one would be doing something worse), it still remains something that is the wrong sort of thing to do.

The moral relevance of the injunction not to steal rests on the moral justification for the existence of the institution of property. Because of the biological needs of human beings, and because of the restricted availability of things that can meet those needs, it seems as though some system of assigning and transferring property rights is needed in our lives if people, in their efforts to get what they need, are not to be harmed, and if they are to be helped when help is needed. The world's present institutionalized system of assigning and transferring property rights may warrant radical criticism and reconstruction, but some system seems necessary. The same holds true of many of the social roles, economic practices, and political arrangements that people find it necessary to set up if they are to avoid being harmed and to receive the help they need. Some morally fair and institutionalized system of distributing benefits and burdens needs to be devised. John Rawls suggests that the fair thing to do is to distribute them so that they serve the best interests of the least advantaged in society, because even selfish-minded people would approve of setting up an institutional system aimed at this end if they did not know where they would find themselves in the system and if the distribution practice gave priority to their personal freedom over meeting their needs.[190] Iris Marion Young quite correctly points out that power and respect are not sorts of things that can be distributed, and yet some social practices and institutions need to be branded as unjust if people are denied power and respect though domination and oppression.[191] The Buddha's injunction not to steal is really an injunction to constitute just social, economic, and political practices and institutions and then to act appropriately within them. The injunction is grounded in the Buddha's call to be compassionate toward all people.

The injunction to abstain from lechery likewise needs to be expanded in order to appreciate its significance. Meeting one's ethical responsibilities means compassionately helping those in need of help, not because of what they are, but just because they are. People are not merely biological and psychological creatures, they are singularly unique persons. Prior to any moral requirement to enable people to meet their biological needs, and beyond the moral obligation not to take their lives, is the moral obligation to respect their singular uniqueness. This means never treating them as mere means to use in achieving our ends. Lecherously seeing them just as sexual objects is only one of many ways of showing disrespect to people. Seeing them as mere human resources to be used to maximize profits in some business or seeing them merely as consumers are further examples. Seeing them merely as citizens, tax payers, clients receiving government assistance, potential military personnel, or voters so that the power or prestige of a nation-state can be served are still more examples of disrespectfully using people rather than letting them live in their singular ethical uniqueness. The Buddha's call for right behavior is a powerful and complex call for compassionate personal action and social justice.

The fifth fold in the eightfold path, *right livelihood,* provides further understanding of what is required in order to live with others justly and compassionately, thereby extinguishing Tanha and cravings for comparative worth. We all find ourselves occupying social roles. Before we can get to the social and change the social order, the social has gotten to us. Extinguishing Tanha and cravings allows the nonfinite aspects of our lives to be liberated from living merely as the suffering-causing persons we and our social and cultural practices have constituted us to be. This does not mean that we cease living within social roles. We will still have jobs and be employers and employees; be parents, children, and siblings in a family; be students and teachers; be neighbors and citizens. Seeking a right livelihood, first of all, means selecting the right roles available in our social environment. If the only way to keep one's job is by deceiving, dominating, and oppressing people, then that is not a right livelihood for one seeking to extinguish Tanha. Second, it means that we have to imaginatively create new roles and reconstruct existing roles. In our contemporary world, so many roles seem to need reconstruction. What it means to be a husband, wife, father, mother, son, daughter, brother, sister, or grandparent seems to need critical appraisal and imaginative redefinition. The same holds true at the economic and political levels. Managers who always give orders and workers who only take orders have to be replaced by roles that end such asymmetrical power relationships of domination. Citizens need to reconceive their roles, doing more than just receive government services and perhaps vote; and elected representatives have to reconstitute those practices that seem aimed more at getting reelected than reducing injustice in the world. Third, calling for right livelihood means that we cease locating social roles on a scale of better and worse, measuring the worth of ourselves and others by where our respective social roles place us and them on that scale. If we think that we are better than others (or worse than others) because of our jobs, or our place in the family, or our political power, then we are feeding Tanha and not extinguishing it. The right livelihood for us is the one in which we make maximum use of our ability to enjoy life, interact interpersonally with others, resist injustice, and compassionately respect and care for others. If we have this way of living socially, then concern about what others think of our social status can be extinguished.

Right endeavor is the sixth fold in the eightfold path. Ending Tanha and its cravings takes strenuous and persistent effort. We have been living Tanha lives for so long and so persistently that the background presumptions that frame our perceptions, evaluations, judgement, emotions, and conscious and unconscious desires have been thoroughly infected with its deadly influence. The same holds true for the many practices in which we have been trained to participate. Extinguishing Tanha requires putting to death so much of what we have become in order that a new way of living can be permitted to prosper. This requires painful self-examination and the rejection off many of our taken-for-granted practices and ingrained habits. We have to renounce so much of what we are. We have to stop further Tanha contamination of our way of living. We have to establish, enlarge, develop, and perfect a Nirvana way of living. With total commitment to an understanding of the four noble truths, with continual critical self-reflection, with the strongest of will power, with unreserved expenditure of all the energy we possess, we have to struggle against what is and strive for what can be. Wishing it were so is not good enough; right endeavor is required.

By contributing to right understanding and resolve; right speech, action, and livelihood; and right endeavor, we can incorporate the last two folds in the eightfold path. The notion of *right mindfulness* needs to be interpreted in two ways. On the one hand, it signifies the need to keep in mind the general, four noble truths, right understanding of which we must show in our daily living. On the other hand, it signifies that we must remain ever alert to where we are in our movement from Tanha living to Nirvana living, what the special problems, are that we must face because of our particular set of cravings and senses of self and self-worth, where we are being successful in dealing with these problems and where we are not so successful. One must be alert to the possibility that at times we have not succeeded in extinguishing cravings and comparative evaluations, but have only transformed them into unconscious motivations. Mindful of what needs to be done, and mindful of how

easy it is to kid ourselves into thinking that we have done what is needed, ardent and alert self-evaluation, self-criticism, and self-transformation must continue until Tanha is truly extinguished. Finally, it is vital
to remain mindful of the fact that right mindfulness is not a matter
of taking control of our lives so that we can become self-made people,
thus meeting in this way our craving for power and control. That kind
of ascetic self-denial is exactly what the Buddha found unacceptable in
Jainism. Instead we need to remain mindful of the fact that extinguishing Tanha is a matter of extinguishing the craving to control things, a
matter of having faith in things when we simply let them be, when we
let our Tanha-free, joyous, compassionate lives be.

The last of the eight folds, *right absorption,* is the fold enfolding all
the other folds and being absorbed in Nirvana living so that the extinguishing of cravings and a comparative sense of self and self-worth are
not felt as losses, but as arriving on the shore of a world of joyous ecstasy
and peaceful nonalienation, having sailed away from a world of suffering, frustration, fear, and anxiety. In this new world, we can let things
in our natural environment just be, free from craven, driven categorization, thereby setting us free to enjoyably encounter their nonfiniteness.
The starry skies, the billions of galaxies; the mighty mountains, rivers,
plains, and deserts; the billions to the power of thousands of electrons,
protons, and quarks; the energy equivalent to mass times the speed of
light squared—simply let all of this be in its regularities and, for us, in its
chanciness. Do not postulate super metaphysical beings, forces, purposes
behind it or beneath it. Just let it rest on Sunyata, no-thingness, the void,
Mu, the empty sky. This means letting it rest in its own suchness. Let it
be, and do not lament that it is as it is. Do not crave to explain it away
or to gain overall control over it. Let it be and learn to live in harmony
with it, using our finite knowledge about how to live as a part of it in
order to live as well as we can within it. Encounter it as something always
other than what our words and concepts can exhaustively classify and
individuate. Live in faithfulness to such encounters with its infinite otherness to our meager efforts to conceptually master it, and thus realize
the wonderful fruits of such encounters and such faithful responses.

Our simple and yet wonderful seeing of sunrises, sunsets, fall leaves
and winter fields, white birch and bamboo trees, roses and orchids,

white clouds in blue skies, mountain ranges and waterfalls; our listening to birds singing, the wind in the trees, the rain on the rocks, our smelling of the air after a rain, the wheat in the field, the cherry blossoms; our tasting of cool water, red apples, wild berries, stems of wild grass; and our feel of the cool wind in our face and the warm sweat on our bodies—this is the enjoying of our encounters that is a vital aspect of Buddhist religious life, the aspect that Zen Buddhism accents so strongly. Also, in the new world of Nirvana we will cohabit interpersonally with other people in our families and communities in ways that words and symbols cannot adequately capture. We will cook and eat, work and sleep, comfort and be comforted, laugh and dance, give birth, heal, and die together, without comparatively evaluating or seeking to control one another. We will live in harmony. In addition to this kind of interpersonal living, which is presupposed by all language and conceptualizing, we also will encounter one another ethically, and in that encounter with the nonfinite, we will be bound together by uncountable obligations not to harm but to care for one another. We will respect the singular uniqueness of one another by compassionately being committed to that maintenance of our relationship that is love, a love that is absolutely dependable and will not be broken at any price. We will continually engage ourselves in resisting oppressive and dominating social practices, while recognizing that there is no one big, grand project that will end injustice. Human cravings and ways of seeking comparative self-worth take thousands of forms, old ones living on and new ones being constituted, and thus so do the kinds of unjust social practices that flow from them. The faithful Buddhist does his best to resist and transform such practices, and then he lets them be, refusing to let injustice turn him into a frustrated cynic or nihilist. Instead, faithful Buddhists live joyfully with natural delights, appreciatively within family and community, ethically and compassionately with people who are immeasurably valuable in their singular uniqueness, and meaningfully by resisting injustice. In reflection and action, in joy and peace, Buddhists let themselves be absorbed into Nirvana.

Our understanding and appreciation of the four noble truths and the eightfold path can be deepened if we look at two major developments that took place in the historical development of Buddhism as a social/

cultural effort to faithfully respond to encounters with the call of the infinite to extinguish Tanha. First, accenting different ways of faithfully responding to this call, two forms of Buddhism developed: *Teravada Buddhism* and *Mahayana Buddhism,* each borrowing and accenting different aspects of the Hinduism that always remained as the background to Buddhist reformation efforts. Second, a need arose to remind intellectuals who were trying to give metaphysical and epistemological interpretations of Buddhist religious life of the Buddha's injunction to stay away from cravings for such theories, to maintain a noble silence that lets things rest on nothing, lets things rest merely in their suchness. The prophet Nargajuna rejected all sides in the debates that arose among competing defenders of such interpretations and theories.

Buddhism in general rejects the Vedas and the Upanishads, as authoritative religious texts. The four noble truths are all that need to be understood in order for Tanha to be extinguished. Theravada Buddhism, however, still thinks that it is important to keep in its new Buddhist traditions a new authoritative canon of the Buddha's teaching. This it believes is necessary if those teachings are not to be misunderstood and corrupted. Thus, for the Theravada Buddhists in South and Southeast Asia, the oldest Buddhist texts available, the *Pali* texts, have become the authoritative yardstick for evaluating the correctness of any teachings called Buddhist. Quite understandably, therefore, in this tradition the Buddha is seen primarily as a teacher, and the leaders of Buddhist communities are seen as interpreters of these texts, faithful practitioners of what the Hindus would call jnana yoga. Furthermore, Theravada Buddhism accents the inescapable necessity of each person, all on one's own, following completely the requirements of the eightfold path. Sensing that extinguishing Tanha requires full-time effort, an understanding developed in Teravada Buddhism that this could only be achieved by people in the Buddhist-constituted orders of monks and nuns. For this reason, Mahayana Buddhists referred to this tradition as *Hinayana Buddhism.* "Hinayana" means "the lesser raft" and "Mahayana," "the greater raft." From the Mahayana viewpoint, few people in the Hinayana tradition will travel from the shore of Tanha living to the shore of Nirvana living. Mahayana Buddhism promises that far more people can make the journey if they cross on its raft.

Mahayana Buddhism accents bhakti yoga rather than jnana yoga. As was the case with Hinduism, Mahayana Buddhists claim that few people seem able to successfully practice jnana yoga, but many seem able to transform their lives through bhakti yoga, worship, and devotion focused on a socially constituted incarnation of the infinite. Thus, they focus on the compassion of the Buddha, rather than on Buddha as a teacher. Out of his love for people, the Buddha wants to do anything he can to help people end self-inflicted suffering by extinguishing Tanha. By focusing on the compassionate spirit of the Buddha and by responding in turn with love and devotion, Mahayana Buddhists find that the Buddha can help them on the eightfold path, so much that they rightly can call him their savior. While still remembering the Buddha's injunction never to call him a metaphysical god but only a person who is awake, Mahayana Buddhists find that the masses of people, whose lives can be controlled by their emotions, can extinguish their cravings for comparative worth by lovingly adoring and devoting themselves to the Buddha. Rather than trying intellectually to interpret ancient texts, they find that chanting the Heart and Diamond Sutras of early Buddhism in a worshipful spirit of love and compassion for the Buddha and for what he loved can help them cross the river from Tanha living to Nirvana living. A crucial part of Mahayana practice is the role played by bodhisattvas, enlightened persons who choose to not live simply in the joyous life of Nirvana, but rather to share compassionately the sufferings of people still trapped in Tanha living.[192] Many of these bodhisattvas also have become the focal points of Buddhist practices of devotion and emulation. One Mahayana tradition, the Pure Land tradition, accented faithful devotion to the Buddha of infinite light (called Amitabha in India, Amitofo in Chinese, and Amida in Japanese). They expressed their worshipful devotion by repeatedly chanting the Buddha's name. Another tradition popular in China and Japan focused their worship on Kuan-yin, the Bodhisattva of mercy. Just as the Hindu bahkti form of yoga found space for different gods being constituted to meet the needs of different kinds of people, so Mahayana Buddhism made space for different groups of people to devote themselves to different bodhisattvas.

Since Mahayana Buddhists found that people could be engaged

in the eightfold path by devoting themselves to any number of Bodhisattvas, they did not accent the early Buddhist Pali texts the way that Theravada Buddhists did. The words of the Buddha take on importance only because of the spirit of Buddha that motivates their utterance. That spirit is shared by all bodhisattvas, and therefore their utterances and writings may be added to the texts to be cherished by Buddhists. Although in its historical development the Buddhist tradition too often was fractured by traditions trying to exclude other traditions, today most of the leaders in the Theravada and Mahayana traditions recognize that they simply embody different ways of putting into practice the eightfold path. The four noble truths give all of them a unifying identity, even as their differences become respected and cherished ways of living out the eightfold path. The marvelous tolerance and respect of differences found within Buddhism is today extended to the different religions of the world. The goal of ending self-inflicted suffering and achieving joyous living, by faithfully responding to the encounters with the nonfinite that extinguish Tanha, is viewed by Buddhists as a goal common to all the world's religions. Only the ways of faithfully responding are different, because of the social and cultural history of the people involved. All these ways of responding religiously are to be cherished and allowed to be what they are.

A second kind of competition threatened to distract Buddhism from the practical, religious task of extinguishing Tanha and self-inflicted suffering. As was noted above, intellectuals who called themselves Hindus had been carrying on metaphysical and epistemological debates with philosophers supporting Carvaka materialism. With the birth of Buddhism in the sixth century BC, these "Hindu" philosophers developed six different metaphysical and epistemological schools as alternatives to both Carvaka and Buddhism. Rather than heeding the Buddha's advice to maintain a noble silence on all such matters, a number of intellectuals who counted themselves as Buddhists formed themselves into schools of "Buddhist philosophy." They couldn't resist the temptation to enter into the game of engaging in metaphysical debates. They attempted to reply to the "Hindu" philosophers who defended theories about atomic substances, about Brahman being an eternal being and Atman being one or many eternal souls. They claimed that nothing is an enduring substance, because everything is always changing, and everything is dependent on everything else. Since they focused on change and process rather than permanence, they found it necessary to offer their own metaphysical theories about the status of events and moments of time and the connections between them. They became captured by the metaphysical project and locked themselves in fly bottles of confusion and intellectual cravings.

In an effort to re-establish noble silence on metaphysical matters, Nargarjuna, in the second century AD, pointed out the need to extinguish all these cravings for metaphysical and epistemological theorizing.[193] He emphasized again following a middle way that dissolves rather than solves metaphysical puzzles. He rejected as extreme the Carvaka materialist position, especially its claim that bodily identity is our only identity, with us becoming extinct when we die. He recognized that Carvaka materialism denies at a theoretical level what Buddhists understand at a practical, living level. We do not just have bodily identity. Human beings have a karma inheritance and legacy; their very identity is tied to the past and the future. Human beings are ethical persons who live on as they parent others to continue to meet the obligations that give each of them their unique identity. Nargarjuna also rejected as extreme in the opposite direction the postulation of an eternal being behind perceptual appearances and an eternal soul that never began to exist and never can be extinguished. Neither we nor the things we perceive rest on anything metaphysical. Everything rests on Sunyata, nothing. He called for Buddhists to remember the need to let things simply be in their pragmatic interdependency.[194] Nargarjuna also rejected the whole debate among "Buddhist" philosophers about whether or not time is divisible into metaphysically atomic moments of time. First, it is incoherent to turn time into a substance in this way. Second, engaging in such debates just generates destructive cravings. Nargarjuna also called for Theravada and Mahayana Buddhists to cherish their shared core and their understandable differences. In the historical development of Buddhist traditions, internal critics like Nargarjuna have appeared again and again to keep the tradition focused on the four noble truths. Among these critics we will find the founders of the Mahayana movement called Chan in China and Zen in Japan, a movement best examined after looking at the Taoist religious tradition in China.

3. Taoism

By the time Buddhism eventually worked its way around the Himalayas from India to China in the second century AD, there already existed in China the indigenous religious tradition of Taoism, which provided Buddhism with friendly soil in which to grow. Taoism has no single founder and does not get treated by the Chinese as a single religious tradition until the second century AD[195] Two names, however, Chuang-Tzu and Lao-Tzu, traditionally have been treated as the leading voices giving expression to this Chinese religious challenge to the adequacy of the social philosophies competing intellectually and politically during the period of social chaos in China, from the fifth through second centuries BC The writings of Chuang Tzu probably date from around 320 BC and over the next century get joined with other materials to form the book *Chuang Tzu*. The book *Tao Te Ching* appeared around 250 BC and was written by an anonymous religious thinker who listed as its author Lao Tzu (old master), who was understood to be Lao Tan (old man) whom to, it was said, Confucius himself had come for instruction. Not until the second and third centuries AD, with the rise of organized Taoist temples and the breakdown of the Confucian Han Dynasty, do these two books and commentaries on them begin to form a common tradition of religious literature.

To understand Taoism it is necessary to locate its critique within that historical context in which the Chinese were seeking for a way to move from social chaos to social order and harmony. There has not been in the development of Chinese social and cultural practices any metaphysical tradition of seeking ultimate explanations of natural and historical events by postulating some metaphysical supreme being as the cause of such events. In India, the Buddha had to call for noble silence in order to keep Buddhism free from the tendency of "Hindu" philosophers to offer such explanatory theories. In China, Taoism develops as a religious critique of the efforts of intellectuals and politicians to solve the problem of social living by remaining wholly within the domain of the social. Taoism will point out that successful human living depends upon rejecting the notion that the social is exhaustive and self-sufficient, calling instead for people to live well by encountering the social's other and by living in faithfulness to such encounters.

The Chou Dynasty began as a rather prosperous and unified regime from the time in the tenth century BC when it replaced China's first dynasty, the Shang Dynasty. By the middle of the eighth century, however, nomadic invaders from the northwest had driven the rulers of the Chou Dynasty to the east, and the central government had lost its ability to maintain control over China. Many independent and quasi-independent states arose, and continual, brutal warfare broke out among and within these smaller states. This era of social chaos lasted for five hundred years until the Chin Dynasty was established in 221 BC, and then the Han Dynasty replaced it in 202 BC. The central concern of most thinkers during these five centuries was finding a way to move China from social chaos to social order and harmony. Three major social philosophies presented their recommendations of ways to constitute social worlds in which people could live without suicidal social war. Legal Realism, suggested by Kung-sun Yang, Lord Shang, in the fourth century BC became the social/political basis of the Chin Dynasty. The teachings of Kung Fu Tzu (*Confucius* in Latin) (551–479 BC) were developed by Meng Fu Tzu (*Mencius* in Latin) (371–289? AD) and Jusun Tzu (298–238 BC). They became established as China's ruling philosophy during the Han Dynasty (202 BC–220 AD) and remained its official ideology until the end of the Ch'ing Dynasty in 1911 AD. Even today, Confucianism is a dominant force in determining social life in China and in the Chinese diaspora throughout the world. A third social philosophy, Mohism, was articulated by Mo Tsu (470–391 BC) and expressed in a book also named *Mo Tsu*, never became the ruling ideology of any dynasty, but it was a strong intellectual competitor against whom Legal Realism and Confucianism had to defend themselves. All three of these social philosophies attempted to solve China's social problem by staying within the realm of the social, offering different plans for the constitution of the social world. It is Taoism, however, that claims that the problem cannot be solved by staying within the social because treating the social realm as exhaustive and self-sufficient is what the problem really is.

At the base of the Legal Realists, recommendations is their belief that people universally and inescapably are greedy, jealous, selfish, and lustful. What Hindus saw as the result of being caught up in the illusion of Maya, and Buddhists saw as the Tanha nature of people that could be extinguished, the Legal Realists saw as the unavoidable nature of human beings living in chaotic China. In order to gain social order, therefore, the Legal Realists claimed one needs to give such selfish people an external motivation for living in a socially orderly way. The orderliness will come, they claimed, when all people are treated first and foremost as citizens of the state; when official agents of the state are chosen solely on their willingness and ability to serve the interests of the state; when there is established a rule of impersonal law governing all citizens except the supreme law giver, the emperor; when the point and purpose of all laws is the strengthening of the power of the state to maintain law and order; and when rewards and punishments are used to provide the motivation needed for people to be law abiding citizens. (The similarities between the position advocated by the Legal Realists in China and Thomas Hobbes's position set forth in his *Leviathan* are clear to see.) Punish all lawbreakers. Punish small crimes severely, and there won't be big crimes. Even punish those who knowingly do not turn in lawbreakers. Reward those who not only obey the law, but who also show willingness to sacrifice themselves and their families in order to preserve the rule of law and the power of the state. People must be given the motivation to prize the rule of law and to respect the supreme lawgiver over everything else. They must be motivated to recognize that what makes harming other people wrong is that it is a matter of breaking the law and committing a crime against the state. If one is realistic about what social life is like, then one will recognize that people must be seen only as citizens and that the production of loyal, law-abiding and law-respecting citizens is the only way to go from social chaos to social order. The state must become the people's god.

Mohism recognized the threat that such worship of the state posed. The goal of establishing lawfulness must not be just that of enhancing the status and power of the state. If all states operated only on that principle, then a continual state of war would exist between states. Orderliness at home would be purchased at the price of world chaos and would motivate each state to seek the destruction of all other states, hoping thereby to create one world empire. States would be unable to recognize that peace among states is better for the people in all the states than continual war among states. When the state itself and its power is seen as the point of governing, then lost sight of is the very reason for creating a world of social order rather than social chaos, and that is so that people can be better off, and not just so that the state can be more powerful. Just living an orderly life is not enough. The supreme law giver must recognize that laws are to be established for the sake of the well-being of the people, and not for the sake of ever-increasing state power. Moism charges that concern for all the people, with each person seen as of equal value, must be the guiding principle of state action.[196] This is what rulers must be concerned about in ordering life within their state and in their dealings with other states.

This concern, as interpreted in Mohism, calls for rationally calculating how to apply the utilitarian principle in the making and enforcing of laws and the carrying out of foreign policy. This supreme moral principle calls for creating the greatest amount of good for the greatest number of people, with all people being treated as one and only one. The Mohists did not argue that by some sort of election procedures people should themselves determine what is best for all the people. They argued that rulers, drawing upon the best calculations of consequences that experts could provide, should use this principle in making their decisions. They acknowledged that sometimes in order to maximize what is good for the many, the well-being of some individuals would have to be sacrificed. Well-being, for the Mohists, did not include recognizing that persons in their unique singularity possessed an ethical identity and significance that took priority over the kind of well-being that could be shared in common with all other people. Mohists did not entertain any notion of individual personal rights that prohibited using some people as mere means to the achievement of a maximization of collective good for all people. The collective good of people—a good capable of being rationally calculated and a people stripped of any nondescribable, infinite otherness—becomes the ultimate object of devotion in Mohism. This worship of the finite will be challenged by the Taoists.

Confucianism rejects two main themes in the Mohist position. First, it rejects the idea that morality consists of one supreme abstract principle (the utilitarian principle), which then is to be applied to concrete cases, by experts in rational calculations of consequences. Morality, for Confucianism, begins in the skillful resolution of conflicts in concrete cases and then rises only to those levels of abstraction necessary to solve the practical problems. Second, Confucianism rejects the idea that people are to be universally treated in one and only one way, as people who are potentially victims of future harms or recipients of future benefits. In Confucianism, people's different identities come from their different social positions and roles in different social environments. Furthermore, morality must not only be future oriented; many obligations stem from receiving benefits in the past and from having made commitments and promises in the past.

Confucianism levels two charges against the efficacy of the Legal Realist schema. First, it charges that Legal Realism only provides people with external motivation for obeying the law, and thus people will always be trying to break the law if they think they can get away with it. To try to prevent this, a huge price would have to be paid in order to be constantly watching people to catch lawbreakers, a tyrannical price that will make the world worse than the cost of the social chaos they are trying to prevent. Motivation for harmonious social living has to be internalized. (Confucianism charges that Mohism also fails to provide people with motivation to judge everything in terms of the utilitarian principle.) Second, Confucianism charges that one can never pass enough laws to govern the uncountable number of ways that people deal with one another. If one were to try to have the law settle every potential conflict between people, the people and the law enforcement agents would be so overwhelmed that no one would know what is legal and what is not. Not huge law books, but people skillful in living harmoniously is what is needed.

Confucianism does share with Mohism opposition to the Legal Realist's pessimistic claims about the selfishness of human beings. Mohists claimed that people can be motivated to act justly with other people if the compassionate feelings of people are just given a chance, a claim challenged by Legal Realism and Confucianism. Some Confucian philosophers claimed that human nature is plastic, with social nurturing and training determining whether people end up selfishly warring with one another or living harmoniously together. Others claimed that people, unless corrupted, are basically good, and thus able to be socialized to desire to live properly and harmoniously. Both groups charged that the Legal Realist position would only produce the tyranny that actually came about when Legal Realism operated in the short-lived Chin dynasty. This is because in Legal Realism, the great lawgiver stands unconstrained by law or by any moral requirements that restrain this absolute sovereign from constructing laws that primarily serve the interests of the sovereign, and not the people bound under the law. (This criticism is reminiscent of Locke's reply to Hobbes, that it is better to have ten thousand people each with the power of one, than one person with the power of ten thousand.) Also, since the goal in a Legal Realist society is only order, there need be no laws offering the compassionate help often needed by the powerless.

Confucius believed that communities could exist in social harmony if and only if a moral educational system were developed that trained people to identify with social roles which specified their obligations and prerogatives, with these roles existing within a harmonious social whole. People are to be so socialized and culturally trained that they will desire to rectify their names; that they will be the family members, friends, and political subjects that they are; that they will carry out the duties and obligations that are a definitive part of those roles. People are to be nurtured to be able and willing to live successfully as the social persons they have been constituted to be in a social world constituted for harmonious social life. People must come to have a sense of identity that is derived from their place within such a social and cultural whole. A community exists only if people act, think, and feel as though it exists, and only if people participate in its self-constituting practices as if it is the most natural and obvious thing to do, as if doing anything else is betraying themselves and what they are. All the practices constituting a social community must be aimed at meeting the community's first and primary obligation to preserve itself and re-create itself perpetually in every new generation, through a program of moral education, social and cultural training, and personal identity constitution. All resources of the community are to be aimed at achieving this result, including the use of textbooks, folk songs, games, stories, plays, festivals, funerals, choice of officials, rewards, punishments, and above all else, having parents, teachers, and government officials serve as moral exemplars.

The purpose of the Confucian program of moral education is the replacement of social chaos with social harmony. The penultimate goal of the program is to nurture and train people to live successfully as the social persons they are with other people who are the social people they are. There are five major virtues, established and habitual ways of acting that will enable people to live well as such social beings, thereby rectifying their names. Confucianism presents a morality of social-role fulfillment and a virtue morality aimed at producing people who successfully carry out their role assignments. People must be reared to possess these five virtues and to constitute and carry out the role assignments required to overcome chaos and preserve harmony. In the Confucian understanding of things, such social nurturing and training is not a matter of brainwashing and mind control. It is socialization that constitutes homo sapiens as persons with brains and minds capable of acting freely or of being controlled. The choice is not between being socialized or not being socialized. The choice is between being socialized as warring individuals or as people willing and able to live in social harmony as they rectify their names.

At the center of the Confucian set of virtues is *Li*, propriety, the character trait of desiring to do what people know is the right thing to do given their social status and the social position of the people with whom they are dealing. The primary example of these sets of social positions is the family and the duties that husbands and wives, parents and children, brothers and sisters, cousins, aunts and uncles, nephews and nieces, grandparents and grandchildren have to one another. Friends are to be treated similarly to brothers, sisters, and cousins. The emperor is the father of the whole Chinese family and is to be treated as such, even as he is to rectify his name and fulfill his social obligations to the people he rules. Strangers and foreigners are to be treated as guests in your home, and when you are in foreign places you are to treat them as hosts welcoming you into their home. One of the most crucial Li proprieties is respect for age. Older persons cannot carry out their primary responsibility of providing moral nurturing and training to the younger generation unless they themselves are respected. There are other Li proprieties that apply to the way things are to be done (in dress and speech; at meals, festivals, and funerals), which stem from the practice of utilizing all aspects of social and cultural life in the project of moral education.

Living harmoniously with other socialized people requires possessing the virtue of Jen, living in a courteous and civilized manner with other people. Confucius said that there is one principle that will guide the behavior of people with Jen: "Do not do to others what you do not want them to do to you."[197] This does not call for people to do to others what they want done to themselves (we don't want masochists treating us that way). It calls for people to not force their will on other people, except when we want other people to do that to us. There are times when the people who prize a virtuous life of Li and Jen might ask other people to help them to live up to their obligations, even if it means forcing them to do something that they at the moment cannot motivate themselves to do. The ideal, of course, is motivating ourselves to rectify our names.

People with the virtue of *Chun-tzu* will have mastered the art of living well as the social persons they are. They will be competent, poised, and graceful in being who they are socially, not needing to be petty, brusque, vulgar, violent, boastful, or despondent. They will know who they are and how to be what they are, and they will carry this knowledge and skill with them wherever they go, thus being at home in any and all situations.

The rulers of the people will understand that real power, *Te*, does not come by exercising force or violence on the people being ruled. It comes when the people confer upon the government the authority to rule. This will be done when people have been trained to be proper subjects, and when rulers are rectifying their names, meeting their obligations to be a proper, caring, teaching, father to the people being ruled. Subjects and rulers alike must come to understand that social harmony and personal well-being depend upon people being trained in the creative, cultural arts of music, art, and poetry. It is the cultural life of a community that gives it its distinctive character. It is the cultural life of a community that is the key to a community's international success in history. Countries can be invaded and governments can be overthrown, but the superior culture will win out in the long run, as was discovered again and again in Chinese history. The northern invaders during the Chou Dynasty became Chinese, as did the Mongols and the Manchu. The cultural arts are *Wen,* the arts of peace that can pacify the most horrible barbarians.

The Confucian morality of role fulfillment and virtue is similar in many ways to the Indian Code of Manu, except for one major difference. Confucianism always recognized that social roles, names to be rectified, are socially constituted by people and must always remain open for reconstitution when they no longer serve their purpose of producing a socially harmonious communal way of living. The Confucian thinker who accented the social and historically variable nature of names, role definitions, is Hsun Tzu (298–238 BC).[198] He recognized that in a world of changing circumstances, conflicts and dilemmas could arise as people try to rectify their names and carry out their obligations. He therefore provided for a procedure for creatively reconstructing these role definitions. Persons familiar with the traditional role assignments and the considerations that led to their constitution, and committed to resolving conflicts in new cases so as to make possible once again socially harmonious living, will creatively construct solutions to the problem. These new decisions and role constructions will become a part of the traditions that are to remain until new hard cases again arise and create a need for further imaginative, moral reconstruction.[199] In a similar manner, people must continually be engaged in recreating and reconstructing their personal habits (virtues) as new circumstances arise. People are virtuous not so much because of what they are, as because of what they are striving to be.[200]

Confucian morality, therefore, is quite similar to English and American common law in which judges have to creatively rework earlier decisions in order to resolve new, unanticipated problems, with these new decisions joining earlier decisions in what becomes traditional common law. There is no one universal principle (e.g., the utilitarian principle) on the basis of which applied decisions are made, and there is no felt need for some nonsocial, metaphysical principle or power to legitimize this social practice. There are just people seeking social harmony, trying to solve concrete problems. The Confucian world is social through and through—socially constituting people as role occupants, socially rearing them to live so as to willingly meet their obligations, socially developing cultural practices that will aid in moral education and living well in such a social world, and engaging in a social practice of reconstructing roles when needed. It is just this treatment of the social as self-sufficient and exhaustive of human life that Taoists challenged.

From the Taoist point of view, all three of these social/political philosophies fail to recognize that the conflicts within and among people cannot be removed simply by better social engineering. Only by encountering and living in harmony with that which is other than what is socially constituted can people find what they need and want. All three of these social philosophies take something constituted by people and turn it into an ultimate that is given infinite significance, thereby preventing people from living harmoniously with what is actually other than what is man-made. Legal Realism made the state into a god, and thus a tyranny of power politics and unrestricted dictatorial rule was produced. Mohism took as its ultimate the human effort to maximize collective good for people as a whole through the use of calculative reasoning about consequences. This makes the good of some abstract social collective more valuable than individual people who, therefore, can and at times should be sacrificed for the common good, when this is necessary. The Taoist reminds us, however, that people are singularly unique, other than what can be pigeonholed with a name, and thus their significance is other than what calculative reason can measure, compare, and add up. In Mohism, the infinite is denied, and the finite is absolutized.

Confucianism, Taoism charges, by striving to make people's finite, social identities their only identities, denies people their singularly unique identities. This never succeeds in producing harmonious life. The social worlds constituted by finite, socialized people are always flawed worlds filled with conflictual assignments of obligations. Chinese literature is filled with tragic dramas of people being caught in inescapable dilemmas about how to be a loyal wife and mother or son and friend. Confucianism is to be praised for recognizing the need to continually reconstitute the social world to resolve such conflict, but such reconstruction projects never touch the core issue that people are not just social functionaries. The attempted socialization of people to see themselves as nothing but the social masks they are asked to wear never works completely. Again, Chinese literature is filled with examples of husbands warring with wives, children warring with parents, officials warring with one another and misusing their power. As actually practiced in China, Confucian moral education projects were always backed up with Legal Realist external reward and punishment motivations, often producing thereby tyrannical parents and officials. Taoist temples were often treated by Chinese officialdom as sanctuaries for people who wanted to or had to drop out of the whole social role playing game. From the Taoist point of view, Confucianism prizes too highly socially constituted worlds, and thereby fails to understand the need to let the finite and social rest on the nonfinite and nonsocial, the infinite. Doing this does not deny the significance of the social, but it will produce a different attitude toward the social and a different way of living socially.

The word "tao" means "the way." In Taoism, this word is used in a variety of different ways. It is used repeatedly to indicate that our socially constituted worlds of objects, characteristics, and people are not ultimate, self-sufficient, or exhaustive. Human conceptualizing, naming, is the key to the constitution of the myriad creatures we deal with in our social lives. The Taoist claims, however, that other than the socially constituted there is "the nameless," "the darkness upon darkness," "the empty," "the nothing," "emptiness." If "earth" is used to refer to the socially constituted world, and "heaven" is used to refer to the necessities and accidents that people cannot control, then "the way" is used to refer to the empty space between heaven and earth.[201] To live in faithfulness to encountering the finite world's otherness is to live without absolutizing the finite, the socially constituted. This otherness is not another being or realm. Encountering the nameless is encountering the limited, historically changing, and socially variable character of the myriad objects and subjects in the world, and letting them be what they are, merely limited, finite, historical, and social. Letting them be means not seeking ultimate explanations or justifications for their being what they are. Talking about living in harmony with the infinite Tao means letting the finite simply be what it is.

In order to indicate what it might be like to simply let things be, rather than see things only as socially constituted beings, Taoism often speaks of living in harmony with the "way of nature," in contrast to living in continual conflict in the "way of social living." Many thinkers, in rebellion against the confinements of living only in accordance with social norms, have looked to nature to find an alternative way of living. So much of our daily living is done in worlds that seem totally filled with materials and objects manufactured by us. Getting to nature has appealed as a way to escape this all-to-human world. To appreciate the Taoist strategy of living in harmony with nature, however, we have to go beyond this romanticist tendency. It is also necessary to not see the things and ways of nature as just a subset of things in the world of socially constituted objects. An objectivisitic approach to nature, its objects, and its laws will not provide the way of nature about which Taoism is talking. It is necessary to recognize that our names and descriptions cannot exhaust what is encountered when one lives harmoniously with nature as a part of living harmoniously with the infinite Tao, the nameless, the no-thingness other to constituted objects. This Taoist approach comes close to the romanticist appreciation of the sublimity of nature. For the most part, our use of names leads us to see nature as consisting of independent objects that we treat as substances, classifiable into sets on the basis of similarities and distinctions between them, and usable by us as natural resources and raw materials. In order to accent the merely historical, social, conventional, desire-driven character of such ways of seeing and treating nature, Taoists accent how nature is to be seen and treated once we let nature be free of our attempts to describe, explain and control it. In contrast to the fixed objects of socially constituted nature, Taoism suggests considering the flowing, ever-changing character of nature. In contrast to seeing oneself as a rational or social being standing outside of nature and trying to master it cognitively and control it technologically, instead see oneself as a part of nature living in harmony with its regularities and irregularities. See oneself as a self and nature as a nature that never can be captured by descriptions and should never be overpowered by socially constituted people. See the tao of nature as an incarnation of the way of the nameless Tao.

Taoism charges that it is because people do not know how to live harmoniously with the way of things that is other than the social way of living, they turn to social engineering in their attempts to solve the problem of living harmoniously with one another. Merely turning to social engineering, however, Taoists claim, will not solve the problem. It will only add to the problem, because it still places its ultimate trust in mere social living. It still remains a secular humanism which does not religiously understand that humans are people who encounter the infinite in themselves and their interpersonal and natural environment. Taoists do not advocate trying to live without linguistic and other social practices, without social identities and socially constituted objects. They do reject, however, trying to absolutize these social projects, thereby refusing to let things be in their otherness to such socialization. People must learn how to live in a way that allows them to encounter the unspeakable otherness to the socially constituted and to live in faithfulness to that encounter, in harmony with the infinite way of things that permeates all of the finite ways of things.

Stop warring against nature and trying to control it. Stop cursing nature for its unstoppable regularities and unavoidable accidents. Stop trying to be better than nature or other people. Stop absolutizing one's criteria of good and bad. Stop creating ever more social regulations and complications of social roles in a effort to achieve harmonious living, an effort doomed to failure. Perfect a life of *wu wei,* creative quietude, in which one masters the skill of living effectively, gracefully, simply, and spontaneously, by not trying to control things but by trusting what one is, social and other than social, and by accepting what one's environment is, finite and infinite. This will be a life in which one lets other people be more than mere socially constituted persons. Letting them be will mean giving them an ethical status as singularly unique individuals under obligation to let all other people be in their finiteness and infiniteness, respecting their otherness to all social categories, and not harming them in their finite precariousness. In Taoism there is an ethical accent that takes priority over Legal Realism's laws, Mohism's utilitarianism, and Confucian social norms, an ethical accent that enables Taoism to critique the deficiencies in all three. Recognizing that all people have ethical significance in their singular uniqueness that is other than their social status, in following the nameless way, all people will be treated equally and equitably.[202] Faithfulness to the Tao involves not harming other people,[203] meeting one's ethical obligation to carry out the highest of benevolent acts without any ulterior motive,[204] and living with compassion for all people.[205] Such benevolence involves letting people, in their ethical uniqueness, be free from domination and oppression, free from having others meddle in their lives when they are meeting their ethical obligations, free so that they can prosper in their own way.[206] It means not abandoning anyone, but doing good to all people, even to those who do not do good to you.[207] It means being able to live with ethical spontaneity; and by simply being what one really is, a person with a unique identity that is ethical, one can meet all of one's moral requirements not to harm and to help others, and to go beyond that to do good even to one's enemies. What social ordering cannot do, religious faithfulness to the Tao achieves.

Living in harmony with the Tao means that far fewer conflicts among people will arise, and thus that far fewer social constraints and less governmental apparatus will be necessary. The ruler following the Tao prevents problems from arising, thus removing the need to solve problems. Not seeing the ruler as a problem solver, people will think that the ruler has done nothing and they have done everything by themselves.[208] The Taoist ruler has no objection to that, because he is not striving for superior comparative worth. Living harmoniously with the Tao means living without all the conflicting and competitive aspects of what Buddhists called Tanha living. Living harmoniously with the Tao means being free from all those craving desires for comparative superiority,[209] and thus from constantly contending with other people to gain superior status and to avoid inferior status.[210] It means being inactive in the whole game of securing social status and thus achieving a calmness and contentment in which one cannot experience disgrace.[211] By seeing the way of nature as an incarnation of the infinite Tao, one can see in nature many examples of what it is like to live without cravings for comparative social worth. Rather than socially attempting to control nature, let social living simply be instances of living harmoniously with the tao, even as rivulets and streams flow into rivers and the sea.[212] In social relationships, be submissive and weak like water, not contending and craving for status, and like water one will wear away what is taken as hard and irremovable, the whole social world constituted out of Tanha craving.[213]

There is a Taoist story that helps us understand the difference between the people who live for the most part as socially constituted persons and the individuals spontaneously living ethical and joyous lives in harmony with the Tao. A person, Chuang Chou, dreamt that he was a butterfly enjoyably flying around without any planned route. When he awoke and began to live again as the person Chou, socially graded as venerable, he wondered, as Taoism would have us wonder, whether he was really a socially constituted person who had only dreamt he was a butterfly, or a butterfly now living the waking nightmare of social life.[214] For the Taoist, we really are butterflies who can enjoyably fly without craving social status or imprisoning ourselves in social roles. The problem is to wake up from our current nightmare and let ourselves be what we are. Let ourselves live as something other than merely a socially constituted being. Let ourselves be ethical persons, ready and willing to be joyful lovers of life.

In Taoism, freeing oneself from craving and confininement within a world of socially constituted objects, roles, and subjects, not only means being able to live with ethical spontaneity, but also with more joyful spontaneity. Gaining such spontaneity means increasing one's power to live well, increasing one's enjoyment and love of life, and enabling others to gain similar freedom, power, and joy. The Chinese call this power to live well Chi. Acquiring and exercising this power is at the center of Taoist religious practice. In religious meditation upon the way that the infinite Tao permeates everything socially constituted as finite (practicing what the Hindus call jnana yoga), Taoists seek to remove the social impediments to spontaneous ethical and joyful living. In carrying out a program of concentration comparable to the practice of what the Hindus call raja yoga, Taoists seek to increase their Chi, their power to live well. Similar to the final stage of raja yoga, Taoists trustingly release themselves into the way of the Tao, which is a seeking that ends up in ceasing to seek, ceasing to be in control.[215] Just as Confucianism has discovered that the presence of moral exemplars in a community have great power in raising the moral quality of the lives of others in the community, so Taoists have discovered that the mere presence in a community of spiritual exemplars who are living in harmony with the Tao can be of great aid to other people seeking to follow the way of the Tao. Taoists are enjoined to be spiritual saviors of other people.[216] In many historical communities, Taoist sages, especially Lao Tzu, have been constituted as focal points for religious devotions. This is similar to the manner in which bhakti yoga is practiced in Hinduism and bodisattvas are constituted in Buddhism.

This interpretation of Taoism leaves two major problems that need to be addressed if we are to appreciate the religious significance of Taoism. First, how is a Taoist to live in a world in which people for the most part are not living in harmony with the Tao? Two options seem available, both of which have historically been chosen. One could choose to drop out of the social world as much as possible and create a small world of one's own in which to live. Taoist temple life was often embraced by people choosing this option. Alternatively, one could remain in the social world, but not be of that world, functioning as a critic of existing social regimes, reminding them of their finiteness and insufficiency and of their need to respect the infinite otherness of people. Numerous Taoist writers, poets, and painters, chose have this option.[217] They were quite successful in the sense that the Confucian, Mohist, and Legal Realist aspects of Chinese social and cultural life felt compelled to provide space for Taoist dropouts and critics, and most cultured Chinese prized what these Taoist critics were saying, even if they could not go all the way with them. Taoist reflections are today an inseparable part of Chinese culture.

Secondly, Taoists recognized that their critique of the adequateness of linguistic distinctions also required that they critique their distinctions between the social and the natural, the finite and the infinite, the one constant way of the Tao and the innumerable ways of social living.[218] These distinctions also must not be made metaphysically absolute. This can be achieved if we recognize that Taoist speech here has a practical and not a theoretical function. There are not two realms, the finite and the infinite. There is only the infinite otherness that the finite cannot escape, which we can encounter even as we perceive the conceptualized finite. Encountering nature's infinity is encountering nature as something that cannot be exhaustively captured by social classifications. Encountering the infinite otherness of every socially constituted person is to encounter that person ethically, as someone who is more than what can be socially classified, but as someone who is social and who faces threats to that person's biological life and who faces social and psychological oppression and humiliation. In order to make practical use of its distinctions without turning them into absolutes, Taoism often affirms both sides of linguistic binary oppositions, and then proclaims that both reside in darkness. What is important in Taoism is not its vocabulary, so easily mistaken for metaphysical vocabulary, but the religious way of life that it proclaims to be a way to live harmoniously with ourselves, our environment and other people.

4. Chan/Zen

Taoism prepared fertile soil in which Chan (Zen in Japanese) could grow and flourish in China. After appropriating many Taoist accents in China, Chan again found fertile soil for creative development in the indigenous Japanese religion, Shinto, when it was transplanted there and became Zen. Before examining Chan/Zen itself, it will prove helpful to gain a little understanding of the religious tradition of Shinto and why it made it so easy for Confucianism and Buddhism to take root in Japan. The word Shinto is the Japanese rendition of the Chinese words "shin tao" and often is referred to with the Japanese words *kami no michi*. Both usually get translated as "the way of the gods," but this can be a troublesome translation. Shinto sees kami in all things in nature as well as in the social descendants of the sun goddess (the Yamato clan and its emperor), the storm gods (the Izumo clan in western Japan), and the gods of the sea (the Kyushu clans). If treated as individual beings, the Kami would number in the thousands, and such a multitude of beings is not what fits our normal use of the word "god." It is much more helpful to interpret Shinto talk about kami as talk about the way trees, mountains, rivers, fish, and birds are to be treated.

There is something precious and sacred about them, and they are not to be treated without respect, not as mere natural resources that people can use as they please. Human communities, in turn, are inescapably linked to nature and its sacredness. The myths about the formation of Japan can all be interpreted religiously as efforts to point to this sacred otherness to what otherwise would be mere raw natural and human resources, capable of being used as mere means because they had no intrinsic significance. That Shinto became corrupted into a mechanism for legitimating aggressive nationalism and militarism should not blind us to its religious significance. Its accent on the sacredness of nature is very similar to the Taoist accent on the unspeakably infinite character of everything we encounter in nature. Its accent on the relationship between social authority and the sacred of nature resembles the Chinese claim that the authority of the emperor depends upon a mandate from heaven, upon dealing with floods and droughts, except that in China emperors could lose this mandate, whereas in Japan the emperor never lost social authority, even when he lost political power. It is these aspects of Shinto that made it very easy for Confucian culture and Buddhism and Chan/Zen to move from China to Japan.

As unique a Buddhist tradition as Zen is, it is crucial to remember that it is still one of the Mahayana Buddhist traditions. In Zen, as in all Buddhism, religious understanding and practice begin with the four noble truths. Suffering is the problem to be solved. Craving, grounded in comparative evaluations of self-worth, is the cause of suffering, and it can be extinguished by means of the eightfold path. In the Mahayana tradition of Buddhism, transmitting from generation to generation the spirit of Buddha (in enlightened ones who woke up) is prized over studying Pali texts. In Chan, this accent remained in its stress upon the historical sequence of masters passing on the "mind of Buddha." Chan/Zen tradition stresses this line of masters from Siddhartha Gautama to his foremost disciple, Mahakaysapa; then through other masters to Nargarjuna in the second-century AD in India; through the early masters who brought Chan to China in the fourth and fifth centuries; through Bodhidharma, the first Chan patriarch in the early sixth century, through the fifth patriarch, Hung-Jen, who gave to Chan a distinctively Chinese flavor in the seventh century by fertilizing it with

Taoists accents; and then to his two students, Shen-Hsiu and Hui-Neng, who founded the northern and southern schools of Chan practice in the late seventh and early eighth centuries; and so on down to masters in this age.[219] Differences that appeared in Chan simply exemplify the Mahayana understanding that new Buddhas in new ages and circumstances actualize additional possibilities present in the four noble truths.

It is understandable that the Chan/Zen tradition looks back to Nargarjuna as one of its founders. Nargajuna had rejected the metaphysical speculations that had developed within Buddhism in India, stressing the Buddha's call for noble silence on metaphysical questions and the need for focusing on the practical work outlined in the eightfold path. When Buddhism came to China, it was engaged once again in metaphysical speculations and debates that had no appeal to Chinese thinkers debating social philosophies or reflecting on Taoist critiques of absolutizing the social. Buddhism flowered in China when under the leadership of Hung-Jen in the seventh century, it utilized three characteristics of Taoism. First, it accented the similarity between Taoist talk about the unnameable Tao and Buddhist talk about the no-thingness, the void, upon which all things rested. Second, it sided with Taoism in rejecting intellectualization as a way to gain spiritual liberation. Third, it blended Buddhist characterizations of compassionate daily life in Nirvana with the Taoist accent on how the person (living in harmony with the Tao) lives bodily and practically while encountering the unnameable Tao in oneself and in everything with which one lives—the Tao that is universally present in all people and things.[220] Chan reached the height of its development and influence during the Sung Dynasty (920–1279) and was treated in China as virtually synonymous with all of Buddhism during the Yuan (1279–1368) and Ming (1368–1644) dynasties. It was during the Sung Dynasty that two traditionally trained Japanese priests, Eisai (1141–1215) and Dogen (1200–1253), journeyed to China, studied Chan/Zen, and brought it back to Japan.

The uniqueness in Chan/Zen comes from three of its distinctive characteristics. First, it emphasizes a nonverbal approach to spiritual enlightenment. Second, it declares that Buddhahood is always already present in everyone and everything. Third, it proclaims the wondrous and beautiful nature of all the daily things and activities of life available after enlightenment, when we let ourselves and everything we encounter be in their Buddha suchness. The first emphasis manifests itself in the Chan/Zen claim that enlightenment occurs like an explosion in which a world of craving and alienation gets replaced by a world of compassionate and harmonious life filled with unimagined wonder, beauty, and peace. The second declaration points out that enlightenment does not have to take us to a new transcendent realm of selves and things; it only consists in extinguishing what is preventing us and everything else from being what we and they would be if our cravings were not messing things up. The third proclamation points out that life after and with enlightenment simply lets us live in a radically different way as embodied, compassionate persons doing in a radically more wonderful way all the ordinary things we must do as such persons. Looking in detail at these three characteristics should help us demystify this religious tradition and thus grow in respect for it and cherish its way of responding to its encounters with the infinite.

Chan/Zen tradition has it that Sakyamuni (the Buddha) passed on to his disciple Mahakasyapa the task of continuing the Buddhist tradition when Mahakasyapa showed that he understood the core of the Buddha's teachings about the four noble truths. This happened when the Buddha simply lifted up a bouquet of flowers. Although there is no historical evidence of any linkage between Mahakayapa and the Chinese patriarchs of Chan, the presence of this story in the Chan/Zen tradition illustrates its emphasis that gaining a practical religious understanding is more important than passing on verbal teachings. Having merely intellectual understanding of what the four noble truths are saying is never sufficient for extinguishing Tanha cravings and suffering. Enlightenment, *wu* in Chinese and *satori* in Japanese, consists of a cataclysmic change in oneself and how one lives with everything else. Zen is not saying that after enlightenment words will not be used.[221] Rather it is reminding us of the large extent to which our cravings for comparative worth and power control the way we use words to rigidly classify and individuate things and to attempt to give ultimate explanations and justification of things. Words, claims, and arguments serving

Tanha cravings never can bring people to enlightenment.

The Chan/Zen use of koans aims at getting a person to see the need to get beyond reliance on such words and arguments. When the master says to the student, "What is the sound of one hand clapping?" he is not asking a question, nor directing the student to provide him with information expressible in the same sort of language he used in speaking. He is inviting the student to recognize the presuppositions of such speech. Most talk about clapping presupposes accepting the existence of the things we classify and individuate as hands, my hands or your hands; classification and individuating practices tied to our substantializing things; and our assignment of possession rights. The master is inviting the student to recognize that such talk is tied to Tanha cravings that must be extinguished. The master is trying to help the student break through the bottom of the pail imprisoning his life in such cravings and conceptualizations.[222] The master is looking for the student to show his understanding by beginning to carry out the ordinary activities of living in a totally new, non-craving way. In "The Way of the Inzan School," it is reported that the response given to the master's inquiry about the sound of one hand clapping consisted of merely thrusting one hand forward.[223] The sound is silence, the silence in which one hears the rain falling outside as one thrusts one hand forward, falling rain that does not feed any of our Tanha cravings.

In "The Platform Scripture of the Sixth Patriarch," Hui-neng reports how the fifth patriarch, Hung-jen, passed on to him the mantle of leadership when he went beyond writing a verse that said that the original Buddha nature of people is always clear and pure by going back to work in the rice-pounding area.[224] The moment of awakening is often compared to a stone being thrown into the water, and having its ripples extend outward to encompass all of one's thinking, believing, feeling, acting, or to a knock at the door of one's gate which is so loud that its vibrations are felt throughout the house.[225] The attainment of a way of life free from Tanha cravings can occur in many ways. It need not come as a result of responding to a koan. It could come by letting a bouquet of flowers, a bamboo leaf, garden moss, or the odor or taste of tea be what they are independent of our Tanha way of treating them. Encountering anything as other to what we experience them under the influence of Tanha can be the occasion for encountering everything in this nonfinite otherness, this original suchness.

Some of the Chan/Zen texts talk about enlightenment coming gradually and others talk about suddenly becoming enlightened. This easily can be misunderstood. A person might break through the bottom of the pail suddenly, but usually this only follows long periods of concentrated meditation *(zazen)* and repeated sessions with a master *(sanzen)* in which the student responds to a koan given by the master. Furthermore, Chan/Zen does not claim that nothing worthwhile happens when Chan/Zen training sessions do not produce a total extinction of Tanha cravings and an explosion into a way of life in which all things are allowed to be in their suchness. Chan/Zen temples provide for many groups of people short-term training sessions, recognizing that many sincere people only succeed in ending cravings in one aspect of their lives and then in another, or only lessen their cravings little by little. When Hui-Neng and the Southern School of Chan in China emphasized sudden rather than gradual enlightenment, the issue at stake was the status of masters and how Buddhist enlightenment is to be preserved from generation to generation. Since what masters are to be sure is present in the next generation is a living understanding of a life totally liberated from Tanha, only a master who has undergone the breakthrough of the bottom of the pail and an explosion into a way of life in which everything is different is going to be able to recognize that a student has done the same and now is a master.

There are many ways in which Chan/Zen tries to get us to understand that spiritual liberation is a matter of letting ourselves and everything else simply be what we and they are, when we no longer constitute ourselves as Tanha through our cravings for comparative worth and power, and when things no longer are treated as objects constituted to satisfy these cravings. Hui-Neng talks about recovering our original mind, our original nature that is pure and undisturbed by cravings.[226] Shen-Hui writes of the mind being void of cravings and its effects from the beginning.[227] Chan/Zen is radically universalistic in that it keeps emphasizing that Buddhahood, living with Tanha cravings being extinguished, always already resides in everything. Mountains and valleys, trees and flowers, air and water, humans and mosquitoes, food and excrement—all would be in that suchness that always was there and will be there again for us once our Tanha selves and cravings are extinguished. Shen-Hui writes that when we attain enlightenment, then all living things are again allowed to have their Buddhahood, their luminous nature.[228] Spiritual liberation does not take us outside of time or the materiality of daily living. It allows us to live in time, among the elements, with things in their suchness, as we encounter the non-Tanha-finiteness of ourselves and everything else. First we empty ourselves of Tanha craving and living. Then we empty this emptiness by letting our original self stand in its native suchness, naked without any Tanha clothing, thus allowing us to encounter everything else in its marvelous suchness.[229] The Chan/Zen talk about emptying one's emptiness plays the very important role of reminding us that enlightenment is not an achievement for which we can take credit, thus puffing us up into thinking that we are better than those still trapped in Tanha living. Enlightenment and revolutionary change in our lives take place when we, as Tanha-constituted selves, get out of the way, when we extinguish Tanha cravings, when we just let ourselves and everything else be in their original suchness.

Life after enlightenment, satori, Chan/Zen tells us, is awesome, wondrous, exhilarating, joyful living in which every encounter with things in their suchness is living a radically different kind of life encountering a radically different kind of world. We no longer are trapped in the endless task of repaying the debts to the past with which karma has burdened our lives. We pass through the Great Death (of Tanha living) into the Great Life, free from all comparisons, free from all sense of superiority or inferiority, free from guilt or resentment, free from shame and fear, free to live a life in which every day is a good day.[230] We can become like the pine tree that has no sense of superiority or like a dolphin who does not think of itself as better or worse than a bass or a horse. Now we can throw ourselves into living playfully, the way a child is totally involved with seriousness and earnestness in its joyous play, without looking for any metaphysical answers to whys and wherefores of life. [231] We simply can let things be. Extinguishing our Tanha self and cravings and letting things be has radical aesthetic and ethical implications.

When Tanha cravings are extinguished, then nothing about ourselves or anything else needs to be abjected as evil, unclean, or ugly.

The human body in its suchness, is not evil, and it is only our cravings that lead us to treat things as disgusting. Just as Chuang Tzu said that the infinite Tao resides even in human excrement and urine, so Chan/ Zen promises us that satori will allow us to find beauty in what once we thought was ugly.[232] Japanese Zen masters have developed an aesthetic in which things that Tanha-enslaved people find ugly are transformed into beautiful works of art. Zen built upon the earlier Japanese Buddhist aesthetic principle of *mono no aware*. This principle recognizes the impermanence of things. It finds that the most beautiful of things are always experienced with a sense of sadness because they exist only for a marvelous moment and then are gone like the waning moon, cherry blossoms, a young woman's face. Zen adds the aesthetic principles of *yugen, wabi, sabi,* and *shibui* which allow Zen poetry, painting, No drama, wet and dry gardening, tea ceremony, and flower arranging to be practices leading to enlightenment and practices in which people can celebrate the beauty of living after satori.

All these Zen aesthetic practices accent process art over product art, thereby undercutting Tanha tendencies to substantialize things for which one then develops cravings. It is the creative activities of writers and readers of poetry; of painters and viewers; of gardeners and meditative viewers of gardens; of writers, actors and viewers of dramas; of flower arrangers and tea ceremony participants on which aesthetic attention is directed. The No actors move with slow deliberate steps and body motions, with the slightest hand motion requiring concentrated, creative, interpretive work on the part of the viewer. Everyone is a participant in the tea ceremony, as the marvelousness of simple sights, sounds, feels, smells, and tastes become exhilarating, as craving is extinguished. In all the Zen art forms, what previously was shunned or overlooked is found to possess great aesthetic value. Fog, early mornings, and late afternoons are accented to give a yugen aesthetic treatment of the profound, the subtle, the deep, the mysterious. Bamboo forests capture this sense of beauty. Moss, weeds, silence, the poor, and the forlorn are turned into expressions of wabi beauty. Thatched roofs, old wood, brown leaves, old women, and cripples give vent to the sabi sensitivity, to the Zen demonstration that the old, the aged and the worn out shine forth beautifully when Tanha comparative evaluations are

extinguished. The shibui accent brings out the same aesthetic appreciation for the dark, dull, shadowy character of the clay and dirt of the
material world. When everything is allowed to be in its original suchness, no room for nihilistic despair remains, and no need arises to go to
some metaphysical realm so that things might have significance. Zen
emptiness is aesthetic fulness.

Letting things be in their suchness not only lets them be in their aesthetic richness, but it also frees people to live ethically and to transform
social practices. Tanha-driven unjust ways of living are changed into a
new compassionate involvement in resisting injustice. When we empty
ourselves of Tanha cravings, then we encounter each person and thing in
its singularity. In Nirvana life, differentiating and individuating things is
radicalized. This person is not encountered as just one more homo sapiens, and this rose is not encountered as just one more rose. We encounter
them in their singular uniqueness. True freedom for the liberated person means living with absolute autonomy, but by letting oneself become
nothing in the Tanha world, one finds oneself equal, but no better or
worse, than everything else. This call to treat all people equally, however,
does not produce homogeneity. Rather, it is a call to let all people live in
their singular uniqueness. It is a call for all people to become servants to
every other person, thereby letting all others be their moral masters.[233]
One can let people live in their singular uniqueness only if one actively
involves oneself in resisting the injustice of domination and oppression.
Zen Buddhism does not call for retreat from the world. Zen Buddhism
does not just call for living a new simple life in nature or a life of just
enjoying the aesthetic fruits of extinguishing Tanha. Zen Buddhism
remains a part of Mahayana Buddhism accenting the compassion of the
Buddha. As part of liberated Zen, Buddhist life is participation in a continual project of social transformation.[234]

There are many ways in which such participation can be carried
out. Some persons may remain as teachers in temples. Others may
grow rice. Others may become artists and poets. Others may live as
professionals or homemakers. Others may join resistance movements
in businesses or governments. Most will combine in their lives many of
these activities: quietly meditating, creating gardens, arranging flowers,
participating in tea ceremonies, writing and reading poetry, chanting

the Sutras. Freedom, peace, joy, beauty, love, and service will be joined together. For most people, it remains a program in progress, letting go of a craving here and a craving there, realizing deeper enlightenment in one area and then in another, living more and more at peace with life and coming to love life more and more.

Hinduism, Buddhism, Taoism, and Chan/Zen are four religious traditions that demonstrate that religious life can remain very much a live option for postmodern thinkers who have moved beyond the metaphysical game of postulating super beings in the hopeless effort to explain why everything is as it is and not otherwise. Reciprocally, the postmodern interpretations of these four Asian religions offered here aim to show participants in these religious ways of life that their faithfulness does not need to carry any metaphysical baggage, and that they will prosper religiously much better without it. In addition, these interpretations hopefully show that these four religions of the world are not competitors with one another. They, and all the differences existing within each of them, are only different historically and socially specific ways of faithfully responding to the infinite otherness inescapably permeating everything that people tend to treat as merely finite. In the next section, an attempt will be made to show that the same holds true in the case of the religions born just east of the Mediterranean Sea: Judaism, Christianity, and Islam.

Section Three

THE ABRAHAMIC RELIGIONS

Encountering what is other to everything that is secularly finite. Hearing the call of this infinite and responding faithfully by constituting a religious form of life, a religious way of thinking, judging, feeling, desiring, expecting, and acting. This is the common core in all the religions of the world. What are the Jewish, Christian, and Islamic religious ways of life? In some ways these three religious ways of life that were constituted by people living on the eastern shores of the Mediterranean Sea are strikingly similar to the religions of Asia. All of them offer alternatives to unjust, nihilistic, despairing, existentially unworkable secular ways of life. The two sets of religious ways of life, however, are also strikingly different. There are four major ways in which they differ.

First, the religions of Asia focused directly and systematically on identifying the inadequacies in ways of life not hearing or responding to the call of the infinite and on how to remove these inadequacies. In the three Middle Eastern/Western religions that claim Abraham as the founder of their religious ways of life, no such systematic treatment is constructed because the focus is on the drama of encountering the infinite and striving to faithfully respond to God's call. This focus on drama rather than analysis and instruction differentiates the Abrahamic religious ways of life from the religions of Asia.

Second, encountering the infinite and responding to its call become such dramatic events because central to that response is the constitution of the infinite as a personal God who is faithfully worshiped and served. Hindus involved in bhakti yoga and Buddhists worshiping bodhisattvas also constitute gods and respond to the call of the infinite by worshiping them, but this is not the defining center of their religious ways of life. Worshipfully constituting the infinite as the God of the Fathers, Yahweh, Elohim, the Father of Jesus Christ, and Allah is the defining center of the Abrahamic religious ways of life.

Third, this worshipful constitution of a personal god is refined over a long period of time. It is vitally linked to the constitution of worshiping religious communities whose very identities are formed by preserving accounts of the dramas of encounters with the infinite and efforts by these communities past and current to respond faithfully to its call. These constituting accounts get preserved in oral traditions and written books, whose recitation, reading, and study are crucial aspects of their constitution of the infinite as God, their worshipful response to the call of the infinite (the revealed voice of God), their constitution of themselves as worshiping communities, and the reconstitution of these communities generation after generation. The differences between these three Abrahamic religious ways of life can be traced back to the different accounts and different books residing at the heart of their faithful responses to the call of God. These three religious ways of life consist of many worshiping practices other than remembering, preserving memories, and reciting and studying these preserved memories, but all of these other practices depend for their constitution and legitimacy on these preserved memories. Although the Vedas, Upanishads, Sutras, and the *Tao Te Ching* function as sacred and at times canonical literature in the Asian religious ways of life, they are radically different from the recorded accounts of religious dramas found in the Bible and the Qur'an.

Fourth, whereas the religions of Asia were constituted by religious people who continually had to resist temptations to permit metaphysical theorizing to corrupt their faithful responses to the infinite otherness of everything finite, this was not a major concern of Hebrews, Christians, and Muslims. Their attention was focused on literature that was narrative drama and poetry and not metaphysical speculation. The poet writing Job may have been warning about not buying into Greek metaphysical wisdom ideas, and the Christian Paul clearly was warning against confusing the religious wisdom of Christian foolishness with the foolishness of Greek metaphysical wisdom. For the most part, however, the religious literature of the Bible and the Qur'an is neither presenting nor refuting metaphysical theories. This is why postmodern thinkers find that they can turn back to such literature as they engage in a revival of religion after the death of the metaphysical god.

Given the centrality of the Bible and the Qur'an in the Abrahamic religious ways of life, two major hermeneutical questions confront the postmodern interpreter of these texts. First, are these texts actually free of metaphysical contamination? In spite of the fondness of postmodern thinkers for portions of the Bible, does the Bible also need to be deconstructively cleansed? Second, how are these texts to be read so as to hear their religious utterances? How is one to deal with the manner in which they originated out of oral traditions, lost written versions, and final written and edited versions of these texts? To what extent must these texts be historically contextualized in order to hear what they are saying? To what extent must one rely upon the work of experts involved in historical and literary criticism in order to do such contextualizing?

The first problem can be stated this way. Although the literature of the Bible and the Qur'an may not be historically linked to Greek metaphysical literature, the question still remains whether they can be treated as containing only metaphysically free religious literature or whether they also contain within them ontotheological aspects not derived from the Greeks. John Caputo thinks this is so in the case of the Bible, given that many of the things said in it appear to be about an all powerful God creating the world and causing supernatural things to happen.[235] It is certainly possible to read the Bible and the Qur'an as containing a great deal of material in which there is some metaphysical or superstitious writing mixed in. The issue is whether these two works have to be read this way. Since they do not contain any systematic presentations of metaphysical theorizing or any debates about the existence of a powerful metaphysical god, it seems reasonable to look for a nonmetaphysical religious interpretation of them, if one can be found. The question then becomes: "What is the religious significance of constituting God as powerful when this is not a matter of asserting the existence of a metaphysical being causing things to happen, but is instead a matter of faithfully responding to the call of the infinite other of everything finite. Caputo himself seems to give the answer to this question when he treats the word "God" as the name of what religious persons in these traditions take to be the unconditional goodness of life, that which we love and desire unconditionally, and in that sense is all powerful in determining the quality of their religious way of life.[236]

The second problem deals with the issue of whether these two texts need to be contextualized in order to be interpreted as literary aspects of a religious response to the call of the infinite. Given that they apparently have very complex histories of birth, moving from oral status to written status to edited status to translated status, it is useless to attempt to describe the intentions involved in the original speech acts that produced them. Searching for original intentions is fruitless and irrelevant. The question is: What do these texts mean to the people reading them? One need not deny that these texts have appropriated a great deal of nonreligious material circulating during the centuries when they were written. Some of those materials may have been expressions of beliefs in supernatural, powerful beings. What is at issue, however, is whether and how these materials were used as literary parts of faithful responses to calls of the infinite other of all beings, natural or supernatural. What is at issue is whether the Bible and the Qur'an can be read as parts of such faithful responses and can serve as religious instruments of the call of the infinite, with such reading itself being a part of the reader's faithful response to the call of the infinite. The interpretations contained here attempt to show that this is possible. The Bible and the Qur'an can maintain their canonical status in our postmodern age after the death of the metaphysical god.

The Bible is a whole set of different orally communicated utterances and written and edited documents. Many of the writers and editors of these documents were people who had religiously listened to the oral traditions and had religiously read parts of the Bible and the Qur'an written before their time. When the great epics were written about the dramas of Abraham, Moses, and the occupation of the promised land, their writers were listening to the accounts of these dramas that had been orally transmitted. The later Hebrew religious dramatists, poets, and prophets heard or read these epics before saying what they had to say. The Christian writers knew the Hebrew Bible and the orally circulated religious accounts of the life, death, and resurrection appearances of Jesus Christ. When Mohammed let himself be used so that the infinite might speak the words of the Qur'an through him, he did so as one who had been listening to what the Bible had to say.

These oral and written texts are inescapably tied to the historical, social, and cultural contexts in which they were spoken or written. Hebrew, Greek, and Aramaic languages were used, not Chinese or Japanese. The words were produced at specific times when they had specific uses. They were produced against a dateable background of nonlinguistic practices and shared taken-for-granted presuppositions. They may be literary forms of faithful responses to encounters with the infinite, but they are not the infinite; they are finite, historical, and socially and culturally situated. Using the work of literary and historical interpreters of these texts is helpful, even crucial, to being able to read them religiously as religious responses to the call of the infinite. The texts themselves provide these historians with some of the best evidence for reconstructing the context in which they were produced, but historians also use other forms of archeological and historical evidence. Having some interpretation of these contextual settings is needed if one is to interpret these texts. One need not resolve all the unfinished debates in the literary and historical critical study of these works, but one cannot hear anything from these texts if one does not contextualize them.

Claiming that one is just going to listen to the Bible and the Qur'an, without deliberately locating them in a historical context is placing them in the context of one's own unexamined presuppositions. This means that one is not hearing what they have to say, but is merely reading into them what one's presuppositions allow them to say, presuppositions that might be very metaphysical, superstitious, and oppressive. The interpretations offered below are being made while operating on the conviction that they can and should be interpreted religiously, and they will be based on efforts to historically and linguistically contextualize them in the way that seems most justified, given this writer's lack of historical and textual expertise and dependence on the work of the experts with which I am familiar. Some experts most likely will challenge some of these contextualizations. The effort here to contextualize and interpret is grounded on the conviction that better accounts of these contexts may modify but they will not nullify the religious significance of these texts. Historical and literary studies by themselves will not introduce the metaphysical contamination that is the real threat to understanding their religious meanings. The interpretations offered here will attempt to show the powerful religious significance of these texts when they are interpreted without any ontotheological or superstitious presumptions or entailments. What is religiously crucial are the religious ways of life they make possible. This is Kierkegaard's great insight and the reason why he never feared that objectivitistic historical study could threaten the Christian's religious modes of subjectivity.

The story of the three Abrahamic religions is, as has been stated, the story of people giving to themselves religious personal identities by constituting religious communities, prophetically critiquing the shortcomings in these communities, and then reforming and reconstituting them. Islam grew out of its critique of what it saw as the Jewish and Christian religious traditions existing in the sixth century, traditions that it found inadequate to meet the needs of the people living in Arabia. The Islamic critique found its voice in what the community of Muslims took to be the pronouncements that Mohammed transmitted to them, having heard them when listening to the voice of the infinite, which bore in the Islamic religious world the name of "Allah." Like all reformation movements, it preserved within itself many Jewish and Christian traditions. Christianity grew out of its interpretation of what it saw as Hebrew and Jewish religious life. Much of what it saw it liked and appropriated, but some of it was seen as corruptions of authentic religious life and was rejected. In particular, it appropriated the Jewish hope for a suffering-servant messiah and found this hope fulfilled, first, in its resurrection faith in Jesus as humanity's savior and Christ and, second, in its constitution of the Christian church as the living body of Christ filled with his messianic spirit.

All three religious communities look back with religious eyes to the figures treated in the Hebrew/Jewish tradition as the persons who constituted its historically developing religious community out of faithful responses to encounters with that which is other than anything merely finite. All three look back to Abraham and Moses. All three communities ground their religious identities in the telling and retelling of religious narratives about their communities' religious histories. Judaism maintains its identity through three religious narratives (the JEP epic of life from Abraham to Moses, the Deuteronomic history tracing events from the occupation of Israel to the fall of Judah, and the Chronicler's history of exile in Babylon and the return under Ezra and Nehemiah to establish Judaism as a worshiping community). Christianity preserves in the synoptic gospels and the book of Acts religious narrations of the life of Jesus and the founding and spread of the Christian community. Islam provides a religious narration of the life of Mohammad and the early spread of Islam. Although these narratives at first lived only as religious oral traditions, eventually they were written down and in many cases edited and re-edited. To these written narratives were added written versions of other religious utterances: the sayings of prophets, the psalms used in worship, poems, letters by Christians, apocalypses, and what Mohammad spiritually heard. Reading, interpreting, and expounding these texts became religious practices central to the identity of these communities. These faiths became religions of the book: the Hebrew Bible for Jews, the Old and New Testaments for Christians, the Qur'an for Muslims.

One cannot understand these three religious ways of living without developing one's own religious interpretations of these texts, even as participants in the three traditions worship through the use of these texts. It is crucial, therefore, to remind ourselves of two things pointed out in section one. First, these are religious texts and not metaphysical texts. Religious talk about Yahweh, Elohim, God the Father, and Allah is to be interpreted as talk that is part of a religious response to encounters with the nonfinite otherness of what nonreligious people treat as finite beings. Second, it must be remembered that the literal meaning of what is said in these texts is a literal religious meaning. Only when literal meaning gets identified with the meaning of nonreligious narratives or science do we end up trapped into either reading these texts as superstitious explanations or magical claims that conflict with historical and scientific scholarship and knowledge or as metaphorical or allegorical presentations of metaphysical, sociological, or psychological claims. These religious narratives might provide nonreligious historians with data to be included in their stories, but it is crucial not to try to reduce the religious to the nonreligious by refusing to let this religious use of language keep its religiously literal meaning.

In the interpretations of these three religions that follows, no attempt will be made to participate in the huge industry of debating alternative interpretations of the Bible and the Qur'an.[237] All that will be attempted will be to offer a postmodern interpretation of these religious texts as faithful verbal responses by Hebrews, Israelites, Jews, Christians, and Muslims to their encounters with the infiniteness of themselves and the worlds in which they live. The aim is to show that people living in a postmodern world after the death of the metaphysical god can be faithful participants in these three great religions. The aim is to show that these religious communities can sustain themselves and prosper even more once they themselves cry out, "The metaphysical god is dead. Long live Yahweh, the resurrected Christ, Allah. Long live the Hebrew/Jewish community of the exodus. Long live the Christian resurrection community. Long live the world of Islam."

1. Judaism

In order to understanding the Hebrew/Jewish religious way of life (mode of subjectivity) it is necessary to interpret the biblical material that both bears witness to that way of life and was involved in its formation and preservation. In the interpretation offered here, attention will be focused on how this way of life is constituted by remembering the epic that dramatically presents the founding moments of the Hebrews as a religious community, the creation and paradise accounts added as preludes to this epic, the covenant renewal ceremonies that made the liturgical remembering of these founding dramas the means for keeping this way of life alive generation after generation, the psalms that functioned in Hebrew worship ceremonies, the judgements offered by prophets on the implications of the failures of the Hebrew people, the reformation movements within the Hebrew/Jewish communities, the messianic call to the Jewish people, the worship practices establishing Judaism after the return of the Jews from slavery in Babylon, and the defense of religious wisdom over secular wisdom. No attempt will be made to offer interpretations of anything like the entire Hebrew Bible or the Old Testament of the Christian Bible. The variety of textual materials chosen for interpretation here are done so that it is possible to show that many different portions of these Bibles can be interpreted in a postmodern manner, that is, without tying them to beliefs in or presuppositions of the existence of a metaphysical god, a supernatural ultimate cause. Of course, many not-unjustified interpretations different from this one can be produced by other postmodern thinkers. The goal here is simply to show that at least one such interpretation is possible. The interpretations offered here attempt to show that although the Jewish religious way of life is as complex as the biblical literature that gives it life, still it is manifesting the same core features of all the world religions. It consists in rejecting the adequacy of any purely secular history, nature, social order, joy, or suffering. It consists in responding prayerfully, worshipfully, ethically to the call of the infinite, constituted as God, so that people can be liberated from treating anything as absolute or ultimate, as an idol to be served unconditionally, and so that people can live with religious joy and hope no matter what is happening.

The place to begin this interpretation of the biblical material is with the epic that sets forth a dramatic account of the founding moments of the Hebrew/Jewish community and way of life. This is no easy thing to do. One must start with the final version edited by captive Jewish priests in Babylon in the sixth century BC, go back to the text written in the late eighth century that these editors took with them to Babylon, go back to two versions of the epic written by different people in the mid-tenth and early ninth centuries, and then go back to the oral accounts of this epic that circulated for hundreds of years before anything was written down and after the events dramatized in the epic. No attempt will be made to check out whether the events depicted in the epic are accurate representations of the religious encounters and responses of the founders of this religious community. Not only must we remember everything Derrida has taught us about the non-existence of presences that can be represented by texts, but we must understand that it is the oral traditions and texts themselves that are the instruments by which these religious communities continually reconstituted themselves and that religious way of life we are trying to understand. It is on the text itself and the context of its production that we must focus.

At each stage of the construction of the final text, people located in different historical settings and working against backgrounds of different presuppositions are linguistically producing and reproducing parts

of the epic's final narrative. Understanding this epic and thus understanding the religious way of life creating the text and being sustained
by the text requires working through the stages of its development,
historically contextualizing these stages, and interpreting what the epic
is saying about the founding of the Hebrew/Jewish religious way of life.
The focus will be on what the epic means to those religiously writing
and reading it. Let the story begin.

While in exile as slaves in Babylonia, after the southern kingdom
of Judah had been conquered and destroyed by Nebuchadnezzar at the
end of the sixth century BC, a Jewish priestly writer (or more probably,
a group of writers) produced an edited, redacted version of the great
epic written earlier, a text carried by Jews into exile with them. This "P"
edition composed in Babylon incorporated an older written version
of the epic material that had been preserved in priestly circles, and it
added to the epic religious interpretations of ancient religious material
(paradise and creation stories) circulating in Babylonian. The version of
the epic that the priestly editors in Babylon worked with had itself been
written around two hundred years earlier. After the fall of the northern
Kingdom of Israel in 721 BC, an editor in Jerusalem in the southern
kingdom of Judea worked with a text that had combined into one
religious epic two separate written versions of the religious narrative of
the history of the Hebrew people, versions that appropriated material
that had been circulating through oral transmission for hundreds of
years before being written down. One version had been written in the
north and one in the south. There was a great deal of overlap of appropriated material, but each written version included some material not
contained in the other.

The northern version of this epic had been written soon after the
division of David's and Solomon's empire into northern and southern
halves (around 900 BC). The southern version had been written down
a little bit earlier during the height of David and Solomon's reigns
(1000-922 BC). The two writers used different words to name their god
(Yahweh in the south and Elohim in the north) and thus these two texts
have become known as the Yahweh text and the Elohim text. (Because
German scholars studying these texts used the name "Jehovah" for
Yahweh, these two texts now are called the "J" and the "E" texts, with

the priestly edition in Babylon being called the "P" edition.) The unification of the two texts around 700 BC is now called the "JE" text. The Jerusalem editor (or again, editors) after 721 BC added to the JE text a primordial paradise and fall story As stated earlier, although biblical scholars may disagree about the accuracy of the details in this historical account, this and any similar historical contextualization will serve the purpose of helping us to recognize that this biblical dramatization of the life of the biblical community is a historically, socially, and culturally specific linguistic aspect of a people's religious response to the call of the infinite.

Not only did the material in the northern and southern texts circulate at the oral level for centuries before they were written down, but at the oral level many of the pieces combined into this epic circulated as separate religious stories, songs, credo confessions, instructions, and liturgies. In addition and most importantly, although these two oral versions of the epic center their attention on the exodus of the Hebrews from slavery in Egypt and their development as a tribal confederacy before its unification into David's empire, they also include much earlier orally preserved accounts of the religious status of the Hebrew people prior to their enslavement in Egypt. These accounts accent Abraham's constitution of the Hebrews into a community whose identity stemmed from focusing their worshipful response to the infinite on one named in the tradition only as the God of the Fathers.

To understand, therefore, the encounter by the Hebrews, Israelites, and Jews with the infinite and to understand their faithful responses to these encounters, let's turn to this multilayered religious epic. Having done this, we can then move on and turn to the religious critiques of the faithlessness of people supposedly in this community of the faithful. These critiques are already present in the J and E narratives, but they become the central focus in the Deuteronomic history, in the written record of the works of the Prophets, and in the book of Job. Finally, we can look at Jewish worship in the period after the exile in Babylonia, especially at the much older songs and prayers collected at that time in the book of Psalms. We will leave to last a look at the religious significance of the wisdom literature and the apocalyptic work, Daniel.

The JE narrative is a religious narrative of the history of a religious people. Different interpreters of the three Abrahamic religious ways of life have accented different aspects of this narrative as the focal point around which these ways of life are centered. Merold Westphal accents the creation stories, charging that claiming that God is a creator God is a necessary condition of all authentic forms of the Jewish, Christian, and Muslim faiths.[238] Derrida identifies the Abraham-Isaac sacrifice story as most central to these three religious ways of life.[239] Caputo attends only to the creation, paradise, and Abraham-Isaac stories in the epic [240] The biblical scholar, Bernard W. Anderson draws upon many forms of literary evidence to support the claim shared by many other biblical scholars that it is the exodus that functions as the axle around which the epic turns.[241] The interpretation offered here, accenting as it does the importance of interpreting biblical texts for understanding the Abrahamic religious ways of life, will go with Anderson and the need to interpret the narrative by looking from the event of the exodus back hundreds of years to Abraham and then back towards primordial time, and then to look forward from the exodus toward life in the promised land, culminating with the reigns of David and Solomon.

Although it probably is Moses and the Hebrews delivered from slavery who constituted Yahweh and Elohim as the God they would worship, in the JE narrative the Hebrews enslaved in Egypt already were a religious people, faithful to the God constituted as that of the Hebrews by Abraham and the other legendary patriarchs. Even though JE has Moses introduce Yahweh as the name of the Hebrew God, JE identifies Yahweh with the God of Abraham, Isaac, and Jacob, and thus the epic narrates the life of one continual religious community whose identity stemmed from living faithfully to this one God. JE views Moses as someone reconstituting what Abraham had constituted, the Hebrew way of life centered on the worship of this one God. Thus, prior to examining the drama of Moses and the exodus, it is necessary to examine the epic's tale of the dramatic events surrounding the event of Abraham entering into a covenantal relationship with his God. As already mentioned, the JE narrative also has another prelude, this one dealing with a primordial time before even Abraham. This prelude shows that humans, were it not for their unfaithfulness to the call of the infinite (God), would live in a paradise of joy. Finally, we need to keep in mind that the P editor of the

JE text adds a third prelude, a creation story which shows that nothing is merely finite, because everything finite points to the nonfinite without which it cannot be anything. In this great epic, therefore, thankfulness for their very existence becomes a part of Abraham's response to the call of his God and Moses' response to the call of Yahweh/Elohim.

This interpretation of the JEP epic will begin by looking first at its treatments of Abraham, then secondly, its treatment of Moses and the exodus, and it finally will turn its attention to the incorporation of paradise and creation materials. While following this plan of initial interpretation, it will always be necessary to keep in mind that the various parts of this epic are hermeneutically interconnected. The account of Abraham may have to be reinterpreted in the light of what is learned from interpreting the account of Moses and the account of primordial times. The account of primordial times may have to be reinterpreted in the light of interpretations of the narrations dealing with Abraham and Moses. The account of Moses may have to be reinterpreted in terms of the interpretation of primordial history. It must be remembered that the authors of this epic had all parts of the epic before them as they constructed the narrative, even as Shakespeare had the final scenes of *Hamlet* in mind when he wrote the opening scenes.

The epics treatment of Abraham begins with a group of nomadic, gypsy-like shepherds tagging along with the Ammorite migration from the Arabian desert into the agriculturally rich valleys of Mesopotamia during the eighteenth century BC While moving along the fertile crescent from the lower Tigris-Euphrates Valley (the city of Ur) to the southern part of Canaan along the Mediterranean, this extended family of nomads, under the leadership of Abraham, constituted themselves as a people whose very identity came from their unique form of religious faithfulness. In Genesis 15, JE tells of Abraham entering into a very personal, covenantal relationship with what was encountered as totally other than anything perceptible in waking life, as what filled Abraham with dread and darkness. This covenant is to be with the God who will be the patriarchs' focal point of thankfulness and hope, with what will be named at first only as the God of Abraham, Isaac, and Jacob. In this covenant, Abraham and his family constitute themselves as a religious community by pledging to worship only this one God they have constituted, who will be for them the faceless face of the infinite. Covenanting to worship only one God, this God becomes for them the one and only God. Through such worship they express their trust that a spiritually bountiful future awaits them and their posterity because of their worship and loyalty. As we have seen, the JE epic interprets the Abraham oral tradition by viewing it through a series of historical periods, the David-Solomon empire, the tribal confederacy, the occupation of Canaan, and the exodus from slavery in Egypt. The epic's narration of the religious achievements of the Hebrew people allows the epic to show that Abraham's trust was not in vain.

The J tradition in Genesis 18:16–33 tells the reader that Abraham wrestled with the ethical implications of his faithful worship of his God. Abraham shows that he knows that worshiping his God requires combating injustice, which causes suffering to both the just and the unjust. However, he wonders whether it is right, whether it is his God's will, to cause suffering to some people in order to combat injustice being done to other people, especially whether religiously righteous people should be harmed in this effort to fight injustice. The epic makes this point by having Abraham spiritually draw near to his God and question whether any number is too large to make unjustified such a sacrifice. (fifty, forty-five, thirty, twenty, ten). Put into Levinas's language, the epic writer senses that faithfully responding to the call of the infinite through worship of one's God cannot conflict with the ethical obligation one incurs when encountering the infinite in the face of another, in the singular ethical uniqueness of another, especially the face of a religiously righteous person who poses no threat to anyone else.

The E tradition in Genesis 22:1–18, in the narrative dealing with Abraham and his son Isaac, illustrates how radical indeed is the faithfulness that encounters with the infinite calls forth from us. This is the narrative that Derrida claims is central to all the Abrahamic ways of life. The narrative here makes two extremely important points. First, religious faithfulness takes precedence over adherence to any nonreligious social norms. This is the great event that opens up a new religious horizon of possibilities above all secular horizons, which Caputo accents. Second, religious faithfulness never calls for violating the obligation not to kill or harm that is integral, as Levins would put it, to encountering the nonfinite singularity of the face of another. Abraham hears two calls from his God that encompass these two crucial aspects of remaining faithful to one's God. The two seem to conflict with each other. It seems as though one must be sacrificed in order to remain faithful to the other. The E narrative shows that the conflict is only apparent. There seems to be a conflict only because social morality is being confused with the ethical responsibilities one has when encountering the non-social, singular uniqueness of people.

Every socially constituted morality prohibits murder, although different social worlds have different specifications of what constitutes murder. Also, as E points out, in Abraham's social world nothing is more important to a father than his son, in whom the father's achievements need to historically survive. The first call of the infinite reminds Abraham that unless one becomes a total hostage to one's encounter with the infinite God, then tragically something finite will become one's ruling lord and master—one's social norms or one's attempt to control the future, especially one's own future as one seeks to have one's own offspring carry out one's will after one is dead. Without faithfulness to one's encounter with the what is other than secular, social morality, the ethical sacredness of people will not be guaranteed. Human sacrifice would become justifiable for so many secularly constituted projects. Without faithfulness to one's encounter with the infinite, one will never be able to pass on through one's ethical children what is timelessly valuable. Rather, what one will pass on will prove to be a curse on the world. E portrays Abraham as steadfast in his religious faithfulness in spite of all the irrelevant secular rationales for doing otherwise.

This makes it possible for Abraham to hear the second call that is sounded every time we encounter the infinite in the face of another. He hears his name called, "Abraham." We are called by our proper name, proper to our particularity as one called to meet unique responsibilities. E has Abraham respond in the only way one can faithfully respond to such a call, "Here I am." Here I am, as the singularly unique ethical individual that I am, able to accept all the responsibilities involved in such a response of faithfulness. Abraham then understands what those responsibilities are in the concrete situation in which he finds himself: "Do not lay your hands on the lad or do anything to him." Thus, in the J and E narrative treatments of the Abraham tradition, it is pointed out that from its founding beginning, the religion of the Hebrews is rising above the secular, while also remaining religiously ethical through and through.

The treatment in the JE narrative of Moses as reconstituting the Hebrew people as a religious community basically begins with Moses's condemnation of the slavery of his people in Egypt. The enslavement of the Hebrew people in Egypt was judged to be unjust for at least two reasons. First, people were being used as mere means in order to achieve Egyptian ends. This violates the ethical uniqueness of people as they are, regardless of their social circumstances. Little by little this understanding of the ethical status of people as singular individuals, born out of their experience as slaves in Egypt, will be deepened and expanded until at last the Hebrew people will recognize that all people possess such ethical status, and that their deliverance from slavery in Egypt carried with it the responsibility to aid all people to gain such understanding and to live as ethical persons. Second, slavery was seen as wrong because it prevents the Hebrew people from carrying out the mission that is an intrinsic part of their living faithfully in response to the call of their God. As we have seen, encountering the infinite is intrinsically tied to being obligated to compassionately meet the real needs of all people for similar encounters and faithful responses. The JE narrative is an expression of thanks for the faithfulness of Moses and his followers in Egypt to their encounters with Yahweh, a faithfulness that led to the deliverance of the Hebrews from slavery, faithful actions which neither Moses nor his followers would take credit for because it was their becoming hostages to Yahweh that produced their actions.

Descendants of the Hebrew patriarchs probably tagged along when the Hyksos invaded and occupied Egypt in the seventeenth and sixteenth centuries b.c. JE dramatizes this migration with the accounts of the lives of Jacob and his son Joseph, who prospered because of the protection of the Hyksos (Genesis 37–50). When the Hyksos occupation force was driven out of Egypt, the Hebrews left behind were enslaved for almost two hundred years. JE tells of the rise of a pharaoh who did not know Joseph, and of Moses being raised by the daughter of the very pharaoh enslaving the Hebrews. JE narrates that Moses, finally having "grown up," sees the injustice of this enslavement of the very people he now learns are his people. He actively resists this injustice, thereby placing his life in danger. He goes off into the desert to come to terms with how he should live now that he ethically has awakened. After living with the Midianites and marrying the daughter of one of their shepherd/priests, Moses comes to recognize that he does not belong in the land of the Midianites, because his very ethical identity ties him back to the Hebrews who do not belong in Egypt as groaning slaves. JE, using the common Hebrew image of fire to indicate encounters with the God of the fathers, tells how Moses, at the foot of Mt. Horeb, found in the groaning of his people a voice calling out to him personally, "Moses, Moses," and placing upon him the singularly unique responsibility to lead his people out of slavery. Moses made the faithful response that destined him to a life of service to his people by replying, "Here I am" (Exodus 3:4).

The response by Moses takes its particular form under two influences. Horeb probably was the mountain that was the focal point for the Midianite worship of their God called Yahweh. This is the name that the JE narrative has Moses use in naming the god of Abraham, Isaac, and Jacob, whom he now hears calling out to him. Faithfulness to the god of the patriarchs means accepting the responsibility to constitute and reconstitute the Hebrew people as a community of religiously faithful worshipers. For Moses to be instrumental in doing this, he has to lead the Hebrews out of slavery in Egypt and then re-form them into a community of the faithful. To do that, he has to secure the consent of the enslaved Hebrews for him to be their leader in this project of deliverance and reconstitution. According to JE, Moses recognizes the radical character of his encounter with Yahweh and this call to service. The responsibility it places on his shoulders seems almost too much. "And Moses hid his face, for he was afraid to look at God" (Exodus 3:6). The radicalness of this encounter with the God of the fathers dawns upon Moses in another way. Yahweh, the name of the focal point of Moses's worshipful response to the infinite other to all socially constituted beings, cannot be described with any of the vocabulary used to describe such perceptible objects. How then can Moses aid the enslaved Hebrews to have the name of God, Yahweh, come to mind? How can the nonfinite be indicated using language descriptive of the finite? In his faithful response to the call to serve his people, JE says that Moses hears Yahweh's self-characterization, "I am who I am" (Exodus 3:14).

Moses understands that his God is not this thing or that thing, and it is not describable like all beings are describable. (Yahweh is not a mountain or a statute, and it would never have occurred to Moses to think of Yahweh as a supernatural, metaphysical being.) Yahweh is what Yahweh is. Don't describe Yahweh. Yahweh is too holy to be contaminated by word classifications. Yahweh is other to the whole universe of classifiable beings. Simply let Yahweh be what Yahweh is, nonfinite. Thankfully, worshipfully, just surrender to Yahweh, thereby guaranteeing that one will not unconditionally surrender to any describable being. Just surrender to Yahweh who comes to mind when one ethically encounters face-to-face people in their nondescriptive singularity. Let things happen as they happen when people faithfully respond to Yahweh by accepting the responsibilities that are placed upon people who encounter people face-to-face. Let these happenings not be seen as accomplishments of people without faithfulness, but rather let them be seen as things that Yahweh does through his faithful servants. Yahweh is what Yahweh is, and Yahweh does what Yahweh does. Yahweh is the God of the fathers, the God of the Hebrew people, a people and a God whose very identities are tied constitutively to their faithful covenant relationship with each other, a faithful relationship that requires the Hebrews to accept the responsibility to constitute and continually reconstitute themselves as an ethically religious community. Moses is called to lead in carrying out this responsibility.

J, E, JE, and P construct a narrative about the deliverance of the Hebrew slaves out of Egypt by incorporating many units circulating at the oral level. One of the oldest of these is the Song of Miriam, which JE says Miriam sang as she danced and played timbrels. In this song she thanks and praises Yahweh because "the horse and his rider he has thrown into the sea" (Exodus 15:21). The one emphasis that dominates the narrative of the deliverance of the Hebrews from slavery in Egypt is that this must not be interpreted as an accomplishment of their own of which they can be proud. Thanks must go to what called them and their leaders to be religiously faithful and therefore ethical, even as thanks must go beyond themselves for the very goodness of life. This deliverance from slavery is much more than deliverance from the tyranny of the Egyptians. It is deliverance from everything in their all-too-worldly lives that prevents them from being a community of faithful worshipers and servants of Yahweh. Pride in one's own self-sufficiency certainly prevents one from understanding that one's unique singularity comes not from one's achievements but from the unique set of responsibilities placed on one by one's encounter with others face-to-face.

Praise and thankfulness, offered to Yahweh by the Hebrew people for being enabled to be Yahweh's ethical hostages, is at the heart of Hebrew worship and their religious way of life. The promised land into which liberated Hebrews are invited is indeed a land of joy, but it is a land in which that joy cannot be separated from accepting the ethical responsibilities placed on all people. No earthly powers can prevent the faithful followers of Yahweh from entering this promised land, from replacing earthly horizons with religious horizons of possibilities. Moses and the Hebrews were not the ones really battling Pharaoh and his magicians (Exodus: 7–12:32). The infinite and indescribable otherness of worldly finiteness cannot be enslaved by pharaohs or overpowered by magicians. The JEP narrative shows that cruel and oppressive pharaohs and nonethical magicians who do not acknowledge the call of the infinite for radical humility and compassion always will fail to find bliss in their way of life. Pharaoh admits that he does not know Yahweh (Exodus 5:2), and he refuses to let the Hebrew slaves reconstitute themselves as a worshiping community that accepts the responsibilities intrinsic to worshiping Yahweh (Exodus 5:4–5). The JEP narrative makes Yahweh's deliverance of the Hebrew people from slavery into a life of faithful worship and service the lens through which everything in its narrative is interpreted. Nothing provided the Hebrew people with a better reminder of this than the Passover rite, celebrated generation after generation (Exodus: 12:1–36). Interpreters of the JEP narrative must always focus on this lens when seeking to understand how and why JEP is selecting and ordering the oral materials into its final narrative. It is the lens and not the details from the oral tradition that are viewed through it that makes the religious tradition of the Hebrews what it is.

Once delivered from slavery, Moses faces the daunting task of reconstituting these people into a community whose identity comes through faithful worship and service to Yahweh. This task is accomplished in a number of ways. JE narrates how the Midianite father-in-law priest of Moses, Jethro, meets Moses near the mountain where Moses first accepted the name Yahweh for the one calling him to save his people. Moses hears from Jethro that Yahweh, who saved the Hebrews from slavery and delivered them into the promised land of service, is the greatest possible God, the only proper focus of worship. (Exodus 18:10–12). Returning to the mountain where his earlier awakening to the suffering of the Hebrew slaves led to his encounter with the nondescribable infinite and its call to assume responsibility to serve the mission of saving the Hebrews—Moses now hears a call to reconstitute the Hebrew people as a holy nation of priests worshiping and serving Yahweh (Exodus 19:3–6). Again the call comes from what never can be a conceivable perceptible being, but always remains as a call coming through a thick cloud that prevents the infinite from ever being turned into a worldly (or super-worldly) being (Exodus 19:9). To even try to gaze at some being hidden in the cloud is to show that one is not willing to acknowledge the nonfinite origin of the call, and this guarantees that one will perish religiously (Exodus 19:21). As an instrument for reconstituting the Hebrews as a community of faithful people, Moses sets forth the declaration of independence and the constitutional prescription for faithful service that he hears from the same voice that originally called him to accept his responsibilities. Moses transmits to the Hebrews the ten commandments.

To remain free from slavery and for life in the promised land of joyful service, the Hebrews are to find their very identity as individuals and a community in worship of and service to Yahweh. They are to worship and serve no other god than the greatest possible God, the one who saved them from slavery when Moses let their deliverance be worked out through his faithful response to the call of Yahweh. Nothing that can be descriptively identified, whether it be some describable natural phenomena, some supposedly supernatural magic worker, some king, some nation, or some social institution (even if it be called religious), is to be worshiped as a god. The secular ones are all graven images, and religious ones are icons pointing to the infinite, as Marion points out.[242] Treating them as gods to be worshiped and served will guarantee that one will never be faithfully responding to the call of the infinite God. In order to focus their worship and service, the infinite can be constituted as a personal God, but one always must add a footnote to all such talk that the infinite as God lies beyond all description. This is the insight of the great negative theologies that talk about the indescribable godhead pointed at by the constituted God. The infinite can be constituted as God only through the use of finite, human language, but forgetting that such language only points beyond itself to the unspeakable otherness of the infinite is to end up worshiping one's own conceptual powers and not God or the infinite. Talking religious talk in order to serve one's own vain desires will guarantee that one is not responding to the call of the infinite, and one will be guilty of not meeting one's ethical responsibilities to others. Instead of racing down counterproductive pathways, the Hebrews are called by the infinite to respond faithfully by worshiping Yahweh daily in their faithful service and to worship Yahweh collectively at periodic times in order to maintain the community as a faithful community. The community is called to worship so as to sustain the religious life of its members, whose unique identities result from their encounters with the infinite and whose social identities are derived from their religious functioning in the community of the faithful. Let the name of Yahweh come to mind in one's prayers and praises and not by attempting to make descriptive representations of Yahweh.

Living faithfully, accepting the responsibilities given by encountering people face-to-face, means that people's freedom is only restricted by what is involved in meeting those responsibilities: honoring those who parent us ethically and religiously, not killing others, not stealing, not deceiving, not sacrificing covenanted love relationships for petty sexual pleasures, not desiring what ethically belongs to others (Exodus 20:1–17). Moses surrenders as a hostage to Yahweh so that Yahweh may offer through him the ten commandments as a declaration of independence and a constitution that gives communal identity to the Hebrew people. This constitution was surrounded by supporting religious practices and institutions, icons in Marion's sense of the word: a sacred ark on which the invisible Yahweh was enthroned, located in a sacred tent that went with the Hebrew people wherever they traveled, indicating that Yahweh's call for faithful service always remains with the Hebrew people.

As narrated in JE, Moses found in the ten commandments the basis for reconstituting the Hebrew people as a community whose very identity is tied back to Abraham's community. Another covenant is established between God and the Hebrew people. JE also narrates how difficult it was for Moses and for all the religious voices who came after him in later centuries to keep religious faithfulness flourishing in this community, how difficult it was for this community to rectify its name. The actual community of Hebrews always was a conflicted community, with faithful servants of Yahweh repeatedly finding it necessary to call people back to faithfulness. JE illustrates this problem with its narration of the building of a golden calf, which could be for some of the former slaves the focal point of their worship (Exodus 32–34). This is just one example of the problem of maintaining the communal religious identity of the Hebrews while migrating into Canaan where different religious traditions existed, traditions reflecting their agricultural form of life. There may have been praiseworthy aspects to Canaan religious traditions (Taoist, Zen, and Shinto traditions, for example, accented the need to see the infinite in the natural), but JE focuses on the vain effort by Canaanites and people duped by them to use rituals to acquire power to control nature so as to guarantee agricultural prosperity. By condemning the use of a golden calf, JE is condemning all practices constituting bellhop supernatural magicians as the focal point of their worship and devotion. Yahweh is not a bellhop god. Prayer is not calling down (or up) for room service. Moses's Yahweh calls people to faithfully be delivered from slavery to desires to control the world and to accept responsibility to serve Yahweh by acting to free people from all forms of slavery.

In dealing with the problem of people worshiping false gods and graven images, JE draws out other, extremely important implications of Yahweh worship. JE narrates how Moses comes to hear that the thankful, humbling religious response to inheriting Abraham's trust and to being delivered compassionately from slavery includes recognizing that this compassion involves steadfast loving forgiveness, even for those who do not remain thankful and humble. Just as Yahweh is the name for what in principle cannot be seen with nonreligious eyes, so Yahweh will not be bound by nonreligious human standards of retributive justice or tit-for-tat forgiveness. Yahweh will be be gracious and show mercy on whomever he chooses to show mercy, forgiving iniquity and transgression, even before forgiveness is requested. At the same time, however, as the JE narrative reminds us, actions and practices guilty for being unjust have their consequences, and in karma-like fashion, these consequences continue generation after generation, as people are nurtured and socialized to live with these unjust practices and are constituted to have desires causing suffering (Exodus 33:17–34:7). With its narration of the conversion of Jethro (a non-Hebrew) to Yahweh worship, and with this affirmation of Yahweh's forgiving love, JE is ever expanding the ethical responsibilities of those faithfully responding to encounters with the infinite other to all images.

The writers of J extend this expansion even further in their prelude to the narratives about Abraham and Moses, in which they draw on non-Hebrew oral traditions and about primordial times prior to the ages of Abraham and Moses. In Genesis 2:4–11:32, J provides an analysis of the human situation that is applicable to all human beings. First, people are characterized as having a dual nature. On the one hand, they are dust and when dead will return to dust (Genesis 2:7, 3:21). On the other hand, they are created in the likeness of Yahweh who is unlike any perceptible physical being, whose name came to Moses's mind when he encountered the suffering of his people and when he was called to take responsibility for serving as an instrument of their liberation. J is saying that people are finite, like dust, and infinite, with their unique particularity being determined by their ethical lives of encountering people face-to-face and of being under infinite responsibility to deliver them from the many forms that slavery and suffering take.

Second, people are characterized as individuals who have "original" natures very similar to that which is described in Buddhism. People would be living in a paradise Garden of Eden, filled with joyful love of life (eating from every tree, enjoying every fruit of such living), and without alienation from others (even the great sexual difference is founded on ethical sameness) (Genesis 2:8–25), if only they had not messed things up. What people are in their primordial suchness is marvelous, but people refuse to let themselves be simply what they are. People refuse to be physically finite and yet singularly unique and infinite because of ethical worth and responsibilities. People throw away what is primordially theirs because they refuse to respond faithfully to the call of the ethical infinite in the face of others and thus to live bound to the unlimited responsibilities one has to all other people. Instead, people constitute secular social norms that supposedly enable them to know how to live; social norms grounded in desires for controlling power, a superior sense of self-worth, and the social approval of others; social norms which cause them to feel shame when they think others know they have not lived up to these social standards (Genesis 3:1–7). Having rebelled against the call of the infinite for faithfulness to our ethical responsibilities, we even try to deny that we personally are responsible for this rebellion and try to excuse our action by blaming someone else: "The smake made me do it" (Genesis 3:8–13).

As an inevitable consequence of our rebellion, paradise is lost, and our lives are filled with suffering (Genesis 3:6–19). Appreciating the ethical sameness of brothers gets replaced by murderous efforts to destroy those who are different: sheep herders versus tillers of the land (Genesis 4:1–17). Seeking to be towering masters of the world, constituting social worlds of our own, and treating these worlds of Babel as self-sufficient and totally exhaustive rather than accepting our ethical condition as hostages with unlimited responsibilities to all people, regardless of their different places in different social worlds, we end up imprisoning ourselves in our social worlds, unable to understand or respect people with different social inheritances (Genesis 11:1–9).

The J narrative, as edited by P, says that human corruption is so deep and so widespread that it might be best to wipe out the whole world constituted by rebellious people and let some person of faith start all over again. Using an old oral tradition incorporated also in the Summerian "Epic of Gilgamesh" (2000 BC), JEP make this point in the narrative of Noah and the flood (Genesis 6:11–9:17). A critical part of the narrative, however, lies in the message of hope that appears with the rainbow at the end of the story. Abraham's trust in the religious fruitfulness of faithfulness and Moses's reception of the message of steadfast love and mercy even for the unfaithful, get reemphasized as Noah enters into a new covenantal relationship with Yahweh, and the promise to Abraham is read back as the primordial promise to Noah.

The P editor of the JE narrative adds a prelude to J's prelude, which expands beyond the encounters of Abraham and Moses with their constituted God, so that now everything in nature becomes an icon pointing to the infinite, so that all of nature is seen as being what it is only because of its relation to the infinite (Genesis 1:1–2:3). When lived with religiously, nature is not what it is when viewed nonreligiously. Taoism, Zen, and Shinto have their ways of proclaiming the religious attitudes we should take toward natural phenomena. P uses the language of creatures being created to proclaim that a nonreligious approach to the natural elements that bring us such joy and awesome beauty will not produce the thankfulness and humbleness needed to prevent us from using nature as mere raw materials servicing our passion for power and control. P's prelude helps us see nature as having significance that is other than the value we place on what we secularly constitute socially to satisfy our cravings. There is an infinite otherness to the sun, moon, and stars; to the earth; to all living things; to all people. It is this undescribed and indescribable otherness that gives them their original suchness, prior to and apart from our categorization schema. One lives in faithfulness to this other when one lives thankful for the goodness of all things in their original suchness, prior to being touched by human rebellion and self-enslavement, prior to being socially constituted as items falling under our classification vocabularies. This prior-ness expresses the religious priority of things in their suchness to things cravenly constituted by us in our will to power. It is true that P declares that people are authorized by God to live by means of natural creatures (have dominion over them), but this is an authorization given to people living faithfully with thankfulness and respect, for people who will be stewards over what is given as a gift so as to meet their ethical responsibilities to deal justly with all other people in all generations.

In order to understand P's creation story, there is no need to introduce metaphysical notions of ultimate causes or first moments of time. There is no need to talk about an all-powerful, supernatural being creating the natural world out of nothing. As Caputo points out, the theological doctrine of *creation ex nihilo* did not arise until the second century AD by thinkers who thought they had to defend metaphysically the biblical narrative of creation against the metaphysical claims of the gnostics.[243] The gnostics had claimed that the metaphysical god's omnipotence excluded the possibility that there could be uncreated materials, something they thought was asserted in P's creation stories when it is said that land, water, and wind are there before God forms them into a cosmos. There was no need to engage in such a metaphysical debate. The crucial religious point is that P is proclaiming that the cosmos with its formed materials is good, and that responding to the call of God is to consist of offering thanks for the goodness of life.

P adds more than a creation story to the JE narrative. Besides editorially working out linkages between the J and E versions of the narratives about the patriarchs and the exodus, this priestly work folds into the narrative an understanding of the liturgical worship practices and specific community regulations that century after century added daily solidarity to the Hebrew community.[244] Again and again, people heard together the same liturgical blessing, "Yahweh bless you and keep you: Yahweh make his face to shine upon you, and be gracious to you: Yahweh lift up his countenance upon you, and give you peace" (Numbers 6:24–26). Some of these practices have lived on for thousands of years, and their observance still provides the Jewish community with its ongoing religious identity. Whereas the ten commandments functioned as constitutional authority in the community, these further specifications of worship routines and moral codes functioned as case law, with the past standing as precedents that need to be creatively applied and augmented as circumstances change. They were binding only on members of the Hebrew community and always subject to constitutional interpretation. In spite of its accent on later temple and priestly life, the P edition further amplifies the ethical focus that dominates Moses's encounter with Yahweh. P narrates that Moses tells his people that faithful worship of Yahweh requires providing food for passing strangers, aiding the blind, treating the poor and the rich equally, not taking vengeance, and loving one's neighbor as oneself (Leviticus 19:9–18). Moses's encounter with the ethical infinite always determines the authority and applicability of Aaron's priestly injunctions.

JEP provides the religious framework within which all other Hebrew and Jewish narrators, prophets, and poets will express their faithfulness in their writing. Judaism is the religion of a community founded on the faithful responses of Abraham and Moses to their encounters with the infinite. It is founded on a loyalty to that which is other than any secularly constituted norms, on a trust that such loyalty will give birth to a religious family rewarded with spiritual lives of milk and honey. It is a community united by mutual covenanting to have one unique, indescribable focal point of religious worship and service, one God. It is a community founded on an encounter with the infinite ethical significance of all people, even slaves, and on a faithful response to this call from the infinite, now named Yahweh, a faithful response of accepting the responsibility to be a vehicle through which people can be delivered from spiritual enslavement because of desires for power. It is the religion of a community freed and bound by the memory of its exodus from slavery and into the promised land of spiritual rejoicing and service, and bound by a constitution requiring it to not give supreme loyalty to anything secular and finite, and by those ethical responsibilities necessary for communal religious life. It is a religion founded on an understanding of the joyful, harmonious life that would be everyone's if their cravings for power were not to prevent them from recognizing their encounters with the infinite. This original way of life always remains as an open option if one permits oneself to be delivered from spiritual slavery. At the end of the rainbow one finds not a pot of social currency, but a messianic promise always open to fulfilment. It is a religion grounded in confessions of guilt for what we have done with our human lives, and it is a religion which understands that mercy and compassionate forgiveness are always available. It is the religion of a people united within a self-imposed discipline of worship and compassion. It is a religion that sings hymns of praise and thanksgiving for things being as the are in their original suchness, that confesses its guilt for corrupting things, and that proclaims its acceptance of the ever-present opportunity to try again to live faithfully.

It is back to the memories preserved in the JEP narrative of its formation that the Hebrew community returned again and again as it took its historical journey from being constituted as a people by

Abraham and as a community by Moses into being a confederation of twelve tribes; into being the united kingdom of Israel under David; into being the divided kingdoms of Israel in the north and Judah in the south; into remaining only as Judah, the southern kingdom, when Israel, the northern kingdom, is destroyed by the Assyrians; into being forced to live as exiles in Babylon as Judah is destroyed by the Babylonians; into being only a worshiping religious community under the political domination of Persians, Greeks, and Romans.

After settling in Canaan, faithful leaders assembled yearly at Shiloh and recited together the narration of how a wandering Aramean started the spiritual journey that took them out of slavery into a land of milk and honey. They finished their recitation by promising again to worship and serve Yahweh (Deuteronomy 26:5–11). At the birth of the twelve tribe confederacy, the leadership of the tribes gathered at Shechem and made a similar narration of their origin as a religious community, and pledged that all of them would remain united in their worship and service to Yahweh, no matter how differently they would exercise their autonomy as separate tribes in the confederacy (Joshua 24). The same memory is invoked when Saul and David transform the confederacy into a united kingdom and empire. Samuel recites the narrative of the exodus before he agrees to anoint Saul as king in order to remind the people and Saul that they must continue to serve Yahweh (I Samuel 12:1–15). When David wants to consolidate his power by centralizing all worship of Yahweh in a new temple in the city of Jerusalem, which had not been under the jurisdiction of any of the twelve tribes, Nathan reminds David of the history of the exodus and the confederacy when Yahweh tabernacled in a tent that could be pitched anywhere. Around 621 BC, after the land of the ten northern tribes had ben turned into Assyrian provinces, King Josiah of Judah instituted sweeping reforms to try to drive out all influences from Assyrian religion. He summoned the people of Judah and Jerusalem to the temple Solomon had built in Jerusalem for a ceremony of covenant renewal at which he read an ancient book (probably Deuteronomy 12–26), which most likely goes back to Northern covenant renewal ceremonies at Shechem where the exodus narrative was repeated. (2 Chronicles 34:14–33). When Ezra returned to Jerusalem after the exile in Babylonia, he collected the people together in Jerusalem and carried out another covenant renewal ceremony, reading all morning to them from the JEP narrative edited by priests while in Babylonia. The narrations by J, E, JE, and JEP of the religious encounters by the patriarchs and Moses that resulted in Yahweh worship have always remained as the foundation of the religion of the Hebrews, Israelites, and Jews and at the center of their religious ways of living.

Filled with the spirit of Yahweh, prophets appeared whenever the Israelites were failing to remain faithful to Yahweh, criticizing those failures and striving to replace faithlessness with faithfulness. By interpreting these prophetic texts, we can deepen our understanding of what such faithfulness means. Some of the prophets will accent the need to trust in religious faithfulness rather than political and military strategies. Some will stress the acceptance of the ethical responsibilities to all people who Moses found to be at the core of Yahweh worship. Some will accent the openness of the future for new lives of faithfulness, no matter how rebellious people have been in the past. Some will proclaim that faithful service to Yahweh requires surrendering oneself to the mission of aiding all people to gain liberation from spiritual slavery. Some will proclaim that remaining faithful to Yahweh through all the suffering that others cause will in fact be a successful tactic for providing aid for them to carry out their spiritual-liberation mission. Consider the following prophetic mosaic.

Elijah, a semi-nomadic Tishbite living on the edge of the desert, went up to the capital of Israel in the eighth century BC and condemned kings Omri and Ahab for entering into entangling alliances with the Phoenicians and Syrians against the Assyrians, alliances cemented by Ahab's marriage to Jezebel, the daughter of a Phoenician king. Through this marriage Ahab permitted the introduction of the worship of Baal and the mother goddess, Asherah, which Elijah saw as a rejection of faithfulness to Yahweh in favor of social practices and myths serving the human craving to control everything (1 Kings 17–19, 21:17–29) This Phoenician religion was part of a widespread cultural phenomenon throughout the agricultural regions of the fertile crescent, worshiping Osiris and Isis in Egypt, Tammuz, and Ishtar in Babylonia, and Baal and Asherah in Canaan. Elijah's objection is not that this tradition finds a sacredness in the cycles of nature. He still affirms that nature is Yahweh's creation. Elijah's objection to Baal worship is that through its ritual sexual practices it seeks to exercise power over the agricultural fertility of the earth. Elijah not only shows that such rituals have no power, but he shows that Yahweh worship does not feed people's craving to have total control over nature. Rather, it calls for people to humble themselves so as to let nature live in its original suchness. It calls for people to be thankful for the joy of living with the natural elements and to surrender as a hostage to their ethical responsibilities to respect people in their singular uniqueness. Yahweh cannot be likened to agricultural products that die in the fall and come back to life in spring. Yahweh cannot be pictured by any graven image, because those who have encountered the infinite through their worship of Yahweh hear only the voice of stillness through which Yahweh speaks (1 Kings 19:11–13).

Moses's mission began when he awoke to the suffering and enslavement of his people in Egypt. Amos's mission began when (around 650BC), as a shepherd and farmer living near Jerusalem, he awoke to the economic oppression of poor people in Israel during times of great prosperity under the reign of Jeroboam II. Amos reiterated the intimate relationship between Yahweh and the religious community of Hebrew people living in the southern and northern kingdoms (Yahweh "knew" them as husbands and wives intimately "know" each other [Amos 3:2]. Amos echos Elijah's proclamation that the Syrians, Egyptians, Phoenicians, and Canaanites will suffer the tragic consequences of pursuing power rather than justice (Amos 1:3, 2:3). He warns the northern Israelites not to be tempted into thinking that their current prosperity, and the temporary vacuum of foreign power in the region which seemed to invite Israeli military adventures, indicates that a great "Day of Yahweh" is about to arrive. The Day of Yahweh, that Abraham and Moses promised, is a day of spiritual liberation, a day when the call to accept ethical responsibility is accepted. For Israel with its rampant oppression of the poor, the Day of Yahweh is a day of darkness (Amos 5:18). While the rich possess summer and winter homes (Amos 3:15), lie on luxurious beds of ivory eating lamb and drinking wine (Amos 6:4–6), and become fat cows (Amos 4:1), the poor are trampled upon (Amos 5:11), oppressed, and the needy are crushed (Amos 4:1). The rich use all sorts of deceitful tricks so that the poor must virtually sell themselves to get sandals and even the worst remnants of wheat (Amos 8:5–6).

Amos proclaims that the ethical core of Yahweh worship condemns these rich exploiters who "turn justice to wormwood" and who completely abandon the pursuit of righteousness, which calls for people to seek good and not evil and to establish justice (Amos 5:7, 14–15). Worship of Yahweh is not a matter of simply presenting offerings or singing hymns, but rather is a matter of being faithful to the call, "Let justice roll down like waters, and righteousness like an ever flowing stream" (Amos 5:21–24). The blessing that is a consequence of faithfulness to Yahweh is not the satisfaction of the cravings for power and status that people think comes with monetary wealth and military power. Just as there are no religious rituals that give people the power magically to control nature and agricultural prosperity, so there are no religious ceremonies, supposedly praising Yahweh that give to people the power to guarantee economic prosperity or national power. Yahweh is not that kind of magical, supernatural power. There are blessings that come to those who live faithfully responding to the call of Yahweh, but they are the blessings of living joyfully with the elements and harmoniously with ourselves and one another, blessings that are available to all people regardless of their economic or social status or the position of their nation in international affairs. There is suffering that results when craving desires enslave people, suffering that is self-inflicted by that socially and personally constituted self that hides from us our original nature and its joyous blessings. We receive rewards when we faithfully respond to the call of Yahweh, rewards that are a gift for which we must be thankful and not an achievement of which we can be proud. We suffer when we do not respond faithfully, suffering we bring upon ourselves by closing the door to the joyous living possible when we let things, including ourselves, be what we are, suffering we cause when we live unjustly rather than resist injustice.

Moses encountered the infinite in awakening to the suffering of his people, and it was an ethical infinite that called for people to respond, "Here I am," "Use me to liberate people to seek justice and righteousness." Amos heard the same call, went north to condemn unfaithfulness and injustice, and called for people to return to authentic worship of Yahweh. While accenting the destructive consequences of their betrayal of their religious inheritance, Amos also proclaimed that not even the unfaithfulness of the Israelites can end the process of spiritual liberation that has lived on since the days of Abraham and Moses. The plowman ever sowing new seeds of liberation will always overtake the reaper of the consequences of rebellion and injustice (Amos 9:13). The prophet who makes this promise of hopefulness the cental theme of his work is Hosea.

Speaking forth just after the death of Jeroboam II in 746BC, during a period of palace murders and chaos when Israel had become a vassal state to Assyria and just before Assyria destroyed Israel and resettled the Israelites throughout the fertile crescent, the northerner Hosea echoed Amos's charges of unfaithfulness against Israel; but he emphasized much more strongly that there still is every reason to hope that Yahweh's true blessings will come. Hosea indicts Israel for making empty oaths in their covenant renewal ceremonies (Hosea 10:4). because instead of intimately living with Yahweh there is lying, stealing and murder (Hosea 4:1–2). Like Amos, Hosea points out that his fellow Israelites do not know what worshiping Yahweh is all about. They offer sacrifices rather than steadfast love (Hosea 6:6). Nevertheless, the project of spiritual liberation, begun when Moses surrendered to the call to compassionately deliver his people from slavery, still remains operational. Yahweh is not a destroyer, no matter how much people destroy themselves through their unfaithfulness. Rather, out of love for people's real well-being, Yahweh will remain steadfastly loving and trustworthy (Hosea 2:19, 11:1–4, 8–9). Drawing upon his own experience with his wife Gomer, whom he took back after she had run off to other lovers, Hosea proclaimed that Yahweh would never stop loving Israel but would always work to bring her tenderly into a relationship of faithfulness (Hosea 2:14–23). Accepting the continually open opportunity to be true to one's original self, and to live up to the responsibilities to provide loving care stemming from one's encounter with the ethical infiniteness of people's unique singularity, is all that is required. That, however, is a requirement to give up the self and life constituted by one's cravings for power and status. The opportunity to be delivered from enslaving alienation from oneself and others, even after breaking covenant oaths, is not something to be purchased simply by saying, "I'm sorry." Rather, it is freely available to anyone willing to accept it as an ever-present gift, an acceptance that consists of a radical self-transformation for which one can only say, "thank you."

The judgements leveled by the prophets Elijah, Amos, and Hosea, get repeated by Isaiah and Jeremiah in new historical settings. Speaking from Jerusalem, Isaiah renders his judgements on the northern kingdom of Israel just at the time she is being destroyed by the Assyrians (721BC), and on the southern kingdom of Judah at the time Jerusalem was almost captured by the Assyrians (701BC). Jeremiah's judgements center on conditions in Judah during the final years of its life (626BC–587BC). In each case, the people of Israel and Judah are declared to be faithless perpetrators of injustice who still disastrously crave gaining national power through military alliances. In each case, these prophets reassert what faithfulness to Yahweh requires and that the blessings of spiritual liberation are always available to those who choose to respond faithfully to the call of Yahweh. In addition, each of these prophets has something additional to add to our understanding of what it means to encounter the infinite and to faithfully respond to that encounter.

Like Abraham and Moses before him, when Isaiah hears himself called to serve Yahweh, he replies, "Here I am" (Isaiah 6:8). It is in the temple in Jerusalem that Isaiah encounters the infinite that fills the whole earth with glory. This infinite still remains an ethical infinite. It leads Isaiah to recognize that he, too, is guilty of merely giving lip service to Yahweh. Experiencing the holiness of Yahweh, he recognizes both his faithlessness and the opportunity for service that still is his as his guilt is taken away as irrelevant (Isaiah 6:1–7). He therefore makes his prophetic judgements. He declares that the whole land, north and south, is sick (Isaiah 1:3). People are being oppressed, the needy, the poor, the widows, the orphans are all being treated unjustly (Isaiah 10:2), and bribes lead to the guilty being acquitted and the innocent being left empty handed (Isaiah 5:23). He again points our the ethical character of worship of Yahweh, which does not consist of trying to buy supernatural favors with offerings and incense. Yahweh is calling people to seek justice and to correct oppression (Isaiah 1:13, 17). Worshiping Yahweh means ceasing to think Yahweh will help satisfy military cravings for power; Yahweh wants peace and having swords turned into plowshares and spears into pruning hooks (Isaiah 2:4). Once again Isaiah proclaims that all is not lost because of the unfaithfulness of Israel and Judah. The opportunity for faithfulness always remains open. Just draw out the reasonable implications of the ethical significance of every person, which is more than any social mask can represent, and one can see that the most scarlet of any person's past history of causing suffering does not destroy the snow-white purity of that person's original ethical status and the opportunity it provides for voluntarily surrendering to the call to be compassionate and just (Isaiah 1:18–19).

Furthermore, Isaiah offers the reassurance that no matter how much injustice exists in the land and how much Israel and Judah are threatened by foreign armies, still the righteous will bear the natural fruit of that righteousness (Isaiah 3:10), the joys of simple living with the elements, the peace of harmonious living with oneself and others, and that special joy that comes from compassionately pursuing justice and resisting injustice, a timeless joy that the chanciness of events in life cannot take away. Isaiah trusts that nothing in the future can extinguish the spiritual mission begun by Abraham and Moses. A remnant of faithful worshipers of Yahweh will always remain (Isaiah 10:20–21). A new kind of kingdom of David, a spiritual kingdom of liberated and righteous people, will be established. Out of the spiritual and ethical riches inherited from Abraham and Moses, new children will be born who will father further generations of faithful champions of righteousness and peace. By accepting this inheritance, one will be encountering the infinite who called Moses to be compassionately responsible, the infinite whom Moses named Yahweh (Isaiah 9:6–7). New shoots will sprout from the stump that remains after Israel is destroyed. These shoots will be filled with the spirit of Yahweh, and they will delight in fearing Yahweh, for this is really fear for people who are suffering, a delight and a fear that makes faithfulness to Yahweh constantly meaningful and significant (Isaiah 11:1–5).

Jeremiah's prophetic judgements run through a forty-year period from the time of the Deuteronomic reformation to past the fall of Jerusalem to the Babylonians and the exile of its citizens to Babylon. The same injustices condemned by the other prophets still need Jeremiah's condemnation: oppression, stealing, murder, bearing false witness, and worshiping Baal (Jeremiah 9:6, 7:8). In addition, there are also the practices of the religious leadership in Jerusalem, which he denounces as failures to understand what faithfulness to Yahweh involves. First, there are scribes who claim that they are wise because they are experts at interpreting the many prescriptions for communal life that have developed over the years. Jeremiah, however, charges that they do not understand that Yahweh wants kindness, justice, and righteousness and not simply the feeding of such scholarly pride (Jeremiah 8:8, 9:23–24). Second, he condemns the many false prophets who were appearing during these very troubled times, making a living by telling people, "Don't worry. Everything is going to be all right. Yahweh will save you from the Babylonians" (Jeremiah 2:11, 14:14, 23:16, 27:16). The benefit from faithfulness to Yahweh, however, is not the military defeat of invading armies. Yahweh is not that kind of commander-in-chief. To make this prophetic judgement as clear as possible, Jeremiah proclaims that Yahweh is going to make a new covenant with his people, but this one will be written in their hearts, because it is there that the problem lies(Jeremiah 31:31–34). People have a rebellious heart, and this must be acknowledged before worship of Yahweh is possible (Jeremiah 5:23, 3:13). People crave power to control their lives, and they think they can bribe a supernatural power to satisfy that craving, but Yahweh's voice calls for surrender to a life of justice (Jeremiah 22:3) and the kind of inner peace that worship of Yahweh brings (Jeremiah 7:22, 14:13).

Jeremiah himself did not always experience such peace. There is a troubling religious question that Jeremiah raises, a question born out of his own experience, a question that challenges all faithful servants of Yahweh surrendering themselves to carry out Yahweh's mission of liberating people. Why does the faithful servant of Yahweh, compassionately trying to liberate people from slavery, end up as a laughing stock, being mocked by the very people the prophet is trying to aid (Jeremiah 20:7)? Jeremiah senses that his very identity is tied up with being a prophet carrying out Yahweh's will, an identity that ties him back to the efforts of Abraham and Moses (Jeremiah 1:4–5). He has tried again and again to carry our his unique responsibilities to meet the real needs of the people. People, however, will not listen and change. His efforts seem fruitless, only motivating others to do evil to him, while those he is criticizing seem to gain worldly prosperity (Jeremiah 12:1, 18:20). His sense of failure brings him to curse the day that he was born, suicidally wishing that he never had been born (Jeremiah 20:14–18).

Jeremiah's frustration is understandable, but he does not let it destroy his trust in the always future messianic mission begun by Abraham and Moses. Jeremiah recognizes that the spiritual benefits of faithfulness will not be available to the person who has thrown away a glorious life with Yahweh for what does not profit a person at all (Jeremiah 3:15). Just as the Hebrews suffered under slavery in Egypt, so the people of Judah will suffer when Jerusalem is destroyed and they are carried away into slavery in Babylon. There will be no balm in Gilead (Jeremiah 8:22). This is not a reason for the faithful to despair, however. First, faithfulness to Yahweh makes available absolutely dependable consolation, joyful living, and peace with oneself and others, no matter what Babylonia does, just as it makes these available to the blind, the lame, and those in travail (Jeremiah 31:8–9). Second, the compassionate love that resulted from Moses's encounter with the suffering of his people and his acceptance of the call to serve Yahweh's will (Jeremiah 2: 2-3), now will give rise to new shepherds who will heal the people's unfaithfulness and feed them with living knowledge and understanding of what Yahweh worship really demands and promises (Jeremiah 3:15, 22). Among those who will feel the heavy boot of Babylonian power there will be some who will remain faithful, not despair, and find the peace and joy that boots cannot crush. A remnant will remain and this remnant will be the loving shepherd that people need to permit the new covenant to be written on their hearts (Jeremiah 23:3–4, 31:34). Just as Yahweh worship does not guarantee abundant harvests or military protection, so Yahweh service does not guarantee that this loving service will yield the intended results. Love, however, is not instrumentally motivated. Parents do not love their children only when their children are obedient. To love someone is to place one's relationship to that person beyond price. Worshipers of Yahweh are related by infinite responsibilities, by love, to the singular uniqueness of all people, and that love does not end when the people being loved cover up their uniqueness with social masks serving destructive cravings, and when they reject that love and seek to harm those who love them. Serving Yahweh is serving such love.

"Judaism" is the name coined after the Romans dispersed the Jews in 70 AD, but it traditionally has been applied to their religious way of life after the Babylonians twice deported the rebellious leadership of Judea, first in 597 BC and then again in 587 BC It is the religious of life of the Judeans, the Jews. Only the top leaders of Judea were deported in 597 BC (the king, the priests, the aristocracy), and among them was the priest, Ezekiel. After the second deportation, many Jews migrated because of the harsh conditions under Babylonian rule in Judea, with many going to Egypt. It is with the priests in Babylon, however, that the mission of Yahweh primarily was continued, although now in a very different form. Although life for the Jews exiled in Babylon was quite comfortable, the priests assumed leadership to reconstitute the Jews as a community, now simply a religious, worshiping community. Ezekiel is one of the founding fathers of this new religious community. The Jews will not again be a political community until 1948, when the modern state of Israel is established.

After five years in Babylon, thirty-year-old Ezekiel began his twenty year mission as a prophet to the exiles in Babylon. Echoing the creation story added in Babylonia by the priestly editor(s) of the JE epic, Ezekiel describes his call by Yahweh as a call from above the heavens covering the four corners of the world (Ezekiel 1). Exekiel reports that the spirit of Yahweh, compassionately seeking to deliver people from spiritual slavery and death, enters him, although he is only a "Son of Man" (Ezekiel 2:1–3). He is to be a "watchman" condemning injustice and lack of faithfulness (Ezekiel 33:7). He condemns not caring for widows, taking bribes, extorting, and being false prophets of hope (Ezekiel 22:6–12, 13:2, 17). He condemns those who abandon Yahweh worship and trust their own power and beauty (Ezekiel 6:15). Before the second expulsion, he warned those back in Jerusalem not to do what they did do, conspire with Tyre (the Phoenicians) and Egypt to try uselessly to revolt against Babylonia, because all three national powers eventually would be destroyed (Ezekiel 26:7, 28:2, 29:2).

Ezekiel also proclaims, however, that Yahweh does not want those he loves to die spiritually; he wants them to live and enjoy the spiritual benefits that faithfulness brings (Ezekiel 33:11). Therefore, echoing earlier prophetic words of consolation and hope, Ezekiel proclaims that the hope for deliverance instilled by the faithful responses of Abraham and Moses will not be extinguished (Ezekiel 20:5–7), because the love of Moses's God, Yahweh, will search for his people, be their shepherd, and form a new covenant in their hearts (Ezekiel 43:25, 34:34, 17:60–63). The lives, which have become dead and dry bones because they craved power and the wrong kind of benefits (Ezekiel 37:1–14), will become a worshiping community as they respond faithfully with justice, righteousness, making peace offerings, celebrating the Passover feast, and remembering the Sabbath (Ezekiel 45:9, 46:4). This new religious community will not receive national power or material possessions, but it will receive only Yahweh and the ethical responsibilities and joyous life that Yahweh brings (Ezekiel 44:28). These are benefits that come only by not aiming at them; they come by focusing on worshiping and glorifying Yahweh and the compassionate service he calls forth from his people (Ezekiel 36:22–32). People should not complain that they are suffering the consequences of their leaders' rebellions against Babylonia, because no matter what one's material, social and cultural inheritance is from one's forefathers, one always has the power to let Yahweh deliver one into a spiritual land of milk and honey (Ezekiel 18:2–32, 33:17–20).

A second prophet rose up during the exile in Babylon, and he proclaimed that the very material weakness of the Jews in Babylon and throughout the diaspora and their very suffering would be the instrument by which Yahweh would carry out his mission of spiritually liberating the people. This anonymous prophet, named by scholars "Second Isaiah" because his message is preserved as chapters 40–55 of the book of Isaiah, proclaims the radically ethical character of encounters with and worship of Yahweh, the awesome mission to which his servants must now commit themselves; and he proclaims that his servants are not to be dismayed by the hugeness of the task before them because it is a joyous mission that they are uniquely able to carry out and because it will bear glorious, life-transforming fruits.

Second Isaiah proclaims that the spirit of Yahweh is upon him as Yahweh's servant (Isaiah 41:9), and it will be upon those who respond faithfully in that spirit (Isaiah 42:1). He makes it very clear what that spirit is and what Yahweh is not. Yahweh is not some thing that can be likened to anything that can be seen. He hides himself from sensory vision, and thus all attempts to image him by necessity will be graven (Isaiah 40:18, 42:8, 45:15, 46:5). His spirit is higher and other than any earthly or supernatural being (Isaiah 55:9). His spirit motivated Abraham to trust that his service would produce a community of people delivered from slavery into faithful service, faithful servants for generations and generations (Isaiah 51:1–2). As Moses understood in his encounter with the infinite significance of every unique, particular person, Yahweh helps the poor and needy (Isaiah 41:17), feeds the hungry, houses the homeless, clothes the naked (Isaiah 58:6–7), does not harm but brings justice (Isaiah 42:1–3), opens the eyes of those spiritually blind and locked in their petty, self-constituted prisons (Isaiah 42:6–7), and gives the spiritual water people need to live (Isaiah 43:20). Focusing one's worship on some other type of god cannot save people from spiritual rebellion, blindness, and injustice (Isaiah 43:11).

The new mission for the worshipers of Yahweh is a consequence of their inescapable need to respond faithfully to the ethical call spoken loudly and clearly by every person we meet face-to-face, and by extension to every person they meet face-to-face, and so on throughout all humanity. Second Isaiah proclaims that worshiping Yahweh means being a light to all nations (Isaiah 42:6, 49:6) and singing a new song that will liberate them from spiritual darkness and into joyous and responsible living (Isaiah 42:10). All peoples in all nations are to be empowered to be part of Yahweh's worshiping community (Isaiah 43:9, 45:22). In the wilderness where the worship of Yahweh has not tamed the hearts of people, Yahweh's faithful servants are to build a highway on which anyone, anywhere, can travel from enslavement to joyous milk and honey (Isaiah 40:3).

Yahweh's faithful servants in Babylon are especially well equipped to meet this terrifying and marvelous challenge. Having had Judea conquered and the temple in Jerusalem destroyed, and having to live on as a new religious community in a foreign land, no longer expecting to again have a political empire, has refined the understanding of Yahweh's faithful servants (Isaiah 48:10). Having lost so much, having experienced so much sorrow and grief themselves, they can show that identification with the sufferings of others which is a crucial ingredient in encountering them ethically face-to-face. By their intimate knowledge of suffering and Yahweh's love, these righteous servants can make many others become righteous (Isaiah 53:11). By proclaiming Yahweh's compassion and by being faithful to the call to be ethically responsible to everyone, these suffering servants of Yahweh, despised and rejected by the world, have a chance to enable people to encounter a nonthreatening love, wake up, be delivered from cravings for power and status, become ethically responsible, and live in joy, meaning, and hope (Isaiah 52:1–6). The world might despise those electing to hear the call to build this highway and walk with those who are newly awakened, but to Yahweh their feet are beautiful and all those in his new worshiping community can break into joyous singing (Isaiah 52:7–9).

Second Isaiah's call to all of Yahweh's worshipers to be Yahweh's suffering servants, carrying out this messianic mission of universal deliverance, sometimes seems to suggest that there will be one particular person who will lead them in building this spiritual kingdom (Isaiah 42:1–4, 53:4–6, 10–11). It is suggested that there will be a second Moses, a suffering-servant messiah, savior, who will build a proper spiritual replacement for David's political kingdom. In the centuries that followed, many different groups with a Jewish inheritance came to hold many different ideas about what such a saving messiah would be like and what kind of kingdom this "Son of David" would establish. Many, still longing for a political nation of their own, expected a messiah to arise who would defeat militarily the Hellenists and Romans who later ruled over them. Second Isaiah, however, clearly seems to be talking only about a new spiritual kingdom of Yahweh worshipers that will ignore national boundaries. It is in the early Christian appropriation of Second Isaish that we find the clearest proclamation that the messiah, the suffering servant, the second Moses, the Son of David, is a particular person. Christians will proclaim that Jesus, who after suffering through rejection and crucifixion was resurrected in the hearts and lives of the new Christian community of Jews and non-Jews as their savior, is their Messiah, filling them with the spirit of Yahweh, thus accomplishing what Second Isaiah said was the will of Yahweh.

The Jews in Babylon, when granted permission to do so by the Persian emperor Cyrus, who had defeated the Babylonians, did return to Jerusalem in 538 BC to build a new temple and a new worshiping community. The basic character of the Jew's faithful response to their encounter with the infinite had been settled in the JEP epic and the judgments of the prophets. Three distinctive features of Jewish religious life, however, got constituted after the Jews returned from exile in Babylon and fleshed out their response in these new circumstances. These three are: (1) temple worship, (2) the teaching and preaching of the Torah in synagogues, and (3) the presentation of a Jewish religious understanding of wisdom in contrast to Babylonian, Egyptian, and Greek claims of wisdom.

Within twenty five years of their return to Jerusalem, a modest temple had been constructed, and very quickly the chief priest of the temple became the authoritative voice for the returning Judeans. Northern remnants who had remained after the old kingdom of Israel had been destroyed, now called Samaritans, again challenged the authority of Jerusalem and built a rival temple on Mt. Gerizim. At the center of the many religious practices conducted by the priests in the temple was the celebration of Passover, in which worshipers yearly reframed their lives as thankful inheritors of the exodus from spiritual slavery into that joyous land of milk and honey now found in their worship of Yahweh. That worship, thankfulness, and joy often found expression in the singing of Psalms, many originating five hundred years earlier in the days of David and Solomon. In the Psalms one finds all the elements of worshiping Yahweh and praying with Yahweh. The worshipers are called to sing to Yahweh (47, 81, 89, 95, 98, 100), to praise him (34, 146–150), and to proclaim his glory and majesty (8, 29). The entire universe praises Yahweh, the God of spiritual liberation and ethical justice (19, 50). Worshipers declare that they remember what their religious forefathers taught them about deliverance from slavery in Egypt and Babylon (44, 66, 77, 80, 105, 114), and they express their thanks to Yahweh (9, 75, 138). They confess their continued need for deliverance from cravings for power and status (22, 38, 139), and they express their understanding of their need for a mercy and forgiveness that enables them to be delivered again into faithfulness and righteousness (32, 51, 57, 73). They thank Yahweh for the great joy that they will now experience in worship and service to Yahweh. (42, 50, 62), in considering the poor (41), and in delighting in the law (1), in worshiping in the temple that is Yahweh's house (84, 122). They thank Yahweh that this joy overwhelms any fears they may have about life (27), because Yahweh provides a timeless help and refuge that they can trust no matter what happens (7, 23, 25, 27, 46, 121). The worshipers will sing a benediction proclaiming that Yahweh will be gracious and will give spiritual blessings (67).

The importance that many Jews placed on temple worship led to a series of events that eventually produced one of the most important religious ceremonies in Jewish life, the celebration of Hanukkah. After having been left religiously undisturbed under the Persians, things changed after Alexander the Great conquered the region. After his death, Judah and Samaria came under the governance of the Seleucid throne in Antioch, Syria. In 175 BC, Antiochus IV decided to use coercion to get everyone to give priority to Greek culture and to do so by requiring worship of Zeus. After rebellion broke out over his appointment of a high priest for the Jerusalem temple, he sent troops to Jerusalem and built an alter to Zeus on the altar used for showing loyalty to Yahweh. A village priest, Mattathias, and his five sons began active guerilla warfare. His eldest son, Judas, nicknamed "the hammer," Maccabeus, defeated a Syrianian army on December 25, 165 BC, and carried out a ceremony of rededication (Hanukkah) of the altar to Yahweh. Yearly since then, a similar festival of lights permits Jews to rededicate themselves to Yahweh.

Also, during the Maccabean war when Jews were being persecuted, an unknown writer wrote the apocalyptic book of Daniel as a coded effort to encourage Jews to resist the tyranny of the Syrians. Only the Jews would know how to decipher the code. The story of Daniel is set back in the time of the Babylonian exile. It tells of visions of Daniel, in which the Babylonian, Midian, Persian, and Greek empires are symbolized as evil beasts, and it tells of the great courage of Daniel and his friends in resisting this evil, resistance that succeeds in preserving the Jewish tradition. It elevates the conflict between the Maccabees and Syrians into a worldwide conflict between religious faithfulness and antireligious oppression, and it proclaims that faithfulness will live on and bring its blessings.

As religiously powerful as temple worship can be, it has two limitations. First, sincere institutional practices can too easily slip into spiritually empty formalities. It is against just this kind of distortion that the prophet Malachi spoke out. Without faithfulness to Yahweh, formal ceremonies are just cases of reverting to magical cravings for control, and they cause the faithful to weep because of the way they vaccinate people against faithful surrender in thanksgiving and service to Yahweh (Malachi 2:13–16). Second, not everyone can get to the temple in Jerusalem to participate in these worship services. This problem was addressed by the constitution of synagogues in local communities outside Jerusalem. This especially was the solution for the Jews spread out throughout the fertile crescent. More Jews had found permanent homes in Egypt, the old Assyria, and Babylonia than were living in the old Israel and Judah, and the synagogue provided them with a way to maintain their identity as a religious community. Once the second Jerusalem temple was destroyed by the Romans in 70 AD, and the Jews were dispersed from Judea throughout the Mediterranean world, the synagogue became the center of Jewish religious communal practice for Jews in the diaspora. A key to understanding the character of synagogue practice is found in the reforms that Nehemiah and Ezra introduced when they returned to Jerusalem from Babylonia.

In 432 BC Nehemiah introduced requirements for official membership in the Jewish community. One of these was a pledge of loyalty to the proclamations in the Torah (the pentateuch—the JEP narrative plus the book of Deuteronomy). In 398 BC Ezra lead a covenant renewal ceremony in Jerusalem in which he read extensively from the Torah, and people pledged their faithfulness to Yahweh as spelled out in the Torah. With the Torah now occupying such a crucial place in Yahweh worship, it became crucial for people to know as well as possible what was being said in it. Thus, a rabbinic tradition was constituted in which interpretations of the Torah and the way it was to be followed were introduced and became precedents for further interpretations and applications in new settings. The synagogues became the centers for these rabbinic studies and for local worship services that accented the teaching of the Torah and preaching about what the Torah requires of

Yahweh's faithful followers. For some rabbinic scholars, the study of the Torah and its interpretations became a way of worshiping Yahweh.

There was a second condition for official membership in the Jewish community that Nehemiah stipulated: the requirement of being born of Jewish parents. He also prohibited marriage to non-Jews. In his eyes, perpetuating a faithful community of Yahweh worshipers required a unified parental effort. This practice, however, led to practices of exclusion that seemed to run counter to Second Isaiah's call to worship Yahweh by liberating all people. As a quasi-prophetic critique of this goal of exclusiveness, three old stories circulating at the oral level were used. The stories of Ruth, Jonah, and Esther all seem to be reminders of Second Isaiah's call. The story of Ruth is the story of a non-Jewish Moabite who adopts her husband's worship of Yahweh and pledges to go with him anywhere, a Moabite who it turns out is one of David's ancestral grandparents. Jonah is the story of a man who does not want to help bring Yahweh's deliverance to the Assyrians in Nineveh, but whose forced efforts produce that result. Esther is the story of a non-Jewish woman who becomes queen of Persia and risks her own life by going unannounced to King Xerxes and persuades him not to carry out his plan to kill all the Jews because they would not be assimilated. The critiques by Malachi and the writers of Ruth, Jonah, and Esther remind us of how easy it is for social practices, constituted as faithful responses to encounters with the infinite, can be divorced from their religious significance and take on lives of their own, lives that often hinder rather than help such faithfulness.

Again and again, reflective Jewish servants of Yahweh had to instruct people not to be taken in by what was being called wisdom in Egyptian, Babylonian, and Greek circles. The wisdom writers in these circles were engaged in two sets of practices whose presuppositions Yahweh worship challenged. First, all sorts of practical advice was being given, based on the common sense of experienced people, common that is to people who had not encountered the infinite, been delivered from slavery to common cravings, and had not responded positively to Yahweh's call for surrender of the finite in service to the ethical call of the infinite. The wisdom writers also were trying to find a rational explanation and justification for the suffering in the world, for the benefits and burdens in life not being fairly distributed according to how morally virtuous or vicious people were, and for death seeming to be able to nullify the meaningfulness of life. The books of Proverbs and Ecclesiastes and the Job poem reject the very project of trying to find such wisdom through the use of nonreligious rational reflection, rather than through surrendering in faithful service to Yahweh. The book of Proverbs includes many pieces of practical advice also found in other wisdom literature (Provers 10:1, 14:11–25, 15:1–5, 17, 18, 22:1–11, 23:1–9, 26, 27, 31). It also places these inclusions, however, in the framework provided by pointing out that wisdom begins in the fear of Yahweh, in fearing for all the people who need liberation and justice, in fearing that we may not be responding faithfully enough to Yahweh's call. (Proverbs 1:7, 8:29, 16:1–6, 28:14, 30:5–14). Only by focusing on our ethical responsibilities to people in their singular uniqueness can we learn what advice is practical for carrying out this mission. Only by finding the joy of responding faithfully to our encounters with the infinite can we know what is and what is not practical and sensible. In the language of Judaism, only by knowing how to worship and serve Yahweh, do we have the practical skills and the wisdom needed to live well.

It is in Ecclesiastes that we hear an anonymous preacher proclaiming that the wise fear of Yahweh is infinitely superior to any wisdom supposedly found by people asking and trying to answer what they call the great questions of life: Given the chanciness of life and the inevitability of physical death, does human life have any significance? Given that trying to be ethical gives no assurance that one will prosper more than people who harm others, is ethical life worth living? The preacher acknowledges the existence of the conditions that motivate many people to ask these question. Many reflective people end up in nihilistic despair, crying out "vanity," "worthlessness" (Ecc.1:2). Life for many people is a wearisome treadmill in which nothing really new ever happens (Ecc. 1:8). Some might gain wealth, but they lack the power to really enjoy it (Ecc. 6:2). People just can't get enough to satisfy their appetites (Ecc. 6:7). Nothing really gets accomplished, and soon after our death no one will remember most of us or what we have done (Ecc. 1:11). Everyone ends up with the same fate as everyone else, being dead (Ecc. 2:14, 16). It doesn't pay trying to help others and not hurt them. Often doing this just hastens one's own destruction and death while those who do not help but do harm prolong their lives by acting that way (Ecc. 7:15). The conditions of life lead many reflective people to recognize despairingly that the dead are better off than the living, and that it would have been still better not to have been born at all (Ecc. 2:20, 4:2–3).

The preacher does not challenge these conditions, but he does challenge the presumption that being wise means admitting that this makes life meaningless, and that meaning must and can be given to life by finding some big rational explanation or justification that explains away or justifies human suffering or the apparent unfair treatment of caring and uncaring people. The preacher says that he, too, once sought such wisdom, and his achievements surpassed all those in Jerusalem, but he found that this kind of search for wisdom was also worthless. Trying to answer the big questions is fruitless; it is endlessly chasing the wind (Ecc. 1:16). One cannot gain wisdom for living by rationally seeking to answer such questions. (Ecc 8:17). If one stays at the level of nonreligious reasoning, one cannot know who Yahweh is or why Yahweh is not Baal controlling human life and history (Ecc. 3:11, 11:5). True wisdom comes when one's words become few (Ecc. 5:2), one stops talking and one listens in the house of Yahweh (Ecc. 5:1), and when one wisely comes to understand that what all people need to do is to fear Yahweh (fear for all people in need) and keep Yahweh's commandments (Ecc. 12:13).

Yahweh is not in the business of answering what people who need deliverance take to be the big questions (Ecc. 8:17). Worshipers of Yahweh know that life is filled with chance (Ecc. 9:11), and there is no big reason why everything is as it is and not otherwise. There are times when people are born and times when they die, times of harvesting and planting, times of killing and healing, times of destruction and construction, times of weeping and laughing, times of mourning and dancing, times of speaking and of keeping silent, times of loving and hating, times of war and peace (Ecc. 3:1–9). That is simply how life is. The nonreligious person seeking wisdom asks, "How can you worship God when there is so much suffering and unfairness in life?" The worshiper of Yahweh responds, "How can you live non-despairingly in a world filled with suffering and unfairness without worshiping Yahweh?" The preacher proclaims that all is beautiful in Yahweh's time (Ecc. 3:10) and that all will be well for those who fear Yahweh (Ecc. 8:12). Yahweh's gift to people is for them to take pleasure in all they do (Ecc. 3:13). Being quiet in order to hear and surrender to Yahweh's call for service is better than striving after the un-catchable wind of seeking answers to ill-considered questions (Ecc. 4:6). The simple joys of living with the elements and cohabiting with others, and the timeless happiness of living a life of service to Yahweh, which is found in the living of the life and not in its results, are joys and a happiness that endure no matter what the times are like. (Ecc. 3:14, 22) The conditions that drive some to seek big explanations and justifications do not make life meaningless, but they are the occasions on which people like Moses encounter the ethical infinite in all people and find joy in surrendering in service to Yahweh's will.

Another powerful rejection of the whole project by the nonreligious wisdom writers is the poem that makes up most of the book of Job. (Job 3:1–42:6). Job rejects all the attempts by his "friends" to show that his life of misery only illustrates the thesis that there is a distribution principle working in the world, assigning material benefits to people who do what is right and material burdens to people who do what is wrong. Job must have done something wrong, for which he now is being punished. Job says, "No!" The temptation that Job faces is not that of remaining faithful in the face of suffering and injustice, but rather it is the temptation to search for wise, justifying reasons for suffering and injustice instead of simply worshiping and serving Yahweh. The satanic alternative to Yahweh worship is the metaphysical craving for ultimate explanations and justifications that exalts human intellectual control and thereby excludes the surrender needed in the worship of Yahweh.

Job at first expresses the nihilistic lament heard in Ecclesiastes that death is better than life and that best of all is never having been born (Job 3:3, 11). The same kinds of considerations are also introduced for judging that life is empty and meaningless (Job 7:3). We seemingly are born for trouble (Job 5:7). The world is filled with violence and empty of justice (Job 19:7). Terrible things are done to orphans, widows, the hungry, and the poor who are cold and wet and without food or clothing (Job 24:1–12). There is no proportionality between moral worth and the distribution of benefits and burdens (Job 6:2, 21:7). Death makes the whole human enterprise seem pointless (Job 4:22, 14:11–16). Job adds his own personal life as evidence that such nihilism seems reasonable. He is an innocent person; why should he suffer (Job 9:21)? He has done everything humanly possible to carry out Yahweh's command to care for widows, the blind, the lame, the poor (Job 29:12–20). Still, he is the laughingstock of everyone (Job 12:4, 30:1–15), and his spirit is broken (Job 17:1).

Job will not accept the claims of his friends that he must have done something wrong, and thus wrongs are being done to him; and he rejects the general thesis that this implies—in the big picture—that people's suffering and injustice really serve some worthy end that justifies them. Job charges his friends not to lie for Yahweh by offering supposed justifications for what happens in human life (Job 13:7). Job wants nothing to do with such "wise" rationalizations. Instead, he joins the preacher in Ecclesiastics in proclaiming that it is fear of Yahweh that is the beginning of wisdom (Job 28:28). Job promises Yahweh that he will stop complaining and will become silent so that he can be taught (Job 6:24). In prayerful reflection he hears Yahweh tell him that his complaining comes from his failure to understand what faithfulness to Yahweh requires and promises (Job: 38:2). In his spiritual ears he hears Yahweh tell him that Yahweh requires surrender and not faultfinding and contentiousness (Job 40:2). Job acknowledges that previously he spoke without understanding (Job 42:3), but now he will argue no more (Job 40:3–5). Yahweh has never promised that faithfulness to him will produce material benefits or an avoidance of physical death. Yahweh is no metaphysical god justifying human suffering and injustice. Life needs no justification, and faithfully responding to the infinite guarantees nothing except its own kind of joyful living and the lasting impact that one's service to Yahweh has on generations to come.

Throughout its history Judaism has faced the challenge of not permitting its religious faithfulness to be turned into metaphysical theorizing about supernatural beings. This was a challenge before and after the biblical times. It was difficult not to turn the promise of a land flowing with milk and honey into a metaphysically legitimated nationalism. It was difficult not to turn religious creation stories into metaphysical theories about a supernatural artisan creating an earthly artifact, or theories about a being who could meet the explanatory demands of the Greek principle of sufficient reason. It was difficult not to turn religious trust in Yahweh's mission of liberating people into a metaphysical theory about a supernatural being determining human history in such a way that people only become pawns moved around on this being's chessboard. Some great thinkers reared in the traditions of Judaism did go metaphysical (Philo, Maimonides, Spinoza), but nevertheless they never came to dominate. Judaism maintained its identity as one of the world's great religious responses to the call of the infinite. Christianity and Islam will grow out of the religious traditions constituted by the Hebrews, Israelites, and Jews.

2. Christianity

The religious interpretation of the exodus provided the frame within which Hebrews, Israelites, and Jews constituted their historically particular response to their encounters with the infinite. The religious frame within which Christians constituted their response is their faith in the resurrection of Jesus as the Christ, the Messiah, their savior. Understanding Christianity means first and foremost understanding its resurrection faith. It is within the framework of that faith that all the narratives of the life of Jesus are told; all the extremely influential letters of Paul are written and read; and all the other materials in the Christian's New Testament Bible are offered and received. Likewise, all the religious practices of Christians in remembering, proclaiming, teaching, and serving are done in the name of the resurrected Jesus Christ. Soon after the death of Jesus around 30 AD, the earlier companions of Jesus and the convert from Judaism, Paul, began to focus all their worship of Yahweh on Jesus, whom they proclaimed to be Yahweh's Messiah, the suffering servant who would carry out the saving mission set forth in Second Isaiah. Jesus was proclaimed to be this savior (in Greek, *Christos*). The driving force leading to this constitution of Jesus as the Christ was the resurrection faith that developed among his followers and filled them with the spirit of Yahweh.

Trying to specify in the twenty-first century what the resurrection faith was that Christians held in the first century is a difficult undertaking for a number of different reasons. First, for over two thousand years, people with many different cultural backgrounds have been talking about the resurrection of Jesus and interpreting it in terms of unexamined metaphysical assumptions commonly held in those cultures. That makes it very difficult for people to rethink what a purely religious interpretation of this faith might be like once the metaphysical god is dead. Second, Christianity was born in a mixed Jewish/Hellenistic world just before and after the destruction of the temple in Jerusalem by the Romans and over three hundred years after Plato and Aristotle gave birth to the metaphysical project in the West. Soon after Christianity's constitution, some thinkers in the Christian community began to give the resurrection faith a Greek metaphysical interpretation. Thus, interpreting the resurrection faith without contaminating it with Greek metaphysical claims about "first causes," "immaterial souls," or "minds" is as difficult as it is necessary. Third, one cannot pinpoint any specific time when the resurrection faith originated. Furthermore, it is difficult to give one specification of what this faith involves, since different oral traditions and texts say different things about the resurrection of Jesus as the Christ. Although the resurrection faith was communicated in oral form soon after the death of Jesus, written enunciations of this faith first appeared about twenty years after his death, and seemingly different written characterizations appeared during the next fifty years after that. Examining the resurrection faith with a fresh religious eye may be very difficult, but it is not impossible. By looking carefully at the textual presentations of this faith, and by refusing to surrender its religious meaning to metaphysical interpretations, it is possible to identify the main characteristics of the unique Christian reconstruction of its Jewish inheritance.

The earliest written mention of someone encountering Jesus as the resurrected Messiah is found in Paul's first letter to the Corinthians, written around 55 AD, twenty-five years after the death of Jesus. This letter, like all the writings in Christianity's New Testament Bible, is written out of that resurrection faith that is the presupposition of all Christian thinking, writing, worship, and practice. Paul writes that after the death of Jesus, Christ, their savior who is the Messiah, appeared to Jesus's companions and to Paul himself (I Cor. 15:5–8). It is clear that Paul is talking about appearances that occurred long before he wrote his letter. The book of Acts, which is the second half of the text Luke/Acts, was written somewhere around 80-90 AD, but it presents a Christian narrative of events that happened soon after the death of Jesus, a narrative based on material circulating at the oral level in the Christian community for around fifty years. A major portion of Acts is a narrative of Paul's life, and it makes reference to Paul's encounter with the resurrected Christ.

Paul was born a little after Jesus (5–15 AD) into a well-to-do family with Roman citizenship, in Tarsus, a city in which Greek culture had a strong presence. As a young man he went to Jerusalem to study the Torah. Paul had a short, youthful career opposing the new group calling themselves Christians. He opposed them because he saw their claim that Jesus had been resurrected as the Messiah as a direct threat to the religious status of the Torah in the Jewish religious way of life. After being present at the stoning of a courageous young Christian, Stephan, Paul, however, had a religious conversion experience around 38 AD This happened while he was traveling to Damascus to further the campaign against Christians (Acts 22:6–21, 26:12–23, 8:1). As probably told by Paul to the author of Acts, Paul claims that this experience was an encounter with the resurrected Christ, although he had never met Jesus during his lifetime and had no idea what he looked like. The author of Acts, conveying what Paul reported remembering about what happened, writes that a heavenly light blinded Paul, one that his traveling companions did not see, and he heard a voice that claimed to be Jesus tell him to stop persecuting Christians, but to go to Damascus to receive instructions about what he was to do with the rest of his life (Acts: 9:3–9). Slight variations of this account appear when the author of Acts narrates what are presented as two speeches that Paul had given. In one case, Paul is reported to have said that his companions saw the light but heard nothing (Acts 22:9). In the other case, Paul says the light engulfed his companions as well as himself, and that Jesus, the Messiah, instructed him right then to carry out the mission of Second Isaiah to bring deliverance to non-Jewish Greeks and Romans. The variations are much less important than the fact that this experience of seeing the wonderful light that Jesus is the Messiah continued to be the centerpiece of his Christianity. Paul, in his letters to various Christian communities, says almost nothing about the life or teachings of Jesus. It is the resurrected Christ, the Messiah, that is the focal point of his worship of and service to Yahweh, and it is to this that he returns again and again to explain how deliverance is gained through worship of Yahweh and through worship of Yahweh's Messiah, Yahweh's offspring, Yahweh's son, Jesus Christ.

Paul made Christology (not Jesusology) the center of the resurrection faith of the Christians. One might say that, similar to those Hindus who gained spiritual liberation through worship of a personal god, Abraham and Moses, by making Yahweh the central focus of their worship, made bhakti yoga the core of the way in Western religions of faithfully responding to encounters with the infinite. Also, similar to Mahayana Buddhists, who sought and maintained spiritual liberation through focused worship of a bodhisattva, so Christians responded to the call of the infinite through focused worship of Yahweh, through focused worship of and service to Jesus resurrected as the Christ, Yahweh's Messiah. Judaism, Christianity, Hinduism, and Buddhism, in spite of their very important differences, share enough important features to make understanding one of them helpful in understanding the others. That is why creative dialogue between them can be very fruitful. During the past two thousand years, many people who have called themselves Christians succumbed to the temptation of advocating the kind of exclusiveness that Ruth, Jonah, and Esther warned against, often because of succumbing to the temptation to pursue the kind of metaphysical wisdom that Proverbs, Ecclesiastes, and Job warned against. There are no good religious reasons, however, for doing so. Different historically constituted ways of responding faithfully to encounters with the infinite are just that, different but not superior or inferior.

Paul acknowledges that some of the people who had been Jesus's companions when he was alive had encountered the resurrected Christ before he did, and their encounters may have been different from his, but he insists that his encounter was as genuine as any of theirs. The earliest written religious narrative of the life of Jesus that Christians read within the framework of their resurrection faith was the book of Mark, written around 70 AD, before Acts was written but thirty years after Paul's religious experience. The early version of Mark, before later editors added a new ending, does not say that Jesus appeared to anyone as a resurrected Messiah. It only says that three women companions of Jesus went to what they thought was the tomb where Jesus was buried after his crucifixion outside Jerusalem in order to anoint his body with funeral spices. They found the stone door to the tomb rolled back, and instead of a dead body they saw a young man in a white robe. He told them that Jesus had risen, and that they were to go back and tell his other companions to leave Jerusalem and go north to Galilee where they all came from to meet the risen Jesus there. According to Mark, the women at first were too afraid to tell anyone.

Three other religious narratives of Jesus's life and death do contain reports of Jesus the Messiah appearing to some of his companions who thereby became disciples of the risen Messiah: Matthew (85 AD), Luke, the first half of Luke/Acts (90 AD), and John (around 100 AD) Significant differences exist between these reports of the appearances of the risen Christ, the Messiah, but even more significant is the common religious import of the reports located in these narratives that all presuppose the resurrection faith.

Matthew, writing out of his resurrection faith, concludes his narrative by including, with slight modifications and additions, Mark's writings about an empty tomb. Instead of writing about two women meeting a young man dressed in white, however, Matthew writes about two women being shaken by an earthquake before meeting, in a flash of lightning, an "angel of Yahweh" dressed in snow white clothing, events that scared to death two men guarding the tomb. Also, instead of the women telling no one right away about the instructions to go to Galilee, Matthew has them run to tell the disciples of Jesus, whom, he writes, then meet and worship the resurrected Christ, who at that time appears to them and tells them to go to Galilee (Matthew 28:1–10).

Luke, writing out of his resurrection faith, also uses the materials in Mark's text, but then makes major additions to them so as to fit these materials into what he will be writing in Acts. He writes that three women go to a tomb, find it empty, meet a young man dressed in white (no guards are mentioned), who this time does not tell them to go to

Galilee, but asks them instead to remember that Jesus said in Galilee that the Messiah, the son of man, must die and be resurrected. The young man gives no further instructions. Luke writes that the women told the disciples but no one believed them, even though the disciples went and checked the tomb and found it empty (Luke 21:1–12, 22–24). Later that day, Luke writes, two disciples are walking seven miles from Jerusalem and having a conversation about the life and death of Jesus, whom they think of as having been another prophet. A man joins them, someone they do not recognize at all, and he instructs them about everything that had been said from Moses through Second Isaiah about how the Messiah must suffer in order to gloriously attain his goal of delivering people from spiritual slavery. Then, while participating in an evening meal in which the man functions just as Jesus did at their last supper with them, they recognize him as the resurrected Messiah, after which he immediately vanishes. These two men go back and tell the other disciples (Luke 24:13–35). Luke then writes that, immediately following this, the resurrected Christ appears among them, convinces them that he is not some metaphysical spirit by asking them to look at him, by eating before them, and by again instructing them about what the Jewish Torah and prophets had said about the Messiah. He then instructs them to remain in Jerusalem until Yahweh fills them with his spirit.

In Luke's writing out of his resurrection faith, being filled with the spirit of Yahweh becomes a crucial feature of being a Christian. It is crucial to keep this talk about the spirit of Yahweh from being confused with any popular notions about supernatural spirits. Luke's accent on receiving the spirit of Yahweh probably was inherited from Paul. Again and again, Paul accents the importance of receiving and living by the spirit of Yahweh, seeing the community of Christians, the Christian church, as the new body of the resurrected Messiah, the new embodiment of the spirit of Yahweh, worshiping and serving Yahweh. Luke begins the book of Acts with a narrative of how the people sharing the resurrection faith are filled with the spirit of Yahweh and begin to carry out his work of deliverance. A vital part of that work is participating in worship services in which a leader plays the priestly role of enabling people to participate in a replica of Jesus's last supper while alive, the very religious ritual that led the two young men to see before them the resurrected Christ, who vanished once the meal was over. This practice becomes the Christian mass or communion, in which a priest or priesthood of believers, by "eating" the "body of Jesus" enables worshipers to encounter the resurrected Christ. The Eucharist is, according to Marion, the icon pointing to the resurrected Christ, who is the icon pointing to God and his messianic activity, who is the icon pointing to the infinite other of every being. It is in worship centered on the Eucharist that the Christian community is constituted to become the body of the resurrected Christ filled with God's messianic spirit.[245]

John also retells and reworks the empty tomb narrative first present in Mark's text. John writes that Mary Magdalene discovers the stone rolled away from the tomb. She does not enter but runs to get the companions of Jesus who do enter, see that it is empty except for the linens in which Jesus's dead body had been wrapped, and then return home (John 20:1–10). Mary stays on and then sees two angels in white who merely ask why she is crying. Then she turns around and sees someone whom she recognizes as "the Teacher" when he calls her name. He tells her not to touch him, because he is ascending to Yahweh. She goes back and relates this to the disciples (John 20:11–18). According to John, on the evening of that day, which became the Christian's Sunday worship day, the resurrected Jesus Christ stood among all the disciples except Thomas; gave the benediction, "Peace be with you"; breathed the spirit of Yahweh into them; and sent them out to carry out the mission of the Messiah. (John 20:19–23). When told this, Thomas said he would not believe it unless he could actually touch the resuscitated dead body of Jesus. Eight days later, with Thomas present, the resurrected Christ stood among them again and gave the benediction, "Peace be with you." He chastised Thomas for thinking that touching a resuscitated body had anything to do with faithfulness to Yahweh or his Messiah, and blessed those who would be faithful, not wanting to see any such irrelevant body (John 20:26–31).

John also then narrates an account of Peter and his companions going out after Jesus's crucifixion on the northern Sea of Galilee to resume their old job of fishing. They see someone on the beach whom they do not recognize, hearing him tell them to do the same thing Jesus had told them years before about how to catch fish, and then recognize him as Yawheh's Messiah, "the Lord." After again eating with the resurrected Christ, they hear him tell them that if they love him, they must follow him and serve his messianic mission to feed and tend Yahweh's beloved children (John 21:1–19). That is to be their only concern, extinguishing all cravings to be superior to other disciples and all envy for benefits and honors they might gain, but that the other disciples do not acquire (John 21:2–23).

In spite of all the variations in the narratives of the appearances of the risen Christ, probably explainable in terms of different oral traditions available to them and different rhetorical goals being pursued in writing to different kinds of readers, the same basic features of the resurrection faith get proclaimed. Jesus of Nazareth, who was crucified outside Jerusalem, now lives in the lives of Christians as Yahweh's Messiah, their religious savior. In spite of the death of Jesus, his presence as Yahweh's Messiah, their savior, their Christ, lives on. They can encounter and meet him as their savior, resurrected in their lives, especially in the worship practices that replicate key activities in his life prior to his death. In their resurrection faith, Christians are proclaiming that no crucifixion or tomb can prevent Yahweh from pursuing his messianic mission of delivering people from spiritual slavery. Trusting Yahweh's promise of deliverance, as old as Abraham and Moses, now becomes for Christians trusting his Messiah's work, especially as spelled out by Second Isaiah, through his new body, the community of Christians filled with the spirit of Yahweh. The Hebrews, delivered from slavery, constituted themselves as a religious community by focusing their faithful response to encountering the infinite on worship of one named "Yahweh." Since Christians constituted themselves as a religious community by focusing all their worship and service on Yahweh's messianic servant, Jesus Christ, they did not feel any need to hesitate in calling the resurrected Christ "the son of Yahweh." If one focuses on the role of the resurrected Christ in the religious life of Christians and how worshiping Yahweh through him fills people with the spirit of Yahweh, then one need not get caught up in metaphysical puzzles about how three beings can be one being. Neither Yahweh, his Messiah son, nor his spirit are beings, and the infinite cannot be counted as one or more than one being.

Two big questions remain to be answered if even an introductory understanding is to be gained of the faithful response of Christians to their encounters with the infinite. First, why is it that Jesus is the one constituted by Christians as the resurrected Messiah? Second, how has Christianity's acceptance of Second Isaiah's messianic challenge to be God's agent in delivering non-Jews from spiritual slavery influenced their religious practices. It will be necessary to examine the four narratives of Jesus's life to get an answer to the first question, and it will be necessary to examine Acts and Paul's letters to get an answer to the second. In both cases it is going to be necessary to historically contextualize these texts in order to understand the issues and audiences that form the background and inform the character of these narratives and letters. Although Paul's letters were written earlier than the narratives, we need to look at the narratives first because they arise out of oral traditions that are expressions of the resurrection faith that led Paul to join the Christians. In interpreting these narratives it is crucial to remember that they are writing within the framework of the resurrection faith. They will not provide, nor should they provide, what historians today would call an objective narrative of the historical life of Jesus. They will tell us what different Christian writers had to say to different sorts of audiences about the life of Jesus in order for them to faithfully carry out their mission as followers of Yahweh's Messiah. It will be necessary, however, to rely on what historical and literary scholars say about the probable construction and setting of the narrative texts. It will not be necessary to engage ourselves in all the debates these scholars are having with one another, but it is necessary not to ignore their work.

Mark's text probably was written earlier than the texts of Matthew, Luke, or John. Matthew and Luke seem to have copied a great deal of Mark's text. Matthew and Luke also seem to have used another source, named by scholars as Q because the Greek word for source is *quelle*. It is not settled whether Q was an actual text or only an oral tradition. Since Mark was written about forty years after the death of Jesus, it is probable that the Q tradition predates Mark's written text. Q is a good place to begin looking at Christian accounts of the life of Jesus.[246]

Q makes it clear that early Christians and probably Jesus himself, following the tradition of earlier prophets, were very critical of what they perceived as the practices of many Jews at the time. Cities in Galilee are judged as being unfaithful (Matt. 11:20–24). Jerusalem is condemned for its treatment of the prophets (Matt. 23:37–39). Q narrates that Jesus warned about false prophets who mouth religious words but do not do what Yahweh instructs (Matt. 7:18, 21–23). Jesus criticizes Jewish leaders for only studying the Torah text and for not living with justice and mercy as the Torah demands (Matt. 23:1–7, 13–15, 23–28). Jesus returns to Abraham to legitimate his charge that supposed followers of Abraham must show their faithfulness by the fruits of their actions and not just by words and ritual performances (Matt. 3:7–10). Q offers as legitimation of Jesus's prophetic judgements a genealogy that traces him back to Abraham, calling Jesus a son of Abraham and a son of David (Matt. 1:1–16). Furthermore, Q tells of the genuine nature of Jesus's faithfulness to Yahweh by narrating how Jesus turned down temptations to become economically successful, to impress people by being a magic worker, and to be ruler over a political kingdom (Matt. 4:3–10). He also narrates how Jesus was fulfilling the prophetic call to help the blind and poor (Matt. 17:2–6). For Q, Jesus was a prophet like the great prophets of old.

According to Q, Jesus was not just a prophet; he also was the leader of a movement dedicated to carrying out Yahweh's mission of liberating people. It points out that Jesus trained and sent out seventy people to Jews throughout their region to proclaim Yahweh's call to service (Luke. 10:1–16). Jesus instructed them to drop all other concerns and give top priority to this mission (Matt. 8:18–22). Get yourself spiritually ready to leave at any time (Matt. 24:43–51) To do what was needed, only Yahweh could be their master (Matt. 6:24). Jesus cautioned them to be ready to leave family behind; to be rejected by those one cares about and by those one is trying to help, thus creating divisions in their families; to be ready to take up a cross of suffering (Matt. 10:37–39). Q also makes it clear that Jesus is committed to carry out Second Isaiah's call to bring deliverance to non-Jews as well as Jews. Q tells of a Roman centurion who becomes a faithful follower of Yahweh because of Jesus's own faithfulness (Matt. 8:5–13). Q narrates two parables told by Jesus in which outsiders are brought into a banquet to eat food in the kingdom of Yahweh (Matt. 22:1–14). Q has Jesus instruct these seventy missionaries that, although their specific ministry is to the Jews, still they are to be the salt that the whole earth needs, and they are to bring light to the whole world (Matt. 5:13–16).

The content of the teachings of Jesus that Q accents is a blend of the proclamations of Abraham, Moses, and the prophets, and a spelling out in radical form what kind of love is involved in being Yahweh's suffering servant to the world. Q has Jesus instructing people to pray a Yahweh prayer (the Lord's Prayer), praying silently to Yahweh, letting the past not prevent them from serving Yahweh in the future, not letting past harms one has caused and past harms caused to oneself enslave oneself. People should focus instead on Yahweh's love in order to better understand how to carry out Yahweh's will, knowing that there always will be sufficient joy in living and serving Yahweh to have the bread one needs for loving life (Matt. 6:9–15). Jesus, according to Q, drops from Yahweh's call to pursue justice any notion of seeking retributive justice, any notion of seeking an eye for an eye (Matt. 5:38–42). Yahweh and those who worship him are not to be in the judging business (Matt. 7:1–5), but are to stay in the loving and saving business, loving people in their unique singularity and infinite significance. regardless of what we or they have done in the past (Matt. 5:39–41, 43–45). Let the past be the past and live for the future, knowing that in Yahweh's love you are forgiven, and in worshiping Yahweh you are to forgive others again and again and again (Matt. 18:15–22). As one worshiping Yahweh, as one who knows that one is loved regardless of one's social and historical condition, love others as now you are able to love yourself (Matt. 7:12).

In responding faithfully to the call of Yahweh, Q's Jesus reminds people that although they must let one life die off (the rebellious life driven by cravings for power and status) in order for another life to begin (the life of surrendering in worship of Yahweh), they should not be fearful or anxious because Yahweh's love shows their singularly unique value (Matt. 10:26–33, 5:13–16). The relationship which the faithful have to the infinite through worship of Yahweh cannot be destroyed even by physical death (Matt. 10:26–33). One can ask for any of the gifts that Yahweh's love can give and one will receive them (Matt. 7:7–11). One can live in total confidence that living with

Yahweh means enjoying life without anxiety, even as the lilies in the field so live (Matt. 6:25–33). Worshiping Yahweh brings blessings on people whom the world normally thinks are people to be pitied: people who were poor in spirit, who mourned for loved ones, who were meek and not striving to be kings of the hill, who hunger and thirst for righteousness, are merciful, pure in heart, peacemakers, and persecuted for Yahweh's sake (Matt. 5:3–12).

Given Q's portrait of Jesus as the new prophet of Yahweh, proclaiming the radical nature of Yahweh's love and the spiritually rich form of life waiting for those who will worshipfully serve him, it should not be surprising that these followers would find active in their community a risen savior, Messiah, as they remember and celebrate his life of faithfulness to Yahweh and love for people. Q does not narrate any encounters with the resurrected Christ, but Q does proclaim that just as the will of Yahweh was done by Jonah, even after three days in the whale, so Yahweh's mission will be done through a resurrected "son of man," Messiah, after three days in a tomb (Matt. 12:38–40).

Mark provides additional reasons why the new Christian community, filled with the spirit of Yahweh and dedicated to the messianic mission of suffering service, should look back and see in Jesus the one who is now their resurrected savior, their Christ. First, Mark constructs his narrative of Jesus's life so that everything he does and says is leading to his rejection by the Jews and his closest companions and then to his crucifixion, thereby stamping him as the suffering servant who remains loyal to Yahweh's call through all challenges. Also, Mark's narrative of the failures of his closest companions to understand what Jesus was doing or to remain loyal in the face of danger reinforces the determination of his readers to now rectify that misunderstanding and disloyalty by making Jesus as the resurrected Christ the focal point of their worship and service.

Around 70 AD, the year when the Romans destroyed the temple in Jerusalem and dispersed the Jews throughout the Mediterranean world, Mark drew together different oral traditions and composed a text that Matthew and Luke would also incorporate in their narratives of the life of Jesus. It is not known where Mark was located when he wrote or for what specific audience he was writing. It is clear that he is writing from the perspective of the resurrection faith and for people living in the new Christian community.

Mark, at the very beginning of his text, informs his readers that he is proclaiming the good news, the gospel, that the resurrected Christ is the Son of Yahweh (Mark 1:1, 11, 3:11, 5:7, 9:7, 15:39). and that Christ calls Yahweh his father (Mark 14:36). Obviously, talking about being a father and son here does not refer to a genetic, biological relationship. Neither can its religious significance be preserved if it is interpreted as being some kind of relationship between metaphysical beings. Just as ethically the identity of parents is preserved by nurturing their children to continue to carry out their unlimited responsibilities to other people, so the resurrected suffering servant and Messiah, worshiped by the Christians, is the spiritual child of Yahweh, the focus of Moses's faithful response to his encounter with the infinite. When Mark narrates that Jesus calls Yahweh father, Mark shows that from within his resurrection faith he confesses that Jesus is the suffering servant carrying out the mission that Second Isaiah proclaimed to be Yahweh's mission(Mark 1:2–3). The spirit of Yahweh lives on in Jesus Christ and in those who are his living body, the Christian community (Mark 1:10–11, 8). Those who faithfully endorse this good news live right now in the spiritual kingdom of Yahweh (Mark 1:15).

Throughout his narrative Mark uses literary irony in writing about the parables Jesus told. The readers, because their resurrection faith is the key to deciphering these parables, understand what mystery the parables illustrate, but the people to whom they are told in the narrative do not understand. Mark narrates that Jesus made many enemies in the established Jewish leadership by attempting to reform what he saw as abuses and as an overly legalistic interpretation of the Torah. By narrating how Jesus taught through parables that his enemies did not understand, Mark can show and the Christian community can understand that something radically new has occurred in their worship of Yahweh through Jesus Christ. Mark and the Christian community can also look back and see that it is loyalty to Yahweh that produced Jesus's enemies, and thus his suffering-servant life of rejection, crucifixion, and resurrection as their savior. It is quite probable that Mark, similar to the other narrators of Jesus's life, wanted to draw a sharp distinction between Christians and the leadership of the old Jewish community. Mark wanted to do this because, after the destruction of the temple in Jerusalem, he was afraid that the Romans would treat Christians the way they were treating the Jews.

Jesus, according to Mark, is a religious reformer and purifier. Jesus sought to keep the temple purely as a place for worshiping Yawheh, and so he drove out of the temple those businesses selling temple offerings and making a profit changing money (Mark 11:15–19). He condemned the leaders who craved honor by wearing fancy robes and saying long prayers, but who stole from widows (Mark 12:38–40). He rejected overly legalistic demands not to help people on the Sabbath (Mark 3:15) and to be more concerned with hand washing than with having a pure spirit (Mark 7:1–8). He rejected the claim by some Jewish priests that Yahweh can forgive the past only through them by himself forgiving people (Mark 2:6–11). Mark says that the leadership was determined to destroy Jesus (Mark 3:6). They claimed that he was not filled with Yahweh's spirit but with the spirit of opposition to Yahweh, satan (Mark 3:22). They tried to show his lack of understanding of the Torah or Jewish tradition by asking him trick questions about divorce (Mark 10:2) and the status of marital people after being resurrected (Mark 12:18–23). Mark shows that Jesus understands the Torah by having him refer back to the requirement in the ten commandments to maintain the family (Mark 10:3–9). Mark has Jesus show that those opposing Jesus do not understand what the resurrection faith is all about, because Yahweh is worshiped by the living, and those resurrected from slavery are resurrected while still biologically alive into a heavenly, joyful life of worship and service. The religious enemies tried to trick Jesus into arousing in the Roman authorities opposition to him by trying to get him to say that people do not have to pay taxes to Caesar. But Jesus responds that Yahweh wants their worship and service, and Caesar can keep his taxes (Mark 12:13–17). Mark has Jesus sum up his response to these attempts to trick him by summarizing Yahweh worship in one great commandment. Be totally faithful to Yahweh in all aspects of one's life, and love every neighbor as such lovers of Yahweh would love themselves as they worship and serve Yahweh (Mark 12:29–31).

According to Mark, Jesus's companions during his lifetime also did not really understand his parables, because they did not fully understand the radical kind of suffering-servant loyalty that Yahweh was demanding of them. Mark's message to his fellow Christians is that they, too, are called to be suffering servants and that nothing short of faithfulness to their resurrected savior, Christ, can enable them to do this. Simply having walked with Jesus was not enough. Had it been enough, then their loyalty would have been an achievement of which they could be proud. It would not have been achieved by surrendering to Yahweh, by letting die one's rebellious life in order to be raised to a new life filled with joy, even when it is filled with suffering service. Mark guarantees to his readers that everything will be understandable to them and no secrets will be hidden (Mark 4:21–5). Again and again, however, Mark narrates how Jesus observes that his closest companions do not understand his parables (Mark 4:13, 6:52, 7:18, 8:21). He rebukes his companions for wanting special status because of their association with him (Mark 9:33–34, 10: 35–37) or for thinking that only they are entitled to carry out his mission (Mark 9:38). Mark narrates that as Jesus is taken away for crucifixion, they all forsake him (Mark 14:50). Even Peter, who will become the leader of the Jerusalem community worshiping the resurrected Christ, does not understand the suffering-servant mission that Jesus has accepted as his own (Mark 8:32–33), and in the end he even denies that he knows Jesus.(Mark 14:66–72).

Mark tells his readers that the resurrected savior whom they worship is the Jesus who remained loyal to Yahweh as his suffering servant, even though no one understood what he was saying and doing and even though he ended up all alone, abandoned and then crucified (8:31, 9:31). Mark makes it dramatically clear to his readers that Jesus's loyalty to Yahweh was purchased at a great price. He was not some masochist who found secret enjoyment in suffering. He was not someone with a messianic complex who craved for glory by being the savior of the world. He prayed to Yahweh that if there is any way he could do the will of his father without being crucified, then let him do it, but if not, then let the messianic mission of the suffering servant be carried out (Mark 14:35–36). John Caputo makes a great deal out of the synoptic gospel's characterization of the passion of Jesus. Here, he claims, we have an account of a man who did not want to be crucified and whom God who is love would not want crucified. Nevertheless he is crucified, and he becomes the great symbol to Christians of all the unjustified suffering in the world. Still more importantly, Jesus, in the spirit of agape love, forgives those who crucify him, even though they neither understand that they are performing an extremely unjust act nor ask for any forgiveness. He thereby becomes for Christians the embodiment of the agape love, which Marion names God, which is to be the ruling spirit in the lives of Christians.[247] Mark reminds his readers that they are called to be the spiritual bothers of Yahweh's suffering servant, whom they worship as their resurrected savior; they are to be the communal body filled with his spirit, remaining joyful and loyal even when they, too, must suffer for their faithfulness to the will of Yahweh (Mark 3:35).

Fifteen years after Mark wrote, and the Romans destroyed the Jerusalem temple and dispersed the Jews, the book of Matthew was written. The author of this text incorporates, elaborates, and edits a great deal of the material from Mark and Q. The book probably is a teaching manual containing a great deal of material used liturgically in worship services by Christians. It seems to have been written in Antioch, Syria, to Christians who were having to deal with a certain historical crisis. After the dispersal from Jerusalem, Jewish worship in places like Antioch was centered in the synagogue and focused heavily on studying the Torah and trying to live in conformity with its instructions. At first, Jewish Christians also carried on their worship services in these same synagogues. In 85 AD, however, in the Birkat-ha-minim directive, Christians were no longer permitted to do so, probably because of opposition of Jewish leaders to what Christians saw as the need to reform and purify Jewish practice. From then on, Christian churches were established in close vicinity to the synagogues where they previously worshiped. The need arose to provide these Christians with instructions and practices that would establish their own unique identity. The book of Matthew tries do this first by showing that faithfulness in their resurrection faith is, in fact, faithfulness in the Exodus faith proclaimed in the Torah; Christianity is only a reform and purification movement of Jewish practice. Second, Matthew proclaims that

Christianity also embodies something new and wonderfully different by being a new kind of presentation of the Torah and the prophets.

What is wonderfully new, Matthew proclaims, is that Jesus Christ is the very embodiment of the Torah (Matt. 11:28–30). The book of Matthew is composed of five teaching discourses, each preceded by a narrative introduction. Looking back from fifty-five years after the death of Jesus, the book of Matthew presents a narrative of Jesus as one who teaches the meaning of the Torah by what he says and by what he embodies. Understand what the Torah is narrating about Yahweh's promise of deliverance and call for loving service and you understand why it is Jesus who is proclaimed by the Christian community as the resurrected Messiah. Understand, from within the framework of the resurrection faith, this Jesus who is constituted as the resurrected Christ and you understand what the Torah is saying about worshiping Yahweh. Matthew writes that by worshiping and serving Jesus as their resurrected savior, Christians gain a full understanding of what the Torah teaches about worshipfully serving Yahweh. In Jesus Christ one sees everything the Torah is trying to say. In being suffering servants like Jesus Christ, Christians are living in loyal obedience to the Torah. The narrative in the Torah and the proclamations of the prophets are about absolute and total surrender to Yahweh's will, to deliver all people from spiritual slavery, to be just to all people, to care for and love all people. Ecclesiastical laws and regulations have a point only when they serve this larger project of surrendering in worship of Yahweh all of one's desires and their consequent beliefs and actions. Matthew proclaims that Jesus Christ is not rejecting anything in the Torah (Matt. 223:3); he is only revealing with his teachings and his life what it means to worship and serve Yahweh through the study of the Torah. Just as two or three can gather together to worship Yahweh by studying the Torah, so two or three Christians can gather together and find there in their midst Jesus Christ, the Torah become flesh in the body of Christ which is the Christian church (Matt. 18:20). Their identity as a Christian community, and their identity as individual Christians is tied to the presence in their midst of the Torah, Jesus the Christ. Only by focusing their worship on Jesus as their resurrected savior can they rectify their names and be who they are.

In Mark, the identity of Christians living within the framework of the resurrection faith is established by contrasting their understanding and faithfulness to the lack of understanding and faithfulness of the Jewish leaders and Jesus's companions while he was alive. The author of Matthew establishes this identity by drawing a contrast between those scribes and pharisees who focus on the letter of the law and not its Yahweh spirit, together with Jewish leaders who prevent Christians from using their synagogues, and the Christians who worship Jesus Christ as the Torah. The book of Matthew does not exhibit any of Mark's literary irony. In Matthew, the resurrection faith of the author dominates the narrative, and thus the companions of Jesus are characterized as disciples who understand the parables that Jesus teaches and who refer to him as Lord and not just teacher (Matt. 8:25, 14:28, 16:22, 17:4, 18:21). In Matthew we read of the contrast between what "they" say (don't kill, don't commit adultery, don't swear falsely, an eye for an eye, hate your enemy) and what Jesus Christ says (don't be angry or insulting, don't lust, answer truthfully, don't seek revenge, love even your enemies). Matthew has Jesus tell his followers to love, without preconditions or reservations, all people, even as Yahweh, on whom Moses focused his worship, loves all people in their singular uniqueness (Matt. 5:21–48). Looking back to Jesus and the way he took on the role of suffering servant in order for them to know Yahweh's love for them as unique individuals, the Christians in Matthew's world do not even entertain the possibility that the Messiah might be someone other than Jesus as the resurrected Christ.

In fleshing out the teaching that Jesus Christ reveals the full implications of the Torah, the writer of Matthew presents a narrative that ties Jesus and his mission as a suffering servant back to all the pivotal figures in the development of Judaism. A genealogy ties Jesus to David and Abraham (Matt. 1:1–7). Jesus is born in Bethlehem, David's city (Matt. 2:1). He is saved from being killed by an evil king and then comes out of Egypt, where he fled, to be a deliverer, just like Moses (Matt. 2:3–23) Jesus, just like Moses, delivers from a mountain a discourse on what will be constituted a faithful response to the call of Yahweh to surrender and thus be his servant in delivering the people from slavery (Matt. 5:1–7:29). Jesus goes up a mountain, is transfigured, meets with Moses and Elijah, and has Yahweh call him his beloved son (Matt. 17:1–8). Jesus rides triumphantly into Jerusalem, just like King David (Matt. 21:2–11). For its Christian readers, the book of Matthew makes clear that the religious significance of the whole Torah is revealed in Jesus their savior, revealed for all to see who look through the lens of the resurrection faith.

Luke/Acts probably was written a few years after Matthew. It also incorporates, expands, and reworks materials from Q and Mark, as well as drawing upon other oral traditions. Thirty years after the death of Paul, more than fifty years after the constitution of the Christian community in Jerusalem, and sixty years after the beginning of the work of the adult Jesus, the author of Luke/Acts writes this two part narrative. The first part narrates the life of Jesus as he moves from Galilee in the north to Jerusalem in the south; the second part narrates the establishment of the resurrection faith community in Jerusalem, its expansion under the leadership of Peter to Samaria in the north, and then, under the leadership of Paul, its extension to Syria, Greece, and finally Rome. The first half of the narrative is an interpretation of the life and death of Jesus as seen from the perspective of the second half of the narrative. This narrative is not only framed by the resurrection faith shared by all the narratives of the life of Jesus, but it is given a specific structure by the way the Christian community is born in Jerusalem and then expands from there. Everything in the first half directs the reader's attention to Jerusalem and what will happen there, and everything in the second half points from Jerusalem to the whole world beyond it.

To understand the Luke/Acts narrative of the life of Jesus, therefore, it is necessary to focus on two aspects of its narrative of the life of the Christian community. First, it is necessary to look at its narrative of the specific character of the birth of the Christian community in Jerusalem. Second, it is necessary to examine the challenge that Roman destruction of Jerusalem and the Christian expansion into non-Jewish worlds makes to understanding the faithful responses of Abraham, Moses, and the prophets in their worship of Yahweh. At the very time when Judaism seems at its low point, Christianity is rapidly expanding. How come this is happening to Christians at this dark hour for Jews, given what Abraham heard as a promise to his children, and what

Moses did to deliver his people from slavery, and what the prophets charged as the mission of Hebrews, Israelites, and Jews?

In the Luke/Acts narration of encounters with the resurrected Christ, the companions are instructed to remain in Jerusalem until they are filled with the spirit of Yahweh (Luke 24:49–52; Acts 1:4–5). In the narrative, this occurred fifty days after the empty tomb was discovered. There, of course, is no need to give a metaphysical reading of this narrative, thereby turning a very important religious event into a made-for-movie story about ghosts and spirits. Being filled with the spirit of Yahweh is being filled with a sense of ethical responsibility and love for all people and a dedication to meet those responsibilities. It is being filled with a spirit of nonalienation from nature, a spirit of thankfulness for the joys of life that not even the suffering produced by the necessities and accidents of nature can erase. It is being filled with a sense of universal brotherhood in which alienation from other people is replaced by living together in a mutually supporting home and by reaching out to all people, regardless of their social status or past histories, and lovingly serving as Yahweh's instruments of delivering them.

Luke/Acts narrates that all this happened in Jerusalem at Pentecost. Thunder, wind, and lightening filled them not only with fear of Yahweh, but also fear for the well-being of those he loves (Acts 2:2–3). People, alienated and unable to understand one another since the time of the tower of Babel, now could understand one another, because in the spirit of Yahweh one sees, respects, and cherishes people in their unique singularity and seeks to deliver them from all forms of slavery that prevent them from enjoying life and Yahweh forever (Acts 2:4–21). People filled together with the spirit of Yahweh shall live together as one family, sharing all the burdens and benefits of daily living (Acts 2:43–47). Filled with resurrection faith and the holy spirit of Yahweh, Peter interprets in cryptic fashion the meaning of the life, crucifixion, and resurrection of Jesus as their savior, just as the writer of Luke/Acts will do in his much larger narrative (Acts: 2:22–36, 38–39). Again and again, Luke/Acts narrates that being filled with the spirit of Yahweh defines who Jesus is (Luke 1:15; 3:16, 22; 4:1,18; 9:3–5). The narration has Jesus say as he is dying that he commits to Yahweh his spirit (Luke 23:46), commits it for safekeeping until it again fills his body, the Christian community, at Pentecost.

The narrator in Luke, writing decades after the birth and spread of the Christian community, has Jesus during his lifetime deputize his companions to be the disciples they would be after they are filled with the holy spirit of Yahweh, carrying on his mission, Yahweh's mission, of delivering all people from spiritual slavery (Luke 5:10; 6:13; 8:10; 9:15, 28–35; 10:1–20, 23–24; 22:28–30; 24:49). Luke/Acts is written to a Christian community that knows that the Romans in 70 AD destroyed the Jerusalem temple and dispersed the Jews (Luke 19:41–44, 21:20–24). The narrator senses that it is necessary to reassure Christians that, even though the Jewish community constituted out of loyalty to Yahweh now lays crushed by the Romans, they as Christians should remain confident that their community, constituted out of loyalty to Jesus as the resurrected Christ, will not suffer the same fate. The narrative of Jesus's life and death is constructed so as to demonstrate that this is so.

The text proclaims that everything that Abraham, Moses, and the prophets trusted would happen because of their worship of Yahweh really in fact did happen and is happening. The narrative presents a Jesus, together with his teachings and actions, and a community worshiping Jesus the resurrected Christ, which is everything that Abraham, Moses, and the prophets trusted would happen. Filled with the spirit of Yahweh, Jesus is filled with the spirit of Moses, and his disciples are filled with the spirit of the prophets. The narrator has Stephen identify Jesus with the prophet that Moses said Yahweh would produce (Acts 7:37), and he has the people in Galilee say about Jesus that a great prophet has arisen among them (Luke 7:16). The disciples are portrayed as sons of prophets and sons of the covenant (Acts 3:25–26). Just as Moses was at first rejected by the Hebrews in Egypt, so Jesus was rejected during his life. Just as Moses was rejected once again in the wilderness, so the disciples of Jesus are rejected by the Jewish leaders in Jerusalem. Therefore, the trust of Abraham and Moses has not been compromised by the actions of the Romans in Jerusalem. Rather, their goals have been achieved in the establishment and worldwide enlargement of the Christian community. The existence of Christians filled with the spirit of Yahweh, faithfully serving Yahweh through their worship of Jesus as the resurrected Christ, is in the Luke/Acts resurrection faith interpretation a demonstration that Jesus was Yahweh's second Moses and suffering servant. In the eyes of the first leaders of the Christian community, only the extraordinary person who was their companion, teacher, and model of loyalty to Yahweh could be the one who was their resurrected savior, their Messiah, their Christ.

The narrative presented in the book of John is quite different from the narratives presented so far. Not only is the chronology of Jesus's activities different (he takes three trips to Jerusalem instead of one, over a three-year period rather than one year), and allegories replace parables, but everything the Christian community came to believe about their savior after the birth of their resurrection faith is attributed to Jesus before his crucifixion. Many of the symbols used in Jewish worship services become names for the Christ: the lamb of Yahweh (John 1:29), the bread of life (John 6:32), living water (John 7:38), the light of the world (John 8:12). His followers call him "son of Yahweh" (John 1:34), "Messiah" (John 1:41). Jesus, in the book of John, is not seen as being resurrected as their Messiah and Christ, but as having been already from before the beginning of time the son of Yahweh. This book, probably written around 100 AD, is more a pastoral work aiding Christians to continue believing all they believe about Jesus the Christ than it is a narrative of the life and death of Jesus. Q, Mark, Matthew, Luke, and John are all written from within the framework of the resurrection faith, but John takes everything Christians are proclaiming about their resurrected savior and attributes it back to Jesus before his crucifixion. In the book of John, many of these later claims become claims that Jesus actually makes about himself. In John's text, Jesus identifies himself as the bread of life (John 6:32), light of the world (John 8:12), door of the sheep (John 10:7), good shepherd (John 10:11), the resurrection and the life (John 11:25), the way and the truth and the life (John 14:9), and the true vine (John 15:1).

In the long discourses that make up this book, we find a Christian thinker systematically presenting in quasi-narrative form a Christology, a sort of theoretical interpretation of the nature of the one the worship of whom makes the Christian community what it is. In time, John became one of the favorite texts used by Christians in their worship services and their evangelical work of bringing people into the Christian community. The presentation of this Christology is not done to satisfy some purely intellectual interest, but it is done to help maintain a faithful, worshiping community, because according to John, it is in this community that one finds the kingdom of Yahweh being realized. In the worshiping Christian community, one finds much of what Abraham, Moses, and the prophets trusted would eventually be achieved. Living in the Christian community is living in a land of spiritual milk and honey, living in heaven on earth. From before time began, this is the highest achievement of human living. The book of John presents a realized eschatology.

In the life of the Christian community is to be found the end, the goal, that all of the worshipers of Yahweh were hoping would come. Christians may live in a dangerous world in which outsiders constantly are threatening them, but still, living together with fellow Christians in their worshipful relationship to Christ and thus to Yahweh and thus to the eternal itself, they taste the eternal happiness that cannot be destroyed by such external dangers, the eternal happiness that Kierkegaard said is the object of the desire defining the Christian way of life. Kierkegaard also said, however, that one can never cease striving to attain spiritual liberation and eternal happiness. In their resurrection faith, Christians proclaimed both that the Messiah had come, that life in the church meant life in the messianic age, and that the Messiah would come again, at a second, undatable time. Yahweh's mission is never finished. Any person's faithfulness can be deepened and strengthened. Many people still are trapped in merely secular worlds, people who need to hear the call of Yahweh and to respond faithfully. There still is so much nihilism and existential anguish and anxiety. There still is so much intellectual confusion and spiritual ignorance. There still are so many people being treated unjustly and so many secular practices that produce domination and oppression. Something marvelous has occurred in the messianic event that founded the Christian faith and community, but the fullness of the messianic age is something that is always in the future. The second coming is a transcendental ideal drawing Christians to continue to hope and strive for greater spiritual emancipation and loving care for other people.

This accent on realized eschatology is crucial to keep in mind when reading the last book written in the John tradition, the book of Revelations. This is not a book about metaphysical beings. It is an apocalyptic book written in the symbolic, coded style of Daniel, using symbolism from Jewish mystical traditions developed from Ezekiel, in order to encourage Christians to remain faithful in spite of the suffering they are undergoing in the Roman empire. The number seven stands for the seven churches to which it was sent, the number four for the four gospel narratives of Jesus's life, and the number twelve for the twelve apostles. Babylon is the code name for the Romans. The book calls for Christians to continue to judge the world the way the prophets did and to live in the midst of Roman persecution as saints already living in the joyous kingdom of Yahweh, having been filled with the spirit of the resurrected Christ, the spirit of Yahweh.

The book of John begins by proclaiming that Jesus Christ is the word that is the call of the infinite which is timelessly prior to all time. This is the call Moses heard when encountering the suffering of his people and when he faithfully responded to this encounter with the infinite by focusing his worship on the one named Yahweh. In encountering Jesus Christ, John proclaims, one encounters the word of the infinite spoken outside temporal changes calling for surrender and dedication to deliver all people, beginning with oneself, from out of slavery to their rebellious ignorance of the infinite and from all the suffering and injustice that follows from such ignorance. In worshiping Christ one lives joyfully in the light of understanding the dependence of the finite upon the infinite, and in an understanding of what faithfulness to hearing the timeless word of Yahweh's call requires and promises. For John God is a Word, a Call, and not a metaphysical cause. In constituting and worshiping the resurrected Christ, and in being his living body filled with his spirit, the spirit of Yahweh, the word of the infinite becomes flesh and dwells among Christians, and Christ is glorified as the son of Yahweh. By being constituted as their focus of worship, the resurrected Christ is the only son of Yahweh, because in the Christian community is found the final spiritual deliverance that Moses, in his faithful responding to the call of the infinite, began in his worship of Yahweh (John 1:1–14).

In naming Jesus Christ in so many different ways, the book of John wants to point out that everything hoped for by Hebrews, Israelites, and Jews worshiping Yahweh is achieved in the community worship-ing the Christian's savior and Messiah, Jesus the resurrected Christ. This religious proclamation can be understood without trapping one-self in counterproductive metaphysical theorizing. The writer of John may have been familiar with the Greek philosophical use of the word "Logos," "word" (the supposedly eternal unchanging principle in terms of which all change can be explained), but in his text it is given a com-pletely Jewish and Christian religious meaning. John is not involved in giving metaphysical explanations that can satisfy the principle of suf-ficient reason. Although he focuses on the resurrected Christ in every-thing he says about Jesus, this does not mean that Jesus was some meta-physical being pretending to be a flesh-and-blood human. It is a very real human who is portrayed in the book of John as the Christ, and it is as their religious savior that he is identified with the word of the infi-nite, calling out to people to be religiously humble, loyal, and ethical and to joyfully love life as it is when not contaminated by human rebel-lion, craving, alienation, ignorance, injustice, guilt, and suffering. That for Christians Jesus Christ is the only son of Yahweh does not mean that Yahweh (or Allah) cannot be worshiped and served in other ways. It means that they cannot be the people they are, with their identities being determined by their Christian way of life, without Jesus Christ and only Jesus Christ being the defining center of that way of life. It does not mean that the only form of bhakti yoga that can liberate peo-ple from suffering and craving is the bhakti yoga of Hebrews, Israelites, Jews, Christians, and Muslims who worship Yahweh or Allah. Hindu worship of Krishna and Buddhist worship of bodhisattvas can also be instances of faithfully responding to the call of the infinite. In addition, as Hindus, Taoists, and many Buddhists point out, bhakti yoga is not the only way to faithfully respond to encounters with the infinite. The book of John is presenting pastoral discourses to Christians in order to strengthen their ability to continue worshiping their resurrected savior, Jesus Christ. It is not presenting a dissertation about all the possible ways people in all times and social/cultural circumstances can respond to the call of the infinite.

The letters of Paul try to carry out many of the same pastoral func-tions as John's discourses. Written more than fifty years before the book of John and after ten years of work by Paul in converting non-Jews to Christianity, they consist of an expression of Paul's interpretation of Christianity and his advice to new Christian communities on how they are to deal with specific problems that these communities face in Greek and Roman environments. Paul's letters have played a powerful role in determining the character of the Christian way of life, determining how Christians respond to the call of Yahweh and how they live with Jesus as their resurrected savior. Examining these letters provides an excellent summation of this study of Christianity.

Paul's first letter, in 50 AD to the Christians in Thessalonica, the home capital in Macedonia of Alexander the Great, is the earliest text we have of Christian writing. In both it and his second letter to them, Paul is warning them not to misunderstand what it means to say that soon their enemies would be destroyed and the kingdom of Yahweh would be established in all its glory. As we have seen, Luke/Acts at first has all the Christian leaders waiting in Jerusalem for the end of the world. Only gradually, as Roman ruthlessness increased and Christianity spread throughout the Roman empire, did Christians come to understand fully the significance of having received the holy spirit of Jesus Christ and Yahweh. The enemy to be destroyed is not Rome but their own rebellion against Yahweh, their own cravings and misguided thoughts. The kingdom that was to come was already significantly present in their new lives in the Christian community. People in Thessalonica were quitting their jobs and sitting around waiting for something to happen. Paul writes this letter, meant to be read to the whole community, and tells them to get back to work, to live quietly, and to help one another (I Thess. 4:1, 11, 5:13–14, II Thess. 3:6, 12). They are not to worry about fellow Christians who have already died because they will be the first to be resurrected as they live on in the community they helped constitute (I Thess 4:13–18).

Paul spells out in his letter to the Colossians what kind of death, resurrection, and kingdom Christians are talking about. Yahweh, Paul writes, is invisible, not some metaphysical being, and their resurrected savior is like Yahweh (Colossians 1:15–20). People living alienated from Yahweh, unable to hear his loving call to love and instead causing injustice, are spiritually dead; they understand nothing about the infinite they encounter or the joyous life that could be theirs (Colossians 2:13, 3:5). In their resurrection faith, however, Christians know that Christ died to the elemental spirits of the world and was raised from that death as his spirit lives in the body of the Christian community (Colossians 2:9, 3:1). Christians then must put to death the rebellious death they are living (Colossians 3:5) and rise with their savior into a life of compassion, kindness, lowliness, meekness, and patience, joyfully singing and giving thanks (Colossians 3:12–17). The living and the dead live on in the Christian community.

A different problem confronted Christians in the city of Corinth, a major, cosmopolitan Greek port city. In this letter Paul urges his readers not to begin to play the Greek philosophical game of metaphysics. Greek thinkers were choosing up sides and forming Platonic, Aristotelian, Stoic, and atomistic schools that debated the supporting arguments presented in each school. Paul warns the Christians at Corinth not to do the same (I Cor. 1:10–17), because Christianity is not a matter of debating competing theories, but it is a matter of worshiping Yahweh through worshiping Christ in their resurrection faith. For those seeking ultimate explanations that meet the demands of the principle of sufficient reason, Christianity is utter foolishness. (I Cor. 1:20–25). Christianity worships and obeys Yahweh and Christ; it does not theorize. Worshiping Yahweh and his suffering servant resurrected as their savior allows Christians to understand how foolish it is to ignore and reject encounters with the infinite in favor of relying on secular, socially constituted concepts and canons of reason, which prevent surrender to the call of the infinite, but instead feed the craving to be intellectual masters of everything (I Cor. 1:26–30).

One cannot comprehend Yahweh and what he calls for people to do by metaphysical theorizing, but only by being reborn with the spirit of Yahweh, as one lives in that community which is his Messiah's body filled with his spirit of surrender, thankfulness, joy, and loyal service (I Cor. 2:6–16; 3:16–17). In service to the resurrected Christ, Christians gladly are metaphysical fools in order to live by the understanding gained through their resurrection faith (I Cor. 4:10). Metaphysical knowledge puffs people up so that they disastrously think that their concepts and reasoning are self-sufficient, but love builds up joy, un-alienated lives, and loving respect and care for all people (I Cor. 8:1). Different Christians will make different sorts of contributions to the life of the community. Some may seem major and some minor, but all are invaluable and united in possessing the same spirit of Yahweh and Christ (I Cor. 12). The most vital characteristic of those possessing the Christian spirit is lovingly living with and for other people, being kind to them, patient with them, not being jealous or boastful, not insisting on one's own way, not being irritable or resentful, not rejoicing in acting unjustly or seeing people treated unjustly, but rejoicing in serving justice and seeing it being served, trusting in Yahweh and being filled with hope, and enduring anything in order to remain faithful to Yahweh and his redemptive work through the resurrected Messiah (I Cor. 13:4–7). Worshiping and loyally loving Yahweh, and ethically loving all people in their singular uniqueness, is the core of responding faithfully to encounters with the infinite and of living filled with trusting hope in the joyous kingdom that comes through such love (I Cor. 13:13). When one is living faithfully, hopefully, and lovingly within the body of Christ and filled with the spirit of Christ, then the death of Jesus and one's own certain death is swallowed up in victory (I Cor. 15: 54–55).

Perhaps the best summary proclamation of the Christian way of life is found in Paul's letter in the late fifties to the Christian community in Rome, a community he did not found and he had never visited, but whose help he needed as he prepared to take his missionary work west to Spain. Paul is writing to explain his understanding of Christianity so as to persuade these Christians that he deserves their support. He proclaims that faithfulness to the resurrected Jesus Christ, because of the faithfulness of Jesus to the will of Yahweh that led to his death, provides Christians with faithful, worshipful obedience to Yahweh's righteous call to deliver his people from spiritual slavery and injustice (Romans 1:16–17, 3:21–31). Paul contrasts the life of Yahweh's faithful servants with the lives of people who do not respond faithfully to their encounters with the infinite. Such people serve idols they have constituted: a finite nature of necessities and chances that supposedly is self-contained, without any dependence on anything infinite and timeless; rulers of nations and empires supposedly supremely sovereign, religious texts and practices that supposedly deliver spiritual fruit, even if their readers and participants lack the spirit of Yahweh (Romans 1:18–25, 2:13, 25, 10:3). He contrasts the lives of those (like Adam) who rebelliously proclaim their autonomy and leave a corrupting, unjust and alienating inheritance, and those (like Jesus the Christ) who remain faithfully obedient, because they have endorsed their inheritance of the resurrection faith and live in a community of joyous, loving servants of Yahweh and his Messiah (Romans 5:1–19; 8:28; 12:9–21). The faithful loyalty that Jesus demonstrated in his life and death is the same kind of faithfulness that Abraham demonstrated in offering up for sacrifice his son, trusting fully that he would be restored, offering him up in sacrifice because only Abraham's faithfulness could make Isaac a spiritual son who would live continually in his spiritual offspring (Romans 4:1–35). Paul, who was Saul the Jew, acknowledges that those Jews who practice righteous loyalty to Yahweh will reap the spiritual rewards of such spiritual living (Romans 10:5, 11:1–2, 7; 14:3–8). Paul reminds his Christian readers, however, that just as not everyone who talks Christian talk is righteously loyal to Christ and Yahweh, so not every one who is circumcised or talks the Torah is righteously loyal to Yahweh (Romans 2:13, 25, 14:10, 16:17). Faithfulness in one's whole way of living is what Yahweh calls forth from all his sons (Romans 8:14), and as Paul writes to the Roman Christians, for them this means faithfulness to Jesus as their resurrected savior, Christ, Messiah, son of Yahweh.

Rooted in the resurrection faith as proclaimed by writers of religious narratives and letters, Christianity over its two-thousand-year history has branched into many varieties. Some of the variations emerged because of the development of different traditions of worship and community formation, and some because of nonreligious factors (connections with national identities and metaphysical movements). With the disintegration of the Roman empire, Christianity split into a Western Rome-centered community and an eastern, Constantinople-centered community. Over time community identity in the West depended more and more upon the authority of the pronouncements of a group of leaders who spoke through the voice of the bishop of Rome, the Pope, and accented worship practices led by professional priests, especially the practice of celebrating the mass (reinacting Jesus's last supper as described in the narratives). The Eastern Christian community also maintained a titular leader, but authority rested more with traditional practices than official pronouncements. With the rise of nation-states in northern Europe, the Western Christian community divided again and again. The Church of England rejected the authority of the Pope and began to develop traditions that accented a common book of prayers. In Germany, Luther protested against what he saw as priestly abuses in the Christian community and against letting Greek metaphysics corrupt Christian thinking. He proclaimed that all Christians could be their own priests, directly encountering Yahweh in prayer and the resurrected Christ through the reading and preaching of the Christian's Bible. First in Switzerland and then in Scotland and the Netherlands, Presbyterians and the Reformed Church maintained community identity through a common confession of faith, which was constructed, interpreted, and applied by leaders elected by members of the Christian community. Also in Switzerland, the Baptist movement began accenting the authority of the Christian Bible and the responsibility of every individual Christian and every Christian community to interpret the Bible. In the eighteenth and nineteenth centuries, additional protest movements began by Methodists ethically condemning common economic and class practices among so-called Christians in Great Britain, and by Quakers condemning priestly privileges and complicity with national wars. Spurred on by Baptist individualism, dozens of new Protestant denominations and independent communities were formed. Finally, new branches continued to grow as communities were founded by leaders who made proclamations based on their own personal encounters with the infinite (the Mormons and the Christian Science movement). Much of this branching only demonstrates that there can be many different ways of responding faithfully to encounters with the infinite and worship of Yahweh and his resurrected Messiah.

Unfortunately, during this two-thousand-year history religious proclamations often became mixed up with metaphysical theorizing. In spite of their deep loyalty to Yahweh and Jesus as the resurrected Christ, Augustine used Platonic metaphysical notions in proclaiming the Christian good news, and Aquinas drew upon Aristotelian metaphysical categories and arguments in an attempt to rationally prove the existence of Yahweh as the supreme being who is the creator and ultimate cause of of nature. Also, unfortunately, Christian leaders too often tried to use the power of the state to coerce people to agree in thought and action with the interpretations and applications these leaders presented as theological and ethical truths. Unfortunately, too often Christian communities have interpreted sentences in the Bible using metaphysical and nonreligious historical categories producing what they have called literal interpretations of the Bible. This has become doubly dangerous as these metaphysical fundamentalists and literalists also have tried to use the power of the state to coerce people to obey their proclamations. Take away the metaphysics, and the current battles between evolutionary accounts in biology and creationist accounts in religion would disappear. Take away the metaphysics, and legal discrimination against gender preferences would appear as blatantly unjust. Take away the metaphysics and efforts to justify national wars by claiming that they are the will of the God of agape love would appear to be as self-contradictory as they are.

Christianity, in its many different faithful responses to Yahweh's call to deliver people from enslavement and as a faithful response to the call of Jesus the resurrected savior, proves that there can be many, not-unjustified, different historically and socially constituted faithful responses to people's encounters with the infinite. Loving respect for differences within Christianity can be matched by Christians with loving respect for non-Christian religious responses of faithfulness, without Christians being unfaithful to what makes them Christian. People, in fact, can deepen their Christian faithfulness by entering into dialogue with persons living in other religious traditions. Today, more and more Christian thinkers are discovering this to be correct as they engage in dialogue with Jews and Buddhists. The big challenge in the current world setting is to do the same with faithful Muslims. If bad metaphysical influences can be erased from Christian and Islamic religious traditions, this too can prove to be a very fruitful dialogue.

3. Islam

Is it possible today to locate Islam in a postmodern age? If one were to take a survey of Muslims throughout the world, the vast majority probably would say that belief in a metaphysical god is an essential ingredient in the religious way of life of Muslims. It certainly seems as though the militant Muslims who are willing to kill and die to protect their way of life hold metaphysical beliefs about Allah and his dispensation of heavenly rewards for what they are doing to protect Islam. Few of its religious leaders probably have ever heard of postmodernism. If they have heard of it, they probably lump it together with the European and American secularism and modernism that they see threatening the Islamic way of life. Few Western Muslims are conversant with postmodern texts.[248] Derrida, who grew up in Algeria, quite deliberately avoids talking about Islam. Given the current deadly battle between European and American securalism or metaphysical Christian fundamentalism and metaphysical Islamic fundamentalism, it would be extremely valuable if a nonmetaphysical, postmodern interpretation of the Islamic religious way of life could be offered. This would allow all the religions of the world to gratefully appropriate the Islamic rejection of secularism, while eliminating the dogmatic, metaphysical contamination of the Abrahamic religions that leave people only two options: unconditional surrender or all-out war. In what follows, a postmodern interpretation of the Qur'an will be offered which preserves that which Allah inspired Muhammad to recite to Allah's faithful servants, recitations that are the defining center of the Islamic religious way of life.

In 610 AD Muhammad of Mecca, Arabia, had an encounter with, the infinite for which he and the events surrounding his life had been preparing him since before he was born. In his faithful response to this encounter, he began a life focused on worship of and righteous surrender and obedience to the most gracious and most merciful god, Allah. The name "Allah" had been used by some of the people in Mecca to refer to one among a number of gods that were worshiped. Muhammad had joined company with one group, the Hanifs, who worshiped only Allah, but still seemed to think that there were other gods for others to worship. Muhammad, because of his identification of Allah with the infinite he had encountered, delivered the message that there is only one God to be worshipped, Allah. The name Allah comes from two Arabic words: *Al,* meaning "the," and *Iloh,* derived from one of the Hebrew names for God, Elohim, by dropping the suffix "im," which makes the name masculine. Allah is neither male nor female. Muhammad's encounter with the infinite compelled him to deliver the message that Allah cannot be a visible object (2:2),[249] cannot be an object located at a place in space (2:115), is eternal and not dependent on the changing conditions of life (3:2), is not a superstitious, supernatural magician (5:103), is the presupposition of every constituted being (2:22), is manifested by all the joyous elements upon which we live and for which we should give thanks for Allah's graciousness (6:55), is manifested in Allah's opposition to all injustice (3:108) and in the responsibility Allah places upon every person to be just (4:135). Allah is merciful, not letting past rebellion and injustice prevent people from enjoying the fruits of living faithful to Allah (3:129).

The Buddha woke up to enlightenment when he became fully aware of the suffering in human life. Moses woke up from his spiritual sleep by encountering the suffering of his people and thereby encountering the infinite. Muhammad's encounter with the infinite, in all its awesomeness, mercy, and joy, came after forty years of personally experiencing suffering, observing injustice, and reflecting on what he had heard about the proclamations of Hebrews and Christians. Muhammad's father died before he was born, and he became an orphan at six when his mother died. Then, at age eight his beloved grandfather, who was caring for him, died, and Muhammad had to go and live with an uncle. During his life he suffered through burying many of his young children and his beloved first wife, Khadija. He observed the hellish results of constant tribal warfare on the Arabian peninsula, the slaughter of children, and the treatment of women as being worth less than animals. Although he was barely literate, he had memorized the words orally communicated to him by those who knew many of the great narratives in the Hebrew and Christian Bibles, and when he relayed the messages that his encounters with the infinite, with Allah, provided to him, these messages often consisted of interpretations of biblical accounts of Biblical characters and events. The messages he delivered were in turn memorized by his followers who in that way continued circulating the messages. Eventually they were written down in the Qur'an, which literally mens "recitation." Not surprisingly, the ethical message Muhammad heard in his encounter with the infinite, Allah, contained many instructions for compassionately carrying for orphans, widows, the poor, and the powerless.

The word "Islam" means "the peace that comes to one who surrenders totally to Allah." Both surrender and the peace it produces involve the whole person. To surrender is to say, "I give up." One must give up one whole way of life and live another kind of life. Surrender means conversion, not conversion from one religion to another or conversion from one set of beliefs to another set, but conversion from unrighteousness to righteousness. The way of life that one is to give up is an unrighteous way of living, and the way of life one is to gain in return is a righteous way of living. The unrighteous way of living is not right in two different ways. First, people in such a life do not rightly understand that visible objects are not self-sufficient metaphysical substances and that objects in space and time do not exhaust what can be encountered. In the language of the Qur'an, unrighteous people do not recognize Allah as creator of all such objects (2:22). They do not thank Allah for the graciousness of receiving a marvelous natural world pointing to the infinite without which it would be nothing. Thus, they do not rightly perceive the joyous life that comes to people just by living with the natural elements surrounding them. Again and again, the Qur'an describes the sort of riches the unrighteous are missing out on enjoying gardens near to the infinite with rivers flowing beneath; timeless joy with pure and holy companions (3:15, 4:57, 56:12); tranquility and peace with Allah, with oneself, with one's companions in righteousness (6:127, 9:72, 48:4). Second, the unrighteous way of living is one in which people act unjustly and without compassion toward the powerless and needy, to orphans, widows, the poor, strangers, and slaves. (2:117, 2:240, 4:2-6, 6:152, 7:44, 9:60, 30:38). They play and amuse themselves while suffering surrounds them (6:32). They lose themselves in social practices that cause them and those like them to be miserable (7:44).

The message Allah communicates through Muhammad is that people in their original suchness are not evil. Unrighteous people are false to themselves and suffer from a disease (2:10), a social disease inherited from practices constituted by unfaithful ancestors and endorsed by individuals who do not resist this disease, but choose to continue to be a part of the problem rather than part of the solution. This humanly constituted social disease is greater than the actions of individuals existing at a certain time. People are nurtured and socialized in this disease-ridden social and cultural atmosphere, and unrighteousness and suffering are the result. In Hinduism and Buddhism this corrupting background is called "karma," in Christianity it is called "original sin," and in Islam it is called "Satan." Although they need not do so, people lose out on joyous life by following Satan and deifying themselves and their creations, by cravingly causing others to suffer, thereby harming themselves (3:117). Although the Qur'an points out that unrighteousness is rampant in the world, it does not present a negative evaluation of people or a pessimistic evaluation of human life. People are capable of ending the hell on earth they have created if they will cease rebelling and gain peace by surrendering to Allah. Muhammad recites what he has heard in his encounter with the infinite, what he has heard in surrendering in silence to the call to be righteous. He is to warn people about what is going on and what they have to do in order to avoid the continual, hellish consequences of their unrighteousness (35:23). Everything good in life comes from Allah, and everything evil is produced by unrighteous people (4:79). Unrighteousness carries with it terrible consequences, but Allah is merciful and compassionate. If the unrighteous become righteous, then joyous, tranquil life in the gardens of joyous living is restored to them. Muhammad recites that he is to warn people of the timeless "judgement day," which is leveled on their lives every moment of every day. The righteous shall live joyfully and peacefully, and the unrighteous will suffer the consequences of their rebellious craving to be God (3:30). The unrighteous are slaves to their cravings and they live with the natural, miserable consequences of such slavery. The righteous surrender as slaves to Allah, and they become free to live in joy and peace.

Islam's accent on the differences between righteousness and unrighteousness is a consequence of Muhammad's ethical encounter with the infinite and his surrender to merciful Allah. Muhammad understood suffering, and he surrendered to Allah who loves each and every person equally in their singular uniqueness. In this sense, Islam is very egalitarian. Respecting and loving people in their ethical singularity, however, means recognizing that their uniqueness stems from their unique set of responsibilities. One cannot respect a person as a unique individual without judging the person to be responsible to be just and loving toward other people. Loving the unrighteous means warning them of the consequences of their current way of living and promising them the joy and peace that is available to every single person, no matter what the history of that person has been. Living righteously means surrendering to Allah and loving mercifully as Allah loves mercifully.

Islam's accent on surrendering to Allah as the creator of all finite beings and persons is a consequence of Muhammad's encounter with the infinite other to all finite things. Worship of Allah as creator means living totally surrendered in thankfulness and gratefulness for our original healthiness and the glorious elements within which we live and which give us such joy: the wind and water, the mountains and seas, the sunrises and sunsets, the natural regularities that make it possible for people to live in harmony with nature. (Islamic righteous life bears remarkable similarities to Zen nirvana life.) Worshiping Allah as creator means never confusing Allah with any graven image constituted by unrighteous persons. Allah is not visible and Allah is outside time, but everything visible and changing points to the infinite other, to Allah as their creator.

This is the message that Muhammad heard and recited to others who recited it to more and more others. In ten years after his encounter with Allah, all of Arabia was listening, and in a hundred years people as far away as Spain were listening. In Islam, the Qur'an is a recitation of what Muhammad heard when encountering Allah and surrendering in worship and service to Allah. For Muslims, the Qur'an is much more than a written text expressing Muhammad's thoughts. Again and again the Qur'an says that Muhammad is only the messenger and warner of what is being said through him as he is encountering the wholly other Allah. The thoughts he recites to others are not thoughts over which he can claim property ownership rights. The human being, thinking with socially constituted secular words and canons of reasonableness, is not the author of these thoughts. These are thoughts forced on him as he surrenders himself to the infinite, which he cannot help but understand as gracious and merciful. It is this understanding that leads him to worship and obey Allah and in that worshipful obedience, to assign authorship to Allah. It is not necessary to postulate some metaphysical being magically pouring ideas into Muhammad's head in order to understand Islam's proclamation that the Qur'an is a recitation of what Allah, not Muhammad, is saying. Islam's understanding of the status of the Qur'an can be given a Kierkegaardian interpretation. Independent of his encounters with the infinite, Muhammad can only make nonreligious statements in an objectivistic form of subjectivity, but in responding faithfully to his encounters with the infinite, by surrendering to Allah in righteous worship and obedience, Muhammad can recite what now constitutes his Islamic subjectivistic form of subjectivity. The other of all subjects and objects in an objectivistic form of life is to be thanked and praised for motivating the construction of the Islamic form of subjectivity that Muhammad recites.

At the very beginning of the Qur'an, Muhammad recites that for those who fear (worship and obey) Allah, there is no room for doubt that the Qur'an offers sure guidance (2:2). Listening to the Qur'an allows the faithful to hear two vital messages: what living righteously requires and what such a way of living delivers as joyful living (17:9). There is nothing special about Muhammad as the one who recites what he has heard. He is just a man. What he learned from his encounter with the infinite others can learn by listening to what he is reciting. The ultimate author of the Qur'an is the infinite other of the finite, the infinite that remains an unfathomable mystery to those enslaved in the merely finite, but is encountered as most merciful by those who righteously listen to what Muhammad is reciting (25:6). Wisdom and knowledge about the dependence of the finite on the infinite, and about the responsibility of all people to be just and compassionate to all people, comes from worshipfully listening to the ultimate author of the Qur'an (27:6). What Muhammad heard and recited was in Arabic because this was his language and because this is the language of the specific people to whom he was delivering his message and warning(12:2, 20:113, 41:44, 42:7).

Muhammad does not pretend that he is the first person who communicated to people what was heard in encounters with the infinite. His encounter with the infinite happened after years of medi-tating on what he had heard about the great figures in the Hebrew tra-dition and about Jesus. After his encounter and his surrender to Allah, Muhammad recites what he, in his new Islamic form of subjectivity, hears about these religious giants (40:23–54). Adam teaches us about the marvelous garden in which the righteous live (2:31) and the shame people feel when they rebel out of a craving for absolute power (7:26). Noah teaches us about judgement, the consequences of unrighteous-ness, and about the mercy of Allah (7:59, 11:25–48, 23:23). Abraham, who was neither Jew nor Christian, but the father of Jews, Christians and Muslims, teaches us, through his faithful and trustful offering up of Isaac, what it means to totally surrender to Allah (3:61, 2:124, 3:95, 11:69–76). Isma'il teaches us that through him Muslims in Arabia are recipients of the promises made to Abraham (2:133, 2:136, 3:84, 6:86, 14:39). Joseph teaches us about the dangerousness of the unrighteous and about family loyalty of the righteous (12:4–101). Moses teaches us how Allah delivered his people from slavery (2:50, 7:104–167), gave the law contained in the ten commandments (2:92, 3:3, 5:44), and showed the land of milk and honey waiting for the righteous (5:20–25, 10:75–90). David taught us what is involved in making just decisions in morally complex situations (38.17), and Solomon taught us the kind of riches that come to the righteous (27:16–47). Jesus taught us what happens when people are filled with the holy spirit of Allah (2:87, 2:253), and he asked his disciples to be his helpers in serving Allah (3:52, 61:14). He taught us the golden rule (3:3).

Muhammad recites that he is only a messenger, not the first mes-senger, but the last messenger needed to deliver the message and warn-ing he is reciting in Arabic to the people of Arabia. Given what he hears in his faithful response to his encounter with the infinite, Muhammad recites that the messages delivered in the biblical narratives about the Hebrew fathers and about Jesus are inadequate and incomplete. They are inadequate because they are only narratives and therefore they need to be interpreted in order for one to hear the message Allah is deliver-ing. Interpretations can vary and thus even faithful listeners will be left unsure about what the message is. In the Qur'an, the message and the warning from Allah are transmitted through Muhammad directly to his listeners so that they know exactly what obedience to Allah entails. Biblical messages are incomplete because the ten commandments and the golden rule are very general and need to be supplemented by specific instructions for their application to problems existing in Arabia at the time Muhammad encountered the infinite and transmitted what he heard from Allah to the listeners who faced these problems. Given the specific moral directives he heard because of his encounter with the ethical and merciful infinite, Allah, his listeners would not need another messenger. Muhammad would be the last one. By constituting a religious community of people surrendering to Allah and recognizing Muhammad as the messenger from Allah to them, this community was given a continuing identity that would wash away tribal differences. The world of Islam is a world of Muslims surrendering to Allah and living righteously in the manner spelled out by what Muhammad delivers in Allah's message to them.

The Qur'an makes it very clear that there had been other messengers before Muhammad and that the religious ways of life constituted by faithfully listening to those messages, are some of the many ways that Allah has created different worshiping communities (5:48). Judaism and Christianity may be appropriate ways for Jews and Christians to worship, but they are not the ways appropriate for those responding worshipfully to what the *Qu'ran* is saying. Furthermore, Muhammad recites that from Allah's point of view many people who call themselves Jews and Christians are to be judged as unrighteous because they have forgotten messages transmitted by their Hebrew fathers and Jesus (5:14, 20). Muhammad does hear Allah say that the infinite and invisible Allah must not be anthropologically pictured as a father who had a son. The Qur'an again and again rejects all metaphysical characterizations of Allah as being three distinct beings (father, son, and holy spirit), somehow remaining three while also being one (4:17–61, 5:17–18, 5:72–75, 5:116, 19:92). Such a metaphysical theory of the trinity had become at Muhammad's time almost an orthodox theory among Christian thinkers influenced by Platonic metaphysics. The interpretation of the trinity presented in the previous section on Christianity works without any such metaphysical theory or any anthropological picturing of the infinite. There does not seem to be any conflict between that interpretation of Christianity and the concerns expressed in the Qur'an.

Many of the detailed injunctions that are communicated through Muhammad to his listeners do seem appropriate to a specific audience, one confronted by the horrors present in unrighteous Arabian life. Whenever rules are set up mandating a certain sort of behavior, one can be sure that the practices being prohibited are widespread and the practices being required are not being followed. Otherwise, why introduce the rules? Therefore, one learns a great deal about Arabian life by looking at the injunctions Muhammad communicates. Infanticide is prohibited (6:141). Family-destroying gambling and use of intoxicants are forbidden (5:50). Detailed rules governing the inheritance of property are introduced (4:1–12). Detailed protections for women pledging dowries in marriage and for women during divorces are introduced (2:228–237). Protection for women from the unwanted attentions of the unrighteous are introduced in the form of dress codes. (24:31) Requirements to provide alms for orphans, widows, and the poor are introduced (2:240, 4:2-6, 6:152, 9:60, 30:38). Muhammad hears that rules such as these are necessary for there to exist a unified community of righteous listeners to the Qur'an, a community of righteous worshipers of Allah, who can hear and relate to others Muhammad's communication of Allah's graciousness and mercy. Since the Qur'an says that there are other ways of faithfully responding to the call of the infinite, and that there should be no compulsion in religion, it does seem that some of these and other similar rules apply only to those who choose to surrender to Allah by worshiping in the Islamic community.

Providing additional strength to the bonding of Muslims together into a community with a common identity are the religious practices that have become known as the five pillars of Islam:

(1) Strive continually until one can say with one's whole life and without any reservation, the opening Surah in the Qur'an:

> In the name of Allah, Most Gracious, Most Merciful.
> Praise be to Allah, the Cherisher and Sustainer of the Worlds;
> Most Gracious, Most Merciful;
> Master of the Day of Judgement.
> You do we worship, and Your aid do we seek.

Show us the straight way.

The Way of those on whom you have bestowed Your Grace, those whose (portion) is not wrath, and who do not go astray. (1:1-7)

(2) Engage in a regular routine of prayer at the critical moments of each day: when you wake up, at noon, at mid-afternoon, at sunset, and when you go to bed (17:78–111).

(3) Give alms regularly and proportionately to one's income (2:271, 9:60, 51:19, 58:12–13).

(4) By daily fasting and prayer, remember Ramadan, the month in which Muhammad first encountered the infinite and heard what he was to recite, and the month in which he made his migration (Hijrah) from his original home in Mecca to Yathrib (renamed "Medina," the city of the Prophet) (2:185).

(5) Once in a lifetime, on an equal basis with other righteous Muslims, join for worship at Mecca, where Muhammad's encounter with the infinite first occurred.

By participating in these practices, Muslims reinforce their faithful Islamic response to the call of the infinite, the call of Allah.

Muhammad's encounters with the infinite did not occur just once, but they occurred throughout the last twenty-three years of his life. During those years his life changed dramatically and so did the things he heard and transmitted for his followers to recite. Twelve years after his encounter with the infinite in the cave outside of Mecca, Muhammad accepted an invitation from the people of Yathrib to come north and become the governor of their city, believing that he and his Islamic faith could establish unity in a city split into uncooperative factions. Although few people in Mecca had listened to his messages when he lived there, eight years later he returned as the conqueror of Mecca and saw a majority of the population became Muslims. By attempting to play the roles of religious prophet and political authority at the same time, Muhammad tackled one of the most complex problems facing any religious person. How does one faithfully respond to one's encounters with the infinite as a person responsible for governing a political state? It is one thing for a person to emulate Allah's mercy when just that one person has been harmed by someone else, but it is much more difficult to know what to do to prevent unrighteous persons from harming other people or to know how to deal with people who have caused such harm.

What does Muhammad, focused on worshiping gracious and merciful Allah, hear and communicate about how the power of the state should be used to prevent harm to the citizens of the state and to deal with criminals? How should one deal with criminals in order to minimize the number and severity of the crimes committed? How does the governor of a state balance compassion for the governed with merciful treatment of people who harm the governed? That only the righteous receive the joyous benefits of harmonious life with Allah and other righteous people does not seem to provide sufficient motivation to prevent unrighteous persons who have forgotten this truth from harming other people. Every state seems to need to establish some sort of system of retributive justice. Muhammad heard Allah say the same thing. In his encounter with the infinite and in his obedient listening to Allah's proclamations, it was still Muhammad as a unique ethical, and socially constituted person who listened and transmitted what he heard and could say. As one who had meditated for years on the messages communicated by his Hebrew forefathers, Muhammad heard and proclaimed the retributive principle of an eye for an eye (5:45). Given the world in that he was reared and which he had to govern, and given the social constitution of the people who might harm or keep harming people and thus their ability to respond to what Muhammad the governor might say, Muhammad said what he heard Allah saying to him. Muhammad also communicated, however, the principle of treating mercifully those evildoers who acted in ignorance, an ignorance present in all the forgetful, unrighteous people, and those who then repented and joined the community of the righteous (6:54). One must even thank Allah for this repentance, because Allah's mercy was present before the repentance, and hearing of such mercy led to repentance.

For hundreds of years now, political theorists and criminologists have debated whether a governmental policy of an eye for an eye motivates people to not commit crimes or prevents criminals from committing new crimes. All governmental injunctions have to be proclaimed to historically and socially specific kinds of citizens, who are motivated by beliefs, desires, and habits that also are historically specific and facing historically specific problems in historically specific situations. What Muhammad would hear and communicate as governmental policies of crime prevention were he to be speaking in changed conditions would have to change in order that it could be Allah who was speaking through Muhammad to these people, so different from the ones living in Medina and Mecca in the seventh century. From its earliest inception, Islam has worked out ways to apply what Muhammad heard to new and changing situations. In addition to the authority of the Qur'an itself, the actions of Muhammad and his companions and later followers who were emulating Muhammad's example became authoritative and was called Sunna. Since so many different and seemingly contradictory injunctions claimed admission to the Sunna, the method of Ijima (reaching consensus on interpretation and application) was added to the authoritative tradition.[250]

Muslims, like all people trying to religiously respond faithfully to encounters with the infinite, have always faced the problem of applying universal ethical responsibilities to the particularities of specific historical situations. Trying to apply governmental policies appropriate to seventh-century Arabia in twentieth-century Turkey, Indonesia, or England would not be listening to Allah, but would be applying a human mechanical procedure, rather than listening to what Allah has to say to people in these very different worlds. Not surprisingly, through the centuries many Muslims have tried to find ways to minimize harming offenders while still preserving laws aimed at preventing harm to citizens. (Instead of chopping off the whole hand of a thief, slice off just enough to be a constant motivation to the person to not repeat the action.) There is every reason for Muslims to bring with them the best understanding that criminologists can provide when they struggle to understand what faithfulness to the infinite, gracious, and merciful Allah requires them to hear when the Qur'an is recited in different and changing circumstances.

Even more difficult than understanding what kind of criminal justice system Allah asks his righteous people to establish in a nation-state is understanding how cities and nation-states should use their power in dealing with other states. The Qur'an declares that Allah is opposed to aggressive wars, but governments have the duty to defend their citizens from external aggression (2:190). No sooner had Muhammad assumed the role of political leader in Medina than active, threatening opposition arose among tribes in Medina and throughout Arabia who were opposed to the revolutionary social changes that Muhammad introduced to implement Allah's ethical demands for the just treatment of people. Even though the new constitution Muhammad introduced in Medina called for tolerance and respect for Jews and Christians, still some factions in Medina supported the tribes going to war against the new Islamic Medina. Muhammad heard Allah instruct him to fight a defensive war by stopping the attacking military forces and by punishing those internally threatening the existence of the new state by supporting Medina's enemies.

Again, what Muhammad heard about what to do as the governor of Medina may be applicable directly only to that specific historical setting. It is extremely difficult to know what people striving to faithfully respond to the ethical call of the infinite should believe about "just wars" in general. The nature of contemporary wars of states against states may throw into question the ethical appropriateness of any such wars, even the ethical appropriateness of the whole idea of state sovereignty. The problems become even more complex when people turn to violence in order to oppose oppressive policies of states, when violations of the ethical status of thousands and millions of people are justified in terms of national defense, and when nation-states do nothing to protect these people because this would violate the sovereignty of the offending nation-states. Creating an even more tangled ethical jungle are current practices of states and groups justifying the pursuit of narrow, self-interested goals by using violent means to aid oppressed people. Because it is so easy to try to legitimate the violent pursuit of questionable goals by claiming that religious faithfulness demands it, it probably is best for people trying to respond faithfully to the ethical call of the infinite to be extremely cautious and skeptical about such claims. Given the character of modern warfare by nation-states and terrorist tactics by opponents of state actions, the days of just wars and just terrorist attacks clearly seem to be over. This, of course, leaves us with another vital question: What are ethically acceptable and hopefully effective strategies and tactics for opposing domination and oppression by nation-states and by groups protected and aided by nation-states?

Since its beginning, Islam has wrestled with the challenge of balancing faithful obedience to Allah with governance of nation-states and empires. It is not unique in doing this, but it is unique in continuing to wrestle with this challenge up to the present time. The leadership of the Tibetan Buddhist tradition dealt with this challenge until China took Tibetan religious leaders out of the political governing business. Christians faced this problem until religious pluralism and the rise of sizeable nonreligious populations caused European and American nation-states to take away from religious leaders the political authority to use the power of the state to enforce mandates that could be justified only to religiously faithful people in certain traditions.

In facing this challenge in the contemporary world, it is crucial to distinguish two things. First, there is the call of the infinite to all religiously faithful people to respect and cherish the singular uniqueness of all people. This is the call that can function as the basis of proclaiming universal human rights. This is the religious basis for the charge that every person is ethically responsible to respect equally the inalienable individual rights of every person. Second, there are the religious requirements instituted by a group of people who have constituted a historically specific way for them to respond to their encounters with the infinite. These requirements are binding on those who without coercion identify themselves with such a community and its traditions. For many cultural, social, economic, and political reasons, many "fundamentalists" today in many of the world's religions are trying to establish practices in which the power of the state can again be used to mandate, as requirements and prohibitions applicable to everyone, what are mandates in their specific religious tradition. This is happening with some Hindus, Jews, Christians, and Muslims. The result is violent intolerance, oppressive, tyrannical police actions, and terrorist attacks. These fundamentalists do not know how to distinguish genuine universal ethical fundamentals (cherish and respect singularly unique persons, all of whom are responsible to respect such persons) and the fundamentals of historically and socially specific religious responses to encounters with the infinite (which are binding only on those participating in that way of responding). An ingredient in all the different religious responses is the religious and ethical requirement to respect all the other ways of responding. Commitment to general and specific requirements is part of what it is a to be religious in any tradition, but dogmatic intolerance of other traditions is not to be part of any tradition. People faithfully and joyfully living in one religious way of life do not have to be fearful or envious of people living in other ways of life. They can just let others be as they immerse themselves in their own way of life. That is the word of Allah that Muhammad transmitted in setting up Medina's constitution.

Throughout its history, given its immense geographical spread and its contact with other cultural and religious traditions, Islam has had to face the problem of having its specific way of faithfully responding to encounters with the infinite through worship of Allah corrupted by unrighteous practices. It has gone through a number of reformation movements. Early in its historical development a number of Muslim thinkers outside Arabia attempted to synthesize Islamic religious practice with the rationalistic, metaphysical practices of Plato, Aristotle, and the Neoplatonists. When Islam came to Iraq it encountered a whole variety of religious and philosophical movements: Greek philosophy, Gnostic pursuit of wisdom, Manichaean theories of a cosmic battle between good and evil, and Christianity. While opposing many of these movements, a group called the Mu'tazila (the neutralists) attempted to develop in the early eighth century a rationally systematic system of Islamic thought in which it was claimed that reason was able to discover the moral imperatives Muhammad had heard from Allah. This metaphysical contamination of Islamic religious practice perhaps is best represented in the work of the Turkish thinker, Al Farabi (873–950), who made religion subservient to metaphysics by claiming that religion simply provides symbolic presentations of metaphysical truths. Influenced by Al Farabi's writings, the Persian thinker, Abu Ali al-Husayn ibn Abd-Allah ibn Sina (known in the Europe as Avicenna), appropriated from Plato his theory of immortal souls, from Aristotle his argument for the necessary existence of a first cause, and from Neoplatonism the theory of intellectual and material emanations from an infinite and eternal being. In the late eleventh century, Al Ghazzali (1058–1111) rejected this entire metaphysical project, because it did not recognize that encountering the infinite and worshiping Allah showed that non-religious human reasoning is not autonomous, and it is not sufficient to demonstrate the ethical responsibilities that Allah proclaims that all persons have. He wrote a work, *The Autodestruction of the Philosophers*, which bears remarkable similarities to Derrida's postmodern deconstruction of the metaphysics of presence, and is Islam's counterpart to Luther's and Kierkegaard's attacks on the metaphysical contamination of Christianity. Just as current metaphysicians fail to appreciate the radicalness of postmodernism's critique of metaphysics, so Ibn Rusd (Averroes) (1126–1198) wrote *Autodestruction of Autodestruction* and attempted to show that Al Ghazzali was contradicting himself when he dialectically destroyed from the inside the pretensions of metaphysical rationalism. Showing that metaphysical reasoning reveals its own lack of self-sufficiency, exhaustiveness, and imperial legitimacy is not rationally contradicting oneself. It is only being humble in the face of encounters with rationality's other, with the other of all socially constituted symbolic practices and conceptual categories.

The tradition that Al Ghazzali drew upon in his critique of metaphysical rationalism was the Islamic tradition of Sufi mysticism. In the name of Muhammad's encounters with the infinite and in the name of individual experiences of worshiping Allah, Al Ghazzali also critiqued the impersonal and overly formalistic and legalistic traditions that had crept into Islam. As a critique of the opulent life style of califs and sultans in Islamic territories, he chose to wear the coarse woolen garments from which the Sufis gained their name. (*Suf* means wool.) Very early in the life of Islam, Sufi mystics began to appear. Sometimes, some of them tried to use Greek metaphysical ideas to explain their mystical experiences and their religious significance. Even Al Ghazzali did not avoid using the notion of a world soul to explain his mystical experience. Sometimes the Sufis formed orders and gave to the order's leader absolute authority over those in the order, thus weakening the critical and reformist potential in Sufi mysticism. Through the many changes in its social expression, however, Sufi mysticism has had a profound effect on Islam and Islamic literature and culture.[251]

The development of a mystical tradition in Islam should not

be surprising, because the same thing happened in Judaism and Christianity. In the twelveth century, the mystical Kabbalah tradition developed in Judaism.[252] From the thirteenth through the sixteenth centuries, a whole series of mystics appeared in the Christian tradition: Francis of Assisi, Eckhart, Catherine of Siena, John of the Cross, and Teresa of Avila. There are many difficulties involved in placing all these Sufis, Christians, and Jews in one category and calling them mystics. Having been constituted as different sorts of people because of their different religious inheritances, they seem to have had very different kinds of experiences as evidenced by the very different kinds of reports they give of their experiences.[253] The Kabbalah mystics drew heavily upon the symbolism in the books of Elijah, Ezekiel, and especially Song of Solomon, reporting encountering Yahweh as their lover and interpreting the Torah as a living organism. Christians also drew upon the Song of Solomon and talked about union with Christ (not God the Father) as the bridegroom of their soul; and they talked about experiencing verification of the trinity and sharing in the suffering of Christ upon the cross. Sufis talked about becoming the Qur'an or encountering Muhammad as the spirit of spirits. Most of these mystics drew upon the vocabulary of neo-Platonism and gave metaphysical explanations of their mystical experiences. Needless to say, the reports by these mystics are very different from the reports Hindu mystics give of their encounters with Brahman or of the blinding white light in the final stage of raja yoga, and that Buddhists give of their encounters with Mu, the empty sky, nothingness.

There is good reason to believe that all of these people had profoundly moving religious experiences, but it seems necessary to say these experiences are as socially constituted as all of the other religious responses by people in the world's religions. In spite of the differences between them, there do seem to be sufficient family resemblances between them to call all of them mystical experiences. By examining the similarities and differences, we can see once again in the world's religions different, socially and historically finite faithful responses to encounters with the otherness of the social and finite, encounters with the infinite. We can appreciate the significance of these mystical experiences without weighing down religion with supernatural, metaphysical postulations. Thinking about these mystical experiences can help us better understand what was said in section one about how the world's religions radically critique nonreligious social practices, while also constituting and participating in different religious social practices.

The symbolic, the conceptual, the linguistic are social and historical through and through. Everything symbolically, conceptually, or linguistically experienced is something that is socially constituted. When social and historical practices and socially constituted objects are not treated as merely being social and historical, but are elevated into being a social and a historical absolutes, then religious criticism of such absolutizing of the finite finds in the infinite its motivation for criticism. People do encounter what is other than and primordially prior to the social. They do so when they encounter the ethically unique singularity of other people and when they become radically unique individuals whose identity consists of a singularly unique set of ethical responsibilities. The people they encounter no longer are just instances of a socially classifiable type, and the responsibilities that are theirs are not shared by anyone else, and thus they are different because they are unique, so radically different that they are not just members of a class in which there might be other members. When the merely social and historical is absolutized, then people are pigeonholed and treated unjustly, their uniqueness not being respected or cherished. It is by having these ethical encounters and by assuming their individually unique responsibilities that Buddha, Moses, Jesus, and Muhammad, out of opposition to injustice and out of compassion and love for people in their uniqueness, became the vehicles through which great world religions were constituted as faithful responses to these encounters. In addition to encountering the ethical otherness of the social, we also encounter in other ways what is primordial prior to our socially constituted experiences with socially constituted objects. We joyously encounter the elements we live with and the people with whom we interpersonally cohabitat, encounters that fill us with thankfulness, joys that make it possible to love life even when it is filled with the suffering that natural necessities and chance produce or that we inflict upon ourselves and others by unrighteously worshiping false gods—metaphysical or political or economic or social or cultural demons.

In faithful response to these encounters with the other to the secularly social and historical, social and historical religious traditions were constituted and reconstituted generation after generation, century after century. Being nurtured and socialized into life in these different religious traditions, different kinds of people were constituted, people who find different ways of faithfully responding to encounters with the infinite. Recognizing the historical contingency of their religious tradition, and that their very social identity is tied up with worshiping in that tradition and accepting their ethical responsibility to cherish people in their unique singularity, people in any of the world's great religions can remain totally committed to their own tradition, while respecting and cherishing different religious traditions. Drawing upon their common responsibility to respect people independently of their social masks, they can join together in battling injustice in the world, while still worshiping in their different ways.

Mystical experiences are socially constituted, but they also bear family resemblances to one another. They are all grounded in an attempt to experience the non-absoluteness and non-exhaustiveness of the social, the finite. These experiences involve the use of the religious practices, ideas, and symbols that are their presupposed social and cultural background and which has constituted them as the social individuals they are. As the history of mysticism demonstrates, it is sometimes difficult not to make into graven images what is experienced, and it is difficult to resist attempting to make metaphysical postulations and give metaphysical explanations of what is experienced. It is crucial, therefore, to remember that the names Brahman, Mu, Tao, Yahweh, and Allah are not the names of metaphysical beings. They are names that come to mind when people are faithfully responding to encounters with the nonfinite, the ethical, joyous, interpersonal other of the secular, conceivable, and social.

Section Four

A DECLARATION OF RELIGIOUS FREEDOM

Jacques Derrida has claimed that the movement he began, which others have labeled deconstruction, is a continuation of the enlightenment.[254] The enlightenment project of the eighteenth and nineteenth centuries sought to release European social and cultural practices from superstition and the dogmatic restriction of freedom of thought by ecclesiastical powers. These practices were critiqued by appealing to metaphysical and epistemological theories about a universal, unchanging human nature and universal and unchanging foundations for justifying beliefs, actions, and social/cultural practices. It did so in an effort to reinforce the development of modern science, democratic political liberalism, and economic capitalism. Deconstruction's second enlightenment project seeks to release human thinking from these metaphysical theories and supposed foundations. Many thinkers practicing deconstruction stop there with a new postmodern, secular way of thinking and living. Derrida, however, goes further. He wants to enlighten thinkers so as to release them from their dogmatic limitation of human ways of living to what is conceivable within a secular horizon of possibilities. He wants to enlighten people so that they can be freed for religious living with new horizons of possibilities that are impossible within a secular way of life or mode of subjectivity.

It is out of a desire to participate in this second enlightenment movement aimed at helping set people around the globe religiously free that this book has been written. The words written in this book, of course, do not have the power by themselves to liberate people religiously. They can help in this project only if they function as vehicles through which the nonfinitness of human life is heard by its readers as a call for a faithful, religious response. No writer of words can guarantee that this is what will happen to the readers of their words. If a religious event does happen, certainly the writer cannot take any personal credit. If it happens, then the writer, like Muhammad, is merely functioning as a reciter of what was heard. It is Brahman, Mu, Tao, Yahweh, Christ, and Allah, not writers, who set people free religiously. Writers of books such as this can only hope to open up space for such events to occur. In the hope of providing further assistance in opening up such space, four things will be attempted in this final declaration of religious freedom: (1) provide additional aid in liberating the world's religions from metaphysical dogmatism by showing some of the harms caused by metaphysical beliefs and presumptions;. (2) lend support to the efforts by these religions to liberate people from secularism by specifying some of the secular harms that authentic religious ways of life seek to eliminate or diminish; (3) assist people to appreciate the possibilities that these religions afford to live joyfully and to lovingly care for other people, and to understand how such a religious way of life frees religious and secular people to live good lives in a just social order; and (4) show how the postmodern interpretations of the world religions offered in this text free them from dangerous polemics and for respectful and fruitful dialogue with one another.

1. Freeing the World Religions from Metaphysical Dogmatism

Sam Harris, in *The End of Faith: Religion, Terror, and the Future of Reason*,[255] charges that religious faith is one of the most dangerous social/cultural phenomena in our lives today. In his attack on Muslim suicide bombers and American Christian-fundamentalist, abortion-clinic bombers and political right-wingers striving to create a Judeo-Christian majority-rule theocracy, Harris interprets religious faith only in terms of the metaphysical theology being preached by persons claiming to be authentic voices of Islam and Christianity. He can see only secular rationalism as an alternative to such metaphysical fanatics. Similarly, when the comedian Bill Maher ridicules religion, it is always something that operates only against a metaphysical horizon of possibilities. This book has attempted to show that critics like Harris and

Maher are basically correct in what they are criticizing, but that they are not criticizing religion in its authentic, nonmetaphysical forms. That they find it so natural to tie religious faith to metaphysical stances, and that the people they are criticizing do the same thing, shows how vital it is to free religion from metaphysics.

As we have seen, it is not easy to keep things balanced while walking this tightrope of rejecting metaphysical absolutes on the one side while affirming religious ways of life on the other. Kierkegaard did it and was labeled irrational. Nietzsche critiqued appeals to metaphysical explanatory and justification absolutes, and he found no way to avoid falling into Dionysian secularism. Heidegger critiqued ontotheologies, but he still ended up trapped within worlds limited by the horizon of being and service to a will to power. In this text, an attempt has been made to build upon the work of Kierkegaard and postmodern thinkers such as Levinas, Derrida, Caputo, and Marion in order to show that the major religions of the world can be liberated from metaphysics without falling into secularism. As Harris and Maher point out, the critique of metaphysical absolutes is not just an intellectual exercise. People are doing great harm acting in ways they think are justified by such metaphysical absolutes. Neither is it merely an intellectual matter that space be found for religious ways of life that are free from metaphysical contamination. Religious prophets critiquing contemporary religious pretenses and unjust social, political, and economic practices are vitally needed, but their critiques cannot be justified if they depend on metaphysical assumptions. In addition, authentic religious life has so many blessings to offer to people when they are freed from prisons of metaphysical dogmatism.

It is extremely difficult not to have metaphysical/religious claims end up being dogmatic claims. These claims try to provide descriptions of ultimate reality and final explanations and justifications. If people believe that their descriptions, explanations, and justifications are true, then they will try to live and act on them. This means that they will think that they are correct, and they will have to treat people who do not agree with them as people suffering under illusions or believing and acting in unjustified ways. People with two different sets of metaphysical claims seem destined for polemics and confrontation, since their unjustifiable dogmatism means that they will share no common ground for dialogue. When people hold conflicting metaphysical beliefs that function as the defining centers of their personal and communal lives, then it should surprise no one that both sets of people will try to defend who they are by all means available. Metaphysical differences often turn into power struggles for domination.

Some thinkers, such as Huston Smith and Richard Swinburne, claim that there can be undogmatic metaphysicians. They claim that they are just offering the best hypotheses they can construct; they are not denying that others offering other hypotheses might be correct, even though they personally do not think that they are. Admitting that they are fallible, they therefore call for tolerance of people with other metaphysical/religious opinions. This advocacy of mutual toleration certainly is superior to power clashes between holders of conflicting dogmas. As Seyyed Hossein Nasr, points out, however, this modern, liberal tolerance is dogmatically intolerant of those who live with passionate commitment to religious ways of life that are trying to preserve themselves in opposition to this modern liberalism, which often today is backed up by very intolerant military, economic, and culturally hegemonic power.[256] This also is Zizek's critique of liberal forms of tolerance.[257] Smith's and Swinburne's claims of freedom from intolerance are made against the horizon of dogmatic liberal modernism, founded upon metaphysical theories about human nature. Something more than tolerating different metaphysical opinions is needed if freedom for passionate religious commitment, and thus opposition to secular modernism, is to be preserved. At the core of religious passion itself there must be found the resources needed to defend fundamental human rights, the cherishing of religious pluralism, and a commitment to a deliberative form of democracy in which the use of force and coercion need to be justified by reasons acceptable to everyone included in the deliberations. Metaphysical reasons never can be such reasons. At the core of the world's religions, however, as interpreted here in a postmodern fashion, are just the reasons needed.

Let's consider just three of the metaphysical/religious beliefs causing considerable harm today. These are metaphysical beliefs about creation, souls, and natural rights and laws. As we have seen, creation talk plays an extremely important role in certain religious traditions, as people seek to avoid making an absolute out of nonreligious categorizations of objects, and as they seek to respond with thankfulness for the goodness of life. Metaphysical interpretations of creation talk, however, have been used to try to force public schools to teach this metaphysics as an alternative to biological accounts of the evolutionary development of life forms. Religious creationism is not in competition with scientific accounts of biological changes, and therefore its discussion does not belong in a biology class restricting itself to secular, scientific inquiry and explanation. Metaphysical creationism also is not a competitor with scientific biological accounts, because it does not restrict itself to scientific standards of explanation, which simply try to find general accounts that remove anomalies within data or between data and previous general beliefs. Debates about the intelligibility of metaphysical creationism and about the soundness of arguments trying to defend it belong in philosophy classrooms and texts such as this one, not in biology classes.

Saying that neither metaphysical nor religious creationism belongs in the biology classroom is not to say that the discussion of religious creationism does not belong in any school curriculum. Forbidding such a discussion would be coercively supporting secularism's intolerant attitude toward religion. It is unfortunate that the debate over creationism has become a debate over the separation of church and state. Debating the issue this way lends credence to the claim that metaphysical creationism is religious in nature. Authentic religious ways of life reject any treatment of metaphysical theorizing as a faithful response to the call of the infinite. What the power of the state must not support is metaphysical dogmatism. There is no general need, however, to use its power to forbid reflection in its schools on religious ways of life, although extreme caution must be exercised here, because in our current cultural climate, it is so easy for religious talk to be transformed into metaphysical talk and for talk in the religious way of life dominant in a particular social setting to become an instrument of power used to exclude respecting other religious ways of life.

What about "soul" talk? The language of individual souls is often used by religiously faithful people to emphasize the singular uniqueness of people that everyone is responsible for respecting. As Levinas points out, ethically encountering people face-to-face is encountering them as people whose identity cannot be captured by any secular, descriptive vocabulary. They are not identical to their bodies, their mental skills or dispositions, or their personalities. The religious language of souls is not part of such secular descriptive language; it works against a different horizon of possibilities. The identity of our souls in authentic religious talk is our ethical identity, our identity-defining unique set of ethical responsibilities, our status as ones whom others encounter ethically. Religiously talking about souls is not talking metaphysically about beings among beings; it is religiously and ethically acknowledging the singularly unique and infinitely valuable individual whom one is ethically meeting face-to-face, and it is acknowledging that one is a unique ethical hostage to those individuals.

This ethical/religious talk gets drowned out, however, when metaphysicians introduce the theory that there are empirically undetectable, invisible, immaterial beings called "souls," which get attached to human bodies and that continue to live after human beings as biological organisms die. There are as many different metaphysical theories about such "souls" as there are metaphysicians, metaphysical theologians, and preachers. The reason for the variety is the inherent confusion in the core metaphysical idea of a "soul." Consider the following, seemingly unanswerable questions: First, is the soul the personality of the person, and if it is, then which personality? Is it the one the person had when two years old, twelve years old, thirty years old, forty years old during an emotional breakdown, or seventy-five years old when the person is in the last stages of Alzheimer's disease? Second, after the death of the human, is this soul eternal (timeless) or everlastingly living through temporal changes? If it is the former, then in what sense is it identical to what a human person is who lives through continual changes? One eternal soul couldn't meet another eternal soul (a dead parent or child) because meetings occur at a time. If the soul lives everlastingly after the person is dead, then one of two undesirable things happen. In the first case, life after death is subject to all the chances for suffering and evil occurring during life before death, only now death cannot end the suffering, hardly the metaphysical heaven expected. Alternatively, everything is determined by metaphysical laws guaranteeing nothing but goodness, but then we no longer have people doing things; we only have metaphysical robots or functionaries. The metaphysical problem of evil, then, is just transferred from this life to the next.

In addition to the religious use of "soul" talk, religions also have used resurrection talk to express trust that living in a faithful response to the call of the infinite is not rendered worthless by the fact people biologically die. In their resurrection faith, Christians proclaim that death cannot defeat the messianic work, which they understand to have been part of Jesus's faithful obedience to the will of his Father, Yahweh, and which is now part of their worshipful response as the body of Christ. The Messiah is the resurrected Christ, whose spirit lives in them and whose body is the Christian community as it reconstitutes itself generation after generation. Paul in his Christian faithfulness tells Christians that dead people will not be resurrected as material bodies but as spiritual bodies. How are we to interpret such talk about spiritual bodies? Using Levinas to interpret this claim, we can say that the individual, nondescribable ethical identity of people (their spirit) will be resurrected in their spiritual offspring, the children they have ethically parented. Christians are the first evidence of this as the spirit of the resurrected Christ lives in them. So, like him, they, as ethically and spiritually unique individuals, will be resurrected to continuing life in their ethical and spiritual children. This extremely important religious response of trust in the continuing effect of faithfulness to the call of God, as old as Abraham, gets completely mutilated when metaphysical speculation is introduced about spiritual bodies that are supposed to be some sort of ghost-like, supernatural being. This metaphysical corruption of a religious resurrection faith has disastrous results.

Again and again in recent years, we see how dangerous it is to have people believe in a metaphysical treatment of religious talk about immortal souls or resurrected spiritual bodies. People get persuaded to join groups, sell everything, and wait for the end of the world after which they think they will begin to live eternally or everlastingly as metaphysical souls or spirits. People get persuaded to join groups that then commit mass suicide and murder of children, believing that they then will begin to live eternally or everlastingly. People join groups that participate in military suicide bombings of noncombatant children, adults, and elderly people, because they have become convinced that they are doing the will of a metaphysical god and that after blowing themselves up they will live in a metaphysical heaven. People are trained to live in fear of being punished with everlasting pain in a metaphysical hell, unless they obey what socially constituted ecclesiastical leaders claim is the will of a metaphysical god. People are trained to believe that current wars, AIDS epidemics, and environmental dangers are metaphysical signals that the end of the world is coming, after which they, the select few, will live in a metaphysical heaven. They, therefore, actually seek to use political power to prevent states from doing anything to reduce these dangers. Such metaphysical claims are not religious claims, and they are extremely dangerous. They are tragic examples of worshiping false gods and thinking that incoherent and unjustifiable metaphysical talk is religious. Serving such false gods in many instances creates hell on earth. It demonstrates why it is so important for the world religions to free themselves from dogmatic metaphysics.

Why is metaphysical talk about natural law also dangerous? All the major religions of the world prioritize the religiously ethical over all forms of secularly constituted social moralities. Although it may be trying to say something like this, metaphysical talk about natural rights and laws that is based on metaphysical talk about human beings having a nature that transcends their social nature creates a cloud of confusion around the religious/ethical religious rod used for measuring social practices, destroying its critical power and contributing to skepticism about the availability of any universal measure of the justness of social customs. The religions of the world use talk about universal human rights and responsibilities in order to talk about using the mandate to respect the singularly unique ethical identities of people as the plumb line for measuring the justness of any socially constituted normative rules and principles. Metaphysical talk about natural laws, however, has been used again and again to unjustifiably restrict the freedom of people to act in ways that were deemed unnatural. Such talk often takes what is the statistical norm for behavior in a society and turns it into a normative law prohibiting behavior commonly present without objection in certain minority groups. It is very easy for people to view what is usually done in their society, what is statistically normal for people to do in their world, and turn it into a norm specifying what is moral for people to do. As Nietzsche pointed out, this is one way majorities, or the voices of power groups claiming to speak for moral majorities, out of fear and envy seek to protect themselves against what they see as threats to their ways of life or their hold on dominating power. These minority preferences, however, often are not unjustified according to the religious measuring rod. Rather, it is these restrictions on human freedom that are religiously and democratically unjustifiable. In a deliberative democracy, for example, metaphysical natural law claims coercively mandating heterosexuality as the only acceptable sexual orientation cannot be supported by reasons acceptable to everyone deliberating about the matter. Neither can they be justified by the religious call to respect the unique singularity of people.

The original enlightenment project and its talk about natural law usually aimed at enhancing individual liberty. The postmodern second enlightenment project aims at enhancing individual freedom even further, and it aims at doing so by holding people even more responsible for caring for one another than the original project did. Whereas metaphysical natural law theories have generated ethical skepticism because attempts to justify their claims have come to be seen after the death of the metaphysical god as unsound or implausible, postmodern religious prophetic judgements on unjust social practices will not generate such skepticism. They are not tied to the impossible task of trying to justify metaphysical claims. They are proclaiming that living with ethical responsibilities is prior to any kind of theoretical activity, prior to any metaphysical descriptions of human nature.

Postmodern religious faithfulness in no way conflicts with accepting scientific claims about the regularities of changes that things undergo in nature. The metaphysical theory of natural law, however, is a very different thing. It is really a moral claim, supposedly backed up by metaphysical considerations. Homosexuality supposedly is immoral because it is "unnatural." Gaining genital pleasure without having an intention to conceive a child supposedly is immoral because it is "unnatural." Using contraceptive birth control devices supposedly is immoral because it is "unnatural." These metaphysical "natural laws" cannot really be laws of nature, or they could not be broken and thus would not need to be enunciated as moral laws. One cannot break the law of gravity, the laws of motion, or the gas law. Metaphysical natural law restrictions on human freedom are unjust restrictions because they cannot be justified by the universal ethical, principle calling for respect and care for the singular uniqueness of people. Metaphysical characterizations of the nature of human beings fail to recognize the socially variable and historically changing status of all characterizations. They fail to recognize that natures can never be simply present for description, since all descriptive words and classification criteria are subject to differance and trace. They fail to recognize that it is the ethical nature of people that gives to them their ethically singular uniqueness and identity.

If one strips natural law talk of its metaphysical ties, some very important ethical insights remain. Postmodern religious ethics both deny and affirm John Locke's claim that it is a natural law that ethical and political sovereignty universally resides with the individual, and that only license (failure to respect the appropriate freedom of other people) is universally prohibited. A postmodern religious ethicist like Levinas denies that ethical sovereignty resides with me when I ethically meet someone face-to-face. Rather, it resides with the individuals whom I encounter and who place upon me the responsibility to care for them. Caring for them, however, means respecting their infinite value as singular individuals, and this means respecting their sovereign freedom. Responding to the call of the infinite does what Locke's appeal to metaphysics could not do: transcend the social to protect the individual. The same thing is true of Kant's attempt to locate ethical sovereignty in persons exercising pure, practical reason. I am not the author of the moral mandates that bind me, as Kant thought. Rather it is the other whom I ethically encounter who is the author of such mandates.

Locke's natural law liberalism is flawed in another way. It only binds me not to interfere with the freedom of other people, a mandate I can meet by just leaving them alone. A religious ethic, however, calls for me to care for other people, to care about their freedom and to care about their possessing the material means necessary for living freely. Offering the negative freedom to be left alone is not enough; to it must be added the mandate to do what one can to provide people with positive freedom. Marx saw this need to augment modern liberalism's restriction of ethics and politics to matters of negative freedom, but his secular revolutionary program is unable to offer any justification for the mandate to care for other people. The postmodern interpretation offered here sees in the world religions a call to be ethically responsible that cannot be removed, even if one closes one's ears to it. It is a call to care for other people by not metaphysically restricting their freedom and by enabling them to live in their own singular uniqueness. It is a call to care for the people in the world who are dominated, oppressed, weak, hungry, sick, homeless, forced to the margins, and ostracized. The answer to the question "Who am I?" is not given by a metaphysical description of everyone's human nature, but it is given when one spells out whom one cares about and how deeply one cares about them.

During the past three hundred years the call to guarantee religious freedom has grown louder and louder, and it is now echoing in all regions of our earth. Only with a few Western thinkers, however, has this call been interpreted as also calling for the freeing of religion from metaphysical prisons. In fact, many voices in many ecclesiastical and political circles have used the call for religious freedom as a justification for keeping religion in metaphysical shackles As one might expect, because claims for religious freedom carry so much weight in certain political and cultural circles, people often try to protect all sorts of practices from criticism and restriction by labeling them "religious." Cries for freedom of religion often intimidate people from criticizing what in fact are nothing but dogmatic metaphysical claims. Simply claiming that a practice or belief is part of "my religion" does not make that practice or belief religious, and it should not guarantee it protection from critical examination. As we have seen, many metaphysical claims get passed off as religious claims. Freedom of religion does not entail freedom to hold incoherent or unsound metaphysical beliefs, or to use them in efforts to justify coercing others to act or refrain from acting in ways specified by those beliefs. Keeping these considerations in mind pulls the rug out from under a whole host of metaphysical beliefs being passed off as religious beliefs and tragically being used to persuade people of the correctness of restricting other people's freedom and of even using violent means to attain chosen goals. Metaphysical beliefs about supernatural beings are not expressions of religious faith-fulness, no matter how many times they are presented that way by ecclesiastical powers. Religious and nonreligious people have a right and a duty to criticize and reject such beliefs. If one is going to play the game of metaphysical theorizing, then one has to play the game of trying to justify them, because there are so many reasons for doubting their coherence and correctness. The religions of the world, as inter-preted in this text, are not engaged in the metaphysical project at all, and they are not attempting to coerce anyone to either be religious or to adhere to religious mandates issued to participants in a specific religious way of life. The clearest voices in defense of maximizing the freedom of both authentically religious people and people without any religious form of life are the religious voices calling for religious free-dom from metaphysical dogmatics.

2. Religiously Freeing People from Secularism

That there is trouble in the world of secularism is not news. Thousands of years ago, Hindus pointed out that there are secular ways of life that do not work. Making the pursuit of sensual pleasure the ultimate goal in one's life does not work. Making the pursuit of political and econom-ic power or personal fame one's ultimate goal does not work. Making the fulfillment of one's social roles as one's ultimate goal does not work. Buddhists pointed out that trying to satisfy the cravings created by the pursuit of such goals causes great suffering to oneself and to others. It is neither possible nor ethically permissible to try to coerce people into leaping out of secularism and into a religious way of life. It is religiously unethical, useless, and counterproductive to try to coerce people to aban-don their secular ways of life, as tragic as they may be. Because the infi-nite cannot be boxed in by secular concepts, neither can one rationally prove to the secular world that only life in a religious world can begin to deal with the troubles existing in the secular world. It is useless to offend people by trying to argue them into being religious.

Even when one cares deeply for those living troubled secular lives and for those suffering because of the false gods being served by such secular people, there are only a few things one can do to help them, and none of these are coercive or able to guarantee success. Always in the end, people must leap by themselves from secular ways of life to religious ways of life. One can try to show the failings of secular ways of life: the strife within them, the inability to find existential peace and contentment within them, the inability to satisfy desires for something that one feels is lacking, the suffering one experiences trying to live in such a way of life. One can show that rational efforts to prove that the religious life is irrational are usually grounded in a confused failure to understand that the infinite is not a being about whose existence one can rationally debate. One can attempt to serve as religious exemplars filled with joy and care, but this often will be taken as offensive grandstanding. One can point to other exemplars (Buddha, Moses, Jesus, Muhammad), but these figures are often dismissed by secular people as being irrational, unrealistic, or just plain crazy. One can proclaim the attractiveness of the infinite other to everything finite, but only when a person is in fact attracted by the goodness and love of the infinite will the person endorse the proclamation. Religiously caring for people, therefore, has to mean caring for people lost in secularism, because in our modern world, that is where most people are living their lives. The religious call is to care for them in order to keep alive the possibility that they will make a leap of faith. The call, of course, is not to care for people in order to save them. That would be using them as a means to an end. The call is to care for people in their singular uniqueness, whether they are religious or secular. It is a call to care as much as possible for their freedom and well-being in their secular ways of life.

The current worldwide upsurge in religious involvement, even though it is often contaminated by metaphysical confusion and secular cravings for economic power and political nationalism, shows that many people are being attracted by that which is other than a merely secular way of life, major portions of which they are finding unattractive. The interest in and support of religious ways of life by existential and postmodern thinkers shows that they are being attracted by the promises of the world's religions of deliverance from the pitfalls of secular living and into lives of joyfully loving life and responsibly caring for other people. The difficulties present in secularism are becoming apparent to many people. Also becoming prevalent is the recognition enunciated thousands of years ago by the Taoists that the problems in secularism cannot be solved within secularism because it is secularism itself that is the problem. It is important, therefore, to continue to point out the defects in secular ways of life from which authentic religion can set them free.

Kierkegaard pointed out the self-defeating nature of organizing one's life only around what one finds interesting, because one then has to concentrate on the very uninteresting chore of being sure not to enter into any interpersonal relationships requiring meeting obligations whether one finds them interesting or not. He pointed out that one cannot focus only on the well-being of one's secular social world by fulfilling the duties definitive of one's social role, because the conventional world of role assignments is not a perfect creation, and because one can end up senselessly harming other people if one keeps doing one's social duties when other people are not doing theirs. Kierkegaaard also pointed out the misery experienced by knights of resignation who are resigned to the folly of secular life, and who do not leap in faith to a new religious horizon of possibilities.

Nietzsche pointed out that conventional secular moralizing is motivated by feelings of envy and resentment toward the few people who try to free themselves from turning such moralizing into an absolute, people who end up being severely punished by the envious and resentful herd. He pointed out that most people living conventional lives are fearful nihilists who are unable to joyously love life in spite of what happens to them because of the regularities in nature and the chanciness of life. These nihilists vainly try to make such a life meaningful by constructing metaphysical explanations and justifications, and then they brand as dangerous nihilists those who show that this unworkable metaphysical project is the construction of a sovereign out of a will to maintain power over things, an emperor without any clothes, an impotent emperor who cannot supply what is sensed to be lacking. Nietzsche tried to leap out of his social world, but unfortunately his call for Dionysian spontaneity was issued to people whose very identities were constituted by the secular, social world they were trying to escape. His own secular horizon of possibilities prevented him from leaping to a new horizon in which the identities of people would be freed from everything secularly finite.

Marx pointed out that much of secular living is carried out in a world in which people are economically exploited and dominated and consequently politically and culturally enslaved. Unfortunately, all that he could call for was the destruction of the current system and then waiting for the liberated people to construct in some unspecifiable way a new secular way of life. Furthermore, his revolutionary call to end social injustices authorized, whenever required, taking undemocratic and even violent action against those who resisted this attempt to revolutionize things. Tragically, people allowed dehumanized means to be used and abused in order to reach this new world of secular possibilities. This new world, however, with all of its supposed new freedom would only be one constituted by people with socially constituted identities, by people still being motivated by service to false gods, by people still filled with existential anxiety and nihilistic fears, envies, and resentments and by wills to power. As with Nietzsche, Marx's analysis of the troubled secular world is excellent, but his solution remains part of the problem.

Heidegger pointed out the disastrous consequences of the secular world's being enframed in a technological world in which everything in nature and all people come to be treated as mere natural and human resources available for use by those seeking ever greater control over things. He could, however, offer as a solution to this problem only more exercises of the will to power. By willpower people are to heroically face death and to let themselves be used poetically as new worlds of beings come into being through them. This letting oneself be used is nothing like letting the ethical infinite in the face of others make one an ethical hostage to them and place one under uncountable responsibilities to care for anyone encountered face-to-face. The people whom Heidegger wants to release themselves to be used poetically are still people with identities socially constituted in secular worlds, and the new worlds they constitute will still reflect their anxieties, resentments, and exercises of will to power. It still will be a world of socially constituted, secular beings and not a religious/ethical world in which personal identities are determined by ethical responsibilities. Heidegger calls for waiting for the gods to arrive culturally so that a sense of the holy may be reborn in people. Waiting, however, is not enough. One would be waiting only for more of the same. Responding faithfully to the call of the infinite is required. Here is the act of the will that is required, but it is an act of the will of one whose identity is one of unique responsibilities, one who is committed to do the will of the infinite God.

Michel Foucault pointed out that our secular world is as it is because of all the discursive and disciplinary practices existing within it that enable and reinforce the exercise of dominating and oppressive power. He recommends that we do a Nietzsche-type genealogical study of why these mini practices have developed in the way that they have in order that people get over thinking that things have to be the way they are. He also claims to be continuing the enlightenment project of enhancing human freedom. Such genealogical study is only one of the ways we can resist having our freedom denied us by these practices. In the space opened up by resistance, he recommends that people make themselves into beautiful works of art. He warns us that there is no one program of social change that can end these exercises of dominating and oppressive power. He recognizes that people doing the resisting will still be socially constituted persons and that any reforms they make in the current social world will always face the danger of themselves becoming oppressive and dominating. He is especially concerned about the efforts of social engineers devising programs to help people. First these "helpful" social experts divide people into contrasting classes: the healthy vs the sick, the delinquent versus the law abiding, the dangerous versus the safe, the irrational versus the rational, the degenerate versus the normal. Then they isolate people in the good first class from the people in the second class, until the sick, criminal, dangerous, irrational, and degenerate people can be changed (healed, reformed, educated) to be like the people in the good class. (In the United States today, with the exception of some of the sick, the holders of power do not even try to change them; they simply isolate them for most all of their lives.)

So much of Foucault's diagnosis of the troubles existing in our modern secular social world seem right on target. The weaknesses in his judgements and recommendations, however, show up the weakness of trying to deal with these troubles while still remaining in the world of the secular. Many of Foucault's critics have not been persuaded by his judgement that no justification is needed for the supreme ethical principle of minimizing nonconsensuality that he uses in condemning oppression and domination. Foucault thinks that people never would indict consentuality for being unethical, and therefore his principle needs no justification. The problem with this claim, however, is that many times the people who consent to certain practices are people with the very socially and culturally coded identities that Foucault has pointed out bring them not to resist their own oppression and domination. To encourage resistance to everything ethically needing resistance requires appealing to the ethical, and not just the secularly social identities of people. It requires an appeal to an ethical world, an authentically religious world not found in secular worlds. In addition, like Marx, Foucault assumes that people building a new future after enlightenment and liberation will build lives that are works of art, that will not be violations of the fundamental ethical rights of other people, that will not be expressions of fear, envy, resentment, and a will to power. Given his own reservation about the dangers present in all reform movements and his charge that old social identities can never be eliminated totally, there is little reason to share his assumption that ethically pure works of art will be produced. Once again, ethically responding to the ethical problems haunting our secular, social world seems to require moving beyond the secular and beginning to respond to the ethical/religious call of the infinite issued from the faces of the people we encounter.

It should not surprise us that more and more postmodern thinkers have become convinced that a postmodern thinking requires a postsecular thinking. Caputo points out that secular worlds are breaking down and being broken open.[258] Derrida points out that deconstruction keeps watch over ethical singularities, which because they are singular, cannot be deconstructed. It makes room for a mystical sense of justice focused on the singular, ethical uniqueness of people, a sense of justice that can indict all unjust social practices.[259] Throughout all the interpretations of the world religions offered in this text there has been expressed the belief that an authentic religious way of life and only an authentic religious way of life can free us from the misery and injustice rampant in secular worlds.

3. Religiously Freeing People to Love Life and Care for Others

The world's religions not only try to point out what is wrong with non-religious secular ways of life. All of them also hold out the promise of something positive, a joyous life that fills one with a love of life, a meaningful life of caring for others and for their individual freedom and for their well-being, which sometimes brings with it both the need to sacrifice joy and the opportunity to find joy in that very sacrifice. One of the common challenges in all of the world's religions is figuring out how to do all of this. What are the joys that religious people experience which lead them to love life and the living of it? What are their responsibilities to enable the people they encounter face-to-face to be free? What kind of freedom is involved? Freedom to do what? Freedom from what? What are the responsibilities of religious people to care for the people they ethically encounter and for all other people in the world? How is any of this to be done? These are the questions that ethicists and political thinkers have been discussing for centuries. What do the religions of the world have to contribute to this conversation?

Let's begin with the religious person's love of life. The creation stories not only critique all secular orientations that presume we are powerful enough to control things, but they also proclaim to us that life itself is good and that thankfulness is our proper response. The Abrahamic exodus faith likewise professes not only deliverance from the evils of slavery, but also possession of a land filled with milk and honey. Hinduism proclaims both deliverance from frustrations found in lives focused on pleasure, power, and social conformity and into an incomparable kind of bliss in a spiritually liberated moksa form of life. Buddhism promises deliverance from the hellish suffering of lives enslaved by cravings for power and superior social status, and deliverance into a joyous nirvana form of life in which cravings are extinguished and we live by letting things be in their enjoyable suchness. Taoism not only says that secularism fails to enable us to live harmoniously with nature, other people, and ourselves, but it also says that surrendering to a way of things that transcends all our conceptual and will-to-power activities will give us a peace that is not only the absence of war but also is joyful habiting with everything in our natural and interpersonal environment. The Abrahamic religions not only worship a God who through his prophets condemns injustice, but they also offer a kind of divine mercy and forgiveness free of any painful need to be earned or paid back. This is a mercy full of the power to evaporate all motivation for revenge and retribution on others and on oneself, while never forgetting what was done, while always giving those we have victimized immortality in our memories, while always filling us with the overwhelming joy of being able continually to look to a future of joyful living and loving service.[260]

Levinas not only accented the ethical character of our encounter with that which is other to beings constituted conceptually by people dominated by a will to power. He also accented our preconceptual enjoying of the elements on which we live and of interpersonally cohabiting with other people. He also accented the enjoyment we gain in performing hard work in order to attain and preserve such lives of enjoyment for ourselves, our families, and the people we are called to care for. The responsibilities placed upon us by people whom we encounter fall into two large classes. First, we are to respect their singular uniqueness, and this involves not coercively restricting their freedom to enjoy their lives and to care for other people. Second, we are to care for other people, so that we do not steal joy from their lives or force misery upon them, so that we do all we can to prevent others from harming them, and so that we aid them as much as possible to lead joyful lives.

In aiding people to find joy we need to remember that one of the things people enjoy most is being free from coercion in deciding what to do in their lives. Joyfulness, often called enjoyment, pleasure, and the love of living, is what makes life worth living. As Levinas points out, it is because enjoying things is present in our lives primordially prior to living in socially constituted worlds that suicide is something motivated by a sense that all joy is gone from living, and it has not a chance of coming back. Suicide always is a tragedy, because joyfulness and loving life would always be present in any life if failures to satisfy certain cravings were not allowed to drive them out. Animals other than humans do not despairingly commit suicide.[261]

It is easy to misinterpret this religious accent on the joyfulness of human life. It must be paired with Kierkegaard's accent on the unique kind of suffering present in the life of the religious person. Having heard the call of the infinite, the religious person at first tends to respond with deep feelings of guilt over having refused for so long to hear the call to feel thanksgiving over the joys of life and to responsibly care for other people. Although this memory of past failures must never be lost, Kierkegaard assures us that there is no need to wallow in such guilt and suffering and to be a knight of resignation. One can move on from that religious A form of life to a religious B form of life, which is constituted around acceptance of genuine forgiveness (unmerited and not calling for repayment). Recognition and acceptance of such forgiveness fills people with another, wonderful sort of joy, one motivating people to sing out, "Hallelujah."

The religious accent on the joyfulness of life also has to be paired with a Job-like accent on the unmerited suffering present in life. It is not only our own frustrated cravings that cause us to suffer. Viruses, cancers, and human cruelty also cause immense amounts of suffering. In a religious form of life, however, as Job reminds us, such suffering is never allowed to prevent us from still giving thanks for the good things that always remain in life: sunsets, cool water, and lilies of the field; friends, family and loved ones; and the joy of caring for other people. Kierkegaard reminds us of the eternal happiness gained by religious people in just striving to gain it, the eternal happiness of being thankful for the goodness of life and of striving to love and care for others. This is a joyousness that requires nothing more than striving for it

Religion's two promises—joyful living and caring for other people—face the problem of sometimes coming in conflict with each other. Choosing some joys may require sacrificing other joys. Trying to care for some people may conflict with caring for other people. Caring about joyful living may conflict with caring about individual freedoms. How does one calculate what is the best thing to do? These are the questions around which the theoretical debate about the ethical acceptability of hedonistic utilitarianism has turned for over two hundred years. This is the problem that neither secular hedonistic utilitarianism nor the alternatives offered by its critics seem able to resolve. The religions of the world can enter into a consideration of these questions, and they can show that in a religious way of life these conflicts are only apparent and that joyous living and caring for others can live in harmony.

The utilitarian principle calls for maximizing happy, enjoyable lives and minimizing human misery. Before considering what authentic religions have to say, let's examine John Stuart Mill's presentation and defense of a secular form of utilitarianism.[262] It seems to suffer from three ethical defects.

(1) Mill recognized that in calling for the maximization of pleasure and happiness and the minimization of misery, one needs to differentiate better and worse pleasures and pains. Being a troubled Socrates is better than being a contented pig. The criterion to be used in ranking pleasures and pains, he suggests, is personal preference. Does the person prefer one pleasure over another or the absence of one pain over another, if one and only one of the two options can be realized? The problem with using this criterion, however, is that the preferences of people are the product of socialization practices aimed at ordering pleasures and enjoyments so as to serve the interests of the social order. Without such socialization, people might find more enjoyable what they do not give preference to because of such socialization. Sometimes social practices are training people to be masochists in order for the social order to reproduce itself and the power arrangements it sustains. This criticism does not only apply to the use of preference considerations in hedonistic theories of intrinsic value, but it also applies to their use in teleological ethical principles that call for satisfying personal interests or desires. Interests and desires also need to be evaluated as better or worse, and they also are constituted socially and often serve goals other than the well-being of the people with such interests and desires.

The joys, interests, desires, and preferences of the religious person, however, can escape such personally counterproductive social ordering. The religious lives of people are filled with enjoyments of the elements, enjoyments primordially prior to any social ordering, and they are filled with the joys of giving thanks, being forgiven, and caring for other people in that singularity which transcends social classifications. These are the things that interest them, that they desire, and that decide their preferences. When choices among religious joys have to be made, the preferences of the person involved can be used in making such choices. Acting on such preferences will always serve a person's well-being.

(2) The utilitarian calculus aims at maximizing the overall pleasure and happiness present in an aggregate of people and minimizing the misery. The calculus aims at maximizing the overall good produced and not on how this maximization affects particular individuals in the aggregate. The calculus permits sacrificing a few for the sake of overall benefits. It is this that Kant is criticizing when he proclaims that people must never be used as mere means, but always must be respected as ends in themselves.[263] It is this that Rawls is trying to protect by prioritizing political liberty over economic well-being in any just and fair society.[264] It is this Heidegger is criticizing when he condemns technocratic worlds in which people are treated as mere human resources to be used by a social system that aims at continually increasing its power.[265] These criticisms seem applicable to all the forms of utilitarianism

These secular criticisms of the utilitarian calculus are admirable, but it does not seem possible to defend them at merely the secular level. Kant tries to defend the prohibition never to use people as mere means by appealing to pure practical reason, but practical reason never is pure enough because it either is socially coded or it is so formally empty that it is useless in protecting individual persons from abuse.[266] Rawls claims that all people, acting behind a veil of ignorance about their own abilities or social standing, would choose to give priority to individual political freedom over other forms of well-being. This assumes that only ignorance about their abilities and social standing would affect their weighing of the importance of political liberty versus economic well-being. It fails to appreciate that what individuals count as knowledge and ignorance is influenced by how people have been socially nurtured. People might have been nurtured to think the economic well-being gained by stable social conditions guarantees them more freedom in life than political liberty. Many Chinese today seem to think in just this way, and that is why they do not support democracy movements in China that they believe threaten social stability. Similarly, Rawls fails to appreciate that people reared in American entrepreneurial ideologies and lottery environments might politically choose a Novak[267] risk taking world rather than Rawls's type of welfare state.[268] They might prefer economic freedom over political freedom. Secular choosers never seem able to shed enough social baggage to give

Rawls the choosers he wants—those preferring political liberty over economic well-being. Even Heidegger's poets, who rise above being mere human resources, represent only the empty space between being functionaries in the social, ontological realm they are leaving and being functionaries in the ontological realm being born. There is no guarantee that any new world created by such poets would prohibit using people as mere means or give priority to political liberty over protection against social chaos or over freedom to try to get lucky and make it big. The critics of utilitarianism have something very important to say, but it seems that it can be said and defended only against a religious horizon of possibilities that transcends all secular worlds.

These criticisms apply to the whole variety of different kinds of utilitarianism. Even when the utilitarian principle is not applied directly to actions to decide what is ethically mandated, but rather is used to decide what rules and practices should exist in a society or what virtuous habits of motivation, acting, and feeling a society should nurture in people,[269] it is still the case that the best net worth of consequences may be attained by using people as means to an end.[270] In the religious way of life, however, people are encountered in their unique singularity, and responding to their call to be allowed to live in that singularity requires never killing off that uniqueness and thus never using them as mere means to an end. At the core of all authentic religious ways of life is the endorsement of the universal principle calling for everyone to respect the inalienable right of all people to live in their singular uniqueness. Religion supplies the ethical resource needed to warrant protection for individuals in their infinite worth and dignity.

(3) Mill attempted to provide a utilitarian justification for guaranteeing to people political and social liberty of thought, expression, and association. His difficulty in doing so is tied to his difficulty in protecting people from being used as means to guarantee social ends. It might be the case that one can maximize more net pleasure and happiness by controlling people's thoughts through propaganda and cultural hegemony and by restricting freedom of speech, freedom of press, and freedom of association. In the world's religions, however, there are resources that enable them to ethically justify the liberties that Mill properly prizes so highly, but which his utilitarianism cannot warrant.

In religious ways of life people are respected as singularly unique individuals calling out to be allowed to live as such individuals, and the people being called are placed under obligation to provide that respect. All people are seen as people who might hear this call and might respond responsibly. This is the ethical core of all the world's religions, and it will judge as unjustified any exercise of political or social power coercively preventing people from hearing this call or responding in the many different ways people can faithfully respond. It will demand that people be at liberty to critique privately and publicly the whole secular horizon of possibilities and permissabilities, and to echo with loud and clear voices, written words, and joyful loving, ways of living, the call to live in religious ways of life. It will demand that people be at liberty to constitute and live within any of the many different kinds of religious communities that faithfully are responding to this call of the infinite. It also will demand that even people thinking and communicating secular thoughts and forming secular associations be granted similar liberties, as long as they are not coercively attempting to deny the same liberties to others. Much secular thought, in spite of its limitations, is aimed at caring for others, increasing their joys, reducing their suffering, protecting their liberties. Besides, no one can predict when secular reflection may mutate into hearing the call of the infinite. One can never predict when a person will hear the call of the infinite and respond in new, unexpected ways to that call. Consider what Mark Taylor has been saying about the manner in which new forms of art and music are in fact faithful responses to the call of the infinite.[271] Besides, being religious means caring for other people whether they are religious or secular, and this has to mean caring for their freedom, as well as caring to maximize their joys and minimize their miseries.

How, then, are conflicts between the well-being of some people and the well-being of other people to be handled? How is this potential conflict dealt with in the kind of religious ethic that is at the core of the world's religions? Different kinds of conflict need to be distinguished if this question is to be addressed. First, religious people will never demand that anyone surrender their status as an infinitely valuable, unique person in order that someone else might avoid suffering or might gain joy. That would be using people as mere means. Second, one certainly is not justified in forcing people to suffer in order that other people's joys be increased, and no religious person would ever expect such sacrifices from others. Authentically religious people get joy from assisting others and not from having others be forcibly sacrificed for their own pleasure. Third, is a religious person ever ethically required to surrender some joy and endure some pain in order that others who are powerless or suffering might be helped? Levinas thinks so. Encountering a person face-to-face is having heavy responsibilities placed upon oneself to care for that person as much as is possible. The fourth kind of conflict is the most difficult with which to deal. There are cases where the conflict is not between ethical identity and personal well-being or between causing suffering in order to gain pleasure, but instead is a conflict between different calculations of overall well-being. There are cases where the conflict is between the well-being of people other than oneself, people whom one is not encountering face-to-face, third parties to the people one is encountering. It is at this point, Levinas charges, that we need to move beyond issues of personal ethics and find a political solution to the problem of fairly and justly distributing benefits and burdens, while also protecting the inalienable liberties of all people.[272]

Levinas's charge that we have to go political to deal with this kind of conflict is not hard to justify. Consider the following kinds of conflicts: (a) conflicts between pursuits of well-being, (b) conflicts between pursuits of liberty and well-being, (c) conflicts among people living within secular ways of life or living within religious ways of life, and (d) conflicts between people living in secular ways of life and people living in religious ways of life. It seems that some kind of political state is needed in order to find just ways of resolving these conflicts. Hobbes was at least right about that. Some kind of system has to be set up that specifies how such conflicts are to be resolved, where the authority to use coercion to enforce such resolutions is to reside, and under what conditions that authority may be exercised.

Not only does freedom from unjustifiable, coerced settlements of conflicts require the existence of governments, but freedom to act individually and cooperatively also often requires governing authority. Although rule-ordered life often, even in he best of existing democracies, serves the interests of those profiting from oppressive and dominating power, it also makes possible the modes of freedom and the kinds of cooperative action that produce a more just set of social practices. Without a rule specifying on which side of the road to drive, no one would be free to drive with any assurance of safety. Without outlawing stealing, there would be no ownership of property and the freedom such ownership provides. Without outlawing lying and failures to keep promises and fulfill contracts, there would be none of the knowledge of other people's pledged lines of action that makes it possible to freely carry out projects based on expectations about what others will be doing. Without outlawing forcing one's will on others, without outlawing murder, assault, rape, and slavery, people would have little freedom to do anything. Kant was at least right about that. Without the use of governmental power to provide constitutional protections of freedom of thought, expression, and religious and political association against the tyrannical use of power by majorities in democracies, many people would not be free to be included in the governmental policy-making process. Jefferson, Madison, and the writers of the Bill of Rights were at least right about that. Without compulsory social security and medicare deductions, massive numbers of people would not be free from the powerlessness that handicaps, injuries, illness, and old age force upon people. Progressive liberals at least are right about that. Having governments restrict certain kinds of freedom often is necessary in order to guarantee much more important kinds of freedom.

The question put to the religions of the world is not whether to have government or anarchy. The question is: How should a political realm be constituted so that it will satisfy the ethical demands lying at the core of the world religions, thus enabling religious people to live in such a political world. Religious people know that in a political realm governing people who are living religious and secular ways of life, they cannot justify legally requiring all people to do what is required by their way of faithfully responding to the call of the infinite. Religious people cannot legally require all people to live according to the demands of agape love. Religious efforts to care for people compassionately and charitably will always go beyond justified government efforts to care for its citizens and people in other nation-states. Nevertheless, the religious commitment to respect the precious, singular uniqueness of all people is not just a core religious commitment. It embodies a universal human, ethical right that all people can use to critique government actions. Given the different social and cultural constitutions and historical development of different people, the existence of different nation-states is probably not only an inevitable reality at this time, but it also is a good thing. The ethical responsibilities of citizens, however, are not just to other citizens in their own country. Given the universal human rights of all people, and given the massive interactions and interdependencies of people in different nation-states, people in one state have all sorts of responsibilities to people living in other states. The development of international law, as well as the constitution and support of international governmental and nongovernmental institutions aimed at helping to protect these universal rights and to aid the powerless and suffering masses of people in the world, is an ethical responsibility of all people.

What does an authentic religious ethic have to say about how governments should be constituted within a nation-state? It seems as though only a constitutional democracy can meet the ethical responsibilities imposed on practices of governing. First, individuals need constitutional protections of their universal human rights against tyrannical acts of governments, even governments acting in accordance with the preferences of citizen majorities that authorized such actions. It is the recognition of this need that leads Rawls to give priority to the equal liberty political principle over the economic-difference principle in determining how benefits and burdens are to be fairly distributed. Second, the right kind of democracy must be constituted. Iris Marion Young distinguishes two different models of democracy: an aggregative model and a deliberative model.[273] Both models presuppose the existence of a state whose authorities alone are authorized under a rule of law to use coercion, and they both presuppose the use of voting to authorize coercion when conflicts cannot be voluntarily resolved. The first model views democracy as a means for achieving what is taken as a just political result, the aggregating of the preferences of citizens in selecting government officials and establishing legally binding policies. The second model interprets democracy as a process that produces results which are considered just simply because they have been agreed to after open and critical dialogue by all persons to be governed by the results.

The second, process-oriented conception of democracy seems superior to the first, result-oriented conception. All of the objections to Mill's use of personal preference as a criterion for measuring better and worse pleasures and pains reappear here. Aggregated preferences may conflict with personal preferences and may call for using people as mere means. In addition, the calculative model of reasoning involved in the aggregative form of democracy conceives of reasoning as something that individuals do operating with a certain mathematical rule of calculation, something a computer could do. It does not appreciate that people in dialogue constantly are refining what they take to be practically reasonable and just. The deliberative model will produce just results, however, only to the extent that all people bound by the final policy are included on equal terms in the dialogue leading to the result, a dialogue in which all participants are required to offer reasons supporting their positions, reasons that they recognize can be acceptable to other participants in the dialogue, no matter how different they are from one another. Young's characterization of the deliberative model of democracy is similar in many ways to what Rawls calls the political process of reaching an overlapping consensus.[274]

Young's deliberative model of democracy will remain an avenue leading to just results only if it works with a process rather than a result approach to justice. Deliberation should not proceed on the assumption that all parties share a common good or should aim at producing a common good. Assuming that such a common good exists assumes that all citizens form a common group, but given the differences existing in all nation-states today, this will mean excluding some people from the deliberative process and the kind of dialogue that could mutually change the participants in the dialogue were the discussion not limited to what is thought to be commonly held as good. Likewise, aiming at reaching agreement on some common good will prevent some people from appreciating that people may hold irreconcilably different ways of living well and that the best way to honor such differences is to be satisfied with rough-and-ready provisional agreements always open to further discussion.[275] Neither religious nor secular people need to assume or strive for some common good way of living in order to live with self-integrity in a democratic state. This embodies the wisdom of Hsun Tzu's Confucian advocacy of seeking social harmony rather than social homogenization.

To think that one can find a principle of justice that will totally cover all possible ways of organizing a society and then can provide an automatic decision procedure for selecting out the just ones, is to forget everything Derrida has said about the inherent incompleteness of our concepts and their socially variable and historically changing differences and deferrals. It is to forget what Levinas has said about all coerced totalities ending up being totalitarian. No one substantive principle of distributive justice can govern justly all the impermanent and changing differences within secular ways of life, within religious ways of life, and between secular and religious ways of life. The political handling of conflicts requires that some sort of procedural approach to distributive justice must be taken.

How, then, are burdens and benefits to be distributed justly in a democracy? Distributing them equally does not seem to be the best way to respect people's universally equal status as singularly unique persons. Rawls's second principle of justice, the difference principle, states that an unequal distribution is justified if it does so in order to serve the best interests of the least advantaged people in the nation. Letting some people be free to earn more money and benefits than other people may motivate them to increase the overall amount of national wealth available and thus enable market forces and the government to raise the level of the worst off in the nation. In democratic deliberation, the worst off should find this to be an acceptable justification for the unequal distribution because they end up better off with the unequal distribution than without it. Only irrational envy could prevent them from seeing this. Rawls's principle, however, has limitations. Not all benefits can be distributed according to some general formula. Self-respect is dependent upon the people's very specific and very different locations in families and other interpersonal relationships. And as Foucault reminds us, power is not a substance that can be distributed justly or unjustly among people, because it is not a substance at all. It depends upon all the disciplinary mini-practices and social and economic institutions existing within a nation and between nations. Instead of trying to find a general distribution formula, Young proposes pursuing justice by resisting in specific situations the unjust treatment of people taking place there, the domination and oppression of people that is occurring.

Young identifies two universal values whose institutional arrangements just societies ought to contain and support in order to respect the equal moral status of all people: (1) fostering self-determination by aiding people to develop and exercise individual capacities and the expression of their experiences and preferences in democratic deliberations, and (2) fostering self-development by enabling people to be effectively free to be involved in determining their actions and the conditions of their actions. Domination is unjust because it denies self-determination, and oppression in its many forms (exploitation, powerlessness, marginalization, cultural imperialism, violence) prevents self-development.[276] Religiously responding to the ethical call to be responsible to people in their naked and helpless singularity would involve at least pursuing these two values.

The world religions might criticize the quality of the secular capacities involved in self-determination by some people, but they would recognize that they could not justify on religious grounds government restriction of such capacities because they know that they have no rationales that would be acceptable to secular people engaged in a democratic process of dialogue. Authentically religious people know that no government imposed theocracy is ever justified. They know that no form of a supposedly religious justification of oppression is justified, no matter how much they are convinced that continued development of secular ways of life are disastrous. What holds for the injustice of trying to use state power to force people to be religious for their own good also holds for almost all attempts to use undemocratic means (authoritarian or revolutionary force) to change unjust conditions, The risk that such means will produce or reinforce injustice is just too high.[277] The religious, ethical, and realistic option is to organize resistance to injustice within the constitutional democratic framework.

There is one more major area of religious/ethical conflicts that needs to be considered. The religious love of joyous living depends upon loving life itself and compassionately respecting the elements whose enjoyment fills our lives with such joy. Sometimes our ways of enjoying life may conflict with the well-being of the elements upon which that joy depends. Hence the problem of environmental ethics. Sometimes our ways of joyful living may conflict with the well-being of lives created through joys of our sexual lives. Hence the ethical responsibilities of family planning and the ethical complexities surrounding the tragedy of aborting human life. How are the religions of the world to deal with these problems, and to what extent can democratic governments use their coercive power in these areas?

In spite of denials by those who would see the environment as nothing but raw materials to be used to maximize corporate profits, secure reelection funding, and find personal joy in destroying life, people who care about the future of themselves and those they care about have the best of prudential reasons for protecting their living environment. We and our descendants need clean air, clean water, rich top soil, not an overly heated atmosphere or oceans, and an abundant, safe food chain. There are also non-prudential reasons for protecting our environment. Developing the capacities needed in order to become aesthetically sensitive to nature (curiosity, openness to novelty, looking at things from radically different points of view [those of animals, and of plants, as if they had points of view], empathetic imagination, interest in the details of the many kinds of living species, and becoming free to feel for something that is not immediately self-serving) is at the same time a matter of developing the capacities needed to meet one's responsibilities to other people.[278] Also, animals suffer and strive to act free of restraints. Being thankful for the world in which one lives seems to require caring about the suffering and freedom of animals. In addition, people's ability to empathize with the suffering and domination of other people is greatly strengthened by an ability to empathize with the suffering of animals and the absence of freedom of movement of animals reared in the meat industries.

The religions of the world are some of the best advocates for preserving and cherishing our natural environment. The Abrahamic religions point out that people are to use their ability to have dominion over nature only so that they can care for it as stewards charged with protecting gifts for which they are to be continually thankful and which they are to hand on in good shape to future generations. Buddhism, Shintoism, and Taoism charge that one can extinguish destructive human cravings only if one lets nature be in its suchness, cherishing it simply for what it is and not just for how in can be used by humans. Many of these religions call for their followers to be vegetarians.

Since it is not now possible to get agreement in deliberative democratic societies on the compulsory elimination of meat consumption, vegetarianism cannot at present move beyond being a religious obligation in some religions to being a legal obligation in democratic societies.

Given that people are called to be ethically responsible to all other people in their fragile singular uniqueness—and to be responsible therefore to justify their taking up space in other people's lives—people also bear a heavy responsibility for creating other people who will occupy additional spaces. People always bear heavy reproductive responsibilities and never more so than in this age in which the globe is so heavily populated, so depleted of the essentials for maintaining life, and so cruelly organized socially, economically, and politically as to prevent the distribution of such life-sustaining resources as are available. Never has the call for reproductive responsibility been more needed than in this age in which so many social and cultural practices are producing people craving for more and more sexual pleasure or at least sexual activity, people not wanting to think or bother about preventing the creation of more people. Religious people certainly can reinforce the claim also made by secular ethicists that respect for people as people requires that sexual activity be tied to interpersonal relationships the preservation of which are prized much more than the attainment of sexual pleasure. Because of the protection they offer against sexually transmitted diseases, especially AIDS, condoms should be used when sexual activity is not coupled with an intention of creating new people. It seems as though the only justification that can be offered to support the claim that no birth control devices should be used during sexual activity is the charge that this would be doing something unnatural, violating some natural law. Obviously one is not violating a physical or biological law of nature or one could not do it. As we have seen, the idea that there are natural moral laws is a metaphysical idea subject to the all the criticisms of metaphysics offered in section one. Given that even the leading proponents of natural-law moral theories in the Roman Catholic Church now say that it is permissible to use condoms if this is done in order to prevent AIDS rather than prevent conception, given that many Muslim leaders now give the same authorization, given the recognition that continual sexual activity helps greatly in strengthening relationships of love, and given that good sex contributes so much to human joy and love of life, there seem to be no ethical reasons not to use birth control devices as means of preventing conception. For many different reasons, major segments of the world religions also seem to agree.[279]

It is one thing to prevent the creation of life, and it is quite a different thing to terminate the life of human embryos or fetuses. Opposition to the use of stem cells that never have been implanted in a woman's uterus and are destined to deteriorate or be destroyed, in order to save adult humans with very serious illnesses such as Parkinson's or Lou Gehrig's disease, seems justifiable only by once again making metaphysical claims that cannot be justified. They certainly cannot be justified to all people participating in dialogue in a deliberative democracy. Few people would consider such cells to be of equal worth to one of their children. If a fire broke out and one could save only one of the two, almost all people would save their children.

It is difficult to treat embryos and fetuses, however, the way one treats stem cells. For many people, especially some authentically religious people, it is impossible to look at embryos and fetuses and not sense that they are encountering face-to-face a singular individual of infinite worth. Certainly parents who joyfully await the birth of their child feel this way. No one could ever justify to them the killing off of what is being created in them. In no deliberative democracy will agreement ever be reached on a policy of forced or coerced abortion, no matter how much it might contribute to lessening the problem of over-population. Voluntarily choosing to abort one's own embryo or fetus should never be a painless decision. Respect for life and for human persons must always be factors involved in making such a decision, and if they are involved, then a decision to abort will always be a difficult decision to make. In a deliberative democracy, however, governmental denial of freedom to make such a choice is not justifiable to all the people facing such a choice. For many people in dialogue in a deliberative democracy, the early termination of a pregnancy is not even unethical, believing as they do that determining at what stage in a pregnancy an individual is present with the ethical status of person-hood is not a metaphysical determination, but is instead a social deci-sion to be based on what best protects the clear cases of persons who have responsibilities as well as rights. Forcing women to continue with pregnancies, especially when they are unable to adequately rear what they have created, may show far greater disrespect to the woman than what is shown to the embryo or fetus. One might try to persuade a woman to continue with a pregnancy and then put the child up for adoption, but there may be many women who find that much too painful to do. One of the best religious, nonmetaphysical handlings of abortion may be the Buddhist position. While declaring that abortion is an unjustifiable failure to respect and cherish life, they recommend extending great compassion to the woman who thinks that she would be doing something far worse if she were to proceed with creating a new life. They call for people to compassionately understand what she perceives as an impossible situation and to compassionately love her before and after the abortion.

The ethical core at the heart of all the religions of the worlds calls for protecting the universal and inalienable rights of all people, and they call for participation in deliberative democratic life. By doing this they can maximize their joyous love of life, meet the requirements of legal obligations in a deliberative democracy, and go far beyond such requirements by compassionately caring for other people.

4. Freeing The World's Religions for Dialogue

Hans-Georg Gadamer provides the theoretical understanding needed to understand how the religions of the world living in a postmodern age can enter into religiously fruitful dialogue with one another.[280] Most people most of the time do not engage in dialogue; they engage in intermittent monologues. They do not really listen to the other speaker or allow their own basic assumptions, beliefs, and desires to be changed. In genuine dialogue one always listens as a socially and culturally constituted per-son, but one also puts everything on the line. One enters the dialogue expecting to hear something being spoken out of a different set of background conditions. One enters the dialogue willing for one's own background and thus oneself to be changed in significant and unpredictable ways. One's background is never wiped clean, but it may be changed sufficiently so that what one's old background ruled out as impossible, irrational, or undesirable now becomes possible. The dialogue partners do not become the same as each other; they retain a great deal of their presupposed background and thus maintain much of their previous social identity. In addition, in dialogue one not only listens, but one also answers back. One permits one's background and one's social identity to change only when one is attracted by something one hears. Dialogue broadens and deepens what one is. It does not destroy everything one finds attractive in one's background presuppositions.

Gadamer focuses primarily on dialogues taking place between individual persons or between an individual and a text the person is reading. In the present text, however, the notion of dialogue is going to be enlarged so that we can talk about whole religious ways of life being in dialogue with one another. Religious ways of life have their background presuppositions. Talking about the religions of the world being in dialogue with one another is talking about how one religion can permit itself to be attracted by what is being proclaimed and showed in other religions, and by doing so, broadening and deepening its own religious way of life. Dialogue among the religions of the world does not require any of them to lose their soul. Talking about religions entering into dialogue with one another requires treating religions as having a distinctive set of family resemblances that differentiate them from other religions. It is important to recognize that it is dangerous to categorize religions as having distinct, specifiable identities. This can easily lead to covering up important differences existing in each of the religions and important similarities among different religions. This is a danger, however, that only requires that one proceed cautiously, always adding as a footnote to everything one says: remember the differences, remember the similarities, remember the traces, remember the historically changing nature of things, remember openness to future graftings, remember the unpredictable future.

Gadamer's program of philosophical hermeneutics, of dialogue opening up new worlds of possibilities, is open to the criticism that he does not deal with the problem of motivating people to enter into a form of dialogue that might radically change their motivations. It seems that we need to enter into an endless series of dialogues aimed at changing people so that they will engage in dialogue. The same problem confronts Heidegger's call for people to become poets creating new worlds, of which Gadamer's call for dialogue is a more down to earth variation. What will motivate people, enframed in secular, technological ways of life, to surrender themselves to the process of having new worlds be created through them? As long as dialogue and poetic world building operate only at a secular level, this will always be a problem. What some else is and what someone is saying will appear attractive to me only if it resonates with something that I already am, thus dialogue will never produce radical change.

This criticism of Gadamer and Heidegger is a variation on Kierkegaard's interpretation of what Plato says in the *Meno* about the impossibility of coming to know the truth, since if the truth is not already in us we will never come to recognize it when we see it. So likewise, it seems as though unless we already are the sort of person who is attracted to certain sorts of things, we will not find anything in anyone else that is attractive. Kierkegaard replied to Plato, however, that the truth does not lie in us, but it must come to us from the infinite, something that will happen only of we leap in faith to a radically new way of life in which we respond to the call of the infinite itself, a response motivated by the attractiveness of the infinite's love for us as singularly unique individuals whose identities are not confined within secular social identities and presuppositions. The infinite in the face of another who calls me to care for all people is the infinite of agape love, which can attract me so that I can respond by letting one world die off and another begin. Agape love will be attractive to any and all people, and only active resistance will prevent it from producing a change in us. This is what Augustine was getting at when he claimed that it is only rebellion against the truth that can prevent the truth from being heard by people. One can elect to turn a deaf ear to this quiet call of agape love, but one can also be attracted, hear this call of infinite love, and begin to strive to respond faithfully to this call. The secular cannot motivate anyone to rise above the secular, but agape love can do this if we will not slam the door in the face of its most attractive call. Secular dialogue confronts an impenetrable barrier that religious dialogue does not face. Here is shown another one of the inadequacies of a merely secular way of life.

In their very response to the call of the infinite, religious people can find the motivation for dialogue with people in other religions. The religions of the world share a common core of thankfulness, ethical responsibility, and a recognition of the inadequacies in purely secular living, which allows them to respect different religious responses to the call of the infinite, regardless how different those responses may be, responses containing aspects that they might profitably appropriate in dialogue with one another. Their dialogue will begin by hearing that a precious religious tradition is saying something. Only then will they begin to listen to the specifics of what is being said. As Levinas points out, the saying of the said takes ethical precedence over what is said. Being religious is being a hostage to the call of people we meet face-to-face. Being such a hostage means dialogically opening oneself to the person saying and showing something, respecting the saying of whatever is said and the showing of whatever is shown, and opening oneself up to possibly attractive features in what is said and shown, thus having the background of one's own sayings and showings significantly changed. When the world religions engage in dialogue with one another, most of what was constituted over thousands of years of faithful responding (religious practices, modes of subjectivity, individual and social identities) will probably remain the same. Still, some aspects of religious ways of life different from one's own might appear as religiously attractive, and one religion's frontier of possibilities may be fruitfully modified. Dialogue is not calling for conversion, but it is calling for religious people to be willing to be enriched. As long as people do not confuse encounters with the infinite, which is the universal core of all religions, with socially and culturally variable responses to this call, religious people have no reason to fear dialogue among the world's religions. A few illustrations of what the world's religions might hear if they did engage in dialogue will be offered in the hope that people in the world's religions will be able to supply or discover thousands of other examples.

The Abrahamic religions have focused on praising God as the creator of the goodness of life, on prophetically judging social practices for being unjust and communities calling themselves religious for being inauthentic, on invoking God's mercy and forgiveness, and on hearing a messianic promise for a hopeful future. Until Kierkegaard, however, they had not dealt systematically with analyzing various secular forms of life that are producing frustration and suffering. It seems that these religions can deepen and strengthen their religious ways of life by listening in dialogue to what Hindus have to say about making pleasure, power, and fulfilling the requirements of social roles the ultimate goals that people pursue. Similarly, the Abrahamic religions could deepen and strengthen their ways of life by listening to what Buddhists have to say about the suffering caused by trying to satisfy cravings generated by using comparative criteria of self-worth. These two dialogues could have a great effect on transforming current patterns of prayer, which are now unfortunately too often focused on begging God for goodies or the prevention of harm and on trying to bargain with God, exchanging promises of changed behavior for gaining supernatural intervention in our world of necessities and chances. Prayer could become much more a matter of meditative self-examination and seeking to increase wisdom and motivation to do what people must do to undo the damage they have already done to themselves.

The Abrahamic religions also might profit greatly if they were to hear in dialogue what Hinduism, Buddhism, and Taoism have to say about the joyous and blissful lives people can possess after enlightenment and extinguishing the worship of false gods, and while still biologically alive. Some Jews and many Christians and Muslims get trapped within metaphysical boxes that lead them to focus so much on life after biological death that they deny themselves the joy and peace that can be theirs before they die. Many Christians and Muslims could learn much from the religions of Asia about how to find joy, beauty, and peace in simply letting themselves and the elements in their environment be what they are. To the extent that their love of life will be strengthened in this way, there will be a weakening of their willingness to sacrifice life, their own lives and those of others, in order to receive back as payment earned rewards in some metaphysically claimed life after biological death. This would be a good thing in many different ways. Religion no longer would be seen as validating the use of violence as a way to attain supposedly religious ends. People no longer would look favorably upon human disasters, mistakenly taking them to be signs of a metaphysical end to this world and an inauguration of a new metaphysical world supposedly similar to this one but free of all human suffering and injustice. People no longer will live in fear of burning timelessly in some metaphysical hell, while also believing that a loving God would enjoy such a spectacle.

Taoism and Zen also have a lot to say to the Abrahamic religions about the religious significance of aestheticizing people's environments and lives. Hundreds of millions of people in China and Japan who never participate in Buddhist or Taoist temple services incorporate many of these religions' insights by enjoying the aesthetic beauty of the temples, the dry and wet gardens around their homes, or the paintings on the walls of their homes; by participating in tea ceremonies and flower arranging; by reading and writing poetry, practicing writing of calligraphy, or producing music. Listening to what these Asian religions have to say might lead Muslims to find a way to continue refusing to make any graven images of Allah, while also continuing to creatively develop aesthetic expressions of the Islamic way of life. Christians might find great help in creating a new postmodern era of Christian art and music. As Mark Taylor points out, some of that is already beginning to happen, as change and indeterminacy get accented over the permanent and the closed in postmodern art.

The religions of Asia could probably benefit if they were to hear in dialogue what Judaism, Christianity, and Islam have to say about forgiveness. Although gaining freedom for the present and future from brooding over the past has always been a feature of the Asian religions, the importance of experiencing forgiveness as an aid in ending such brooding has not been accented. It is one thing to tell people about the counterproductive character of letting guilt and shame determine one's present and future options, but it is quite another thing to acquire the power and freedom to extinguish the demands of such feelings. So much of Asian literature is dominated by the despair people feel because of guilt and shame. The mercy of gods worshiped in bhakti worship and the compassion of the bodhisattvas worshiped in Buddhist worship seem quite able to appropriate suitable Hindu and Buddhist versions of a realized eschatology in which a forgiven past opens up fresh pages in life.

Listening to the voices of the prophets might produce some of the most significant areas of enrichment in the religions of Asia. Newly constituted Hindu, Buddhist, and Taoist prophets would have a great deal to say about the unjust governmental and social practices existing in the nations of Asia. They would have a great deal to say about how authentic faithful responses to the ethical call of the infinite in these religious traditions exclude and condemn the metaphysical, superstitious, nationalistic, sexist, and class-privileging factors presently contaminating much of their religions. Already some such prophets are arising. Motivated by the protests of Buddhist priests during the Vietnam war, a number of Buddhist prophets are arising in Southeast Asia who are ethically condemning unjust social conditions and advocating democratic pursuits of justice. Many writers, heavily influenced by their religious backgrounds, are writing prophetic novels and poems. Still, these seem to be the exceptions to the general tendency to focus on personal efforts to diminish jiva and tanha, rather than on public efforts to socially and politically care for other people.

One final example: The religions of Asia, in dialogue with the Abrahamic religions, might hear something about the significance of the shared, communal religious worship and service accented so heavily in Judaism, Christianity, and Islam. In the religions of Asia, communal worship seems primarily to be restricted to communities of priests or monks. Lay persons generally are not involved in communal worship. Sometimes mass collections of people participate in Hindu practices, but this is often a collection of strangers and not an interpersonal communal activity. Without denying the importance of the insight in Asian religions that each person must individually hear the call of the infinite and respond saying, "Here I am," it seems possible also to engage in shared interpersonal activities that will help individuals hear that call and make the leap of faith needed for enlightenment and the attainment of bliss, Nirvana, and harmonious living. It also seems possible that communities of the authentically religious could speak prophetically and act collectively to provide loving care to people who need empowerment and the means for escaping suffering and for enjoying life.

Many more examples could be found of how Abrahamic religions could benefit from dialogue with one another and how the religions of Asia could do the same. Some of that is occurring now, but hardly enough. Again, differences in metaphysical beliefs is a major contributing force preventing significant dialogue. That participants in the postmodern revival of religious interest are engaged in very creative dialogue, even though they represent different Jewish and different Christian traditions, gives us a glimpse of what is possible. Now the dialogue needs to be taken out of the scholarly books and university lecture halls and practiced by people in these worshiping communities. Ordinary Christians and Jews, Christians and Muslims, Muslims and Jews, Hindus and Muslims, Christians and Hindus, Christians and Buddhists, Jews and Buddhists, Jews and Hindus need to engage themselves in dialogue.

In the contemporary world there are many different socially constituted, religiously faithful responses to different people's encounters with the nonfinite other to all socially constituted persons and objects. Six of these world religions, each with many internal variations, have been examined in this text. There are many others that have not been dealt with (for example, Native American and African religions), not because they don't deserve equal respect and treatment, but because of the lack of competence of this writer. All of these religions can be seen as social and historical variations of a common practice, refusing to absolutize any human schema of categorization and individuation and any resultant socially constituted objects and subjects, except as they are constituted in faithful response to encounters with the infinite. All of these religions need to be respected and cherished. It is not enough to merely tolerate them, to put up with them the way the body can tolerate certain medicines. Religious people living in one socially constituted religious world, in faithfully responding in their specific ways to their encounters with the infinite need to respect and cherish the way people live in differently constituted religious worlds.

People who are not living in any religious world also have an ethical responsibility to respect people living in religious worlds, because all people have the responsibility to respect the singular uniqueness of all people; because religious people are striving to be faithful to their responsibility to respect the singular uniqueness of people, including the nonreligious; and because religious people are seeking to resist all unjust practices that create domination and oppression of religious and nonreligious people. Respecting the freedom of all people to practice their way of being religiously faithful is a religious responsibility of all religious people, and it is an ethical responsibility of all people, religious or not. Not coercing nonreligious people to participate in religious practices of any kind is also a religious and ethical responsibility of all religious and nonreligious people. Freedom of religion means respecting all authentic forms of religion, and it means respecting all people, whether they are religious or not. Religious and nonreligious people may face tremendous difficulties in listening to one another in a dialogue, but both can participate in a deliberative democratic process that finds a rough-and-ready way to live with one another in peace.

In a deliberative democratic process that is determining how state or social power is to be used, people must give reasons that other people participating in the deliberations can accept. Deliberations might change people's minds about what reasons they can accept, but if such change does not occur and no such agreement can be reached, the use of coercive power is not justified. This is why in such democratic deliberations one cannot offer as a reason justifying the use of power the simple claim, "Well, that's my religious belief," when that belief is really a metaphysical belief. It is a perfectly good response if the belief is an authentically religious belief, because there is an ethical core in all authentic religions calling for respect for singularly unique people, for prizing universal human rights, and for using deliberative procedures to decide how to care for people.

When it comes to metaphysical beliefs, however, it simply is not true that people have a right to believe anything they want to believe. One does not have an ethical right to believe something that shows disrespect for the singular uniqueness of people and which leads to treating people unjustly, as constitutionally and democratically determined. One does not have an epistemological right to believe something that one can not justify to people who have good reasons for charging that one's belief is false. People within authentic religious ways of life can charge that one does not have a religious right to worship some graven image, some socially constituted institution, practice, or dogma, that is not constituted out of religious faithfulness to encounters with the other of all socially constituted objects and subjects. Respect for religious differences, respect for nonreligious persons, and respect for not-unjustified beliefs and social and cultural practices do not entail losing the ability and obligation to judge metaphysical beliefs as morally, epistemologically, and religiously unacceptable. Many metaphysical and superstitious beliefs are currently trying to hide behind religious masks, demanding that no one criticize them because such criticism would be sacrilegious. The religions of the world need to tear off these masks so that these beliefs can be criticized for what they are.

Perhaps one of the best ways to do this is through the use of the kind of humor that Bill Maher uses. Unfortunately, Maher keeps saying that he is attacking religion, when he is only attacking metaphysicians, magicians, and superstitious people wearing religious masks. Maher might object to my claim that what he is attacking should not be called "religion." Since words are social tools to be used in terms of social norms constituted by how people use words and correct the use of words, and since probably most people call religious' what Maher is ridiculing as religious, there is a sense in which Maher is not misusing the word "religious." The words "religion" and "religious," however, have another meaning, the one aimed at in the expression "authentically religious." One can understand the religions of the world only if one also uses these words in this second way. As used in nonreligious ordinary language discourse and in sociological or historical descriptions, the word "religion" is used to describe practices and beliefs of people and groups that identify themselves as religious. One can, however, use the word religion to refer to people's encounters with the infinite and to the many different socially constituted ways of responding faithfully to these encounters. Without keeping alive this religious use of the word "religious," it will be very difficult to avoid theoretically reducing religion to sociology, psychology, superstition, or metaphysics.

Throughout this text an attempt has been made show that religious encounters, religious faithfulness, religious worship, religious obedience, and religious practices are sui generis. An effort has been made to try to show what that uniqueness comes to and how it involves respecting the ethical uniqueness of people, joyfully loving life, compassionately caring for people, and dedicating oneself to prize eternal happiness above everything else, a happiness found in seeking it, a happiness found in surrendering everything so as to respond faithfully to these encounters with the nonfinite other to all nonreligious objects, institutions, and practices. The declaration that people must be allowed to remain free to be authentically religious in any one of the many ways people do this is also a declaration of resistance to all efforts to coercively restrict people's freedom to be religious and not to be religious. Offering a declaration of religious freedom is a matter of proclaiming, "Long live the religions of the world." Long live their common core and their historical differences. This declaration calls for everyone to endorse the principle of religious freedom: free to be religious, free to be religious in different ways, free to even not be religious. This is a declaration that every religious person can and should make. Let everyone, especially the religious people of the world, endorse the principle of not coercing anyone to be religious or to be religious in a certain way. Religious faithfulness cannot be coerced. Thus, this declaration of religious freedom also calls for people to let the nonreligious people of the world be respected in their suchness, respected as singularly unique persons, religiously to be loved in a way that maximizes the possibility that they, too, perhaps will respond to encounters with the infinite.

NOTES

Section One

1. Using the religious/secular distinction faces a host of problems, as do all binary opposites when interpreted without considering the context in which they are used. Derrida traces the use of the word "religion" to its history of use in the Greek, Jewish, Christian, and Islamic worlds during two thousand years of usage. See Jacques Derrida, "Faith and Knowledge: The Two Sources of 'Religion' at the Limits of Reason Alone," *Religion*, trans. Samuel Webber, in Jacques Derrida and Gianni Vattimo. eds. (Stanford: Stanford University Press, 1998), 4. In the medieval world, the word secular was used to refer to people not in monastic life. Treating church, temple, or mosque life as religious and economic, political, or entertainment life as secular hides the fact that much in the former can be inauthentically religious and much in the latter can be attempts to live in faithful responses to the call of the infinite, the call to love life and the most fragile and unlovely of people. For an excellent discussion of the the problems involved in working non-pragmatically with a religious/secular distinction, see John D. Caputo, *On Religion* (New York: Routledge, 2001), 2, 43. The way that the words "secular" and "authentically religious" are used in this book is similar to the way Caputo distinguishes the faithful and scrupulous lovers of God from the people who do not love God but seek to live in a world in which their power control things (ibid., 1–2, 31, 43, 93, 110–111, 123). Since not all of the world's religions use "God talk," In this book I will use the term "infinite" and designate as authentically religious those who strive to live in faithfulness to encounters with the infinite. I will designate as secular the absence of a life of faithful striving to act out of a desire for the most desirous, the call of the infinite to love life and to meet one's responsibilities to other people. It is crucial to remember that authentic and inauthentic religious practices generally live intertwined in the historical social phenomena commonly named religion, with the former continually critiquing the latter.

2. For an overall characterization of Levinas's efforts to indicate that which is other than the describable, especially the ethical uniqueness of people, see Henry L. Ruf, *Postmodern Rationality, Social Criticism, and Relgion* (St. Paul, MN: Paragon House, 2005), 308–325.

3.   Jean-Luc Marion, *God Without Being*, trans. Thomas A. Carleson (Chicago: University of Chicago Press, 1991), 55.

4.   For extensive treatments of speech acts, see John Searle, *Speech Acts* (Cambridge: Cambridge University Press, 1969); *Expression and Meaning* (Cambridge: Cambridge University Press, 1979). See also Kent Bach and Robert M. Harnish, *Linguistic Communication and Speech Acts* (Cambridge, MA: MIT Press, 1979).

5.   Emmanuel Levinas, "God and Philosophy," in *The Levinas Reader*, ed. Sean Hand (Oxford: Basil Blackwell, 1989), 170–175.

6.   Stephen Katz shows that mystical experiences are always reported in language specific to a particular religion and thus are different sorts of experiences. This, of course, does not show that what is being encountered in these mystical experiences is not the other to all constituted objects and linguistic descriptions. See Stephen Katz, *Mysticism and Philosophical Analysis* (New York: Oxford University Press, 1978).

7.   For a fuller discussion of the need to move beyond tolerance to respect of religious differences, see Henry L. Ruf, "Radicalizing Liberalism and Modernity," in *Philosophy, Religion, and the Question of Intolerance,"* eds. Mehdi Amin Razavi and David Ambuel (Albany, NY: SUNY Press, 1997), 170–188.

8.   For a detailed study of attempts by scholars to reduce religious phenomena to secular phenomena, see D.Z. Phillips, *Religion Without Explanation* (London: Basil Blackwell, 1976); *Religion and the Hermeneutics of Contemplation* (Cambridge: Cambridge University Press, 2001).

9.   Nicholas Everitt, *The Non-Existence of God* (London: Routledge, 2004). Besides examining the supposed proofs of classical thinkers such as Anselm, Aquinas, Descartes, Kant, and Paley, he analyzes recent arguments for a metaphysical god given by thinkers in the tradition of analytic philosophy, such as Plantinga and Swinburne.

10.   Everitt, *The Non-existence of God, 7–8.*

11.   Everitt, *The Non-existence of God*, 16.

12.   Aristiotle, "Metaphysics," in *The Basic Works of Aristotle*, ed. Richard McKeon (New York: Random House, 1941), 689–693.

13.   See Richard Swinburne, "The Argument from Design," in *Contemporary Perspectives on Religious Epistemology*, eds. R. Douglas Geivett and Brendan Sweetman. (New York: Oxford University Press, 1992), 204–5; and William Lane Craig, "Philosophical and Scientific Pointers to *Creatio ex Nihilo,"* in *God*, ed. Timothy Robinson (Indianapolis: Hackett Publishing Co., 2002), 70–71.

14. See the objections to the notion that a timelessly existing metaphysical god can create things in time in Nicholas Everitt, *The Non-Existence of God*, 75–76.

15. For a critique of the claim that a timeless metaphysical god could know what people are now doing, see Norman Kretzmann, "Omniscience and Immutability," in *God*, 167–181.

16. For analyses of the many reasons that arguments for the existence of the metaphysical god do no work, see Michael Martin, *Atheism: A Philosophical Justification* (Philadelphia: Temple University Press, 1990).

17. Without endorsing the pragmatic interpretation of the explanation presented here, a number of other philosophers have also pointed out that there is no good reason to endorse the metaphysical principle that every contingency needs an explanation or that every possibility, actualized or unactualized, needs an explanation. Paul Edwards points out that explanations are complete when phenomena are found to be instances of uniform connections like the law of gravity. See his "A Critique of the Cosmological Argument," in *Philosophy of Religion*, ed. Louis P. Pojman (Belmont, CA: Wadsworth, 2003), 12–13. William Rowe has charged that we do not know that the metaphysical principle of sufficient reason is true, although many people, after centuries of training, suppose it is true. See his "An Examination of the Cosmological Argument," in *Philosophy of Religion*, 22–23.

18. Slavoj Zizek has developed Lacan's distinction between socially constituted "reality" and the "Real," in order to indicate that all in such symbolic reality is not all that needs indication. The Real indicates the traumatic gaps that we have to live with in such a reality, the gaps we try to fill in with social ideologies and fantasies and personal fantasies and small objects treated as having ultimate significance. See his *Interrogating the Real*, ed. Rex Butler and Scott Stephens (London: Continuum, 2005), 347. Zizek, however, also rejects ontotheology and the search for an explantory ultimate reality. What he and Lacan call the Real is what I am calling the other, the Infinite. It is social reality's abyss or void that is not nothing, Nargarjuna's claim that Zizek endorses in his and Glyn Daly's *Conversations With Zizek* (Cambridge: Polity Press, 2005), 96.

19. Aristotle, "Physics, Book VII.1 and VIII.6," in *The Basic Works of Aristotle*, ed. Richard McKeon (New York: Random House, 1941), 340–342, 373–377.

20. Thomas Aquinas, *Summa Theologiae, Questions on God*, Part I, Question II, Third Article, ed. Brian Leftow (Cambridge: Cambridge University Press, 2006).

21. William Craig, "Philosophical and Scientific Pointers to *Creatio ex Nihilo*, 185–200.

22. Dallas Willard argues, like Craig, that every event must be a member of a

series of events with a first member that is self-existent; otherwise it would be trapped in the paradox of completing in time an infinite series. Again, mathematical notions of the infinite are being confused with historical notions of events preceding events endlessly. See Willard's "The Three-Stage Argument for the Existence of God," in *Contemporary Perspectives on Religious Epistemology*, 212–224.

23.   Paul Draper, "A Critique of the Kalam Cosmological Argument" in *Philosophy of Religion*, 44–45.

24.   Paul Draper points out that Craig equivocates in his use of the expression "to begin" when talking about the origin of the universe. When he uses it to talk about our observations of things caused to exist (to which he compares the universe as a whole), then such caused beginnings always have earlier times when they do not exist. When he uses it to talk about the beginning of the universe, he is talking about the universe and time beginning together; there is no universe until changes begin to happen. In this second sense, however, we have no experience of universes together with time beginning to exist and thus have no reason to think that they must be caused to exist. We have no criteria for applying the expression "cause of universes and time beginning to exist." See his "A Critique of the Kalam Cosmological Argument," 46.

25.   Theodore Schick Jr., "The 'Big Bang' Argument for the Existence of God," in *Philo I*, no.1 (Spring/Summer 1998).

26.   Craig's objection to the "vacuum fluctuation" hypothesis again depends on his charge that absurd paradoxes would show up because the hypothesis would be endorsing the idea of an actual infinity of past time, and this would entail that universes would be springing into existence at every point in the vacuum. See his "Scientific Confirmation of the Cosmological Argument" in *Philosophy of Religion*, 34. Craig's objection depends again on confusing mathematical notions of closed infinite sets and the experiential notion of endless yesterdays before yesterday.

27.   Anselm,"Proslogium" in *Proslogium/Monologium*, trans. Sidney Norton Dean (Eugene, OR: Wipf & Stock Publishing, 2003), chapters II and II.

28.   Spinoza, "Ethics, Proposition XI," in *Spinoza Selections,* ed. John Wild (New York: Charles Scribner's Sons, 1930) 103-106

29.   Alvin Plantinga, *God, Freedom, and Evil* (Grand Rapids, MI: Wm. B. Eerdmans Publishing, 1977).

30.   Plantinga chooses to talk about properties rather than predicates, but there does not seem to be any need to make any such commitment to an ontology of properties in order to examine his version of the ontological argument. Just

as pragmatists and postmodernists see no need to buy into the metaphysical assumptions behind endorsements of correspondence theories of truth, so do they see no need to postulate properties as the supposed counterpart of the descriptive terms we use in making claims. Properties are just as much socially constituted as objects. Also, pragmatists and postmodernists reject the idea that one can refer to possible properties and possible worlds that are not worlds possible for socially constituted people. Possibilities and necessities are only contingently so, their specification being contingent on the vocabularies and concepts available to socially constituted people living in socially constituted worlds that are historically changeable in ways not now specifiable. In order to keep this in mind, Wittgenstein recommended that we always inquire about the civil status of contradictions. See Ludwig Wittgenstein, *Philosophical Investigations,* trans. G.E.M. Anscombe (New York: Macmillan, 1953), 121.

31. Aristotle, "Physics, Book II.8," in *The Basic Works of Aristotle*, 249–251.

32. William Paley, *Natural Theology: Or Evidence of the Existence and Attributes of the Deity, Collected from the Appearances of Nature* (Indianapolis: Indiana University Press, 1964).

33. Very readable presentations and strong defenses of scientific, biological explanations for the phenomena that metaphysicians claim they must postulate their god to explain can be found in the following two articles: David Quammen, "Was Darwin Wrong? NO," *National Geographic*, November 2004, 3–35; and H. Allen Orr, "Devolution: Why Intelligent Design Isn't," *The New Yorker*, May 30, 2005, 40–52.

34. See Richard Swinburne, "The Argument from Design," 201–211.

35. See Robert M. Adams, "Flavors, Colors, and God," in *Contemporary Perspectives in Religious Epistemology*, 225–240.

36. See Martin Heidegger, *Being and Time*, trans. Joan Stambaugh (Albany, NY: SUNY Press, 1996), 89–105; and Hubert L. Dryfus, *Being-in-the-World* (Cambridge, MA: MIT Press, 1991), 108–127.

37. See John Searle, *Intentionality* (Cambridge: Cambridge University Press, 1983) and "Analytic Philosophy and Mental Phenomena," *Midwest Studies in Philosophy* (1980): 405–423. Slavoj Zizek, in his discussion of the various philosophical efforts to deal with sentience and consciousness, shows that there are alternatives to Churchland's reductive materialism and Whiteheadian pan-psychism. There is Colin McGinn's emergent but unknowable consciousness, Dennet's treatment of consciousness as the result of evolutionary development, and Badiou's claim that consciousness is an ultimate event unspecifiable with objective criteria. See Zizek's *The Parallex View* (Cambridge, MA: MIT Press, 2006), 174–178). The weakness in the latter three positions is that they fail to preserve

the Wittgensteinian portrayal of the intersubjective character of consciousness, which eliminates any inability to distinguish conscious people from zombies.

38.   Immanuel Kant, *Critique of Practical Reason,* trans. Lewis White Beck (New York: The Liberal Arts Press, 1956), 114–115.

39.   Kant, *Critique of Practical Reason,* 118.

40.   Kant, *Critique of Practical Reason,* 126–136.

41.   Kant, *Critique of Practical Reason,* 115–120.

42.   George I. Mavrodes, "Religion and the Queerness of Morality," in *God*), 74–89.

43.   Mavrodes, "Religion and the Queerness of Morality," 88–89.

44.   Friedrich Nietzsche, *The Gay Science,* trans. Walter Kaufmann (New York: Vintage Books, 1974), 36. See my exposition of Nietzsche's position in *Postmodern Rationality, Social Criticism, and Religion,* 171–184.

45.   Robert Merrihew Adams, "Moral Arguments for Theistic Belief," in *God,* 90–112.

46.   For a fuller defense of a pragmatic, noncorrespondence theory of truth, see my *Postmodern Rationality, Social Criticism, and Religion,* 20–21, 69–73, 127–129.

47.   Jean-Paul Sartre, *Existentialism and Humanism,* trans. P. Mairet (London: Metheun, 1948).

48.   Nicholas Wolterstorff, "Is Reason Enough?," in *Contemporary Perspectives on Religious Epistemology,* 142–149.

49.   Alvin Plantinga, "Is Belief in God Properly Basic?" in *God,* 351–363.

50.   Plantinga's argument, interpreted as a claim about a metaphysical god, has been criticized by a number of philosophers who point out reasons for doubting such beliefs and thus the need to try to justify them. See Stewart Goetz, "Belief in God is Not Properly Basic," in *Contemporary Perspectives on Religious Epistemology,* 168–177; Robert Pargetter, "Experience, Proper Basicality, and Belief in God," in *Philosophy of Religion,* eds. Michael Peterson, William Hasker, Bruce Reichenback, and David Basinger (New York: Oxford University Press, 2007), 273–279; and Michael Martin, "A Critique of Plantinga's Religious Epistemology," in *Philosophy of Religion,* 429–436.

51.   See D.Z. Phillips, *Faith and Philosophical Enquiry* (New York: Schoken, 1971); *Religion Without Explanation; Belief, Change and Forms of Life* (Atlantic Highlands, NJ: Humanities Press, 1986); *Wittgenstein and Religion* (New York: St. Martin's Press, 1993); and *Religion and the Hermeneutics of Contemplation.*

52. See Kai Nielson, "Does Religious Skepticism Rest on a Mistake?" in *Contemporary Perspectives on Religious Epistemology*, 116–127. A similar charge about the inability to supply criteria for identifying God is leveled against Plantinga by Stewart C. Goetz, "Belief in God Is Not Properly Basic." In Plantinga's case, this charge has force only if basic religious beliefs are taken to be beliefs about a metaphysical being, rather than expressions of faithful responses to encounters with the infinite.

53. David Hume, *Dialogues Concerning Natural Religion*, ed. Richard Popkin (Indianapolis: Hackett Publishing Co., 1988).

54. Immanuel Kant, "The Arguments of Speculative Reason in Proof of the Existence of a Supreme Being," in *Critique of Pure Reason*, trans. Norman Kemp Smith (New York: St. Martin's Press, 1965), 495–531.

55. Ludwig Feuerbach, *The Essence of Religion*, trans. Alexander Loos (Amherst, NY: Prometheus Books, 2004).

56. Soren Kierkegaard, *The Present Age*, trans. Alexander Dru (New York: Harper, 1962); *Philosophical Fragments*, trans. David F. Swenson and Howard V. Hong (Princeton: Princeton University Press, 1962); *Concluding Unscientific Postscript*, trans. David F. Swensen (Princeton: Princeton University Press, 1944), 23–35, 115–134, 169–224.

57. Soren Kierkegaard, *The Sickness Unto Death*, trans. Alastair Hannay (London: Penguin Books, 1989).

58. Karl Marx, "A Ruthless Criticism of Everything Existing," in *The Marx-Engles Reader*, ed. Robert C. Tucker (New York: Norton, 1978), 112–15; "Manifesto of the Communist Party," in *The Marx-Engels Reader*, 489–492; *Capital*, Vol 1, trans. Samuel Moore and Edward Aveling (Moscow: Progress Publishing, 1954), 77.

59. Friedrich Nietzsche, *The Gay Science*, Preface, 2, Book One, 1, 48, Book Three, 109, 125, 130, 151, Book Four, 276, 324, 326, Book Five, 343; *Human, All Too Human*, trans. Marion Faher and Stephen Lehmann (Lincoln: NB: University of Nebraska Press, 1984), 28, 34, 108, 114, 117; *Thus Spake Zarathustra*, trans. Thomas Common (Mineola, N.Y.: Dover Publications, 1999) Prologue, 2, 3, First Part, III, IV, IX, Second Part, XXVIII, Third Part, LV, LVII.

60. Martin Heidegger, *Being and Time*, 9–16, 43, 75, 83; "The Origin of the Work of Art," in *Poetry, Language, Thought*, trans. Albert Hofstadter (New York: Harper, 1971) 17–87.

61. Jacques Derrida, *Of Grammatology*, trans. Gayatri Chakravorty Spivak (Baltimore: the Johns Hopkins University Press, 1974); "Differance" and "Signature Event Context," in *Margins of Philosophy*, trans. Alan Bass (Chicago: University of Chicago Press, 1982), 1–28, 307–330.

62. For an extensive discussion of how philosophers in the past 150 years have pulled the rug out from underneath the metaphysical project, see Ruf, *Postmodern Rationality, Social Criticism, and Religion*.

63. See Ruf, *Postmodern Rationality, Social Criticism, and Religion*, especially chapters three and five.

64. Kierkegaard, *Concluding Unscientific Postscript*.

65. Kierkegaard, *The Present Age*.

66. Kierkegaard, *Philosophical Fragments*.

67. Kierkegaard, *The Sickness Unto Death*.

68. Kierkegaard, *Concluding Unscientific Postscript*, 116, 146, 365, 377, 383.

69. Kierkegaard, *Concluding Unscientific Postscript*, 132,138–139, 284.

70. Kierkegaard, *Concluding Unscientific Postscript*, 178, 296.

71. Kierkegaard, *Concluding Unscientific Postscript*, 124.

72. Kierkegaard, *Concluding Unscientific Postscript*, 25–47.

73. Kierkegaard, *Concluding Unscientific Postscript*, 187—221.

74. Friedrich Nietzsche, *The Gay Science* and *Human, All Too Human*.

75. Max Horkheimer and Theodor W. Adorno, *Dialectic of Enlightenment*, trans. John Cumming (New York: Continuum, 1987); Max Horkheimer, "The End of Reason," in *The Essential Frankfurt School Reader*, eds., Andrew Arato and Eike Gebhardt (New York: Continuum, 1982), 26–48; Andrew Arato and Eike Gebhardt, "Esthetic Theory and Cultural Criticism," in *The Essential Frankfurt School Reader*, 185–234.

76. Martin Heidegger, *The Question Concerning Technology*, trans. William Lovitt (New York: Harper Colophon Books, 1977).

77. Michel Foucault, *Power/Knowledge*, trans. Colin Gordon, Leo Marshall, John Mephem, and Kate Soper (New York: Pantheon Books, 1980); *Discipline and Punish*, trans. Alan Sheridan (New York: Vintage Books, 1979); and *Power*, trans. Robert Hurley and others (New York: The New Press, 1994).

78. Martin Heidegger, *Being and Time*, 67–83. See also Hubert L. Dryfus, *Being-in-the-World*.

79. See Martin Heidegger's "The Origin of the Work of Art," What Are Poets For?" Building Dwelling Thinking," in *Poetry, Language, Thought*.

80. John Caputo, *On Religion*, 51.

81. Jacques Derrida, "Faith and Knowledge: the Two Sources of 'Religion' at the Limits of Reason Alone," 30–36.

82. Jacques Derrida, *Adieu to Emmanuel Levinas*, trans. Pascale-Anne Brault and Michael Naas (Standord: Stanford University Press, 1999) 28.

83. John Caputo, *The Weakness of God: A Theology of the Event* (Bloomington, IN: Indiana University Press, 2006), 6–7.

84. John Caputo, "Apostles of the Impossible: On God and the Gift in Derrida and Marion," in *God, The Gift, and Postmodernism*, ed. John Caputo and Michael J. Scanlon (Bloomingtin, IN: Indiana University Press, 1999), 199.

85. Jean-Luc Marion, *God Without Being*, 67, 115.

86. Slavoj Zizek, *The Puppet and the Dwarf: The Perverse Core of Christianity* (Cambridge, MA: MIT Press, 2003), 94.

87. Slavoj Zizek, *On Belief: Thinking in Action* (London: Routledge, 2001), 90.

88. Emmanuel Levinas, *Of God Who Comes to Mind*, trans. Bettina Bergo (Stanford: Stanford University Press, 1998), 67–72.

89. See, in particular, Emmanuel Levinas, *Totality and Infinity*, trans. Alphonso Lingis (Pittsburgh: Duquesne University Press, 1969).

90. See Jacques Derrida, *Of Grammatology*.

91. Jacques Derrrida, *On Cosmopolitanism and Forgiveness*, trans. Mark Dooley and Michael Hughes (London: Routledge, 2003), 31–32.

92. Jacques Derrida, *Given Time: I. Counterfeit Money*, trans. Peggy Kamuf (Chicago: University of Chicago Press, 1992), 7, 11–14.

93. Jacques Derrida, *On the Name*, trans. David Wood, John P. Leavey, Jr., and Iam McLeod (Stanford: Stanford University Press, 1995), 7–9.

94. Jacques Derrida, *Of Hospitality*, trans. Richard Bowlby (Stanford: Stanford University Press, 2000), 75–78.

95. Jacques Derrida, *The Gift of Death*, 49.

96. Jacques Derrida, *The Gift of Death*, 55–68.

97. Jacques Derrida, *On Cosmopolitanism and Forgiveness*, 34–59.

98. Jacques Derrida, "Response to Jean-Luc Marion," in *God, The Gift, and Postmodernism*, 57–61.

99. Jacques Derrida, *Of Hospitality*, 149.

100. Jacques Derrida, "Khora," in *On The Name*, 89–124.

101. It is Derrida's claim that the Messiah is always yet to comew which leads Zizek to attack Derrida's "spirituality" as a deplorable aspect of postmodernism. See Zizek, *The Fragile Absolute* (London: Verso, 2000), 1. He objects to what he thinks is Derrida's passivity, Derrida's thought that the messianic promise will

be destroyed if translated into determinate economic and political action. See *Interrogating the Real*, 340–343. Derrida, however, does not seem to be counseling inaction in concretely resisting political and economic injustices, but rather action tempered by a critical understanding of the dangers inherent in trying to act on the basis of a some blueprint taken as the final representation of the good life. This is just Marx's understanding that communism is not to set forth and act upon such a totalitarian blueprint. One cannot predict how people freed from domination will decide democratically to organize themselves. In section Four I will attempt to show how discursive democracies working with procedural understandings of justice will proceed with concrete actions.

102. Jacques Derrida, "Faith and Knowledge: The Two Sources of 'Religion' in the Limits of Religion" in *Religion*, 17-18.

103. John Caputo, *The Weakness of God: A Theology of the Event*, 1-17.

104. Zizek advocates an interpretation of Christianity that is beyond ontotheology, but which he sees as different from the religious positions presented by Derrida and Levinas, which he finds to be deplorable (*The Fragile Absolute, 1*). God, for Zizek, is not the metaphysical god or some indescribable other forcing infinite responsibilities upon some passive hostage. (*Conversations with Zizek*, 67, 106–107, 162–163; *Interrogating the Real*, 340–341; "Neighbors and Other Monsters," 142–149). For our understanding of religion, the differences between Zizek's claims and those of Derrida and Levinas may be less significant than their common claims.

105. Slavoj Zizek, *On Belief*, 129–130.

106. Slavoj Zizek, *The Puppet and the Dwarf*, 66, 68, 74, 79; *On Belief*, 9.

107. Slavoj Zizek, *Interrogating the Real*, 347; "Neighbors and Other Monsters," 143.

108. Savoj Zizek, *The Parallax View* (Cambridge, MA: MIT Press, 2006), 99, 103.

109. Slavoj Zizek, *The Parallax View*, 110.

110. Slavoj Zizek, *The Parallax View*, 180–182.

111. Slavoj Zizek, *The Fragile Absolute*.

112. Slavoj Zizek, *Interrogating the Real*, 196; *The Parallax View*, 97–98.

113. Slavoj Zizek, *The Fragile Absolute*, 96.

114. Slavoj Zizek, *Interrogating the Real*, 125.

115. Slavoj Zizek, *Conversations With Zizek*, 161-162; *Interpreting the Real*, 125, 197.

116. Slavoj Zizek, *Conversations With Zizek*, 161–162.

117. Slavoj Zizek, *The Parallax View*, 183–184.

118. Slavoj Zizek, *The Fragile Absolute*, 123; *The Parallax View*, 111, 187.

119. Slavoj Zizek, *The Fragile Absolute*, 101; "Neighbors and Other Monsters" 141.

120. Slavoj Zizek, *The Parallax View*, 187.

121. Slavoj Zizek, *The Puppet and the Dwarf*, 116; *On Belief*, 90, 121, 146–7; *The Fragile Absolute*, 127.

122. Slavoj Zizek, *The Fragile Absolute*, 11.

123. Slavoj Zizek, *Conversations with Zizek*, 115–116.

124. Slavoj Zizek, *The Fragile Absolute*, 2, 15, 17–19.

125. Slavoj Zizek, *The Fragile Absolute*, 160.

126. Slavoj Zizek, *The Puppet and the Dwarf*, 9, 101, 130; *On Belief*, 91, 137.

127. Slavoj Zizek, *On Belief*, 68–69.

128. Slavoj Zizek, *The Puppet and the Dwarf*, 13; *On Belief*, 107; *The Fragile Absolute*, 107.

129. Slavoj Zizek, *The Fragile Absolute, 113, 118.*

130. Jean-Luc Marion, *God Without Being*, trans. Thomas A. Carlson (Chicago: University of Chicago, 1991), ix, 47.

131. Jean-Luc Marion, "In the Name," trans. Jeffrey L. Kosky, in *God, the Gift, and Postmodernism*, 25.

132. Jean-Luc Marion, "In the Name," 34–35.

133. Jean-Luc Marion, *God Without Being*, 16, 29, 35, 60.

134. Jean-Luc Marion, "In the Name," 36.

135. Jean-Luc Marion, "In the Name," 32; *God Without Being, 106, 183.*

136. Jean-Luc Marion, *God Without Being*, 117, 100, 111.

137. Jean-Luc Marion, *God Without Being*, 45–47, 86, 100, 106, 114, 128–135, 144, 150, 161, 172.

138. Jean-Luc Marion, "In the Name," 38–42; *God Without Being*, 144.

139. See D. Z. Phillips, *Religion Without Explanation*; *Wittgenstein and Religion*; *Religion and the Hermeneutics of Contemplation*.

140. Emmanuel Levinas, *Of God Who Comes to Mind*, trans. Bettina Bergo (Stanford: Stanford University Press, 1994), 57.

141. Emmanuel Levinas, "Substitution," in *The Levinas Reader*, 92.

142. Emmanuel Levinas, *Alterity & Consciousness*, trans, Michael B. Smith (New York: Columbia University Press, 1999), 4, 19.

143. Emmanuel Levinas, *Totality and Infinity*, trans. Alphonso Lingis (Pittsburgh: Duquesne University Press, 1969), 49.

144. Emmanuel Levinas, *Of God Who Comes to Mind*, 87.

145. Emmanuel Levinas, *Of God Who Comes to Mind*, 121.

146. Emmanuel Levinas, *Of God Who Comes to Mind*, 72; *Totality and Infinity*, 80.

147. Emmanuel Levinas, "There is: Existence without Existents," in *The Levinas Reader*, 30–35; *Alterity and Transcendence,* trans. Michael B. Smith (New York: Columbia University Press, 1999), 99; *Ethics and Infinity*, trans. Richard A. Cohen (Pittsburgh: Duquesne University Press, 1985), 47–52.

148. See Rudolf Otto, *The Idea of the Holy*, trans. J.W. Harvey (New York: Kesssinger Publishing, 2004).

149. Emmanuel Levinas, *Totality and Infinity*, 110–112, 134–135, 140.

150. Emmanuel Levinas, *Totality and Infinity,* 144.

151. Emmanuel Levinas, *Totality and Infinity*, 152–158.

152. Emmanuel Levinas, *Totality and Infinity,* 163.

153. Emmanuel Levinas, *Totality and Infinity,* 156.

154. Emmanuel Levinas, *Totality and Infinity*, 133–6; "Time and the Other" in *The Levinas Reader,* 39–42.

155. Emmanuel Levinas, *Totality and Infinity*, 190–198; *Ethics and Infinity*, 95–107; "Substitution," 109–119.

156. Zizek's many criticisms of Levinas's characterizations of what is other than secular, socially constituted objects and subjects all seem to result from Zizek's failure to understand what Levinas is saying. First, Zizek seems to think that because Levinas is claiming that people are ethically different because they are ethically unique, that they are not flesh and blood, socially constituted beings ("Neighbors and Other Monsters," 146; *The Parallax View*, 111–113). The Holocaust survivors, whom Zizek thinks Levinas can't adequately deal with, are the very people, like Zizek's outcasts, whom Levinas claims we can encounter ethically, face-to-face, whose lives are priceless regardless of their physical and social status. Zizek claims that these survivors cannot call out for ethical recognition, but Levinas points out that being under obligation to respect their ethical individuality does not depend on them recognizing their ethical stratus or on us be willing to treat them ethically. Second, Levinas's phenomenological characterization of aspects of human living that are other that secular, social constitutions cannot be understood if one tries to reductively force them into Zizek's use of Lacan's narrative of subject formation ("Neighbors and Other Monsters," 144–149). Enjoying the elements, cohabiting, being in ethical rela-

tionships are not stages in subject formation. Third, Zizek, fails to distinguish Levinas's uses of the words "ethical" and "moral" when he claims that Levinas misses Kierkegaard's insight that the theological requires the suspension of the ethical and that the religious rests on a radical decision and not just an encounter with a face ("Neighbors and Other Monsters," 145). What Kierkegaard thinks Christianity suspends is what Levinas sees as socially constituted morality, the same thing both he and Zizek think religion transcends. What Levinas calls ethical and religious is what Zizek calls the agape love in the Christian community. Levinas never claims that encountering other people automatically means encountering them ethically in a way in which God comes to mind. As with Kierkegaard and Zizek, a decision has to be made. Often one hears the ethical call only as one commits oneself by saying "Here I am." God comes to mind only when one does decide to change world horizons and commit oneself to be responsible. Third, Zizek claims that God for Levinas is only the name of a law to love one's neighbor, which authenticates the symbolic order ("Neighbors and Other Monsters," 146). For Levinas, however, the ethical is other than the symbolic order, just as is Zizek's concept of the agape Holy Spirit. Furthermore, loving one's neighbor entails a whole religious way of life, as Zizek himself points out, and the God to whom Levinas prays is much more than a law, as we shall see in the treatment of the Abrahamic religons in section three. Finally, Zizek's disagreements with Levinas may stem from their very different interpretations of Moses's constitution of the Hebrew/Jewish community. Zizek sees this as an unacknowledged particular traumatic act of violently imposing universal laws (*The Fragile Absolute*, 99, 109; "Neighbors and Other Monsters," 140; *The Parallaz View*, 182. Levinas distinguishes, however, Moses's hearing of the call of the ethical infinite from laws and norms of the social order that Hebrews established in covenant in their worship of Yahweh, norms which might be quite different for other religious communities. Only the call to respect the singular ethical uniqueness of people is universal; different communities filled with such respect can constitute themselves with many different, not-unjustified norms. This point will be spelled out in section four, Part 3.

157. Emmanuel Levinas, *Totality and Infinity*, 80.

158. Emmanuel Levinas, *Totality and Infinity*, 213–215; *Of God Who Comes to Mind*, 82–85; "Rights of Man," in *Outside the Subject*, trans. Michael B. Smith (Stanford: Stanford University Press, 1994), 116–125.

159. Emmanuel Levinas, *Totality and Infinity*, 50; *Of God Who Comes to Mind*, 67–68, 95.

160. Emmanuel Levinas, *Of God Who Comes to Mind*, 100.

Section Two

161. Much of my interpretation of Asian religions has been heavily influenced by my dialogue with Huston Smith's *The World's Religions* (San Francisco: HarperSanFrancisco, 1991), a book I have taught for years in courses on Asian philosophies. In my dialogue with this and other texts written by Smith, what I have heard being said has always been filtered by my postmodern rejection of the ontotheological and metaphysical aspects of his approach to the world's religions.

162. "The Hymn of Creation," in *A Sourcebook in Indian Philosophy*, ed. Sarvepalli Radhakrishnan and Charles A. Moore (Princeton: Princeton University Press, 1957) 23–24.

163. See "Kaautilya's Artha-Saswtra," in *A Sourcebook in Indian Philosophy*, 193–223.

164. See "The Laws of Manu," in *A Sourcebook in Indian Philosophy*, 173–192.

165. *"The Laws of Manu,"* 189.

166. *"The Laws of Manu,"* 190.

167. See "The Bhagavad Gita," in *A Sourcebook in Indian Philosophy*, 102–163.

168. See Keiji Nishitani, *Religion and Nothingness*, trans. Jan Van Bragt (Berkeley, CA: University of California Press, 1982), 159–160, 243–255.

169. "Katha Upanishad," in *A Sourcebook in Indian Philosophy*, 45.

170. "Katha Upanishad," 46.

171. "Brhadaranyaka Upanishad," in *A Sourcebook in Indian Philosophy*, 88.

172. "Svetasvatara Upanishad" in *A Sourcebook in Indian Philosophy*, 95.

173. "Chandoga Upanishad," in *A Sourcebook in Indian Philosophy*, 66.

174. "Brahman Isa Upanishad," in *A Sourcebook in Indian Philosophy*, 38.

175. See "Carvaka," in *A Sourcebook in Indian Philosophy*, 228–236.

176. See "Vaisesika," in *A Sourcebook in Indian Philosophy*, 387–423.

177. See "Samkhya," in *A Sourcebook in Indian Philosophy*, 426–452.

178. See "The Non-Dualism of Samkara," in *A Sourcebook in Indian Philosophy*, 509–543.

179. See "Jainism," in *A Sourcebook of Indian Philosophy*, 250–271.

180. "What the Buddha Taught," in *A Sourcebook in Asian Philosophy*, 202.

181. "Reason and Wisdom," in *A Sourcebook in Asian Philosophy*, 240.

182. *"Reason and Wisdom,"* 245.

183. "The First Sermon," *(Samyutta-nikaya)* and "The Synopsis of Truth" (*Majjhima-nikaya*), in *A Sourcebook in Indian Philosophy*, 274–278.

184. For a fuller development of Nietzsche's analysis of the human situation, see Ruf, *Postmodern Rationality, Social Criticism, and Religion*, 171–184.

185. See "Dependent Origination: The Middle Way," in *A Sourcebook in Asian Philosophy*, 233–238.

186. For a critique of the metaphysical use of binary oppositions, see Mark C. Taylor, *Erring: A Postmodern A/theology* (Chicago: University of Chicago Press, 1984).

187. "The Theory of No-Soul of Self," in *A Sourcebook in Indian Philosophy*, 280–288.

188. "The Synopsis of Truth," in *A Sourcebook in Indian Philosophy*, 277.

189. See Levinas, *Ethics and Infinity*, 87–89, 99–101.

190. See John Rawls, *A Theory of Justice* (Cambridge, MA: Harvard University Press, 1971, 60–67.

191. See Iris Marion Young, *Justice and the Politics of Difference* (Princeton: Princeton University Press, 1990), 24–33.

192. For selections from the Heart and Diamond Sutras and Mahayana commentaries on them, see "The Rise of Mahayana," in *A Sourcebook in Asian Philosophy*, 148–261.

193. See "Nargarjuna: Treatise on the Fundamentals of the Middle Way," in *A Sourcebook in Asian Philosophy*, 264–271.

194. For a pragmatic interpretation of Nargarjuna's position, see David J. Kalupahana, *Nagarjuna: The Philosophy of the Middle Way* (Albany, N.Y.: SUNY Press, 1986).

195. For a historical and analytic treatment of the founding voices and texts of Taoism, see A.C. Graham, *Disputors of the Tao* (La Salle, IL: Open Court Press, 1989), 170–235.

196. See "The Mo Tzu," in *A Sourcebook in Chinese Philosophy*, trans. Wing-Tsit Chan (Princeton: Princeton University Press, 1963), 213–231. For an analysis of early and later forms of Mohism, see A.C. Graham, *Disputors of the Tao*, 33–53, 137–170.

197. Confucius, "The Analects: 15:23" in *A Sourcebook in Chinese Philosophy*, 44.

198. See "The Hsun Tzu," in *A Sourcebook in Chinese Philosophy*, 122–128.

199. See A.S. Cua, *Ethical Argumentation: A Study of Hsun Tzu's Moral Epistemology* (Honolulu: University of Hawaii Press, 1985).

200. For a discussion of the developmental character of Confucian virtue, see Richard Shusterman, "Pragmatism and East-Asian Thought," in ed. Richard

Shusterman, *Range of Pragmatism and the Limits of Philosophy* (Oxford: Blackwell, 2005), 31.

201. "Lao Tzu: *Tao Te Ching*" in *A Sourcebook in Asian Philosophy*, 445–448.

202. Lao Tzu, *Tao Te Ching*, trans. D.C. Lau (Baltimore: Penguin Books, 1963), Section XXXII, page 91, LXXIX, page 141.

203. *Tao Te Ching*, LX, page 121.

204. *Tao Te Ching*, XXXVIII, page 99.

205. *Tao Te Ching*, LXVII, page 129.

206. *Tao Te Ching*, LVII, page 118.

207. *Tao Te Ching*, XLIX, page 110; LXII, page 123; LXIII, page 124.

208. *Tao Te Ching*, XVII, page 73.

209. *Tao Te Ching* , XXXVIII, page 96.

210. *Tao Te Ching*, XXII, page 79.

211. *Tao Te Ching*, XX, page 76; XLIIIV, page 105.

212. *Tao Te Ching*, XXXII, page 91.

213. *Tao Te Ching*, LXXVIII, page 140.

214. *Taoist Tales*, ed. Raymond Van Over (New York: Mentor Book, 1973), 151.

215. For a Western defense of disciplinary practices called "somaaesthetics," aimed at increasing people's power to live beautiful and enjoyable lives, see Richard Shusterman, *Performing Live: Aesthetic Alternatives for the Ends of Art* (Ithaca, NY: Cornell University Press, 2000).

216. *Tao Te Ching*, XXVII, p. 84.

217. One of the most popular examples of this Taoist/Buddhist critique of Chinese social life is the eighteenth-century novel, *Dream of the Red Chamber*. See Tsao Hsue-Chin, *Dream of the Red Chamber*, trans, Chi-Chen Wang (New York: Anchor Books, 1958).

218. For an extensive discussion of Taoism's treatment of its own distinctions between the nameable and the unnameable, see A.C. Graham, *Disputors of the Tao*, 219–223.

219. For a detailed historical narrative of the early development of Chan, see D.T. Suzuki, *Essays in Zen Buddhism* (New York: Grove Press, 1949), 60, 163–228.

220. The numerous influences on Chan/Zen from Taoism are documented in *A Sourcebook in Chinese Philosophy*, ed. Wing-Tsit Chan, 429–445; and D.T. Suzuki, *Essays in Zen Buddhism*, 109, 173.

221. For further elucidation of the Zen distinction between the use of words before and after enlightenment, see Masao Abe, *Zen and Western Thought* (Honolulu: University of Hawaii Press, 1985), 23.

222. See D.T. Suzuki, *Essays in Zen Buddhism*, where he writes that a master, when asked what Buddhahood was, replied that "the bottom of a pail is broken though," a complete revolution occurs, the cataclysmic birth of a new way living.

223. "The Koan on the Sound of One Hand and the Koan on Mu," in *The Sound of the One Hand*, trans. Yoel Hoffman (New York: Basic Books, 1975) 47–51.

224. "The Platform of Scripture of the Sixth Patriarch," in *A Sourcebook in Chinese Philosophy*, 431–432.

225. D.T. Suzuki, *Essays in Zen Buddhism*, 259.

226. "The Platform Scripture of the Sixth Patriarch," in Wing-Tsit Chan, ed., *A Sourcebook in Chinese Philosophy*, 436.

227. "Recorded Conversations of Shen-Hui," in *A Sourcebook in Chinese Philosophy*, 441.

228. "Recorded Conversations of Shen-Hui," 442.

229. For further clarification of the relation of emptiness to suchness, see Keiji Nishitani, *Religion and Nothingness*, 91, Masao Abe, "Emptiness is Suchness," in *The Buddha Eye*, ed., Frederick Franck (New York: Crossroad, 1982), 203–208.

230. See Masao Abe, "Emptiness is Suchness," 203, 207.

231. See Keiji Nishitani, *Religion and Nothingness*, 252–255.

232. For a further discussion of the similarities between Taoism and Buddhism on sacredness of even excrement and urine, see *A Sourcebook in Chinese Philosophy*, 445.

233. For a full development of the thesis that liberation from Tanha leads to loving service to all others, see Keiji Nishitani, *Religion and Nothingness*, 164, 285.

234. That the pursuit of social justice lies at the heart of Zen practice is stated very succinctly by Kieiji Nishitani, "The Awakening of Self in Buddhism," in *The Buddha Eye*, 22–30.

Section Three

235. John Caputo, *The Weakness of God: A Theology of the Event*, 77.

236. John Caputo, *The Weakness of God: A Theology of the Event*, 87-93.

237. Although this book will not be engaged in debates with scholars studying the Bible and Koran and with historians studying what happened in the fertile crescent, Egypt, and Arabia, during the three thousand years during which Judaism, Christianity, and Islam originated, this interpretation of these religions would not be possible without drawing upon such scholarship. Three excellent introductions to such scholarship are: Bernhard W. Anderson, assisted by Katheryn Pfisster Darr, *Understanding the Old Testament* (Englewood Cliffs, NJ: Prentice Hall, 1998); Luke Timothy Johnson, *The Writings of the New Testament* (Minneapolis: Fortress Press, 1999); Fazlur Rahman, *Islam* (Chicago: University of Chicago Press, 1979).

238. Merold Westphal, "Overcoming Ontotheology," in *God, The Gift, and Postmodernism*, 150.

239. Jacques Derrrida, *The Gift of Death*, 55–68.

240. John Caputo, *The Weakness of God*.

241. Bernhard W. Anderson, *Understanding the Old Testament*, 9–15, 137–163.

242. Jean-Luc Marion, *God Without Being*, 17–20.

243. John Caputo, *The Weakness of God*, 59, 75, 80.

244. The priestly additions of liturgical detail and behavioral prescriptions are located mainly in Exodus 25–31, Leviticus, and Numbers 28–31.

245. Jean-Luc Marion, *God Without Being*, 140–181.

246. Most of the citations for Q will be taken from Matthew, with only a few taken from Luke. To identify the parallel passages in the two books, see *Gospel Parallels*, ed. Burton H. Throckmorton Jr. (New York: Thomas Nelson & Sons, 1949).

247. John Caputo, *The Weakness of God*, 42–45.

248. Akbar Ahmed in *Postmoderism and Islam: Predicament and Promise* (London: Routledge, 1992) deals hardly at all with postmodern thinkers but is concerned with what he calls "postmodern life," especially the role of the mass media in creating false images of Islam. Muqtedar Khan thinks that postmodernism's attack on the secularism and skepticism of modernity can be very helpful to Islam's attempt to defend itself against European and American efforts to force it to replace its religious way of life with modern secularism. See his "Islam, Postmodernity and Freedom, in *Ijtihad*, June 13, 2006.

246. All numbered citations in the text are from the Qur'an, trans. Abdulla Yusuf-Ali (Elmhurst, NY: Tahrike Tarsile Qur'an, Inc., 2005). The first number refers to the Surah, or chapter, and the second number refers to the verse.

250. For a thorough discussion of the development in Islam of the Sunna and the

Ijima, see Fezlur Rahman, *Islam*, 43–63.

251. See Idries Shah, *The Way of the Sufi* (London: Penguin Books, 1968).

252. See Daniel C. Matt, *The Essential Kabbalah: The Heart of Jewish Mysticism* (Edison, NJ: Castle Books, 1997).

253. For excellent analyses of the differences existing between people called mystics, see Stephan T. Katz, *Mysticism and Philosophical Analysis* (New York: Oxford University Press, 1978); Robert M. Gimello, "Mysticism in Its Contexts" and Hans H. Penner, "The Mystical Illusion," in *Mysticism and Religious Traditions*, ed. Steven T. Katz (New York: Oxford University Press, 1983), 61–88, 89–116.

Section Four

254. Jacques Derrida, "Response to Richard Kearney," in *God, The Gift, and Postmodernism*, 75.

255. Sam Harris, *The End of Faith: Religion, Terror, and the Future of Reason* (New York: Norton, 2004).

256. Seyyed Hossein Nasr, "Metaphysical Roots of Tolerance and Intolerance: An Islamic Interpretation," in *Philosophy, Religion, and the Question of Intolerance*, 43–56. Slavoj Zizek makes the same point in *On Belief*.

257. Slavoj Zizek, *On Belief*, 3–4, 118–121.

258. John Caputo, *The Weakness of God*, 290–291.

259. Jacques Derrida, "Force of Law: The Mystical Foundation of Authority," in *Deconstruction and the Possibility of Justice*, ed. Drucilla Cornell et al. (New York: Routledge, 1992), 3–67. See also John Caputo, *Against Ethics: Contributions to a Poetics of Obligation with Constant Reference to Deconstruction* (Bloomington, IN: Indiana University Press, 1993).

260. For a thought-provoking discussion of the relationship between forgiveness, forgetting, and remembering the past and being open for a new future, see Caputo, *The Weakness of God*, 230–231.

261. Emmanuel Levinas, *Totality and Infinity*, 149.

262. John Stuart Mill, *Utilitarianism* (London; Penguin Books, 1987); *On Liberty* (London: Penguin Books, 1974).

263. Immanuel Kant, *Metaphysics of Morals*, trans. Lewis White Beck (Englewood Cliffs, NJ: Prentice hall, 1989).

264. John Rawls, *A Theory of Justice* (Cambridge, MA: Harvard University Press, 1971) 60-61.

265. Martin Heidegger, *The Question Concerning Technology and Other Essays*, 17–28.

266. One of Kant's most sympathetic interpreters, Thomas E. Hill Jr., points out that one major problem in Kant's position is caused by the formal character of his principle excluding any substantive considerations providing reasons for doing things. See Hill's *Autonomy and Self-Respect* (Cambridge: Cambridge University Press, 1991), 97, 174. He also points out the fundamentally flawed character of Kant's attempt to prove logical connections between claims about pure practical reason, autonomy, and substantive moral principles. See his *Dignity and Practical Reason in Kant's Moral Theory* (Ithaca, NY: Cornell University Press), 121.

267. Robert Nozick, *Anarchy, State, and Utopia* (New York: Basic Books, 1974).

268. John Rawls, *Justice as Fairness*.

269. For a presentation and defense of various forms of utilitarianism, see Peter Railton, *Facts, Values, and Norms: Essays Towards a Morality of Consequences* (Cambridge: Cambridge University Press, 2003).

270. For criticisms of the use of the utilitarian principle to justify social practices, see David Lyons, *Forms and Limits of Utilitarianism* (Oxford: Oxford University Press, 1965).

271. Mark Taylor, *Tears* (Albany, NY: SUNY Press, 1990); *Nots* (Chicago: University of Chicago Press, 1993); *Hidings* (Chicago: University of Chicago Press, 1997, *About Religion: Economics of Faith in Virtual Culture* (Chicago: University of Chicago Press, 1999).

272. Emmanuel Levinas, *Outside the Subject*, 116–125; *Alterity and Transcendence*, 170, 176; "Substitution" and "Ideology and Idealism," in *The Levinas Reader*, 118, 242–248.

273. Iris Marion Young, *Inclusion and Democracy* (Oxford: Oxford University Press, 2000), 16–51.

274. John Rawls, *Political Liberalism* (New York: Columbia University Press. 1993), 133–172.

275. Iris Marion Young, *Inclusion and Democracy*, 41–44.

276. Iris Marion Young, *Justice and the Politics of Difference* (Princeton: Princeton University Press, 1990), 37–65.

277. Iris Marion Young, *Inclusion and Democracy*, 35.

278. See Thomas E. Hill Jr., "Ideals of human excellence and preserving natural environments," in his *Autonomy and Self-Respect*, 104–117.

279. See Daniel C. Maguire, *Sacred Choices* (Minneapolis: Fortress Press, 2001); *Planned Parenthood Discusses Sacred Choices* (New York: Planned Parenthood Fed. of America, 2002).

280. Hans-Georg Gadamer, *Truth and Method*, trans. Garrett Bardan and John Cumming (New York: Continuum, 1975) and *Philosophical Hermeneutics*, trans. and ed. D. Laing (Berkeley: University of California Press, 1977).

BIBLIOGRAPHY

Abe, Masao. *Zen and Western Thought,* (Honolulu: University of Hawaii Press, 1985).

————. "Emptiness is Suchness." In *The Buddha Eye,* edited by Frederick Franck, edited by (New York: Crossroad, 1982).

Adams, Robert M., "Flavors, Colors, and God." In *Contemporary Perspectives in Religious Epistemology,* edited by R. Douglas Geivett and Brendan Sweetman. (New York: Oxford University Press, 1992).

————. "Moral Arguments for Theistic Belief." In *God,* edited by Timonthy Robinson (Indianapolis: Hackett Publishing Co., 2002).

Ahmed, Akbar. *Postmodernism and Islam: Predicament and Promise* (London: Routledge, 1992).

Anderson, Bernhard W., assisted by Katheryn Pfisster Darr. *Understanding the Old Testament,* Abridged Fourth Edition. (Englewood Cliffs, NJ: Prentice Hall, 1998).

Adorno, Theodor W., and Max Horkheimer *Dialectic of Enlightenment,* edited by John Cumming (New York: Continuum, 1987).

Anselm. "Proslogium." In *Proslogium/Monologium,* translated by Sidney Norton Dean (Eugene, OR: Wipf & Stock Publishers, 2003).

Aquinas, Thomas. *Summa Theologiae, Questions on God,* edited by Brian Leftow (Cambridge: Cambridge University Press, 2006).

Arato, Andrew and Eike Gebhardt. "Esthetic Theory and Cultural Criticsim," In *The Essential Frankfurt School Reader,* edited by Andrew Arato and Eike Gebhardt (New York: Coninuum, 1982).

Aristotle. *The Basic Works of Aristotle,* edited by Richard McKeon (New York: Random House, 1941).

Bach, Kent, and Robert M. Harnish. *Linguistic Meaning and Speech Acts* (Cambridge, MA: MIT Press, 1979).

Caputo, John. *Against Ethics: Contributions to a Poetics of Obligation with Constant Reference to Deconstruction* (Bloomington, IN: Indiana University Press, 1993).

————. "Apostles of the Impossible: On God and the Gift in Derrida and Marion." In *God, The Gift, and Postmodernism,* edited by John Caputo and Michael J. Scanlon (Bloomington, IN: Indiana University Press, 1999).

————. *On Religion* (New York: Routledge, 2001).

————. *The Weakness of God: A Theology of the Event* (Bloomington, IN: Indiana University Press, 2006).

Craig, William Lane. "Philosophical and Scientific Pointers to Creation ex Nihilo" In *God,* edited by Timothy Robinson (Indianapolis: Hackett Publishing Co., 2002).

————. "Scientific Confirmation of the Coismological Argument," In *Philosophy of Religion,* edited by Louis J. Pojman (Belmont, CA: Wadsworth, 2003).

Cua, A.S. *Ethical Argumentation: A Study of Hsun-Tzu's Moral Epistemology* (Honolulu: University of Hawaii Press, 1985).

Derrida, Jacques. *Of Grammatology,* translated by Gayatri Chakravorty Spivak (Baltimore: The John Hopkins University Press, 1974).

————. "Diffferance" and "Signature Event Context." In *Margins of Philosophy,* translated by Alan Bass (Chicago: University of Chicago Press, 1982).

————. "Faith and Knowledge: The Two Sources of 'Religion' at the Limits of Reason Alone." Translated by Samuel Webber, In *Religion,* edited by Jacques Derrida and Gianni Vattimo (Stanford: Stanford University Press, 1988).

————. *Given Time: I. Counterfeit Money,* translated by Peggy Kamuf (Chicago: University of Chicago Press, 1992).

————. "Force of Law: The Mystical Foundation of Authjority." In *Deconstruction and the Possibility of Justice,* edited by Rucilla Cornell, Michael Rosenfeld, David Gray Carlson (New York: Routledge, 1992).

————. *On the Name,* translated by David Wood, John P. Leavey Jr., and Iam McLeod (Stanford: Stanford University Press, 1995).

————. *The Gift of Death,* translated by David Wills (Chicago: University of Chicago Press, 1995).

————. *Adieu to Emmanuel Levinas, Pascale-Anne Brault and Michael Naas* (Stanford: Standford University Press, 1999).

————. "Response to Jen-Luc Marion." In *God, The Gift, and Postmodernism,* edited by John D. Caputo and Michael J. Scanlon (Bloomington, IN: Indiana University Press, 1999.

―――. "Response to Richard Kearney." In *God, The Gift, and Postmodernism,* edited by John D. Caputo and Michael J. Scanlon (Bloomington, IN: Indiana University Press, 1999).

―――. *Of Hospitality,* translated by Richard Bowlby (Stanford: Stanford University Press, 2000).

―――. *On Cosmopolitanism and Forgiveness,* translated by Mark Dooley and Michael Hughes (London: Routledge, 2003).

Draper, Paul. "A Critique of the Kalam Coslmological Argument." In *Philosophy of Religion,* edited by Louis P. Pojman (Belmont, CA: Wadsworth, 2003).

Dryfus, Hubert L. *Being-in-the-World* (Cambridge, MA: MIT Press, 1991).

Edwards, Paul. "A Critique of the Cosmological Argument." In *Philosophy of Religion,* edited by Louis P. Pojman (Belmont, CA: Wadsworth, 2003).

Everitt, Nicholas. *The Non-Existence of God* (London: Routledge, 2004).

Feuerbach, Ludwig. *The Essence of Religion,* translated by Alexander Loos (Amherst, NY: Prometheus Books, 2004).

Foucault, Michel. *Power/Knowledge,* translated by Colin Gordon, Leo Marshall, John Mephem, Kate Soper (New York: Pantheon Books, 1980).

―――. *Discipline and Punish,* translated by Alan Sheridan (New York: Vintage Books, 1979).

―――. *Power,* translated by Robert Hurley and others. (New York: The New Press, 1994).

Gadamer, Hans-Georg. *Truth and Method,* translated by Garrett Bardan and John Cumming (New York: Continuum, 1975).

―――. *Philosophical Hermeneutics,* translated by and edited by D. Laing (Berkeley, CA: University of California Press, 1977).

Gebhardt, Eike and Andrew Arato. "Estheetic Theory and Cultural Criticism." In *The Essential Frankfurt School Reader,* (New York: Continuum, 1982).

Gimello, Robert M. "Mysticism in its Contexts." In *Mysticism and Religious Traditions,* edited by Steven T. Katz (New York: Oxford University Press, 1983.

Goetz, Stewart. "Belief in God is Not Properly Basic." In *Contemporary Perspectives in Religious Epistemology*, edited by Douglas Geivett and Brendan Sweetman (New York: Oxford University Press, 1992).

Graham, A.C. *Disputors of the Tao* (La Salle, IL: Open Court Press, 1989).

Harnish, Robert M. and Kent Bach. *Linguistic Meaning and Speech Acts* (Cambridge, MA: MIT Press, 1979).

Harris, Sam. *The End of Faith: Religion, Terror, and the Future of Reason* (New York: Norton, 2004).

Heidegger, Martin. *Being and Time*, translated by Joan Stambaugh (Albany, NY: SUNY Press, 1996).

———. "The Origin of the Work of Art," "What are Poets For," and "Building Dwelling Thinking." In *Poetry, Language, Thought*, translated by Albert Hotstadter (New York: Harper, 1971).

———. *The Question Concerning Technology*, translated by William Lovitt (New York: Harper Colophon Books, 1977).

Hill, Thomas E. Jr. *Autonomy and Self Respect* (Cambridge: Cambridge University Press, 1991).

———. *Dignity and Practical Reason in Kant's Moral Theory* (Ithaca, NY: Cornell University Press, 1992).

Horkheimer, Max and Theodore W. Adorno. *Dialectic of Enlightenment*, translated by John Cumming (New York: Continuum, 1987).

———. "The End of Reason." In T*he Essential Frankfurt School Reader*, edited by Andrew Arato and Eike Gebhardt (New York: Continuum, 1982).

Hume, David. *Dialogues Concerning Natural Religion*, edited by Richard Popkin (Indianapolis: Hackett Publishing Co., 1988).

Johnson, Luke Timoty. *The Writings of the New Testament*, (Minneapolis: Fortress Press, 1999).

Kalupanana, David J. *Nargarjuna: The Philosophy of the Middle Way* (Albany, NY: SUNY Press, 1986).

Kant, Immanuel. *Critique of Practical Reason*, translated by Lewis Beck White (New York: The Liberal arts Press, 1956).

———. *Metaphysics of Morals,* translated by Lewis White Beck (Englewood Cliffs, NJ: Prentice hall, 1989).

Katz, Stephen. *Mysticism and Philosophical Analysis* (New York: Oxford University Press, 1978).

Khan, Muqtedar. "Islam, Postmodernity and Freedom." In *Ijtihad,* June 13, 2006.

Kierkegaard, Soren. *The Present Age,* translated by Alexander Dru (New York: Harper, 1962).

———. *Philosophical Fragments,* translated by David F. Swenson and Howard V. Hong (Princeton: Princeton University Press, 1962).

———. *Concluding Unscientific Postscript,* translated by David Swenson (Princeton: Princeton University Press, 1944).

———. *The Sickness Unto Death,* translated by Alastair Hannay (London: Penguin Books, 1989).

Koller, John M., and Patricia Koller, eds. *A Sourcebook in Asian Philosophy* (New York: Macmillan, 1991).

Kretzmann, Norman. "Omniscience and Immutability." In *God* (Indianaapolis: Hackett Publishing Co., 2002).

Lao Tzu. *Tao Te Ching,* translated by D.C. Lau (Baltimore: Penguin Books, 1963).

Levinas, Emmanuel. *Totality and Infinity,* translated by Alphonso Lingis (Pittsburgh, PA: Duquesne University Press, 1969).

———. "Substitution" and "There is Existence With Existents." In *The Levinas Reader,* edited by Sean Hand (Oxford: Basil Blackwell, 1989).

———. *Ethics and Infinity,* translated by Richard A. Cohen (Pittsburgh, PA: Duquesne University Press, 1985).

———. "God and Philosophy." In *The Levinas Reader,* edited by Sean Hand (Oxford: Basil Blackwell, 1989).

———. *Outside the Subject,* translated by Michael B. Smith (Stanford: Stanford University Press, 1994).

———. *Of God Who Comes to Mind,* translated by Bettina Bergo (Stanford: Stanford University Press, 1998).

———. *Alterity & Transcendence,* translated by Michael B. Smith (New York: Columbia University Press, 1999).

Lyons, David. *Forms and Limits of Utilitarianism* (Oxford: Oxford University Press, 1965).

Maguire, Daniel C. *Sacred Choices* (Minneapolis: Fortress Press, 2001).

Marion, Jean-Luc. *God Without Being,* translated by Thomas A. Carleson (Chicago: University of Chicago Press, 1991).

———. "In the Name." Translated by Jeffrey L. Kosky. In *God, the Gift, and Postmodernism,* edited by John D. Caputo and Michael J. Scanlon (Bloomington, IN: Indiana University Press, 1999.

Martin, Michael. *Atheism, A Philosophical Justification* (Philadelphia: Temole University Press, 1990).

———. "A Critique of Plantinga's Religious Epistemology." In *Philosophy of Religion,* edited by Louis P. Pojman (Belmont, CA: Wadsworth, 2003).

Marx, Karl, "A Ruthless Criticism of Everything Existing" and "Manifesto of the Communist Party." In *The Marx-Engles Reader,* edited by Robert C. Tucker (New York: Norton, 1978).

———. *Capital Vol I,* translated by Samuel Moore and Edward Aveling (Moscow: Progress Publications, 1954).

Matt, Daniel. *The Essential Kabbalah: The Heart of Jewish Mysticism* (Edison, NJ: Castle Books, 1997).

Mill, John Stuart. *Utilitarianism* (London, Penguin Books, 1987).

Mavrodes, George I. "Religion and the Queerness of Morality." In *God,* edited by Timothy Robinson (Indianapolis: Hackett Publishjing Co., 2002).

Nasr, Seyyed Hossein. "Metaphysical Roots of Tolerance and Intolerance: An Islamic Interpretation." In *Philosophy, Religion, and the Question of Intolerance,* edited by Mehdi Amin Razzavi and David Ambuel (Albany, NY: SUNY Press, 1997).

Nielson, Kai. "Does Religious Skepticism Rest on a Mistake?" In *Contemporary Perspectives on Religious Epistemology,* edited by R. Douglas Geivett and Brendan Sweetman (New York: Oxford University Press, 1992).

Nietzsche, Friedrich. *The Gay Science,* translated by Walter Kaufman (New York: Vintage Books, 1974).

———. *Human, All Too Human,* translated by Marion Faher and Stephen Lehmann (Lincoln, NB: University of Nebraska Press, 1984).

———. *Thus Spake Zarathustra,* translated by Thoman Common (Mineola, NY: Dover Publications, 1999).

Nishitani, Keiji. *Religion and Nothingness,* translated by Jan Van Bragt (Berkeley, CA: University of California Press, 1982).

———. "The Awakening of the Self in Buddhism." In *The Buddha Eye,* edited by Frederick Franck (New York: Crossroad, 1982).

Nozick, Robert. *Anarchy, State, and Utopia* (New York: Basic Books, 1974).

Orr, H. Allen. "Devolution: Why Intelligent Design Isn't." In *The New Yorker* (May 30, 2005).

Otto, Rudolf. *The Idea of the Holy,* translated by J.W. Harvey (New York: Kessinger Publishing, 2004).

Paley, William. *Natural Theology: Or Evidence of the Existence and Attributes of the Deity, Collected from the Appearances of Nature* (Indianapolis: Indiana University Press, 1964).

Pargetter, Robert. "Expereince, Proper Basicality, and Belief in God." In *Philosophy of Religion,* edited by Michael Paterson, William Hasker, Bruce Reichenbach, David Basinger (New York: Oxford University Press, 2007).

Penner, Hans H. "The Mystical Illusion." In *Mysticism and Religious Traditions,* edited by Steven T. Katz (New York: Oxford University Press, 1983).

Phillips, D.Z. *Faith and Philosophical Enquiry* (New York: Schoken, 1971).

———. *Religion Without Explanation* (London: Basic Blackwell, 1976).

———. *Belief, Change, and Forms of Life* (Atlantic Highlands, NJ: Humanities Press, 1986)

———. *Wittgenstein and Religion* (New York: St. Martin's Press, 1993).

———. *Religion and the Hermeneutics of Contemplation* (Cambridge: Cambridge University Press, 2001).

Planned Parenthood Federation. *Planned Parenthood Discusses Sacred Choices* (New York: Planned Parenthood Fed. of America, 2002).

Plantinga, Alvin. *God, Freedom, and Evil* (Grand Rapids, Mich: Wm. B. Eerdmans Publishing, 1977).

———. "Is Belief in God Properly Basic?" In *God,* edited by Timothy Robinson (Indianapolis: Hackett Publishing Co., 2002).

Quammen, David. "Was Darwin Wrong? No." *National Geographic,* Vol. 206, No. 5 (November 2004).

Qur'an, translated by Abdulla Yusuf-Ali (Elmhurst, NY: Tahrike Tarsile Qur'am, Inc., 2005).

Radhakrishnan, Sarvepalli, and Charles A. Moore, eds. *A Sourcebook in Indian Philosophy.* (Princeton: Princeton University Press).

Rahman, Fazlur. *Islam* (Chicago: University of Chicago Press, 1979).

Railton, Peter. *Facts, Values, and Norms: Essays Towards a Morality of Consequences* (Cambridge: Cambridge University Press, 22003).

Rawls, John. *A Theory of Justice* (Cambridge, MA: Harvard University Press, 1971).

———. *Political Liberalism* (New York: Columbia University Press, 1993).

Rowe, William. "An Examination of ther Cosmological Argument." In *Philosophy of Religion,* edited by Louis P. Pojman (Belmont, CA: Wadsworth, 2003).

Ruf, Henry. *Postmodern Rationality, Social Criticism, and Religion* (St. Paul, MN: Paragon House, 2005).

———. "Radicalizaing Liberalism and Modernity." In *Philosophy, Religion, and the Question of Intolerance,* edited by Mehdi Amin Razavi and Daniel Ambuel (Albany, NY: SUNY Press, 1997)

Sartre, Jean-Paul. *Existentialism and Humanism,* translated by P. Mairet (London: Metheun, 1948).

Schick, Theodore Jr. "'The Big Bang' Argument for the Existence of God." In *Philo I,* no. 1 (Spring/Summer 1998).

Searle, John. *Speech Acts* (Cambridge: Cambridge University Press, 1969).

———. *Expression and Meaning* (Cambridge: Cambridge University Press, 1979).

———. *Intentionality* (Cambridge: Cambridge University Press, 1983).

———. "Analytic Philosophy and Mental Phenomena." In *Midwest Studies in Philosophy,* vol 5 (1980).

Shah, Idries. *The Way of the Sufi* (London: Penguin Books, 1968).

Shusterman, Richard. *Performing Live: Aesthetic Alternatives for the Ends of Art* (Ithaca, NY: Cornell University Press, 2000).

———. *The Range of Pragmatism and the Limits of Philosophy* (Oxford: Blackwell, 2005).

Smith, Huston. *The World's Religions* (San Francisco: HarperSanFrancisco, 1991).

Spinoza. "Ethics, Proposition XI." In *Spinoza Selections,* edited by John Wild (New York: Charles Scribner's Sons, 1930).

Suzuki, D.T. *Essays in Zen Buddhism* (New York: Grove Press, 1949).

Swinburne, Richard, "The Argument from Design," in Contemporary Perspectives on Religious Epistemology, eds. R. Douglas Geivett and Brendan Sweetman (New York: Oxford University Press, 1992).

Taylor, Mark C. *Erring: A Postmodern A/theology* (Chicago: University of Chicago Press, 1984).

———. *Tears* (Albany, NY: SUNY Press, 1990).

———. *Nots* (Chicago: University of Chicago Pres, 1993).

———. *Hidings* (Chicago: University of Chicago Press, 1997).

———. *About Religion: Economics of Faith in Virtual Culture* (Chicago: University of Chicago Press, 1999).

Throckmorton, Burton H., Jr., ed. *Gospel Parallels.* (New York: Thomas & Sons, 1949).

Hau and Yoel Hoffman, *The Sound of One Hand,* translated by Yoel Hoffman (New York: Basic Books, 1975).

Tsao Hsue-Chin. *Dream of the Red Chamber,* translated by ChiChen Wang (New York: Anchor Books, 1958).

Van Over, Raymond. *Taoist Tales.* (New York: Mentor Book, 1973).

Westphal, Merold. "Overcoming Ontotheology." In *God, The Gift, and Postmodernism,* edited by John Caputo and Michael J. Scanlon (Bloomington, IN: Indiana University Press, 1999).

Wing-Tsit Chan, trans. and comp. *A Sourcebook in Chinese Philosophy.* (Princeton: Princeton University Press, 1963).

Willard, Dallas. "The Three-Stage Argument for the Existence of God." In *Contemporary Perspectives on Religious Epistemology,* edited by R. Douglas Geivett and Brendan Sweetman (New York: Oxford University Press, 1992).

Witttgenstein, Ludwig. *Philosophical Investigations,* translated by G.E.M Anscombe (New York: Macmillan, 1953).

Wolterstorff, Nicholas. "Is Reason Enough?" In *Contemporary Perspectives on Religious Epistemology,* edited by R. Douglas Geivett and Brendan Sweetman (New York: Oxford University Press, 1992).

Young, Iris Marion. *Justice and the Politics of Difference* (Princeton: Princeton University Press, 1990).

————. *Inclusion and Democracy* (Oxford: Oxford University Press, 2000).

Zizek, Slavoj, *The Fragile Absolute* (London: Verso, 2000).

————. *On Belief: Thinking in Action* (London: Routledge. 2001).

————. *The Puppet and the Dwarf: The Perverse Core of Christianity* (Cambridge, MA: MIT Press, 2003).

————. *Interrogating the Real,* edited by Rex Butler and Scott Stephens (London: Continuum, 2005).

————. *Conversations With Zizek* (Cambridge: Polity Press, 2005).

————. "Neighbors and Other Monsters: A Plea for Ethical Violence." In *Slavoj Zizek,* Eric L. Santer, and Kenneth Reinhard. *The Neighbor* (Chicago: University of Chicago Press, 2005).

————. *The Parallax View* (Cambridge, MA: The MIT Press, 2006).

INDEX